Ayahuasca Shamanism in the Amazon and Beyond

O | R | S

OXFORD RITUAL STUDIES

Series Editors

Ronald Grimes, Ritual Studies International
Ute Hüsken, University of Oslo
Barry Stephenson, Memorial University

THE PROBLEM OF RITUAL EFFICACY
Edited by William S. Sax, Johannes Quack, and Jan Weinhold

PERFORMING THE REFORMATION
Public Ritual in the City of Luther
Barry Stephenson

RITUAL, MEDIA, AND CONFLICT
Edited by Ronald L. Grimes, Ute Hüsken, Udo Simon, and Eric Venbrux

KNOWING BODY, MOVING MIND
Ritualizing and Learning at Two Buddhist Centers
Patricia Q. Campbell

SUBVERSIVE SPIRITUALITIES
How Rituals Enact the World
Frédérique Apffel-Marglin

NEGOTIATING RITES
Edited by Ute Hüsken and Frank Neubert

THE DANCING DEAD
Ritual and Religion among the Kapsiki/Higi of North Cameroon and Northeastern Nigeria
Walter E. A. van Beek

LOOKING FOR MARY MAGDALENE
Alternative Pilgrimage and Ritual Creativity at Catholic Shrines in France
Anna Fedele

THE DYSFUNCTION OF RITUAL IN EARLY CONFUCIANISM
Michael David Kaulana Ing

A DIFFERENT MEDICINE
Postcolonial Healing in the Native American Church
Joseph D. Calabrese

NARRATIVES OF SORROW AND DIGNITY
Japanese Women, Pregnancy Loss, and Modern Rituals of Grieving
Bardwell L. Smith

MAKING "THINGS" BETTER
A Workbook on Property and Environmental Behavior
A. David Napier

AYAHUASCA SHAMANISM IN THE AMAZON AND BEYOND
Edited by Beatriz Caiuby Labate and Clancy Cavnar

Ayahuasca Shamanism in the Amazon and Beyond

EDITED BY BEATRIZ CAIUBY LABATE
AND CLANCY CAVNAR

OXFORD
UNIVERSITY PRESS

OXFORD
UNIVERSITY PRESS

Oxford University Press is a department of the
University of Oxford. It furthers the University's objective
of excellence in research, scholarship, and education
by publishing worldwide.

Oxford New York
Auckland Cape Town Dar es Salaam Hong Kong Karachi
Kuala Lumpur Madrid Melbourne Mexico City Nairobi
New Delhi Shanghai Taipei Toronto

With offices in
Argentina Austria Brazil Chile Czech Republic France Greece
Guatemala Hungary Italy Japan Poland Portugal Singapore
South Korea Switzerland Thailand Turkey Ukraine Vietnam

Published in the United States of America by
Oxford University Press
198 Madison Avenue, New York, NY 10016

Library of Congress Cataloging-in-Publication Data
Ayahuasca shamanism in the Amazon and beyond / [edited by] Beatriz Caiuby Labate, Clancy Cavnar.
p. cm. (Oxford ritual studies)
ISBN 978-0-19-934120-7 (pbk.)—ISBN 978-0-19-934119-1 (hardcover)—
ISBN 978-0-19-934121-4 (ebook)
1. Ayahuasca ceremony—Cross-cultural studies. 2. Shamanism—Cross-cultural studies.
3. Hallucinogenic drugs and religious experience—Cross-cultural studies. I. Labate, Beatriz Caiuby.
GN472.4.A93 2014
201'.44—dc23 2013039105

1 3 5 7 9 8 6 4 2
Printed in the United States of America
on acid-free paper

Dedicated to Steven Rubenstein
(in memoriam)

CONTENTS

ACKNOWLEDGMENTS

We wish to thank the German Research Council (DFG) and the Collaborative Research Center (SFB) Ritual Dynamics—Socio-Cultural Processes from a Historical and Culturally Comparative Perspective, for their support for the Amazon Conference: Amazonian Shamanism, Psychoactive Plants and Ritual Reinvention, which took place in the Institute of Medical Psychology, Heidelberg University, in December 2011.

We thank Prof. Dr. Rolf Verres for his avid support of the conference, and Alexandra Heidle for her help in organizing it.

We thank Anton Bilton, Giancarlo Canavesio, Kathleen Harrison, Robert J. Barnhart, Botanical Dimensions, and MAPS for their support for this book.

We thank all the authors of this book for their contributions.

We thank Françoise Barbira Freedman for her contributions to the introduction of the book and Oscar Calavia Saéz for writing the foreword.

We thank Andrew Dawson, Kenneth Tupper, Matthew Meyer, Renato Sztutman, Brian Anderson, and Tiago Coutinho for their dialogues during the production of this book.

We also thank Alessandro Meiguins, Lou Gold, Thiago Martins e Silva, Ana Gretel Echazú Böschemeir, Claude Guislain, Frankneile Silva, Billy Fequis, Luana Almeida, Stephen Hugh-Jones, Pierre Urban, Sydney Solizonquehua, and Miguel Alexiades for their permission to use photos and drawings they provided.

Finally, we offer our grateful thanks to Ute Hüsken, Roland Grimes, and Oxford University Press for their consideration of this important topic.

CONTRIBUTORS

Bernd Brabec de Mori is an ethnomusicologist specializing in indigenous music from the Ucayali valley in Eastern Peru. He spent some years in the field and was integrated into the indigenous group Shipibo-Konibo. He now lives in Austria and has been working at the audiovisual archive Phonogrammarchiv of the Austrian Academy of Sciences, at the Centre for Systematic Musicology (University of Graz), and as a senior scientist at the Institute of Ethnomusicology, University of Music and Dramatic Arts Graz. His publications address the fields of Western Amazonian indigenous music, arts, and history as well as the complex of music, ritual, and altered states.

Alhena Caicedo Fernandez received her Ph.D. in social anthropology and ethnology from Ecole de Hautes Etudes Sciences Sociales (EHESS) in Paris. She teaches in the department of anthropology at Los Andes University, Colombia, and is a member of the Centro de Pensamiento Latinoamericano Raiz.AL ("Raiz.AL" Center of Latin American Thought). Her doctoral thesis, entitled "The New Places of Shamanism in Colombia," explored the changing dynamics in the field of yage consumption in that country and examined the processes of urbanization and eliticization on ritual consumption.

Clancy Cavnar is currently completing her postdoctoral hours in clinical psychology at the Marin Treatment Center, a methadone clinic in San Rafael, California. In 2011 she received a doctorate in clinical psychology (Psy.D.) from John F. Kennedy University in Pleasant Hill, California, with a dissertation on gay and lesbian people's experiences with ayahuasca. She attended New College of the University of South Florida and completed an undergraduate degree in liberal arts in 1982. She attended the San Francisco Art Institute and graduated with a Master of Fine Art in painting in 1985. In 1993, she received a certificate in substance abuse counseling from the extension program of the University of California at Berkeley, and in 1997 she graduated with a master's in counseling from San Francisco State University. In that same year, she got in touch with the Santo Daime in the United States, and has traveled several times to Brazil since then. She is also co-editor, with Beatriz Caiuby Labate, of two books: *Prohibition, Religious Freedom, and Human Rights: Regulating Traditional Drug Use* (2014) and *The Therapeutic Use of Ayahuasca* (2014).

Mariana Ciavatta Pantoja graduated from the social sciences program at Universidade Federal do Rio de Janeiro (UFRJ) in 1985. She moved to the state of Acre in 1993, spending two years in the Alto Juruá Extractivist Reserve engaged in political consulting and academic research. In 2001, she defended her doctoral dissertation in social sciences at UNICAMP, which was published as *Os Milton: Cem Anos de História nos Seringais* [The Milton: One Hundred Years of History of the Rubber Tappers Camp] (2nd edition 2008). Since 2004, she has lectured at the Federal University of Acre, where she coordinates the Anthropology and Forests Laboratory (AFLORA) and integrates the New Social Cartography Project, a network of researchers and social movements in Brazil.

Françoise Barbira Freedman received her Ph.D. in social anthropology from the University of Cambridge after doing field research in the Peruvian Upper Amazon. She has been teaching and working in medical anthropology in an interdisciplinary perspective at Cambridge with successive innovative outreach projects, first on the simultaneous use of health services and local healers in the Amazon and the Andes, and later on a comparison of Amazonian couvade with emerging new fathers' involvement in pregnancy, childbirth, and early parenting. Longitudinal fieldwork with the Keshwa Lamas in Peru has resulted in a compilation of a medicinal plant knowledge base, a community forest reserve, and a live "forest pharmacy." Currently still working with Amazonian healers and midwives, she is committed to the parallel development of academic research in ethnobotany and fair-trade applications of Amazonian plant knowledge through the Cambridge University spinout company Ampika. The BBC Channel 4 documentary *Jungle Trip* (2001, accessible online), to which she contributed, offers a zany TV rendering of the interplay between Keshwa Upper Amazon "plant doctors," Mestizo healers, gringo shamans, and a young English shaman apprentice.

Evgenia Fotiou is a cultural anthropologist with an interest in health and healing in cross-cultural perspective. Her teaching and research interests include indigenous religions and gender, and she is currently researching the revitalization of Greek religion in modern Greece. She has lived, worked, and studied in Greece, Austria, Peru, Germany, and the United States and is fluent in four languages. She received her Ph.D. in cultural anthropology and Latin American studies from University of Wisconsin-Madison in 2010. Her dissertation research was on ayahuasca use in the context of shamanic tourism in Peru. After teaching at the UW-Madison departments of anthropology and gender and women's studies (2011–12), she received an ACM-Mellon postdoctoral fellowship in indigenous religions at Luther College for 2012–2014. She has served on committees and as a manuscript reviewer for the journal *Anthropology of Consciousness*, and she was guest editor of a special issue on ayahuasca and healing, published in the spring of 2012. She has presented at several professional meetings and has chaired and organized panels, bringing together scholars from a variety of disciplines.

Beatriz Caiuby Labate has a Ph.D. in social anthropology from the State University of Campinas (UNICAMP), Brazil. Her main areas of interest are the study of psychoactive substances, drug policy, shamanism, ritual, and religion. She is Visiting Professor at the Drug Policy Program of the Center for Economic Research and Education (CIDE) in Aguascalientes, Mexico. She is also Research Associate at the Institute of Medical Psychology, Heidelberg University, co-founder of the Nucleus for Interdisciplinary Studies of Psychoactives (NEIP), and editor of NEIP's website (http://www.neip.info). She is author, co-author, and co-editor of twelve books, one special-edition journal, and several peer-reviewed articles. For more information, see http://bialabate.net/.

Esther Jean Langdon was born in 1944 in Denver, Colorado, and has lived in Brazil since 1983. She graduated in sociology and anthropology at Carleton College, Minnesota, in 1966 and did her master's at the University of Washington. She conducted fieldwork on shamanism and indigenous cosmology in Colombia from 1970 to 1974. In 1974, she obtained her Ph.D. degree at Tulane University. The focus of her Ph.D. thesis was the relationship between cosmology, illness, and the daily practices of the Siona from Colombia. Currently she is full professor at Universidade Federal de Santa Catarina (Florianópolis, Brazil), where she has been working since 1983. Between 1993 and 1994 she conducted postdoctoral research with Richard Bauman at Indiana University, emphasizing studies on performance. She has published several articles in books and national and international specialized journals. The books she has edited include *Portals of Power: Shamanism in South America* (1992), co-edited with Gerhard Baer; *Concepciones de la Muerte y el "Mas Allá" en las Culturas Indígenas Latinoamericas* (1999), co-edited with Maria Susana Cipolletti; *Xamanismo no Brasil: Novas Perspectivas* (1996) and *Saúde dos Povos Indígenas: Reflexões Sobre Antropología Participativa* (2004), co-edited with Luiza Garnelo. She is researcher at the Conselho Nacional de Desenvolvimento Científico e Tecnológico (CNPq) and currently coordinates an investigation on contemporary forms of shamanism. She is also coordinator of Instituto Nacional de Pesquisa Brasil Plural.

Anne-Marie Losonczy is an anthropologist, director of studies at the Ecole Pratique des Hautes Etudes, Sorbonne, Paris, professor at the Université Libre de

Bruxelles, and member of the Mondes Americains-Cerma, École de Hautes Etudes en Sciences Sociales, Paris. After earning a master's in Roman philology and clinical psychology at the University of Budapest, she continued in a master's course in anthropology at the Université Libre de Bruxelles and at the EHESS in Paris. After completing a Ph.D. at the Université Libre de Bruxelles in 1992, she taught at the University of Barcelona, at the University Paris X-Nanterre, and at the Institute of Ethnology at the University of Neuchâtel in Switzerland, which she directed. She has taught as a visiting professor at the National University of Bogota in Colombia, at the National University of Budapest, and at the University of Pecs (EU, Marie-Curie Program), and recently at the University of Florianopolis in Brazil. She is the author of four books in French and Spanish, one of which is on the shamanic practice of the Emberà Indians of Colombia, and about sixty articles. Her fieldwork in Colombia focused on Afro-American groups and local multiethnic societies in the continental and insular Colombian Caribbean and on shamanism and society of the Emberà Indians of the Colombian Choco. In Cuba and Colombia she studied emerging popular rituals of sanctification in urban graveyards. Her more recent research, together with Silvia Mesturini Cappo, uses a comparative approach to focus on certain rearrangements of ritual practice labeled as "shamanic" in urban social environments.

Silvia Mesturini Cappo has a B.A. degree in social sciences from the Université Libre de Bruxelles, Belgium, and a master's degree in social science of religion from the École Pratique d'Hautes Etudes of Paris (EPHE-Sorbonne); she obtained a Ph.D. in anthropology from the Université Libre de Bruxelles, Belgium in 2010. Her thesis, "Espaces Chamaniques en Movement: Itinéraires Vécus et Géographies Multiples" (Shamanic Spaces on the Move: Life Itineraries and Multiple Geographies between Europe and South America) is based on multi-sited fieldwork including European (France, Belgium, Holland, and Spain) and South American locations (Peru, Bolivia, Ecuador, Colombia, and Argentina) between 2004 and 2010. Her research on ayahuasca rituals and their internationalization is part of a wider interest in shamanic practice at large and its recent developments. Her ethnography has had a special focus on ritual interaction, cultural translation, and the interactive construction of legitimized knowledge and meaning.

Daniela Peluso is a cultural anthropologist who has worked over the last two decades in Lowland South America, mostly with communities in Peru and Bolivia. She has been actively involved in various local efforts on issues relating to health, gender, indigenous urbanization, and land-rights and works in close collaboration with indigenous and local organizations. Her publications focus mostly on indigenous urbanization, historicities, economies, and relatedness. She received her Ph.D. in 2003 from Columbia University and is a senior lecturer in social anthropology at the University of Kent.

Isabel Santana de Rose completed her Ph.D. in anthropology at Universidade Federal de Santa Catarina (UFSC, Florianópolis, Brazil) in 2010. Currently, she is a postdoctoral fellow at the Federal University of Minas Gerais (UFMG). Her Ph.D. thesis, "*Tatá endy rekoe*—Sacred Fire: Encounters between the Gurani, Ayahuasca, and the Red Path," focuses on the emergence of contemporary shamanic networks in southern Brazil. She is coauthor with B. C. Labate and R. G. Santos of *Religiões ayahuasqueiras: Um balanço bibliográfico* (2008), which was also published in English (*Ayahuasca Religions: A Comprehensive Bibliography and Critical Essays*, 2009), and author of several articles published in books and specialized journals. She is also a researcher in the Interdisciplinary Study Group of Psychoactives (NEIP), Study Group of Indigenous Health and Knowledge (NESSI/UFSC), and Study Group in Orality and Performance (GESTO/UFSC).

Glenn H. Shepard, Jr., received his undergraduate degree from Princeton University, carried out postgraduate studies in Peru and Germany, and in 1999 received his Ph.D. in medical anthropology from the University of California at Berkeley. He has worked with diverse indigenous groups of Peru, Brazil, and Mexico and speaks more than ten languages. He has published widely on ethnobotany, shamanism, medical anthropology, human ecology, and indigenous environmental knowledge in journals, including *American Anthropologist, Medical Anthropology Quarterly, Journal of Ethnobiology, Journal of Psychoactive Drugs, Economic Botany, Conservation Biology, Science, Nature,* and others. After carrying out postdoctoral research in Manaus at the National Institute for Amazonian Research and in São Paulo at the University of São Paulo, he is currently a curator and researcher in indigenous ethnology at the Museu Paraense Emilio Goeldi in Belem do Pará, Brazil.

Pirjo Kristiina Virtanen is a Finnish Academy researcher and adjunct professor in Latin American studies in the Department of World Cultures at the Helsinki University. She is also an associated postdoctoral researcher at the University Paris Ouest-Nanterre La Défense, Centre EREA. Her research interests are Amazonian indigenous epistemologies, oral histories, mobility, movement, indigenous politics, indigenous youth, and Arawakan-speaking peoples. She has also worked in research projects on pre-Columbian settlements in Western Amazonia. Her articles have been published, among others, in the *Journal of Latin American and Caribbean Anthropology, Identities, Revista Amazônica,* and *Anthropos,* as well as in chapters in edited compilations of Ashgate and the University Press of Colorado. She is the author of *Indigenous Youth in Brazilian Amazonia: Changing Lived Worlds* (2012).

LIST OF ILLUSTRATIONS

FOREWORD

Authentic Ayahuasca

Oscar Calavia Saéz

What is a foreword for? Sometimes it helps a reader to not waste time: in this case, to not waste time reading a good book badly. For it would be a shame to read this dense and coherent group of texts as if it were just an attempt at deconstructing the notion of the "ancient tradition of ayahuasca." Indeed, each of the chapters distances itself from this myth of origin to bring us to some theme of rigorous modernity: ayahuasca as a substitute for prior shamanic systems, its use as a sign of indigenous identity, transcendental tourism, the misunderstandings between local practitioners and global neophytes, life histories of ayahuasca entrepreneurs, gringo shamans, sexual predation insinuating itself into religious practice.... All this might appear disappointing, even scandalous to readers addicted to the notion that the world of ayahuasca is a primordial phenomenon, born from the Amazonian soil like the very vine that nourishes it. Or to those convinced that, although the traces of recent elaborations can be seen in hybrid versions of ayahuasca—more or less Christianized, more or less "New Age"—there always remains in the depths of the forest some native village where it is preserved in its full authenticity, where it continues to be drunk and chanted as it always was.

But in reality, the region's ethnologists have questioned this notion of authenticity for some time. We can no longer ignore the fact that "ancient" ayahuasca has had a tumultuous history, at least for as long as we have known about it. The same can be said about many other aspects of indigenous traditions, which, like all traditions, are subject to constant change that is much faster than usually imagined. So much so that it's worth asking why it is that we insist on seeking authenticity and ancient traditions among precisely those peoples who have not made an effort (unlike certain others) to seek a pure, unadulterated cultural wellspring, unchanging through the centuries. Indeed, indigenous Amazonian peoples have no need to construct such a fantasy because Westerners—or rather, Northerners, as they are appropriately rebaptized by the authors of this book—have provided one ready-made. It was outsiders who characterized Amazonia as a world without history, indistinguishable from its natural environment; where knowledge about plants and ecosystems does not proceed so much from conscious investigation, but rather from a kinship that was never broken—indigenous peoples represent Nature because they never stopped being part of Nature. In some sense, this quest for authenticity and transcendence that takes many travelers and tourists to the jungle and to ayahuasca lodges follows a simple economic law: it is preferable to seek these things out where they can be procured for the lowest cost. Authenticity and transcendence are too *expensive* (and I'm not talking about monetary costs) to acquire in the homeland of the Northerners: there, one pays a high price for such things. Transcendence is in the hands of powerful churches, which dole it out in exchange for obedience to hierarchies and moral systems that most of the population no longer abide by. Cultural authenticity is associated with the dangers of nationalism and memories of tragic wars.

Indeed, as this book shows, a high price is also exacted for these values in Amazonia, even though this cost is easy for Northerners to ignore since the burden falls mostly on those who remain, rather than those who are just passing through. Although transcendental tourists understand ayahuasca as a kind of shortcut from individual to world consciousness (Nature, Great Mother, caring Pachamamma), ayahuasca among forest peoples is mostly about sociality: a negotiation among human and nonhuman companions and neighbors; an activity that establishes networks, sometimes precarious, between kin and affines; masters and apprentices; brothers-in-law, animal spirits and the dead; or a battleground between rival shamans. Euphemisms about medicine and religion obscure a darker and more complex reality in which shamanism necessarily involves witchcraft, or to use less exotic terms, very real microconflicts among neighbors, kin, and rivals over knowledge, power, and economic resources, which the presence of profitable neophytes only tends to intensify.

There is no mystery as to the origins of *vegetalismo*, Santo Daime, Red Path, and other traditions analyzed in this volume: all were created rather recently, and many of their founders are still alive. It is not difficult to identify the sources of the doctrines and rituals that became mixed in a particular combination for each. Yet there is no basis, in the case of indigenous shamanism, to postulate an unchanging tradition, other than the very primitivist bias that makes one read ethnographies as though they were necessarily describing original, primordial states.

A well-known analysis by Peter Gow is surprising at first because it goes against habitual notions: ayahuasca use expanded from the mestizo Amazon world, from major rivers populated with Catholic missions toward the forest interior, and not vice versa. Yet this analysis need not row against the tide of the indigenous worldview: just ask the indigenous people themselves, or check the ethnographies from a few decades ago, and you will find abundant evidence that shamans used to use other substances, or that ayahuasca was once less important than it is now, or that ayahuasca and all its ritual and poetic paraphernalia was adopted from some other group. This information does not even contradict those notions about Amazonian space that are so dear to Northerners, in which the "savages" upriver have a more primeval kind of knowledge. On the other hand, this implies that the most powerful ayahuasqueros are found downriver. It is not the Indians, but rather the recently created ayahuasca churches, that like to spread the idea that their practices are descended from the Inca or from the beginnings of time. The backwoods Indians, on the other hand, prefer to compare ayahuasca with television or the movies, or who knows, maybe even the Internet.

For all of these reasons—and going back to what I said in the beginning—it would be a waste to read this book as just one more volume (and a late one at that) in this vast library on the deconstruction, or invention, of traditions. And yet there can be no doubt: Ayahuasca tradition is a hybrid invention. It seems obvious that some Amerindian someplace in the Amazon invented it; perhaps many centuries ago, perhaps more recently. In any event, we should discard the possibility that the inventor's own descendants, if there are any, preserve the original mode of usage. If Amazonia is as historical as we have just claimed it to be, it is more likely that these hypothetical heirs to Ur-ayahuasca have also adopted one of the all-new ayahuasca variations, after having already forgotten—who knows, maybe long ago—the original version. We will never know. In this sense, the authors in this volume provide us with something more interesting than a deconstruction of ayahuasca: namely, the story of its construction, a work in progress that indeed may be centuries old.

Whatever "authentic" is—and much has been written about this since Sapir's famous article—perhaps what best distinguishes it is *efficacy*: an efficacy, moreover, shot through with impurities. Whatever its origin—ancestral legacy or purchased a few days ago in some bazaar—a magical object is authentic only to the degree that it produces effects; even unintended effects that prove it's not just some placebo, whether medical or cultural. It is difficult to pinpoint why ayahuasca is so efficacious, and why it has been so successful at displacing a whole series of other, older psychoactive substances, at least in certain places; this question appears regularly throughout the volume. A superficial look at the evidence—a more substantial proof would require more extensive pharmacological research—points to the possibility that ayahuasca owes its success to being located midway along a scale running from substances that produce light inebriation to others causing a deeper and more dangerous plunge into other worlds. We note how weaker variants of the brew, which are effective only when accompanied by long and rigorous dietary and behavioral restrictions, are being increasingly abandoned in favor of more concentrated preparations. Ayahuasca appears to offer the perfect median; or, to say it in another way, it is the perfect embodiment of ambiguity. Ayahuasca allows a distinct perception of the other world without losing consciousness of this one. Perhaps for this reason, ayahuasca, better than other substances, supports the hypothesis that another reality can be found just behind the apparent world: Ayahuasca allows a point-by-point comparison.

Beyond this, ayahuasca permits a broad, synesthetic association between visions, music, and verbal creations that is not necessarily forthcoming for other psychoactive substances. There is not, to my knowledge, a coherent genre of graphic art, music, or poetry centered on *Datura, Virola* snuff, or even alcohol. Let me be a bit more specific: For millennia, there have been torrents of poems, music, and artworks that have emerged from visionary and intoxicating experiences. Bach himself dedicated a cantata to his tobacco pipe. Yet I am not aware of another example where, as is the case for ayahuasca, so much attention has been paid to a common, formal template for such creations such that, for example, among the Panoan Indians, graphic art can be seen as a kind of visual ayahuasca song. Maybe this is due to the inherent properties of the substance, or maybe it is the first time that a psychoactive substance has constituted the underpinning for a veritable international network of churches whose priests, followers, and commentators seek to provide the same epistemological value to "The Vision" that other churches give to "The Word."

Ayahuasca is, in sum, a means of communication: among subjects, among worlds, among symbol systems. The very etymological basis of its Quechua name—which has imposed itself over innumerous local denominations—alludes to the contact it permits with the dead. Thus ayahuasca is a privileged means of establishing ties with all categories of Others. And it would be a poor concept of communication indeed if we dismissed the possibility for misunderstanding—the "impurity" we alluded to earlier. A misunderstanding is not necessarily the worst understanding, and even the oft-maligned ayahuasca tourists cannot be dismissed as valid sources of interpretation. The Renaissance, Christianity, Buddhism, and Maoism are all good examples of misunderstanding. Anthropology is about little else.

In the midst of so many attempts at cultural revival and re-symbolization of indigenous cultures, the affirmation of identity by means of ayahuasca has certain peculiar features. Ayahuasca fulfills, to perfection, the purpose of incarnating an indigenous identity, but it does so by means of a much more flexible strategy than dances or traditional body painting, opening out to a broad pan-indigenous identity that goes beyond Amazonia to incorporate Andean, Mexican, and even North American references. It is capable of adapting to the necessities of both indigenous groups and individual indigenous subjects. It also has an expansive potential: other signs of indigeneity are inaccessible to outsiders, but ayahuasca opens the possibility of not only wearing but also conferring these signs. Nothing prevents a gringo from becoming a legitimate shaman in his or her own right. And yet this same expansive capacity that extends to nonindigenous foreigners also confers strength and authority on indigenous claims to autochthony. It is not as paradoxical as it sounds. Ayahuasca is now the motor of a missionary enterprise that indigenous Amazonians have directed toward the same societies that bombarded them with their own missionaries for centuries. The dialog has finally gained some symmetry.

When considering the suspicions and conflicts generated by the commercial use of ayahuasca in local communities, we shouldn't forget that the same cloud of distrust and strife has hung over village shamans since the earliest accounts we have. For example, Júlio César Melatti's study of Marubo leadership published thirty years ago shows that, unlike chiefs who are bound by an ethos of generosity with their subjects, Marubo shamans can, and even should, be stingy, turning their knowledge into profits, and are envied and criticized for doing so. In a word, shamans deal first and foremost with "Others" and hence are perhaps better prepared than other "Others" to take on the role of indigenous entrepreneur. Ultimately, and against the grain of received wisdom, intellectual property is not such a new phenomenon in the rainforest: it exists precisely where the local economy and ethos has tended to deny other kinds of property.

Ayahuasca has always organized social networks and continues to do so. I regard with a certain degree of suspicion those analyses that characterize previous indigenous uses of ayahuasca as involving ritual regulation of relationships between the group and the cosmos. My suspicion is focused on the abstract character of the terms *group* and *cosmos*. It seems clear enough that ayahuasca creates connections between *concrete* subjects: for example, with other shamans, from whom one obtains songs or new cultigens in relationships that can range from patron-client to theft; or with potential allies, who are also probable enemies. Ayahuasca was also related to warfare, providing both the motivations and occasions for it. Among the Yaminahua, I learned during my own research, most of the attacks that occurred decades ago began right after ayahuasca ceremonies. And yet, unlike other psychoactive plants such as *Datura*, with a more unambiguous use in warfare, ayahuasca can be as much a cause for starting a war as a substitute for it. The predominance of ayahuasca might come from its capacity for staging virtual wars in an era when pacification by whites has almost eliminated the relational role—let's not forget that hostile relationships are still relationships—that war once served in Amazonia.

It would be perverse to deny authenticity to the quests and explorations of the travelers and transcendental tourists who also appear on these pages. Centuries before the term *tourist* was invented, and before Burroughs, Ginsberg, and so many others got interested in Amazonian shamanism, a similar kind of disdain was reserved for those in the Christian world or elsewhere who went on pilgrimages to distant sanctuaries or received exotic gurus with open arms and minds. In ancient Rome, the term *superstitio*—etymological source of the modern word "superstition"—could be used to refer to an unwholesome interest in foreign gods. Religious curiosity predated the famous "disenchantment of the world" by many centuries. It is not just in modern times that such curiosity complements or confronts local religions with other traditions from far away, or that such imported devotions cohabitate with, or even change, local practice despite resistance or opposition by established religious institutions, including that peculiar church known as secular rationalism that has waged an ongoing inquisition against "cults." The case of the Guarani people of coastal Brazil, told in this book, is striking in the way that ayahuasca has become sanctified within a religion that before contained no trace of it. No problem: the Guarani have now retroactively remembered ayahuasca in their oral traditions. This kind of rediscovery of the visionary sacred also holds true in other parts of the world. Not so many centuries ago, the concept of Faith—which, as we know, deals with all that we cannot, and should not, see and touch—banished direct sensory encounter with the divine, formerly attained through trance and vision. From then on, contact with the divine could be maintained only through written texts. And yet direct sensory experience remains a possibility or potentiality in any religion. The vestiges of European witchcraft at the dawn of the Age of Reason (which was also the Age of Faith) were nourished by the use of psychoactive preparations. Even if it is impossible to take seriously a direct genealogical link between the modern Wicca movement and pre-Christian magico-religious practice, as some New Age movements postulate, it is also impossible to forget that this past has perpetuated itself in a kind of "return of the repressed." It was only a matter of time before this alternative eventually returned, associated with faraway traditions, and inevitably bathed in forms inherited from centuries of Christianity.

There may well be a series of deep misunderstandings in the stereotypes that Amazonians and Northerners maintain about one another, but the studies that are gathered here reveal that the situation is perhaps not so hopeless as it seems. From the indigenous side, the attitude of Northerners may be strange, even laughable. Local shamans, worried about supernatural predation and magical aggressions, are faced with rich and powerful foreigners who seem more concerned with battling ghosts from their own childhood. But the idea that indigenous peoples are consciously "scamming the gringos" is not an accurate depiction of this encounter. However, one such case is mentioned in this volume, involving a young shaman who is not fully qualified to practice the trade. He tries to justify himself before his own family members by saying he's not misusing traditional knowledge, just making money from foreigners: a good shaman doesn't give too much away, and needs to know what he's worth. But this is just family politics.

Even if some degree of scam or deception is involved, it will be forcibly limited because ayahuasca is *real*. And I am not referring only to its substantive chemical properties, but to the local perception that ayahuasca is a subject in its own right, with its own intentions. The shaman is just a mediator and cannot prevent ayahuasca from choosing to bestow its knowledge on some clumsy-looking gringo. Even the worst kind of experiences—sexual assault or molestation by "spiritual masters" or their assistants, or encounters with unscrupulous, money-hungry shamans—can serve to reintroduce essential conditions into the system. For no religious system can escape the conflicting claims—always relative, always contingent—between true and false prophets, between priests, charlatans, and sorcerers: the tension between ritual purity, political interest, and carnal desire. At best, certain historical developments have facilitated the illusion of pure religious activity, disconnected from the world and the body and free of earthly temptations; of a transcendental "beyond" free from such desires and goals.

If, despite all this deconstruction, we decide to stick with our notion of authenticity—it could be of benefit after all, given the contemporary state of factoid hyperproduction and meteoric trends and fashions—at the very least we should purify it of any archaic residue. The authenticity of ayahuasca asserts itself, on the contrary, by its very modernity. Indigenous people must suffer from a hopelessly exotic view of themselves if they limit their use of ayahuasca to relations with animal spirits and masters of game animals. These are, of course, important, but today (as always), Amazonian peoples interact with many other powerful agents. Ayahuasca would be little more than a folkloric simulacrum if it did not operate in the contemporary context. One might argue that ayahuasca has put Amazonian subjects into direct contact not with global society as a whole but rather with a very specific segment of it: namely, orphaned citizens of transcendence nostalgic for the reenchantment of the world. Although this may be part of the truth, it is not the whole truth. A footnote to one of the chapters mentions that important politicians and Silicon Valley entrepreneurs—hardly your typical dreamers trapped in the archaic past—are among the ayahuasca clientele in the United States. As convinced as one might be that Cartesian rationalistic positivism is the best possible framework for science, to believe it is also the best possible framework for the contemporary world is an act of blind faith in reason that is perhaps not all that rational.

Ayahuasca—who would have imagined?!—is now part of this world, remarkable not because of its archaic and remote origins but rather because of its potentialities, which are very much in harmony with the current times.

—Translated from the Portuguese by Glenn H. Shepard, Jr.

Ayahuasca Shamanism in the Amazon and Beyond

Notes on the Expansion and Reinvention of Ayahuasca Shamanism

BEATRIZ CAIUBY LABATE, CLANCY CAVNAR, AND FRANÇOISE BARBIRA FREEDMAN

This unique collection of chapters focuses on the recent expansion of ayahuasca shamanism both within and outside Amazonia and on the issues that this expansion raises for the study of Amazonian shamanism more generally. In this book we discuss how indigenous, *mestizo*, and cosmopolitan cultures together have engaged in shaping and staging a wide variety of shamanic rituals in which the consumption of psychoactive ayahuasca brews is a central part. All authors draw on firsthand observations of the creation and expansion of these new forms of rituals, as well as on a variety of other sources.

Ayahuasca is a psychoactive mixture typically made from the Amazonian vine *Banisteriopsis caapi* combined with the leaves of the bush *Psychotria viridis*, among other possible admixtures. The beverage contains dimethyltryptamine (DMT), a controlled substance subject to national and international drug laws. Ayahuasca was first used by indigenous Amazonian peoples within a shamanic complex that included both individual and group therapeutic functions, particularly in the areas of hunting magic, warfare, and collective rituals associated with social reproduction. Though little is yet known about the origins and spread of ayahuasca in pre-Hispanic contexts, its use in colonial missions and frontier posts of the Upper Amazon was reported in historical sources before accounts of its wider dissemination in the Amazonian lowlands at the turn of the twentieth century as a result of the social, ethnic, and economic upheavals associated with the Rubber Boom.

Like previous transformations of shamanism in Amazonia since the Hispanic conquest, the recent process of dissemination of ayahuasca has been dialogic among forest people and newcomers in the region. The extent of this transformation of Amerindian epistemology and ontology, involving not only shamanic traditions in

Amazonia but also ways of living in the rainforest that are now threatened, is discussed in several chapters in this volume. In fact, some of the current developments and practices described are still evolving. The influence not only of New Age ideas favored by spiritual pilgrims who flock to the Amazon in search of life-transforming experiences but also of dynamic ongoing interethnic contacts and exchanges is a main theme in the book. The chapters herein highlight the regional and transnational developments that have contributed to this new spread of shamanic ayahuasca rituals, now worldwide, and to what we claim is a "reinvention" of Amazonian shamanism.

There is, indeed, a reinvention taking place, encompassing the diverse meanings of this polysemic concept: the ethnographies collectively reveal both a makeover of shamanic rituals with a new or more intensive use of ayahuasca to fit a more diversified audience with differing expectations, and a recasting of elements of ritual considered as traditional in new versions with a style all their own. In the Amazon, both displaced indigenous people and mestizo rubber tappers are engaged in a syncretic creation of rituals that help build ethnic alliances and political strategies for their marginalized positions. Reinvention also points to the recovery of aspects of indigenous cultures that are brought back into salience in ayahuasca shamanism with the objective of reclaiming native heritage. Reinventing authenticity is instrumental to what some authors have called the "cultural revival of indigenous traditions," as well as to the emergence of new ethnic identities. Although the central place of shamanism in cultural revival has already been documented in Siberia and Central Asia, it has been relatively ignored in Amazonia. This volume opens new possibilities for stimulating comparisons. Reinvention does not occur in a historical or social vacuum.

The emerging rituals are inseparable from tensions arising from the expansion of ecotourism and ethnic tourism, and from more widespread trends in the commodification of indigenous cultures in posttraditional and postcolonial contexts. Ayahuasca shamanism has also gained increasing popularity within a network of services combining alternative healthcare, psychological well-being, and spiritual development, both locally and internationally. Though both anthropologists and some local shamans have criticized the provision of these related services, this development needs to be examined at the point of its cultural emergence in its historical, social, and economic context. This is one of the aims of the contributors to this volume.

Concepts of souls and spirits are fundamental to indigenous ontologies in South America. Humans have souls, and so do spirits, animals, plants, and inanimate substances. Also significant and animate are sacred sites such as trees, mountains, caves, waterfalls, springs, and underground rivers. All communication necessitates knowledge of soul and spirit essences and substances. Ritual—a system of stylized behavior only partially encoded in indigenous exegesis and performance—is the primary vehicle of popular religious instantiation in Amazonia. Music, rhythm, poetry, and aesthetic imagery are all integral components of shamanic performative dramatic art. During indigenous ritual enactment, the cosmology opens up to include all people in the universe, living and dead, Indian and non-Indian, together with animal spirits and souls.

The visionary qualities of ayahuasca offer infinite scope for a dynamic assemblage of symbols and interpretive performances. This book advocates an understanding of the relationships between postcolonial Amazonian cultures as a process of "transculturation," a concept that emphasizes the often-ignored impact of the peripheral culture on the one that assumes dominance. Far from decontextualizing Amazonian shamanism from its various cosmological and ritual dimensions, this volume allows reflection on a multiplicity of aspects involving the transforming practices, ontologies, and cosmologies of intermixing indigenous and colonist Amazonian populations in a globalizing world.

This volume has its origins in the Amazon Conference: Amazonian Shamanism, Psychoactive Plants, and Ritual Reinvention, organized by Beatriz Caiuby Labate at the Institute of Medical Psychology of Heidelberg University, December 6 and 7, 2010. This conference was part of the subproject Ritual Dynamics and Salutogenesis in the Use and Misuse of Psychoactive Substances (RISA), within the larger framework of the Collaborative Research Center (SFB) Ritual Dynamics: Socio-Cultural Processes from a Historical and Culturally Comparative Perspective, which Labate was a member of from 2009 to 2011. The conference included presenters from a variety of disciplines and discussed the contemporary expansion of Amazonian shamanism and the Brazilian Ayahuasca religions, the Santo Daime and the União do Vegetal (UDV), into urban centers in Brazil, Europe, and North America. Cavnar presented a paper on psychological aspects of perception of sexual orientation related to the consumption of ayahuasca in different contexts.[1] For this book, we have chosen to exclude the topic of the overseas expansion of the Brazilian ayahuasca religions and their diverse interfaces. Labate and Jungaberle (2011)[2] have addressed the internationalization of ayahuasca in a recent collection; our aim is to fill a gap in the literature regarding the part played by ayahuasca in current dynamic trends in Amazonian shamanism. We also decided to privilege the anthropological discipline over the original interdisciplinary scope of the conference in order to concentrate on ethnographic insights based on contributors' long-term fieldwork. To complement this focus, we invited scholars who were not present at the conference to participate in this collection. The resulting volume includes contributions from Brazil, Finland, England, France, Austria, Colombia, the United States, Greece, and Belgium. All chapters are previously unpublished, and draw on fresh ethnographic data. Barbira Freedman, an anthropologist with a comprehensive understanding of shamanism in Western Amazonia, who was also present in the conference and is author of a chapter, was invited to contribute to this Introduction, helping to situate current changes in Amazonian shamanism in broader perspectives of social and cultural reinvention.

Our use of the term *Amazonian shamanism* encompasses the cosmologies and shamanic practices of indigenous and mixed colonist communities in the Amazon regions of Brazil, Bolivia, Venezuela, Ecuador, Colombia, and Peru. We deliberately avoid an artificial separation between indigenous Amazonia and the mixed majority of forest dwellers. Whereas this volume concentrates on activities that are taking place in Brazil, Colombia, and Peru, these activities are also present in the other Amazonian countries, and outside South America, as discussed in some of the chapters in this volume.

Amazonian shamanism is widely diverse, and may include the use of several psychoactive plants, or, relatively infrequently, be independent of them. Taking distance from both academic and popular literature on ayahuasca that privilege "altered states of consciousness," this volume situates ayahuasca in the social creation of Amazonian shamanism. Like other shamans around the world, Amazonian shamans perform complex sets of transformative interactions between human and nonhuman agents on the basis of specific knowledge practices that they have acquired in relation to particular constituencies, either local or more remote. Since early colonial encounters, ayahuasca rituals were demonized in an attempt to eradicate shamanism in the Christianization of pacified Amazonian indigenous people. Yet not only were these rituals retained, hidden from probing inquisitors, but they also spread into areas of mixed settlement through the agency of non-indigenous shamans who had learned native shamanic crafts. Those new rituals, developed within mixed urban populations, were then disseminated by being exported back to the forest. This historical process, yet to be documented fully, [3] culminates in the current reshaping of Amazonian shamanism that we address in this volume. Various reinvented traditions straddling indigenous and mixed cultural heritage receive special attention in our collective analysis.

Vegetalismo, an urban healing tradition based on indigenous ayahuasca shamanism in Western Amazonia, spread among mixed forest and urban populations around the main Peruvian Amazonian towns of Iquitos, Tarapoto, and Pucallpa throughout the twentieth century. It is now being remodeled to accommodate social and cultural changes within the wider political economy. In rubber camps of the Brazilian Amazon, indigenous and mestizo ayahuasca rituals became further entangled with diverse Afro-Brazilian and Christian religious traditions, resulting in the founding of several organized religions in which ayahuasca is the principal sacrament, notably Santo Daime and the União do Vegetal (UDV). In Colombia, indigenous uses of ayahuasca still prevail, though rural mestizo forms of ayahuasca shamanism have also spread throughout the country.

The rise of ayahuasca tourism invites special consideration in relation to shamanic reinvention. Inspired by scholarly publications of prominent anthropologists and ethnobotanists about Amazonian shamanic rituals involving the use of ayahuasca, North American and European adventurers in the 1970s began seeking out ayahuasca shamans for novel experiences. This flurry of interest resulted in a mix of research and popular literature that in turn stimulated the local staging of ayahuasca rituals for foreign visitors. By the 1990s, this demand had blossomed into the small-scale industry of "ayahuasca tourism," providing a major nexus for the internationalization of ayahuasca. Today, ayahuasca tourism is a complex and flourishing business that consists of transnational networks of visitors and both foreign and local agents across several Amazonian countries. These networks are activated in organized tours of ayahuasca shamans in the United States and Canada, in various European countries, in Africa, and in Asia, who offer talks and perform rituals that may or may not include the use of ayahuasca. Some of the touring shamans are clearly not indigenous, while others assert authentic indigenous roots. Shamans of mixed blood have to position themselves with constructed images that are of interest to their audience in the multiple recasting of identities presented in this volume. The emergence of Western adepts and apprentices of local shamans—so-called *gringo shamans*—who frequently act as mediators for foreign visitors seeking spiritual insights, medical cures or psychonautic experiences, adds to the complex panorama of contemporary agents in ayahuasca shamanism.

Local shamanism, cosmopolitan biomedicine and psychology, alternative therapies, New Age spirituality, and the tourism service industry have blended in intricate and fascinating ways that challenge traditional ethnographic notions of authenticity, ethnicity, tradition, and place. Indeed, in many cases anthropologists have participated directly in these activities by publicizing and defending ayahuasca use, and sometimes even benefiting themselves economically as they turn into "facilitators" for gringo-oriented shamanic workshops and retreats.

The simultaneous expansion of local and transregional forms of ayahuasca shamanism, compounded by the recent development of ayahuasca tourism, has fueled a rising interest in ayahuasca; yet ayahuasca shamanism has been poorly addressed in the anthropological literature. This is in part because of the essentialist bias implicit in notions of authenticity and indigeneity, along with the relative paucity of studies on mixed forest people in Amazonia. Many anthropologists want to work with "authentic" Amazonian shamans, not tourist-pandering "charlatans"; the chapters in this book explore this territory. The authors give insight into who chooses to become a shaman, what kind of shaman, and why shamanism has become so popular. Shamans act as the intermediaries between worlds that they have always been: either interpreting native tradition for the tourists while navigating the world of gringos, or traveling into the invisible world and back dialoguing with other Indians. At the same time, these contemporary shamans attempt to maintain community and local social ties. The majority of the chapters address how the meaning and purpose of rituals are translated to outsiders and echo back in native contexts.

The role of ritual in mediating the encounter between indigenous traditions and modernity is also considered. Grassroots Amazonian shamans have to contend with an uneasy transition from traditional ayahuasca shamanism, including divination, sorcery, and curing sorcery-inflicted wounds, to using ayahuasca for self-exploration and to cater to Westerners' hopes of healing both physical and emotional ailments. Simultaneously, they are also involved, either directly or indirectly, in local interethnic exchanges among indigenous groups.

We argue that ayahuasca shamanism provides a uniquely rich platform to discuss the complexity of interrelations between Indians and non-Indians, neo-shamans and traditional healers, local people and outsiders, as well as interrelations among indigenous Amazonians. All these actors are involved in ayahuasca shamanism from differing perspectives. Contributors to this volume offer an unprecedented grasp of overall trends in Amazonian shamanism through multifaceted analyses that are based on detailed local ethnographies of ayahuasca rituals. Collectively, the chapters address indigenous and mestizo networks of exchange and alliance that are deeply rooted in the history of the various ethnic groups of the Amazon and in a shared popular cosmology and shamanic culture.

Glenn Shepard, Jr., a North American ethnobotanist and anthropologist who lives in northern Brazil and has done extensive fieldwork in Peru, opens the book. He observes and reflects on the recent introduction of *Psychotria* leaves, one of the most common components of the ayahuasca brew, to the Matsigenka, and the adoption in the late eighties of ayahuasca by the Yora in the Manu river region in Peru. He notes the participation of a charismatic indigenous politician in the spread of the use of the brew, and the ironic role of missionaries in the proliferation of local variations of ayahuasca shamanism. Apart from the historical account, Shepard gives a detailed description of the varieties of plants and ideas associated with them. This chapter introduces new ethnographic data and challenges the stereotypes of ayahuasca shamanism as uniform, static, and millennial that currently circulate throughout the Internet and in the advertising materials of contemporary ayahuasca retreat centers in the Amazon. It attests to diversity and dynamism in indigenous identity, belief, and ritual practices. His chapter invites a relativization of the essentialist conceptions present in models for regulation of the use of psychoactive substances in Western societies. The Matsigenka and Yora's recent adoption of a certain kind of ayahuasca shamanism provokes reflection on the processes through which governments have made legal and cultural exceptions for psychoactive drug use for specific cultural groups associated with a certain "tradition," designated by particular geographic boundaries and temporality.

The next chapter is written by the Brazilian anthropologist Mariana Pantoja, who has been able to observe from the privileged position of her house in the city of Rio Branco, in Acre, new effervescent developments taking place in this area and also in the remote Alto Juruá, in the Brazilian Amazon. Her contribution describes the recent ethnic self-identification of the Kuntanawa people, individuals who were previously known as mestizo rubber tappers and who are reestablishing their indigenous origins as part of a process of local leadership disputes and struggles for territorial rights. She notes the role of ayahuasca rituals in this process of reinvention of ethnic and cultural identity. Interestingly, the Kuntanawa's historical use of ayahuasca has been influenced by the Santo Daime religious movement, alongside indigenous and mestizo references. Pantoja observes that the Kuntanawa have joined other indigenous groups in the promotion of a pan Pano-ethnic alliance through the institution of common festivals. In these, the Indians exchange knowledge, perform rituals, and "share their culture" with an external audience. These events can be placed within larger contemporary processes of objectification of culture, as discussed in the contemporary literature on this topic. The Kuntanawa identity is controversial, with criticisms stemming from both local ideas on indigeneity and traditional anthropological concepts of "culture" as some sort of fixed and coherent unity. It is not by chance that their ethnic (re)construction is done in dialogue with anthropologists (such as the one who writes the chapter) and is highly reflexive.

Pirjo Kristiina Virtanen's chapter follows, continuing the topic of the role of ayahuasca in establishing interethnic alliances in the Brazilian Amazon. This Finnish anthropologist has done fieldwork in Brazil with the lesser-known Manchineri group, and also at the pan-indigenous meetings that currently take place in the city of Rio Branco. She recounts her own experiences as a visitor to ceremonies where alliances are created among indigenous peoples from diverse ethnic groups. This exchange takes place on the intersecting planes of bodies and ritual poetics, which includes the chanting and music that are central to many ritual contexts described in this book. These hybrid spaces where histories and mythologies are communicated allow Indians who live in the cities to learn and affirm their ethnicity, and also to create alliances with non-Indian associates. Virtanen also describes the expansion of these rituals beyond Acre, where ayahuasca rituals seem to be privileged spaces for the communication of an Amazonian indigeneity. Further, she reflects on how traveling shamans and their presumed wealth are viewed—not without controversy—in their own communities. This chapter also adds to the comprehension of classic topics of shamanism, such as the role of ritual in establishing controlled spaces for interaction with dangerous forces, as well as the creation of knowledge as a bodily, collective, and cosmic enterprise.

Esther Jean Langdon and Isabel Santana de Rose are based in the Department of Anthropology of the University of Florianópolis, known to have a rich nucleus for the study of shamanism. Their chapter registers a unique ritual combination of indigenous Guarani Indians from Brazil, the Santo Daime ayahuasca church, and an international neo-shamanic group. The authors reflect on the dialogues established in this dynamic network shaped by multidirectional flows of people, substances, and knowledge. Shared ritual elements of ayahuasca ceremonies and mutually agreed-on concepts are subject to constant change with the introduction of new actors or information. Langdon and Rose argue that contemporary shamanism is dialogical: it cannot be understood as a philosophy or logic in itself, independent of specific social, political, and historical contexts. This case is a great empirical example of multiple exchanges and translations between city and forest; reappropriations that occur throughout diverse spaces and times. On the one hand, the distant northern Amazonian brew helps the southern Indians to "remind them of things from their past, their cultural traditions and history," and, on the other, it contributes to the establishment of ayahuasca as a symbol of a pan-indigenous universal spirituality for an urban, New Age population. Again, the process of cultural revitalization is entangled with tensions and dispute.

Continuing reflections on the transnational circuit, Anne-Marie Losonczy and Silvia Mesturini Cappo's chapter appears next. On the basis of their fieldwork experiences in Peru and Colombia, these French-speaking researchers address what they name "urban and transcontinental shamanism," a phenomenon centered on mobility and networks. The authors identify the genesis of the creation of categories such as "ayahuasca shamanism," and relate it to others such as "altered states of consciousness." In this chapter, they analyze the pattern of communication that is the foundation of the relationships between indigenous people and the Western spiritual seekers who interact with them in the context of ayahuasca rituals. Each party, the foreigners and the ritual experts (indigenous or *mestizo* shamans), seems to interpret the other to mean ideas that are culturally familiar to them, but sometimes very different from what the speaker intended, thus allowing these parties to communicate and achieve common goals while maintaining unchallenged concepts used ordinarily for structuring their worlds. In other words, they argue that these divergent logics may still allow communication through a certain degree of mutual misunderstandings, creating the perception of a shared agreement, and allowing both parties to meet their goals. Needless to say, this paradigm is not without conflict. By addressing the role of ayahuasca as a mediator in the world of the West and its Other, or in interethnic relationships, Losonczy and Mesturini Cappo situate the current transformations of Amazonian shamanism in the historical context of the colonization of the Americas.

The next chapter was written by Françoise Barbira Freedman, a classic Cambridge anthropologist who draws on longitudinal observations as an eyewitness to the transformation of Peruvian vegetalismo since the seventies. She reports on the Iquitos-Nauta road located in Iquitos, Peru, a city that seems to have become the new, internationally known ayahuasca Mecca. In this environment, there is a high concentration of shamans of various ethnicities, backgrounds, and experience levels: a complex range of classification that includes, in her words, "indigenous, covert indigenous, mestizo, and gringo shamans." Some have established lodges to give ayahuasca to seekers who live in the vicinity and who come from afar. She describes the explosive growth of these centers, and their main characteristics, along with their network of alliances and deadly disputes. These spaces are stimulated by the approval of paying foreigners—sometimes identified as "passengers" instead of "tourists"—who gravitate toward those centers, and shamans who vie to appear the most "authentic." In this context, "indigeneity" seems to be the central currency of exchange. Barbira Freedman's chapter is provocative as it addresses both the rich, creative, and dynamic aspects involved in the current internationalization, including the revitalization of aspects of vegetalismo, and its impending conflicts. Like other authors in this volume, she points to the low regard in which shamans who specialize in gringo rituals are sometimes held by communities who accuse them of greed. She also positions this expansion within the history and symbolism of regional shamanism, such as the geography of poles of power in the Upper Amazon. She argues that contemporary "road shamans" and their travels reflect classic motives of Amazonian shamanism, and link trajectories in a forest-urban continuum.

The chapter by Evgenia Fotiou, a Greek anthropologist based in the United States, continues reflections on the activities around this capital of ayahuasca tourism, the city of Iquitos. She examines the motivations of gringos who travel to South America in search of ayahuasca ceremonies, a phenomenon she names "shamanic tourism," characterized by "pilgrimages," in contrast to the seeking of recreational use of drugs. Her work draws on a period of seventeen months of fieldwork in Iquitos. She examines the motivations of these tourists, and how what they find relates to what they had hoped to find, as shamans manage to reflexively tailor their presentation to the expectations of visitors. Furthermore, she identifies some "psychologizing processes" involved in the experiences of these foreigners, and their relationship to aspects such as witchcraft and the vegetalista diets. She also examines an idea popular among foreigners that ayahuasca is a feminine entity, and proposes a more nuanced interpretation in this regard, taking into account native gender concepts. Her balanced approach leads to a picture of shamanic tourism as consistent with the nature of Amazonian shamanism, which has historically involved exchange with the Other. Nevertheless, the danger that these activities further essentialize and marginalize indigenous cultures and their knowledge is pointed out.

Beatriz Caiuby Labate's chapter is the result of many years of this Brazilian anthropologist's travels and research around South America, North America, and Europe, focusing on the relationship of foreigners to Peruvian vegetalismo. Her research gives special attention to ayahuasca use in Pucallpa, a less-touristic town than Iquitos. Labate looks at the activities of various *ayahuasqueros*, including indigenous, poor mestizo, and middle-class Peruvians, and gringos who themselves became leaders of sessions in Peru or in their home countries. She identifies and describes the main processes involved in the diversification and internationalization of Peruvian vegetalismo. This expansion is possible through creative translations performed on both sides, where the foreign references are dynamically incorporated and reappropriated under the logic of vegetalismo and vice versa. This chapter follows others in the collection that identify the contours of transnational networks and circuits that promote the migration and flux of people and "sacred technologies" on a global scale. The author argues that this phenomenon should not be understood as a mere commodification of indigenous spirituality, or neocolonialism, but as a product of deliberate local strategies to adapt to changing socioeconomic conditions. Nevertheless, she recognizes several conflicts and shortcomings. This is the only chapter in the book to address, even if laterally, regulation of the use of ayahuasca, which faces diverse legal challenges in, and outside South America.

Bernd Brabec de Mori is an Austrian ethnomusicologist who speaks from the perspective of an "incorporated gringo" who has married a Shipibo woman and lived among the Shipibo of the Yarinacocha region of Pucallpa, Peru. By outlining six brief life stories, and dialoguing with the literature on Amerindian perspectivism (cf. Eduardo Viveiros de Castro), he attempts to provide an insider's view of how the Shipibo interpret the foreigners who approach them for ayahuasca ceremonies. He echoes the ideas of Shepard in this volume, and authors elsewhere, who suggest that ayahuasca may have been a recent introduction to many of the indigenous groups who currently use it, which is perhaps especially ironic in terms of the reputation that the Shipibo have acquired as some sort of "masters of ayahuasca, the ancient Amazonian tradition" in Northern countries. Brabec de Mori describes the transition from the use of ayahuasca related to warfare, hunting, sorcery, and healing to its use in psychological self-exploration among Westerners, and transitions from the figures of the *médicos* (doctors) to the *chamanes* (shamans). He points out the uncomfortable issues present in this expansion, such as the observation that ayahuasca tourism frequently increases local economic inequalities and challenges the possibility of continuity of treatment for locals; and the fact that Indians, despite what some of us may wish, do not always distinguish clearly between characters such as an ayahuasca tourist, a gringo apprentice, and a researcher—all are identified as the Other. On the other hand, while pointing out the negotiations and mediations between both universes, he suggests that some *rinko* (gringo, foreigner) apprentices can be incorporated into local kinship relationships. He also explores how contemporary Western-oriented ayahuasca rituals might fit into Shipibo cosmology, which plays an important role in defining their positionality in the cosmos and in a globalized world. As has been shown in other chapters of this book, ayahuasca ceremonies are often related to ways of dealing with alterity.

Daniela Peluso also offers a critical view on the expansion of Amazonian shamanism to larger audiences. She is an anthropologist currently based in the United Kingdom, and has worked with indigenous populations in Lowland South America for the last two decades, especially the Ese Eja. Focusing her research in Puerto Maldonado, Peru, she addresses one of the most controversial aspects of the expansion of ayahuasca use and its impact on local communities, one that is among the most feared and talked about, but less concretely researched; her chapter analyzes gender relationships, sex, and seduction between shamans and local and nonlocal women who participate in ceremonies with them. Peluso explains how Amerindians understand sexual abstinence in diets and ceremonies in light of the qualities ascribed to sexual relationships in Amazonia, both on the material plane and in the noncorporeal world. Indigenous practices and symbolism are contrasted with meanings attributed to sexual abstinence by Westerners, such as those informed by New Age ideas on spirituality and healing. Departing from local narratives and from those collected from the Internet, Peluso explores the typical relationships females have with shamans and looks at the factors that contribute to the high number of foreign women who have reported sexual advances by shamans either during or after sessions. Engaging with critical feminism, the author also reflects on the role of the male gaze in touristic settings, especially in those that represent greater economic inequalities. If the meeting of unfamiliar cultures brings up issues of exploitation, misunderstanding, and mistrust, this chapter shows that these are more complicated matters than they first appear to be, since some of these conflicts are historically embedded in shamanism. Peluso's writing makes one wonder if there should be an effort to establish ethical codes of conduct for the interaction of shamans and clients that would be applicable cross-culturally, such as those that guide relationships between doctors and patients.

In the final chapter, the young Colombian anthropologist Alhena Caicedo Fernández considers how the use of yage—the Colombian version of ayahuasca—has spread in that country beyond its rural and urban folk origins. Unlike Peru, the expansion to a middle class and elite clientele in big cities seems to have arrived later, and mestizo shamanism seems less predominant. Yage here is combined with several urban references, such as New Age spirituality, including, for example, practices of North American Indians, holistic therapies, and varying degrees of popular Catholicism. In an environment of great shamanic experimentation that also encompasses, besides yage, the use of yopo, coca, and tobacco, yage remains connected to the images of the indigenous that predominate in national society. Non-indigenous Columbians and a few foreigners, who act as leaders or mediators to the leaders, establish their identity and legitimacy by being associated with a recognized *taita*, or ayahuasca elder, in the Putumayo-Caquetá region. Caicedo Fernández also explores the term *traditional indigenous medicine*, which is part of both a scholarly tradition and this current expansion. As in other chapters of this book, the author shows how the introduction of new actors and forms into the rituals has created tensions among practitioners of competing *malocas* (structures built for drinking ayahuasca), including conflict over the production and distribution of the ayahuasca, a topic generally underrepresented in the literature on ayahuasca.

This volume will be useful to anyone who wishes to understand the current trends of globalization of ayahuasca rituals as well as the contextualized transformations of shamanism in Amazonia that parallel, yet differ from, recent developments in Central Asia. Fueled by contradictions and historic continuities and discontinuities, ayahuasca shamanism has come to stay. This expansion cannot be reduced to some sort of Western cultural cannibalism or obsession with the substance's effects. The versatile appropriation and use of ayahuasca by relatively isolated indigenous groups in Amazonia and by neo-indigenous shamans who are reinventing rituals in a pan-Amerindian cultural context outside Amazonia point to its complex associations with indigeneity. The former favor ayahuasca as a cultural medium of exchange with downriver mixed populations that have access to urban-based power; the latter integrate the brew in their rituals as a portal of power for tapping into deeper sources of indigeneity. In contrast, ayahuasca is a hallmark of syncretism in the new religious movements that have arisen around its use in Brazilian Amazonia. Whether it is a hunter's tool, a sorcerer's weapon, a doctor's medicine, or a Daimista's Eucharist, ayahuasca's mysterious qualities seem to ennoble those who have mastered its power. Wherever it is introduced, the brew appears to elicit engagement with tradition and innovation, and with self and alterity, in ways that soon make it predominant in the contexts into which it is incorporated. Whether gringos opt for going native in Amazonia or choose to "do ayahuasca" with their own Celtic, Wiccan, Native North-American, or Eastern references, they are present in the transformational space of ayahuasca. At the same time, Amazonian indigenous and mestizo people make use of ayahuasca shamanism in novel forms to uphold reinvented traditions and emerging social identities, or to promote new ethnic and political alliances. As ever in the history of Amazonia, cultural transformation is dialogical, downstream and upriver, across towns and forests, inseparable from the cosmopolitan cultural trends enacted in the international political economy.

Notes

1. This paper was based on her Ph.D. dissertation; see Clancy Cavnar, "The Effects of Participation in Ayahuasca Rituals on Gays' and Lesbians' Self Perception" (Psy.D. diss., John F. Kennedy University, 2011).
2. Beatriz Caiuby Labate and Henrik Jungaberle, eds., *The Internationalization of Ayahuasca* (Zurich: Lit Verlag, 2011).
3. For a historical overview of vegetalismo, see: Françoise Barbira Freedman, *Tree Shamans of the Upper Amazon: Lamas in the Historical Emergence of Ayahuasca Shamanism* (CAAAP: Lima, in press).

1

Will the Real Shaman Please Stand Up?

The Recent Adoption of Ayahuasca Among Indigenous Groups of the Peruvian Amazon

GLENN H. SHEPARD, JR.

Ayahuasca use has been adopted, modified, and reinvented in urban contexts around the globe.[1] The dynamism and diversity in contemporary urban shamanism[2] is assumed to stand in contrast with a uniform and ageless tradition of indigenous shamanism "practiced without interruption for at least five thousand years."[3] Yet some authors have noted a great diversity in indigenous shamanistic practices in South America.[4] If anything, tobacco, rather than ayahuasca, seems to be the keystone of South American shamanism.[5] Peter Gow[6] was the first to make the almost heretical suggestion that ayahuasca use in the western Amazon might be a fairly recent phenomenon that spread as a result of dislocation and interethnic contact in the late nineteenth century during the Rubber Boom. At the time, Gow admitted that his hypothesis was "speculative" and "suffers from a lack of hard data to back it up."[7] Bernd Brabec de Mori contributes a considerable amount of "soft data"[8] toward Gow's hypothesis, using historical documents and linguistic analysis to show how the Shipibo ayahuasca complex, widely considered paradigmatic of millennial indigenous shamanism, appears to have been borrowed in colonial times from neighboring peoples. Antonio Bianchi[9] describes two distinctive sets of shamanistic traditions among Peruvian indigenous groups. First, he characterizes a more homogeneous and widespread tradition of *curandero* healers using the standard ayahuasca formula (*Banisteriopsis* vine plus *Psychotria* leaves), which is found among indigenous groups like the Shipibo along the major axes of colonial expansion. Second, he describes a more diverse set of practices using other plant preparations, notably tobacco, found among more remote indigenous groups, associated less with "curing" in the individual, therapeutic sense and more with promoting ecological harmony for the group.

Here I present two cases of very recent introduction of the standard ayahuasca formula in two neighboring indigenous groups of the Manu River region in southern Peru: the Matsigenka and the Yora (Nahua). Although attesting to the historical dynamism of indigenous people and their shamanic practices, the case also raises questions about authenticity, tradition, and culture, and how these concepts are used as a litmus test to judge the *bona fide* status and legality of ayahuasca use in "nontraditional" urban settings around the world.

Manu: Crossroads of the Twentieth Century

Throughout most of the twentieth century, Matsigenka and Yora populations have inhabited the Manu River headwaters in southeastern Peru, a region declared as a national park in 1973 and Biosphere Reserve in 1977. Though occupying overlapping territories, they belong to unrelated cultural-linguistic families (Arawak and Pano, respectively) and were at war with one another for much of the past century. Both entered into sustained contact with the Peruvian state and global society only in the second half of the twentieth century. Both populations were forced to the fringes of their traditional territory as they sought refuge from slavery, ethnic conflict, epidemic illnesses, and other consequences of European contact in the late nineteenth century.

Though touted in tourist pamphlets and wildlife films as a "Living Eden," Manu National Park in the Madre de Dios basin is far from untouched by human interference.[10] Human occupation of the region goes back as far as three thousand years, and the Inca empire built roads and established trading posts to exploit the region's rich resources.[11] Isolated geographically by the Andean cordillera to the west and nonnavigable rapids downstream in Bolivia to the east, the Manu and upper Madre de Dios remained largely free of colonial intrusions through the late nineteenth century. In 1894, the rubber baron Carlos Fermín Fitzcarrald hauled a steamship across an isthmus from the upper Mishagua River (a tributary of the navigable Ucayali/Urubamba basin) into the headwaters of the Manu River (see Map 1), thereby opening the upper Madre de Dios to rubber exploitation and colonization. Fitzcarrald's crew first traded with, but later was attacked by, "Mashcos," fierce Indians of uncertain ethnicity. In retaliation, Fitzcarrald and his crew are said to have killed more than three hundred Mashcos, burning their houses and gardens and sinking their canoes.[12]

The Yora, or Nahua, speak a Panoan language similar to that spoken by the Yaminahua, Sharanahua, and Muranahua of the Purus River. According to their oral histories, they migrated to the Manu-Mishagua watershed soon after the collapse of the Rubber Boom in 1917, when Manu was abandoned by outsiders.[13] The Yora appear to have fled from Rubber Boom–era disruptions in their home region in the Purus basin to the northeast. They came to occupy the demographic and territorial void in the upper Manu left by the massacred Mashcos and the retreating rubber tappers. At first, the Yora obtained metal tools and other trade goods by searching and excavating around the abandoned rubber camps, and ate from the rubber tappers' abandoned banana plantations.[14] Later, the Yora came to satisfy their desire for trade goods by raiding Matsigenka settlements in the Manu headwaters, as well as Peruvian loggers on the Mishagua River. The Yora also attacked seismic teams working for Shell Oil from 1982 to 1984,[15] and in early 1984 made national headlines when they attacked and repelled an expedition of the Peruvian marines led by Peruvian President Fernando Belaunde to the Manu River headwaters, intending to inaugurate construction of the Peruvian leg of the Trans-Amazon highway.[16]

In May 1984, the Yora, faced with ever more frequent incursions by outsiders, finally initiated peaceful contact with loggers and were taken to visit the mission town of Sepahua on the lower Urubamba. Soon after, respiratory diseases decimated them. By 1990, nearly half of the original Yora population was dead.[17] The Yora left Manu to occupy the upper Mishagua in order to receive assistance from Protestant and Catholic missionaries operating out of Sepahua on the Urubamba River. José Choro, an astute and ambitious Yaminahua headman based in Sepahua, served as interpreter for the Yora during the early days of contact, and soon came to be the main intermediary, broker, and benefactor of trade relations between the Yora, the loggers of Sepahua, and missionaries of various denominations. It was also Choro who introduced ayahuasca to the Yora.

Closely related to the Ashaninka, or Campa, of the Ucayali River, the Matsigenka are an Arawakan-speaking people known from early colonial documents to inhabit the Urubamba River and its tributaries.[18] By the early to middle 1800s, they had entered the upper Madre de Dios Basin, where they engaged in both trade and warfare with the native Harakmbut populations of Madre de Dios.[19] During the Rubber Boom, Matsigenka laborers were especially valued for their peaceful and industrious disposition.[20] They were persecuted by frequent slave-raiding expeditions, leading many Matsigenka to seek refuge away from the major rivers in remote headwater regions.[21] The explorer Jorge von Hassel reported on the atrocious conditions of enslaved natives working at rubber camps along the Manu River during this time, and estimated 60 percent mortality owing to disease and mistreatment.[22]

A few Matsigenka remained along the main course of the Manu River in the aftermath of the Rubber Boom, while others from isolated, refuge communities in the headwaters moved further north and east into the Manu Basin, occupying the demographic void left by the slaughtered Mashcos.[23] The Matsigenka came to occupy the upper Sotileja, Cumerjali, and other south-bank headwater tributaries of the Manu River by the middle of the twentieth century, but were stopped in their expansion by the arrival of the bellicose Yora in Manu's northern and eastern tributaries. Both sides experienced numerous casualties during Yora raids.[24] Sometimes the Matsigenka pursued the Yora to punish retreating warriors, but they never managed to mount a counterattack at the Yora settlements. Once the Matsigenka were settled by missionaries in larger, easily accessible villages with greater access to trade goods, Yora raids increased, reaching a peak in the late 1970s through the mid-1980s[25] as the Yora were also experiencing increased pressure from loggers and oil prospectors along the Mishagua.

The Matsigenka, currently the main indigenous population of Manu Park, did not occupy the main course of the Manu River in large numbers until the early 1960s, when Protestant missionaries employed native guides from the Urubamba region to contact remote Matsigenka settlements throughout the region to set up a centralized community at Tayakome. Ironically, given the missionaries' distaste for native religion,[26] it was precisely these native guides who first introduced the Matsigenka of Manu to the *Psychotria* admixture of the ayahuasca brew.

Figure 1.1. Matsigenka man holding ayahuasca vine. The Matsigenka people cultivate several distinctive varieties of ayahuasca, known as *kamarampi* in their language. © G. H. Shepard.

Matsigenka: "The Leaf from Urubamba"

Prior to contact with these native guides from the Urubamba, the Matsigenka of the Manu and upper Madre de Dios made a psychoactive preparation from the *Banisteriopsis* vine that did *not* include *Psychotria viridis* or similar species. Psychoactive preparations of *Banisteriopsis* and related species without *Psychotria* admixtures are reported in other groups of the Peruvian Amazon.[27] The Matsigenka boiled this traditional *Banisteriopsis* preparation for long periods of time—"from early morning until late afternoon," according to accounts, so perhaps eight to ten hours—until it was reduced to a honeylike consistency.[28] They sometimes added other plants to this brew, including *Fittonia albivenis, Geoganthus poeppigi, Biophytum* sp., and an unidentified species of orchid. It is possible that some of these may contain trace amounts of some psychoactive compound. The orchid species, for example, is said to bring the sky down low to the earth, so the shaman can climb up into the spirit realm. However these uses may also reflect symbolic associations: *Fittonia* and *Geoganthus*, popular ornamentals cultivated worldwide, have brightly colored venation and markings on the leaves, which the Matsigenka associate with the colorful patterns evoked in hallucinogenic trance. The orchid grows high in trees and is collected only when a branch falls, providing a symbolic connection with the sky. Whether or not these admixtures have psychoactive properties, prolonged cooking of *Banisteriopsis* may change the chemical composition or raise the concentration of beta-carboline compounds in the brew such as harmine, harmaline, and tetrohydroharmine, known to have psychoactive effects at high enough doses.[29]

The Matsigenka cultivate six or more domesticated varieties of *Banisteriopsis,* all of which belong to the species *B. caapi.* The Matsigenka say each variety has distinctive horticultural properties and pharmacological effects when consumed. The multiple varieties of *Banisteriopsis,* like other Matsigenka cultigens, are said to have been brought by shamans from the sky.[30] The Matsigenka recognize wild *B. caapi* and related species such as *tevuine igamarampite* ("hawk's ayahuasca," probably *Hirea* sp.), but consider these wild species to be unsuitable for consumption. This intensity of knowledge and domestication of *Banisteriopsis* suggests that the Matsigenka have a fairly long history of using the ayahuasca vine prior to learning about the DMT-containing ayahuasca brew potentiated by *Psychotria* admixtures.

Beginning in the late 1950s, native guides from the Urubamba region, particularly the Camisea River, visited isolated Matsigenka settlements of the Manu headwaters and taught them to add *Psychotria* leaves as an admixture to *Banisteriopsis.* For this reason, the people of Manu refer to *Psychotria* as *orovampashi,* literally "Urubamba leaf." The Urubamba populations themselves call the plant "chacruna," reflecting contact with indigenous and mestizo populations further down the Ucayali. Though it grows naturally in the lowland forests along the floodplain of the Manu River and its tributaries, the Matsigenka there were formerly unaware of this use of *Psychotria. Psychotria viridis* is the most frequently mentioned admixture to *Banisteriopsis* noted in the literature on western Amazonian ethnobotany. *P. viridis* is also used by the Yora and Yaminahua in their *Banisteriopsis* brew. The Matsigenka recognize this species but consider *P. viridis* to be a dangerous plant, used only by sorcerers of rival tribes such as the Shipibo and Piro. The Matsigenka name for *P. viridis* is *pijirishi*, "bat *Psychotria*," or *yakomamashi*, "anaconda leaf," since it is said to cause terrifying visions of fanged bats and snakes. The Matsigenka use a different *Psychotria* species or subspecies to mix with ayahuasca. I collected botanical vouchers on many occasions but was unable to identify its species despite visiting several herbaria. According to the Matsigenka, this species or variety, called *orovampa-sano*, "true Urubamba-leaf," causes no unpleasant visions of bats or snakes, but only "good" visions of happy, dancing people. This information suggests that closely related species or subspecies of *Psychotria* may contain different concentrations or chemical variants of DMT with varying psychoactive effects, which are perceived and valued differently according to the cultural group.

The Matsigenka remember the former admixtures and sometimes add them to the contemporary *Banisteriopsis-Psychotria* preparation to enhance its effects. But, other than this occasional and perhaps nostalgic reference to the older tradition, *Psychotria* has completely replaced the prior admixtures. No one has prepared *Banisteriopsis* brew without *Psychotria* since the late 1950s or early 1960s. I have been unsuccessful in eliciting specific descriptions of the prior brew's effects, since the Matsigenka are generally reluctant to speak in detail about such experiences. When I have asked older men about the former brew, they mention that it, too, is strongly "intoxicating" (*kepigari*) and takes the shaman to the spirit world as effectively as the contemporary *Psychotria*-based brew. The main difference they note is the consistency, always referred to as thick and honeylike, and the longer time needed for preparation. The *Psychotria*-based brew, by contrast, can be consumed when still in liquid form after about four to six hours of cooking, with no need to reduce it to a thicker consistency. Although the reduced preparation time is certainly a factor, I assume that the *Psychotria*-based ayahuasca brew is preferred today, indeed used exclusively, because it provides stronger and more consistent intoxicating effects than the older formula.

The Matsigenka currently use ayahuasca only during the rainy season, the season when animals get fat on forest fruits and hunters are most active. The main purpose for using ayahuasca is not for healing in the strict sense, but rather for hunters to improve their aim. In this sense, despite having adopted the *Psychotria*-based ayahuasca brew, the Matsigenka maintain the general features of the "pre-ayahuasca" indigenous shamanic complex described by Bianchi as focusing on ecological, rather than therapeutic, functions.[31] Bouts of vomiting

Figure 1.2. Psychotria leaves. The Matsigenka of Manu learned about the potent *Psychotria* admixture for ayahuasca only recently through contact with neighboring peoples of the Urubamba river. For this reason they call it *orovampashi*, "Urubamba leaf." © G. H. Shepard.

and physical purging clean the hunter of impurities, dietary improprieties, and taboo violations that accumulate in his body.[32] Indeed, the Matsigenka word for both the ayahuasca vine and the brew, *kamarampi*, means literally "vomiting medicine," emphasizing its fundamental role in purging and purification. In addition to physical purification, the visionary state allows hunters to interact directly with spirits that control access to game animals. Throughout the rainy season, groups of related men (especially brothers-in-law) take ayahuasca in group sessions for the avowed purpose of better hunting. The transition from rainy to dry season, and the subsequent cycles of ayahuasca consumption and prohibition, are marked by specific ecological cues. From the time the *puigoro* plant (*Vernonia* sp.) flowers in the dry season until all its airborne, dandelion-like petals are washed away with the first rains, ayahuasca use is strictly forbidden. The Matsigenka claim that fires rage in the spirit world during this season and can burn the ayahuasca taker's soul. It is possible that psychoactive components in the two main plant mixtures change their composition with the season of the year, accounting for these observations. On the other hand, the dry season is also a time of cloudless nights and intense starlight, which may contribute to unpleasant visions of flames. The Matsigenka prefer to take ayahuasca in complete darkness, fearing that the slightest spark of artificial illumination, whether from a candle, match, kitchen fire, or flashlight, will burn the soaring soul. In this deep darkness, which banishes ordinary sight, the Matsigenka achieve "true seeing," *nesanotagantsi*.

Tobacco, rather than ayahuasca, is the quintessential psychoactive substance of the Matsigenka shaman. The Matsigenka word for shaman, *seripigari*, means literally "the one intoxicated by tobacco."[33] Tobacco was traditionally used as snuff (*opane*), or boiled to a paste known as *opatsa seri*[34] and absorbed in cotton balls to be chewed or swallowed as a quid. *Banisteriopsis* vine and even toxic *Bufo* frog eggs[35] are sometimes boiled with tobacco paste to potentiate its effects. Tobacco quid can be taken alone or consumed together with ayahuasca to maximize intoxication. More recently, immigrants from the Urubamba and Ucayali introduced the smoking of cured tobacco in pipes.

The most potent psychoactive plant in the Matsigenka shaman's arsenal is *Brugmansia suaveolens*. It is considered the most "intoxicating" (*kepigari*) and hence the strongest of all Matsigenka plant medicines. The Matsigenka of the Urubamba call it *saaro*, but *Brugmansia* is known in the Manu dialect simply as *kepigari*, "intoxicating," or else *jayapa*, the same name given the plant among the neighboring Harakmbut-speaking groups.[36] Great care is taken in the preparation and dosage of *Brugmansia* because of its high potency and toxicity: a moderate dose can last for several days, and a large dose can last for weeks, even months. Excessive use is believed to cause insanity, and the Matsigenka of the region have reported two deaths caused by overdoses. Young shamans may take a strong dose of *Brugmansia* and wander alone in the forest for several days to establish initial contact with the spirits. An infusion of *Brugmansia* may also be given as a last resort to treat people suffering from incurable illnesses, witchcraft, or severe accidents. Unlike *Banisteriopsis* and tobacco, used often in group rituals, *Brugmansia* is usually taken alone, and only very rarely.

Under the influence of various psychoactive plants, specialist shamans as well as nonspecialist "lay" users gain power through an ongoing relationship with the *Sangariite*: elusive, luminous beings who serve as the Matsigenka's spirit allies. The name Sangariite is derived from the root *-sanga-*, meaning "pure, clean, clear, invisible." The Sangariite reside in villages in the forest that are perceptible under ordinary circumstances merely as small, natural clearings made by mutualistic ants known as *matyaniro* (*Myrmelachista* spp.) around the shrub *matyagiroki* (*Cordia nodosa*).[37] When someone visits these clearings under the influence of hallucinogenic plants, especially *Brugmansia*, they reveal their true nature: large villages full of dancing people surrounded by rich gardens. Entering the Sangariite village, the shaman may obtain novel varieties of food crops or medicinal plants for cultivation.[38] In trance, he or she may convince the Sangariite to release game animals for the Matsigenka to hunt, or enlist their aid to heal the sick.

In keeping with cultural norms of modesty and stoicism, Matsigenka shamans are reluctant to admit their practice. Indeed, to do so could result in accusations of sorcery. And yet, I also get the sense that anyone who uses ayahuasca and other psychoactive plants, especially tobacco, with regularity inevitably builds connections with the spirit world and is, in this sense, climbing the ladder of shamanic initiation even if he or she does not openly admit to being a "shaman." For example, when I have participated in ayahuasca ceremonies and taken tobacco snuff (*seri*), my companions often ask, half-joking, "*Piseripigata*?!" which means both, "Are you intoxicated by tobacco?!" and "Are you (becoming) a shaman?!"

I have observed a curious paradox regarding gender in Matsigenka shamanism and healing. Many female shaman-healers are mentioned in the oral histories of Matsigenka communities in the Manu and Madre de Dios, corresponding to the generation just prior to and during missionary contact in the late 1950s. And yet today, there are sparingly few, if any, female shaman-healers in these villages. Women are reluctant to consume ayahuasca even when their husbands vehemently call them to drink during the ceremonies. Although women maintain an important pharmacopeia of medicinal plants, especially with regard to child health,[39] medicinal plant knowledge and shamanistic healing are largely separate and independent realms of therapy.[40] Where have all the female shaman-healers gone? Though this conclusion is highly speculative, I suspect that the recent introduction of the *Psychotria*-ayahuasca brew, and the concomitant incorporation of the new figure of the ayahuasca curandero as shaman-healer, may have upset the gender balance among traditional healers. Whereas in prior times, male-dominated rituals involving psychoactive plants and focusing on hunting were a realm apart from shamanic healing ceremonies, the two functions have now become fused in the male-dominated ayahuasca ritual.

In Matsigenka communities of the Urubamba, a new breed of folk healer, the "steam bath healer" (*tsimpokantatsirira*), has emerged in recent years as an alternative to the more secretive and less publicly acceptable shaman-healers. Especially where evangelical missionaries have been active, Matsigenka tobacco shamans and ayahuasca curanderos work with extreme discretion, if at all. Steam bath healers, however, generally perform their ceremonies during the day, in public view of the household of the patient. They first heat river stones in a fire and then place the hot stones in a pot full of herbs and water, causing the water to boil and give off steam (*otsimpokake*). The patient stands over the boiling pot under a cotton tunic or blanket in order to bathe in the steam. When the session is over, the healer removes the stones and herbs from the pot and, to the surprise of the patient, finds various foreign items that were supposedly introduced into the patient's body by sorcery and have emerged with the steam. Commonly mentioned intrusive objects include nails, wires, bicycle spokes, empty medicine bottles, and other manufactured goods as well as herbs. By removing these intrusive objects, the healer is thought to relieve the underlying cause of pain and illness. Matsigenka steam bath healers have learned the technique mostly from Asháninka migrants, to whom they must pay significant amounts of cash to learn the secrets of the trade. The removal of the intrusive, illness-causing objects directly parallels the activity of shaman-healers. Steam bath healers are able to operate without the same stigma as the tobacco and ayahuasca shamans, although some Evangelical converts are beginning to denounce steam bath healers as devil worshipers as well. It is also interesting to note that both women and men train to become steam bath healers in roughly equal proportion, unlike the contemporary ayahuasca curanderos, who are almost exclusively male. The steam bath tradition, though very new, harkens back to a prior time when shaman-healers of both genders were common.

Yora: Ayahuasca Express

Prior to their 1984 contact, the Yora were unaware of the hallucinogenic *Banisteriopsis-Psychotria* mixture. Instead, they used a bitter-tasting liana of the genus *Paullinia,* which they call *tsimo* (pronounced "tsee-boh," literally "astringent"). The vine is nearly indistinguishable from a similar *Paullinia* species used by the Yora for fish poison, known as *pora.* (Note that the Yora name for the psychoactive *Paullinia,* "tsimo," is pronounced very much like the Brazilian vernacular term "timbó," referring to a *Paullinia* species used as fish poison.) Tsimo was boiled for several hours to prepare a strongly bitter-astringent beverage, producing nausea, sweating, body pains, blurred vision, and vague, shadowy hallucinations. The beverage was consumed by the Yora in group ceremonies that involved shamanistic chanting and healing. If strict dietary prohibitions were not followed before and after consumption (for example, no catfish, no armadillo, no tapir, etc.), the brew was said to cause severe side effects, among them pustules and lesions on the skin. One Yora man alive today has a chronic and apparently untreatable skin lesion covering most of his ankle that is blamed on improper diet while using tsimo almost thirty years ago.

Yora shaman-healers were known as *kokoti,* a word derived from the verb root "to suck." These ritual specialists, distinct from herbal healers (*nisaya*), healed by chewing tobacco, chanting, and sucking on the patient's body and then spitting, often revealing the presence of blood in their saliva. The blood is a sign that wasp spirits (*wina*) or other malevolent entities have stung the heart, causing illness. With successive healings, the concentration of blood in the saliva slowly diminishes.[41] Though many *kokoti* died during the epidemics of the early contact years, the practice has continued to be an important aspect of Yora medicine, fully integrated with the ayahuasca shamanism that was adopted beginning in 1984. The Yora are enthusiastic chewers of tobacco, kept in great wads nearly the size of baseballs in their swollen cheeks. Yora healers likewise use chewing tobacco and, more recently, mestizo-style pipes to consume tobacco during ayahuasca healing sessions.

José Choro, the Yaminahua headman who served as intermediary throughout the Yora contact, introduced them to ayahuasca early in the process. Within the year, the Yora were consuming ayahuasca almost daily, and the *Paullinia* brew was completely abandoned. Today they refer to both the *Banisteriopsis* vine and the ayahuasca brew by the Yaminahua name *xori.* The Yora claim that ayahuasca gives a more pleasant and vivid sense of intoxication with none of the toxic side effects that the traditional *Paullinia* beverage presented. They say that the *Paullinia* vine was "bad," and this is why they no longer use it. However, the Yaminahua headman Choro may have played a part in encouraging such negative attitudes, as he had a vested interest in asserting complete control over the Yora group. In addition to monopolizing economic negotiations with outsiders for many years and marrying three Yora wives, Choro also retrained the surviving Yora healers in the use of ayahuasca under his tutelage. As captured in Graham

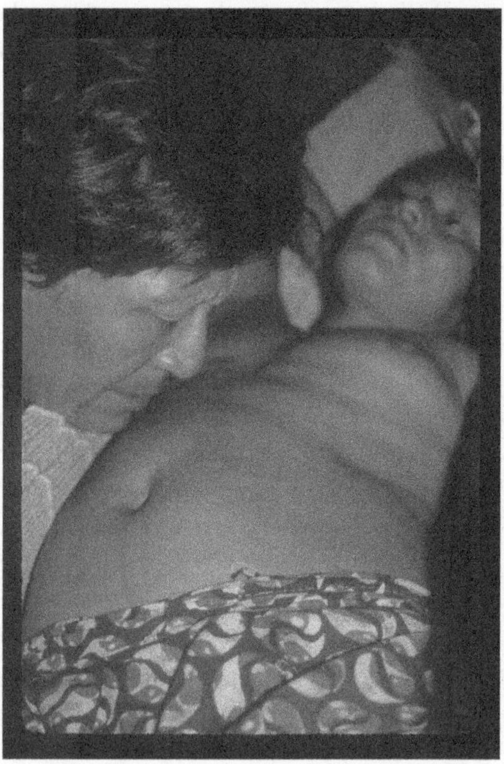

Figure 1.3. Yora shaman singing. The Yora (Nahua) headman Nishpopinima was initiated into ayahuasca shamanism by José Choro, the Yaminahua man who brokered the Yora's contact beginning in 1985. Here, Nishpopinima in trance sings a healing song over a patient. © G. H. Shepard.

Townsley's 1990 documentary film *The Shaman and His Apprentice*, Choro initiates the Yora headman, Nishpopinima, into shamanism. Turning the Yora headman into his shamanic apprentice only solidified Choro's thorough political, economic, and spiritual domination over the group.

The Yora, always fascinated by novelty and the trappings of outsiders,[42] adopted ayahuasca wholeheartedly. During my long months of fieldwork from 1995 to 1997 in the village of Serjali, they prepared ayahuasca nearly every day. Choro and other Yaminahua shamans in the village, as well as Nishpopinima and other Yora adepts, performed public healing ceremonies several times a week. Yora and Yaminahua healers eagerly invite the entire village, as well as resident anthropologists, tourists, or other visitors, to witness, photograph, tape-record, and film their sessions. This openness and enthusiasm about ayahuasca shamanism contrasts sharply with the secrecy and modesty surrounding Matsigenka shamanism and healing.

Unlike the Matsigenka, the Yora do not plant *Banisteriopsis* in their gardens, and instead consume the wild species. Because they use the vine so frequently, *Banisteriopsis* populations have been wiped out near the village, and they must go ever farther into the forest to find more. The Yora mix ayahuasca with several locally occurring *Psychotria* species, known both by their Yaminahua and mestizo Spanish names. They use *Psychotria viridis* and several similar species, including the same variety used by the Matsigenka, although they do not distinguish between the various species or subspecies recognized by the Matsigenka. During the ceremony, the Yaminahua, and now the Yora, pass around a gourd with the fragrant wild basil plant (*Scutellaria* sp.) to inhale at various moments, thereby dispelling foul-smelling demon spirits (*yõshi*) while attracting the fragrant *Xoma*, guardian spirits somewhat like the Sangariite of the Matsigenka. The healer sings poetic couplets that often begin by calling to the demon, animal spirit, or other malignant various forces believed to cause the illness. By calling to these illness-causing forces, the healer is able to draw them together and bring them under his power. Aspects of Western technology, for example, guns, motors, metal tools, and gasoline, are considered to be sources of heat and bad smells, and are therefore invoked in healing songs for treating high fevers and other introduced illnesses. Thus, in the realm of shamanic chants, just as in the realm of herbal medicines, Yora and Yaminahua healing practices reflect a profound "homeopathic" principle of efficacy at work, in the sense that "like treats like."[43] After calling to the objects or spirits believed to cause illness, the healer proceeds to dispel the illness with his own cooling breath and "fragrant songs" (*ini wanane*). An excerpt from a Yora/Yaminahua healing song that I recorded and translated demonstrates how odors, illness, and Western technology become melded in shamanic synesthesia[44] in this rich poetic tradition:

Whose illness is this?
The flaming illness of lightning
Its hot fire burns
Its white smoke
Its boiling fever

The owners of metal
The white people from down river
The metal people are burning
The metal knives are burning
The smell of hot steel

What strange people are these?
Their illness goes to the far reaches
The headwaters of the snaking river
None can escape the fever
How will we put out this fire?

Variations and Common Themes

There are many important differences in how the Matsigenka and the Yora have adopted the ayahuasca-*Psychotria* brew into their preexisting shamanistic and healing traditions, beginning with the brew itself. In my experience, the brew prepared by the Matsigenka of Manu has a much stronger hallucinogenic effect than that prepared by the Yora. Mateo, a Matsigenka companion who went with me to the Yora village and tried their brew, claimed that it got him drunk "just like masato" (manioc beer). He explained that the Matsigenka ayahuasca is stronger (and in his opinion, better) because it is prepared from cultivated *Banisteriopsis* liana, brought down from the sky by past Matsigenka shamans. The Yora, by contrast, use wild *Banisteriopsis*, which has no such divine pedigree. However, my observations suggest the Yora cook their brew a much shorter time than do the Matsigenka, on the order of two to three hours, compared with four to six hours of preparation among the Matsigenka. Furthermore, the Yora seem to add less *Psychotria* than the Matsigenka. The Yora appear to prefer the milder ayahuasca brew because it allows them to remember and sing their complex healing songs. When Mateo prepared his own ayahuasca brew in the village for the Yora, they said it was too strong and intoxicating (*pae*) for their liking, and interfered with their ability to sing: unlike typical Yora sessions, where they sing all night long, not a single Yora man raised his voice to sing during the whole session. The Matsigenka, by contrast, are unable to sing unless the intoxication comes on strong. With a relatively mild intoxication, such as

I experienced in my use of the Yora brew, the Matsigenka say they can't remember the songs, or rather, that the songs remain aloof, far away, buzzing faintly like a hive of bees on the horizon but never coming close enough to inspire the singer to burst into song.

Matsigenka healing sessions take place in absolute darkness, since even the faintest spark or other artificial illumination is thought to burn the souls of the participants, while distracting from the "true sight" (*nesanotagantsi*) revealed in trance. Yora and Yaminahua healers, on the other hand, often sit near a fire, and are not distressed by flashlights, camera flashes, or other sources of artificial illumination. The Yora and Yaminahua, like most Panoans and other Amazonian peoples, value ayahuasca-induced visions of anacondas, believed to be the spirit-owner or "mother" of the ayahuasca plant. The Matsigenka consider birds, for example, hummingbirds and the screaming piha (*Lipaugus vociferans*), to be their principle spirit guides, and consider visions of snakes to be evil omens. The Matsigenka avoid *Psychotria viridis* precisely because they claim it causes "bad" visions of snakes and bats, preferring a second, botanically unidentified *Psychotria* species or variety. The Yora, by contrast, do not distinguish between these several types and use them interchangeably.

The ayahuasca songs sung by the Matsigenka are often difficult to translate, since they incorporate many onomatopoeic, archaic, or nonsense words and are often chanted or mumbled without clear enunciation. It is also difficult to detect a clear narrative structure to any given song sequence. Most songs are improvised from within the depths of trance, combining stock phrases with complex verb suffixes, onomatopoeia, and esoteric vocabulary not found in ordinary language. The songs are said to come from the Sangariite themselves, and are not fully intelligible in ordinary states of consciousness. Matsigenka songs seem to derive their power as much from their acoustic properties, augmented by the hallucinogenic experience itself, as from any overt semantic content. In group sessions, men often sing together in chorus or fugue, or even sing different songs at the same time, further complicating any accurate, direct translation of the song narratives. As noted above, Yora and Yaminahua ayahuasca songs, by contrast, consist of poetic couplets sung clearly and organized into an overarching narrative structure. Yora and Yaminahua healers may spend several hours singing to the patient, who rests quietly in a hammock and may even fall asleep during the therapy. At several key times during the ceremony, the shaman blows onto a small gourd containing a warm infusion made from wild basil, and offers it to the patient to drink. The healer also sucks or massages body parts that are in pain.

Despite these differences, there is much in common between Matsigenka and Yora/Yaminahua shamanism. In the first place, both groups consider herbal healing and shamanistic healing to be separate realms. In the case of the Matsigenka, nonspecialist men and women use herbs to address various conditions that require no specialized intervention, and this knowledge is widely shared. On the other hand, shaman-healers, both in the past and in the present, must apprentice to a more experienced teacher to acquire the specialized knowledge needed to heal. Shaman-healers are invoked for special classes of illness, notably soul loss, the introduction of intrusive objects and, more recently, witchcraft and sorcery.[45] The Yora, unlike the Matsigenka, recognize specialized herbal healers known as *nisaya*, "owners of plant medicines," distinctive from the "sucking shamans" who remove intrusive objects. Despite popular misconceptions in which the shaman is considered the repository of all healing knowledge (including medicinal plants), in fact, many groups throughout South America distinguish between shamanic healing, which involves specialized knowledge (especially songs), and herbal healing, which may or may not be the province of specialists.[46] Note, however, that such a distinction between shamanic versus herbal healing does not necessarily correspond with a distinction between "natural" or "empirical" versus "supernatural" modes of therapy. Herbal remedies may address illnesses with spiritual causes,[47] while shamanistic ceremonies may be used for illnesses a Westerner might consider to be naturalistic in origin.[48] The distinction, rather, is between modes of agency, one construed predominantly through the ritual intervention of the shaman, and the other depending on the inherent, active principles, which can be both empirical and spiritual, of plants.

As in many Native American societies, Matsigenka and Yora/Yaminahua cosmology is characterized by an essential duality. The visible, daytime world of ordinary consciousness exists in parallel with the invisible world of spirits, associated with nighttime, nocturnal animals, the dead, dreams, and altered states of consciousness. Though evading detection by ordinary senses, the spirit world is omnipresent, and decides matters of life and death. Psychoactive plants of diverse species and forms of preparation allow people to access the spirit world while bringing practical outcomes in the realm of daily existence. In pre-ayahuasca times and the present, and unlike the curandero tradition of the Ucayali, both groups show a certain egalitarian ethos with regard to the use of psychoactive plants and the access they provide to the spirit world. In both cultures, psychoactive plants are consumed in fairly regular group rituals without a necessary therapeutic function, and without a necessary focus on the figure of the shaman or curandero as central to the ritual. In the past, these group rituals sought to achieve positive outcomes from agriculture and hunting expeditions (and Yora war parties) as well as on building rapport and solidarity within the group, rather than on healing specific illness conditions per se. Today, both groups, and especially the Matsigenka, consider the shaman-healer to be a rare and qualified specialist. Both groups recognized specialized shaman-healers prior to the introduction of the *Psychotria*-ayahuasca brew. However, their healing skills were more associated with tobacco use and the removal of intrusive objects, and did not necessarily have any relationship with the group consumption of psychoactive preparations in rituals, especially for hunting. Modern ayahuasca practice appears to fuse previously diverse functions and settings of psychoactive plant use for individual healing and group purposes. In the case of the Matsigenka, the introduction of ayahuasca-based curanderismo may have displaced women from traditional shamanistic healing roles.

Within both groups, illnesses that do not respond to other therapies (plants as well as Western medicines) are automatically suspected to have a hidden cause, perceptible and treatable only in the parallel world of spirits. Illnesses involving chronic suffering, wasting, sudden onset, dizziness, pain in the heart or chest, and inexplicable itching, swelling, or body aches are also suspect. During sleep or when walking alone in the forest, human victims may be attacked by vengeful animal and plant spirits, demons, ghosts, or human sorcerers. These malevolent beings may frighten their victims and steal their souls, leaving the body to suffer and wither. Alternatively, malevolent beings may introduce foreign objects (spines, bones, needles, pebbles, stinging insects, herbs) into a person's body, causing pain and illness. No matter what remedies are administered, the painful object remains and the illness continues to get worse. In the case of both soul loss and intrusive objects, only shaman-healers are capable of treating the underlying cause of the illness, and all other treatments are futile until this is achieved. The son of a former Matsigenka shaman-healer explained:

> Ordinary illness hurts, but when you use herbs or take pills, you get better. But if there is something painful inside, you don't get better. No! It hurts even more. Your heart hurts, or your knee hurts, you get tired, you don't eat, you get skinny. As long as the painful thing is there, you don't get better. They say it can be a twig, or a needle, or a bone or herbs. They say sorcerers can shoot them at you like a dart; or demons, or dead people. I don't know anything about that. Only a shaman knows about those things. They can see where the painful thing is when they take ayahuasca, and suck it out, and then show it to you. "Look! Here it is! This is what was hurting you."

"Ordinary illness," *kogapage mantsigarentsi,* is distinguished from supernatural illness not by any particular symptom, but rather by its chronic and unrelenting nature. The "painful thing," *katsitankicha,* must be removed before healing can occur. By massaging and sucking painful parts of the body, the shaman removes the intrusive object, spitting it out to display to the patient. The Matsigenka and the Yora/Yaminahua shaman can call back an abducted soul by singing during the healing ceremony. These common elements of shamanism in the two groups appear to predate the arrival of the ayahuasca brew, reflecting elements of Pan-Amazonian cosmologies, illness concepts, and spiritual practices that may be more ancient. But how much more ancient? The case at hand invites a certain degree of skepticism toward deeming any practice as "ancient," "traditional," "millennial," or "stable" in the lack of more precise historical and ethnographic evidence.

Whatever the status of the pre-ayahuasca shamanic traditions, there are intriguing similarities in the social and historical situation that brought the *Banisteriopsis-Psychotria* brew to the Matsigenka and Yora. Both adopted the brew, melding it with previous shamanistic and healing traditions, during times of cultural contact and change. In both cases, the adoption of the new brew seems to be at least somewhat related to questions of efficacy and convenience. In the case of the Matsigenka, the prior *Banisteriopsis* preparation required much longer cooking times. In the Yora case, the *Paullinia* vine used for group rituals appears to have had numerous and potentially severe toxic side effects. And yet, both groups' (and especially the Yora's) wholehearted and complete embrace of the new ayahuasca brew—utterly abandoning prior plants and modes of preparation (Yora), or reducing prior plant preparations to an occasional, token gesture (Matsigenka)—implies an embrace not just of a new technology but of a new cultural identity in a changing world. Numerous authors, from Gow's pioneering speculation to Mariana Pantoja's chapter in this volume, suggest how ayahuasca has played a role in negotiating new cultural identities in settings of intense cultural contact and ethnic re-identification.

The remote and isolated Matsigenka of the Manu were quick to appropriate the "new" *Psychotria* admixture taught them by their fellows coming from the Camisea River, ironically arriving in their communities at the behest of missionary organizations. The Yora case presents an even more drastic example of wholehearted rejection of a prior tradition and embrace of the new. Certainly, the Yaminahua headman who brokered the Yora contact had a vested interest in asserting his shamanic authority over the weakened, vulnerable, recently contacted group. Introducing ayahuasca and initiating the Yora headman as his shamanic apprentice served the double function of asserting the new leader's political and spiritual dominance over the group. And yet, the Yora need not have embraced the brew as enthusiastically as they have, consuming it nearly every night whether the Yaminahua headman is present or not. Ayahuasca appears to provide them with a context to assert a new, hybrid Panoan identity fusing Yora and Yaminahua elements. Just as Yaminahua healing songs call out to the feverish temperatures and hot, metallic odors of Western technologies such as guns, motors, and gasoline to dominate novel illnesses, so the Yora have been able to appropriate this new shamanistic complex to negotiate a new relationship with the Yaminahua and other neighboring groups.

Western scholarly study and popular fascination with ayahuasca use focuses on its esoteric, spiritual, and therapeutic elements, often overlooking or minimizing the striking and fundamentally important performative aspects. Having participated in rituals among a number of indigenous and urban traditions, I have always been struck by the virtuosic, soulful, and deeply moving aesthetic quality of vocal and musical performances by experienced and respected shamans, healers, and masters; sensations that are of course augmented by, but not solely reducible to, the brew's powerful alteration and heightening of emotional and sensory responses. A key component of attaining status and power within these various traditions is mastery of musical and vocal techniques and repertoire. Indeed, music and other forms of artistic expression are an important part of many religious traditions, and contribute specific aesthetic and emotional qualities to spiritual experiences. In this sense, the spread of ayahuasca and its associated *icaros*, or sung incantations, may have much in common with the history of, say, the blues or gospel music. In this regard, Brabec de Mori's study[49] of ayahuasca as a musical genre that has spread among various indigenous and non-indigenous groups is especially welcome.

Will the Real Shaman Please Stand Up?

Though the *Banisteriopsis-Psychotria* preparation is now central to the shamanistic practices of the Matsigenka and Yora of the Manu region, the brew, and perhaps associated elements, was introduced to both groups in recent decades. I know this only because I was able to interview people who had witnessed the transition themselves. An ethnologist arriving among these cultures a generation later might find little or no evidence that these practices weren't centuries old. These observations underscore the tremendous fluidity of indigenous medical and spiritual practices and musical traditions, and the speed with which novel elements may be adopted and incorporated. The Madre de Dios region was unusually isolated through the middle of the twentieth century, which was due to both geographical and political circumstances. Other anthropologists working in Madre de Dios describe how ayahuasca shamanism was incorporated recently among the Harakmbut[50] and Ese Eja.[51] Taken together, these case histories from Madre de Dios and Manu provide ample evidence to support Gow's pioneering hypothesis[52] that ayahuasca use has spread recently in the Peruvian Amazon, probably in the aftermath of the Rubber Boom. The contemporary ayahuasca-*Psychotria* brew and the associated curandero healing complex was absent among the isolated peoples of Manu and Madre de Dios across all major cultural-linguistic groups (Matsigenka-Arawak, Yora-Pano, Harakmbut, Ese Eja), and only reached these groups when they emerged from cultural isolation at various moments in the middle to late twentieth century. The Matsigenka in particular appear to have arrived in Manu and Madre de Dios by migration from the Urubamba River during the nineteenth century,[53] when the *Psychotria*-based ayahuasca brew does not appear to have been part of their cultural repertoire. Thus the contemporary ayahuasca recipe must have reached the Matsigenka of the Urubamba only after the Manu and Madre de Dios populations had split off. The timing of this split—early to mid-nineteenth century—coincides well with Gow's hypothesis that ayahuasca use spread widely only toward the end of the nineteenth century.

The Matsigenka of Manu adopted the *Psychotria*-ayahuasca formula from their brethren in the Urubamba in the late 1950s to early 1960s, about the time Mestre Gabriel founded the União do Vegetal in Brazil.[54] The Yora began using ayahuasca in the late 1980s, about the same time the first Santo Daime church arrived in Belgium.[55] Of course, the Matsigenka and Yora adopted ayahuasca into diverse, preexisting shamanic traditions that are presumed to have existed for many prior... centuries? Millennia? Or, perhaps again, mere decades? Does learning that the Matsigenka and Yora acquired the ayahuasca brew only recently, through contact with outsiders, fundamentally change how we understand their shamanistic practices and cosmology? Is there anything special, unique, or particular about indigenous people's relationship to ayahuasca when compared to adepts who use it in urban centers? Do the Matsigenka and Yora have an inherently superior moral right to consume ayahuasca within their spiritual tradition when compared with, say, a Belgian Santo Daime member risking incarceration to consume an illegal substance? Such questions raise troubling doubts about our sometimes facile resort to terms such as "tradition," "modernity," "indigeneity," and "authenticity."

Growing numbers of Westerners seek out ayahuasca and various shamanic traditions in search of spiritual insight, healing, or exotic experiences. This phenomenon has generated demand for "shamanic tourism," and sets local religious or therapeutic practices in a strange new relationship with global markets and European esoteric traditions.[56] Emergent religions such as the Native American Church and the ayahuasca religions of Brazil demonstrate how spiritual movements can undergo rapid expansion and change during moments of social upheaval. Indigenous groups, supposedly the millennial caretakers of ancient sacred traditions, are involved in the same dynamic processes of contact, adaptation, and change as everyone else. The arguments for legalization of ayahuasca use in Amazonian countries and across the world focus either on the question of religious freedom or the protection of traditional therapeutic practices. And yet, in both the Matsigenka and the Yora cases, neither religion nor healing was necessarily central to their initial adoption of the new ayahuasca brew. Rather, in both cases, the new brew was perceived as more potent and efficacious than the previously available psychoactive preparations and, for the Yora especially, it provided novel possibilities for negotiating with spiritual and cultural others. Are Europeans who encounter ayahuasca for the first time really so different when they, too, become enthusiasts? Is it possible to imagine a court case for ayahuasca legalization founded on the principal of the right to "novel radical experience of alterity," rather than the established precedents of religious freedom, therapeutic diversity, and millenarian indigenous practice? A closer examination of the diversity and dynamism of contemporary shamanistic practices among urban, and even indigenous, populations calls into question the sometimes artificial boundaries between "us" and "them," between the "global" and the "local," the "modern" and the "traditional," and the "authentic" and the "spurious."[57] And yet, many of the laws that lend authority and sanctify appropriate, legal use of controlled substances in religious or therapeutic settings are built on precisely such fragile notions. Further inquiry into the dynamism of indigenous religious practice will surely confirm these misgivings; but if indigenous people and their cultural practices are not allowed the final safe refuge of exceptionalism, where will they be left?

Notes

1. Beatriz Caiuby Labate, *A reinvenção do uso da ayahuasca nos centros urbanos* (Campinas, Brazil: Mercado de Letras, 2004).
2. Donald Joralemon, "The Selling of the Shaman and the Problem of Informant Legitimacy," *Journal of Anthropological Research* 46 (1990): 105–18.
3. Jeremy Narby, *The Cosmic Serpent: DNA and the Origins of Knowledge* (New York: Tarcher/Putnam, 1998), 154.
4. Esther Jean Matteson-Langdon and Gerhard Baer, eds., *Portals of Power: Shamanism in South America* (Albuquerque: University of New Mexico Press, 1992); Glenn H. Shepard, Jr., "Native Central and South American Shamanism," in *Encyclopedia of Shamanism*, Mariko N. Walter and Eva J. N. Fridman, eds. (Santa Barbara: ABC Clio, 2005), 390–91.
5. Johannes Wilbert, *Tobacco and Shamanism in South America* (New Haven: Yale University Press, 1987).
6. Peter Gow, "River People: Shamanism and History in Western Amazonia," in *Shamanism, History and the State*, Nicholas Thomas and Caroline Humphrey, eds. (Ann Arbor: University of Michigan Press, 1994), 90–113.
7. Gow, "River People," 92.
8. Bernd Brabec de Mori, "Tracing Hallucinations: Contributing to an Ethnohistory of Ayawaska Usage in the Peruvian Amazon," in Beatriz Caiuby Labate and Henrik Jungaberle, eds., *The Internationalization of Ayahuasca* (Zürich: Lit Verlag, 2011), 7.
9. Antonio Bianchi, "Ayahuasca e xamanismo indígena na selva Peruana: O lento caminho da conquista," in Beatriz Caiuby Labate and Isabel Santana de Rose, eds., *O uso ritual das plantas de poder* (Campinas: Editora Mercado de Letras, 2005), 325.
10. Glenn H. Shepard, Jr., et al., "Trouble in Paradise: Indigenous Populations, Anthropological Policies, and Biodiversity Conservation in Manu National Park, Peru," *Journal of Sustainable Forestry* 29 (2010): 252–301.
11. Patricia J. Lyon, "An Imaginary Frontier: Prehistoric Highland-Lowland Interchange in the Southern Peruvian Andes," in Peter D. Francis, F. J. Kense, and P. G. Duke, eds., *Networks of the Past: Regional Interaction in Archeology (Proceedings of the XII Annual Conference of the University of Calgary)* (Calgary: University of Calgary Archeological Association, 1981), 2–16.

12. Zacarias Valdez Lozano, *El verdadero Fitzcarrald ante la historia* (Iquitos, Peru: El Oriente, 1944), 18.
13. Kim MacQuarrie, "Dissipative Energy Patterns and Cultural Change Among the Yura/Parque Nahua (Yaminahua) Indians of Southeastern Peru" (M.A. thesis, California State University at Fullerton, 1991), chap. 7 (Oral History of the Yura): 1–2.
14. MacQuarrie, "Dissipative Energy Patterns," chap. 7: 8.
15. MacQuarrie, "Dissipative Energy Patterns," chap. 8 (History of Yura Contact): 9.
16. Alonso Zarzar, "Radiografía de un contacto: Los Nahua y la sociedad nacional," *Amazonia Peruana* 8, no. 14 (1987): 94.
17. Shepard et al., "Trouble in Paradise," 264.
18. Alejandro Camino, "Trueque, correrías e intercambio entre los Quechas Andinos y los Piros y Machiguenga de la Montaña Peruana," *Amazonia Peruana* 1, no. 2 (1977).
19. Beverly Yvonne Bennett, "Illness and Order: Cultural Transformation Among the Machiguenga and Huachipaeri" (Ph.D. diss., Ithaca, NY: Cornell University, 1991), 87.
20. Bennett, "Illness and Order," 94.
21. Camino, "Trueque, correrías e intercambio."
22. Jorge M. von Hassel, "Los varaderos del Purús, Yurúa y Manu," *Boletín de la Sociedad Geográfica de Lima* 15 (1904): 244.
23. Shepard et al., "Trouble in Paradise," 265.
24. Glenn H. Shepard, Jr., "Pharmacognosy and the Senses in Two Amazonian Societies" (Ph.D. diss., University of California at Berkeley, 1999), 108.
25. Shepard, "Pharmacognosy and the Senses," 108–10.
26. Glenn H. Shepard, Jr., "The Secret Shaman," in Joanne Eede, ed., *We Are One: A Celebration of Tribal Peoples* (London: Quadrille/Survival International, 2010), 130–31.
27. Bianchi, "Ayahuasca e xamanismo indígena na selva Peruana," 327.
28. Glenn H. Shepard, Jr., "Venenos divinos: Plantas psicoativas dos Machiguenga do Peru," in Beatriz C. Labate and Sandra Goulart, eds., *O uso ritual das plantas de poder* (Campinas, Brazil: Editora Mercado de Letras, 2005), 203.
29. Claudio Naranjo, "Psychotropic Properties of the Harmala Alkaloids," in *Ethnopharmacologic Search for Psychoactive Drugs*, U.S. Public Health Service Publication No. 1645, D. H. Efron, B. Holmstedt and N. S. Kline, eds. (Washington, D.C.: U.S. Government Printing Office, 1967), 385–91.
30. Glenn H. Shepard, Jr., "Shamanism and Diversity: A Matsigenka Perspective," in Darrell A. Posey, ed., *Cultural and Spiritual Values of Biodiversity* (London: United Nations Environmental Programme and Intermediate Technology Publications, 1999), 94.
31. Bianchi, "Ayahuasca e xamanismo indígena na selva Peruana," 327.
32. Glenn H. Shepard, Jr., "Primates in Matsigenka Subsistence and Worldview," in A. Fuentes and L. Wolfe, eds., *Primates Face to Face: The Conservation Implications of Human and Nonhuman Primate Interconnections* (Cambridge: Cambridge University Press, 2002), 116–17.
33. Gerhard Baer, "The One Intoxicated by Tobacco: Matsigenka Shamanism," in J. Matteson-Langdon and G. Baer, eds., *Portals of Power: Shamanism in South America* (Albuquerque: University of New Mexico Press, 1992), 80; Glenn H. Shepard, Jr., "Psychoactive Plants and Ethnopsychiatric Medicines of the Matsigenka," *Journal of Psychoactive Drugs* 30, no. 4 (1998): 325.
34. Shepard, "Psychoactive Plants and Ethnopsychiatric Medicines," 325.
35. Shepard, "Venenos divinos," 197.
36. Shepard et al., 2010, "Trouble in Paradise," 265.
37. David P. Edwards et al., "'A Plant Needs Its Ants like a Dog Needs Its Fleas': *Myrmelachista schumanni* Ants Gall Many Tree Species to Create Housing," *American Naturalist* 174, no. 5 (2009): 734–40.
38. Shepard, "Shamanism and Diversity," 93.
39. Glenn H. Shepard Jr., "A Sensory Ecology of Medicinal Plant Therapy in Two Amazonian Societies," *American Anthropologist* 106, no. 2 (2004) 252–66.

40. Carolina Izquierdo and Glenn H. Shepard, Jr., "Matsigenka," in C. R. Ember and M. Ember, eds., *Encyclopedia of Medical Anthropology: Health and Illness in the World's Cultures* (New York: Kluwer Academic/Plenum, 2003), 825, 832.
41. Shepard, "Pharmacognosy and the Senses," 87.
42. Conrad Feather, "Elastic Selves and Fluid Cosmologies: Nahua Resilience in a Changing World" (Ph.D. diss., University of St. Andrews, 2010).
43. Shepard, "A Sensory Ecology," 257–58.
44. See also Constance Classen, "Sweet Colors, Fragrant Songs: Sensory Models of the Andes and the Amazon," *American Ethnologist* 17 (1990): 722–73.
45. Carolina Izquierdo, Allen Johnson, and Glenn H. Shepard, Jr., "Revenge, Envy and Cultural Change in an Amazonian Society," in S. Beckerman and P. Valentine, eds., *Revenge in the Cultures of Lowland South America* (Gainesville: University of Florida Press, 2008), 180–84.
46. Werner Wilbert, "Warao Herbal Medicine: A Pneumatic Theory of Illness and Healing" (Ph.D. diss., University of California, 1986); Kenneth M. Kensinger, "Cashinahua Medicine and Medicine Men," in P. Lyon, ed., *Native South Americans: Ethnology of the Least Known Continent* (Boston: Little, Brown, 1974), 286.
47. Shepard, "A Sensory Ecology," 255–56.
48. Wilbert, "Warao Herbal Medicine."
49. Brabec de Mori, "Tracing Hallucinations."
50. Andrew Gray, *The Arakmbut: Mythology, Spirituality, and History* (New York: Berghahn Books, 1996).
51. Miguel N. Alexiades, "El Eyámikekwa y el ayahuasquero: Las dinámicas socioecológicas del chamanismo Ese Eja," *Amazonia Peruana* 27 (2000): 193–213.
52. Gow, "River People," 92.
53. Bennett, "Illness and Order," 87.
54. See Beatriz Caiuby Labate, Isabel S. Rose, and Rafael Santos, *Ayahuasca Religions: A Comprehensive Bibliography and Critical Essays* (Santa Cruz, CA: Multidisciplinary Association for Psychedelic Studies, 2009).
55. Marc Blainey, "Motivations for Conversions to the Brazilian Santo Daime Religion in Europe." Paper presented at Amazon Conference: Amazonian Shamanism, Psychoactive Plants and Ritual Reinvention (Institute of Medical Psychology, Heidelberg University, Dec. 6–7, 2010).
56. Joralemon, "The Selling of the Shaman."
57. Beatriz Caiuby Labate, "Ayahuasca mamancuna merci beaucoup: Diversificação e internationalização do vegetalismo ayahuasqueiro Peruano" (Ph.D. diss., Universidade Estadual de Campinas, Brazil, 2011).

Bibliography

Alexiades, Miguel N. "El Eyámikekwa y el ayahuasquero: Las dinámicas socioecológicas del chamanismo Ese Eja." *Amazonia Peruana* 27 (2000): 193–213.

Baer, Gerhard. "The One Intoxicated by Tobacco: Matsigenka Shamanism." In *Portals of Power: Shamanism in South America*, edited by Jean Matteson-Langdon and Gerhard Baer, 79–100. Albuquerque: University of New Mexico Press, 1992.

Bennett, Beverly Yvonne. "Illness and Order: Cultural Transformation Among the Machiguenga and Huachipaeri." Ph.D. diss., Dept. Anthropology, Cornell University, 1991.

Bianchi, Antonio. "Ayahuasca e xamanismo indígena na Selva Peruana: O lento caminho da conquista." In *O uso ritual das plantas de poder*, edited by Beatriz Caiuby Labate and Sandra Goulart, 319–31. Campinas, Brazil: Editora Mercado de Letras, 2005.

Blainey, Marc. "Motivations for Conversions to the Brazilian Santo Daime Religion in Europe." Paper presented at Amazon Conference: Amazonian Shamanism, Psychoactive Plants and Ritual Reinvention, Institute of Medical Psychology, Heidelberg University, December 6–7, 2010.

Brabec de Mori, Bernd. "Tracing Hallucinations: Contributing to an Ethnohistory of Ayawaska Usage in the Peruvian Amazon." In *The Internationalization of Ayahuasca*, edited by Beatriz Caiuby Labate and Henrik Jungaberle. Zurich: Lit Verlag, 2011.

Camino, Alejandro. "Trueque, correrías e intercambio entre los Quechas Andinos y los Piros y Machiguenga de la Montaña Peruana." *Amazonia Peruana* 1, no. 2 (1977): 123–40.

Classen, Constance. "Sweet Colors, Fragrant Songs: Sensory Models of the Andes and the Amazon." *American Ethnologist* 17 (1990): 722–35.

Edwards, David P., Megan E. Frederickson, Glenn H. Shepard, Jr., and Douglas W. Yu. "'A Plant Needs Its Ants Like a Dog Needs Its Fleas': Myrmelachista Schumanni Ants Gall Many Tree Species to Create Housing." *American Naturalist* 174, no. 5 (2009): 734–40.

Feather, Conrad. "Elastic Selves and Fluid Cosmologies: Nahua Resilience in a Changing World." Ph.D. diss., University of St. Andrews, 2010.

Gow, Peter. "River People: Shamanism and History in Western Amazonia." In *Shamanism, History, and the State*, edited by Nicholas Thomas and Caroline Humphrey, 90–113. Ann Arbor: University of Michigan Press, 1994.

Gray, Andrew. *The Arakmbut: Mythology, Spirituality and History*. New York: Berghahn Books, 1996.

Hassel, Jorge M. von. "Los varaderos del Purús, Yurúa Y Manu." *Boletín de la Sociedad Geográfica de Lima* 15 (1904): 241–46.

Izquierdo, Carolina, Allen Johnson, and Glenn H. Shepard, Jr. "Revenge, Envy and Cultural Change in an Amazonian Society." In *Revenge in the Cultures of Lowland South America*, edited by Steven Beckerman and Paul Valentine, 162–86. Gainesville: University of Florida Press, 2008.

Izquierdo, Carolina, and Glenn H. Shepard, Jr. "Matsigenka." In *Encyclopedia of Medical Anthropology: Health and Illness in the World's Cultures*, edited by Carol R. Ember and Melvin Ember, 823–37. New York: Kluwer Academic/Plenum, 2003.

Joralemon, Donald. "The Selling of the Shaman and the Problem of Informant Legitimacy." *Journal of Anthropological Research* 46 (Summer 1990): 105–18.

Kensinger, Kenneth M. "Cashinahua Medicine and Medicine Men." In *Native South Americans: Ethnology of the Least Known Continent*, edited by Patricia Lyon, 283–89. Boston: Little, Brown, 1974.

Labate, Beatriz Caiuby. *A reinvenção do uso da ayahuasca nos centros urbanos*. Campinas, Brazil: Mercado de Letras., 2004.

Labate, Beatriz Caiuby. "Ayahuasca mamancuna merci beaucoup: Diversificação e internationalização do vegetalismo ayahuasqueiro Peruano." Ph.D. diss., Universidade Estadual de Campinas, 2011.

Labate, Beatriz Caiuby, Isabel S. Rose, and Rafael Santos. *Ayahuasca Religions: A Comprehensive Bibliography and Critical Essays*. Santa Cruz, CA: Multidisciplinary Association for Psychedelic Studies, 2009.

Lyon, Patricia J. "An Imaginary Frontier: Prehistoric Highland-Lowland Interchange in the Southern Peruvian Andes." In *Networks of the Past: Regional Interaction in Archeology (Proceedings of the 12th Annual Conference of the University of Calgary)*, edited by Peter D. Francis, F. J. Kense and P. G. Duke, 2–16. Calgary: University of Calgary Archeological Association, 1981.

MacQuarrie, Kim. "Dissipative Energy Patterns and Cultural Change Among the Yura/Parque Nahua (Yaminahua) Indians of Southeastern Peru." Master's thesis, California State University at Fullerton, 1991.

Matteson-Langdon, Esther Jean, and Gerhard Baer, eds. *Portals of Power: Shamanism in South America*. Albuquerque: University of New Mexico Press, 1992.

Naranjo, Claudio. "Psychotropic Properties of the Harmala Alkaloids." In *Ethnopharmacologic Search for Psychoactive Drugs*, edited by D. H. Efron, B. Holmstedt, and N. S. Kline, 385–91. Washington, D.C.: U.S. Public Health Service, 1967.

Narby, Jeremy. *The Cosmic Serpent: DNA and the Origins of Knowledge*. New York: Tarcher/Putnam, 1998.

Shepard, Glenn H., Jr. "Psychoactive Plants and Ethnopsychiatric Medicines of the Matsigenka." *Journal of Psychoactive Drugs* 30, no. 4 (1998): 321–32.

Shepard, Glenn H., Jr. "Pharmacognosy and the Senses in Two Amazonian Societies." Ph.D. diss., University of California at Berkeley, 1999.

Shepard, Glenn H., Jr. "Shamanism and Diversity: A Matsigenka Perspective." In *Cultural and Spiritual Values of Biodiversity*, edited by Darrell A. Posey, 93–95. London: United Nations Environmental Programme and Intermediate Technology Publications, 1999.

Shepard, Glenn H., Jr. "Primates in Matsigenka Subsistence and Worldview." In *Primates Face to Face: The Conservation Implications of Human and Nonhuman Primate Interconnections*, edited by Agustin Fuentes and Linda Wolfe, 101–36. Cambridge, U.K.: Cambridge University Press, 2002.

Shepard, Glenn H., Jr. "A Sensory Ecology of Medicinal Plant Therapy in Two Amazonian Societies." *American Anthropologist* 106, no. 2 (2004): 252–66.

Shepard, Glenn H., Jr. "Native Central and South American Shamanism." In *Encyclopedia of Shamanism*, edited by Mariko N. Walter and Eva J. N. Fridman, 382–93. Santa Barbara, CA: ABC Clio, 2005.

Shepard, Glenn H., Jr. "Venenos divinos: Plantas psicoativas dos Machiguenga do Peru." In *O uso ritual das plantas de poder*, edited by Beatriz Caiuby Labate and Sandra Goulart, 187–217. Campinas, Brazil: Editora Mercado de Letras, 2005.

Shepard, Glenn H., Jr., Klaus Rummenhoeller, Julia Ohl, and Douglas W. Yu. "Trouble in Paradise: Indigenous Populations, Anthropological Policies, and Biodiversity Conservation in Manu National Park, Peru." *Journal of Sustainable Forestry* 29 (2010): 252–301.

Valdez Lozano, Zacarias. *El verdadero Fitzcarrald ante la historia*. Iquitos, Peru: El Oriente, 1944.

Wilbert, Johannes. *Tobacco and Shamanism in South America*. Edited by R. Raffauf and Richard E. Schultes, Psychoactive Plants of the World Series. New Haven: Yale University Press, 1987.

Wilbert, Werner. "Warao Herbal Medicine: A Pneumatic Theory of Illness and Healing." Ph.D. diss., University of California at Los Angeles, 1986.

Zarzar, Alonso. "Radiografía de un contacto: Los Nahua y la sociedad nacional." *Amazonia Peruana* 8, no. 14 (1987): 91–114.

2

Kuntanawa

Ayahuasca, Ethnicity, and Culture

MARIANA CIAVATTA PANTOJA,
TRANSLATED BY MATTHEW MEYER

The Kuntanawa indigenous people, I tend to think, are a nascent ethnic group. This view is probably not shared by the members of the group themselves, and they are right. The presence of Pano-speaking indigenous peoples in the Amazon's forests, and particularly in the Brazilian Upper Juruá, is widely recognized and amply documented.[1] The presence of the Kuntanawa, a Pano group, is registered not only in historical-ethnographic documents from the turn of the twentieth century, when the expanding rubber economy overtook the region, but also in the lives of the present group's two principal founders: two women, a mother and her daughter, the first captured around 1910, while still a girl, in an armed expedition against the native peoples, which were very common at that time and known as *correrias*.[2] There is, then, a contradiction: How can the Kuntanawa be a nascent ethnic group if their existence has been attested to for at least one hundred years? What is it that threatens to bring anthropologist and natives to such different points of view? To begin with, it is Theory itself.

The phenomenon of ethnicity is seen by scholars as primarily social rather than biological or, more precisely, as the establishment of social boundaries through which ethnic groups set differences, define belonging and exclusions, and thus organize their mutual interaction.[3] If "origin" is a component of this belonging, it does not necessarily operate according to biological criteria, whose weight becomes relativized in an unequal competition with factors of social and historical order. That is why I can be a Kuntanawa without having blood ties with ancestors in common, or even be from a distant region, if I establish matrimonial ties with a member of the descent group, or align myself with the group when differences are produced in an interethnic context.

Ethnicity is thus something produced in interaction, and is generally linked to social and territorial rights, leading to the phenomenon being identified as belonging to the political sphere, and to ethnic identity being understood as political above all else. Once more, I am doubtful that my Kuntanawa friends would agree with this. If it is clear to them that they are positioned, as indigenous people, in an interethnic field of disputes and rights, and that they undertake vital negotiations with the State for their legal recognition as such and for the conquest of their own land, I believe that the experience of "being Kuntanawa"—again, from their perspective—contains within it other dimensions. Perhaps that is why, from their point of view as Kuntanawa, they were always present—"we are existing Indians, not emergent ones," one of their leaders informed me—and today are recovering their original traditions. This discourse, which draws a line of continuity with the past and could be classified as essentialist or essentially political, can be analyzed in two ways: within an interethnic context, in which signs of Indian-ness must be displayed to prove authenticity before the Other[4]; and from a Kuntanawa pronominal perspective about what it is, from their point of view, to be Kuntanawa.[5]

In this article, I intend to make an experimental incursion into what I would describe as a double process of cultural invention, keeping in mind once more the resistance that this term *invention* will face on the part of the Kuntanawa, who will probably find in it something that conspires against their ethnic authenticity.[6] But this is absolutely not the issue. What I would like to explore in my reflections on the notion of invention is the creative dimension of Kuntanawa culture.[7] The Kuntanawa themselves do speak of their "culture" and are extremely skilled at building it up, laying claim to cultural objects (including the notion of "culture" itself) recognized and legitimated as such in interethnic context.[8] Out of our invention of them, they reinvent themselves, and us as well. But, it should be noted in a more internal context, these cultural objects are experienced not only conceptually but also sensually. They behave, let us say, as "perspectival operators"[9] of Kuntanawa subjectivity.

For the purposes of this article, I will focus on the ritual use of ayahuasca, which is widespread among Amazonian indigenous peoples and is associated with shamanic practices, though not exclusively.[10] It will be seen that ayahuasca, as part of indigenous "culture," occupies a privileged position in situations in which Kuntanawa affirm their identity as *índios* before non-indigenous society, as well as in relation to other indigenous groups, Pano and otherwise. In addition, through the ritual consumption of ayahuasca, Kuntanawa undergo a subjective experience through which they affirm access to dimensions more internal to their existence as a people. With ayahuasca as their guide and teacher, they explore unknown depths, bringing back their people's history and their ancestral traditions from their ayahuasca journeys. Under its influence, they compose songs that testify to their way of life in the forest and reveal a self-image in construction. The use of ayahuasca in the case discussed here, it will be seen, is fundamental not only to the self-construction of a Kuntanawa shaman's personal trajectory but also to the interethnic context of the expansion of a shamanism spearheaded mostly by young indigenous people in which the Kuntanawa are participants. In both situations and at both levels of agency, ayahuasca works by activating perspectives on what it means to be Kuntanawa, perspectives that are not necessarily coincident, but rather coexistent.

This chapter has the form of a chronicle, narrating facts and events and seeking theoretical paths that allow an escape from the duality between a more historical and political perspective on ethnicity as an object of study and a more internal, subjective, or even cosmological perspective from which to conceive of oneself and the other. In this sense, the article is part of ongoing reflections and has an exploratory character as well.[11] The ideas of Manuela Carneiro da Cunha about the reflexive character of the culture concept, which allows "culture" to speak about culture, shed new light on the duality referred to above; so does the optimism of Marshall Sahlins, when he affirms that culture (with or without quotes) is being indigenized, and Roy Wagner's epistemological alert about the culture concept.[12] In some fashion, these formulations structure and guide the following text.

The Kuntanawa in the Public Eye

In January 2005, I received a phone call from representatives of the office of the Indigenous Missionary Council (CIMI) in Cruzeiro do Sul.[13] They wanted to talk about the Kuntanawa. They had just returned from a trip on the upper Tejo River to the house of Milton Gomes da Conceição (seu Milton) and Maria Feitosa do Nascimento (dona Mariana), and they wanted to tell me about what was happening and seek my support. They brought from their trip a petition with forty signatures in which the Kuntanawa demanded that the National Indian Foundation or FUNAI,[14] begin "the demarcation of our land as soon as possible." Other documents had already been sent the previous year. I realized that the area requested would be completely superimposed on the Alto Juruá Extractive Reserve (a Conservation Unit created by the federal government in 1990), which might create conflicts with its residents and with other institutions.

Not long after, I received an envelope from CIMI containing documents that showed that the organization had known of Kuntanawa survivors on the Tejo River since 2001, but only in March 2004 had it been formally sought out by two Kuntanawa representatives, seu Milton and dona Mariana, who were seeking help with gaining ethnic recognition. CIMI sent correspondence to the local and regional offices of FUNAI, requesting any information pertaining to the Kuntanawa. In June 2004, having received no response from FUNAI, another letter was sent to the regional administrator, informing him that another Kuntanawa representative, Osmildo, a son of seu Milton and dona Mariana, had sought out CIMI. In that exchange, CIMI expressed its full conviction of the veracity of the Kuntanawa demands for ethnic recognition, even attaching testimony from other indigenous people, and asking FUNAI to "proceed, according to its mission, with a more complete study aimed at the recognition and consequent demarcation of land." In the same month, Osmildo, the "Kuntanawa chief," sent a letter to the local, regional, and national representatives of FUNAI and CIMI, informing them that the Kuntanawa were 250 people strong, and were "reorganizing as the indigenous people that we are." It acknowledged that, despite having always been considered Indians by the leaders of the Indigenous Territories (TIs) neighboring the reserve, and by the region's non-indigenous residents, they had united themselves with the rubber tappers "for the creation of the Reserve, since we understood that to be a good thing." But the situation had changed. Although they had already held executive positions in the Reserve Association, "currently the folks at the reserve don't want us as members anymore, because we are Indians and they prefer only rubber tappers as members." The letter closed with a request that FUNAI immediately begin the studies "necessary for the demarcation of our land."

Ancestors and Descendants

To better understand the processes discussed above, it is necessary to remember that the region of the Brazilian Juruá Valley began to be occupied by non-indigenous populations at the end of the nineteenth century. These new migrants, most of them from the Brazilian northeast, followed the trail of rubber, which was then an export product with high value on the international market. This encounter between native peoples and migrants, not only in Brazilian lands but along all the Amazonian rivers with concentrations of *Heveas*,[15] was especially tragic for the former group, who saw themselves run out of their traditional territories, persecuted, killed, or forcibly incorporated into the society then in formation.[16]

Seu Milton and dona Mariana are the children, respectively, of a Nehanawa Indian man and a Kuntanawa woman from groups decimated on the Envira River at the turn of the twentieth century by the *correrias*. They were, therefore, survivors. The families that took them in baptized them with the names Pedro Tibúrcio and Maria Regina da Silva. Both formed families through unions with migrants who came to the rubber regions of the Amazon to live and populate the

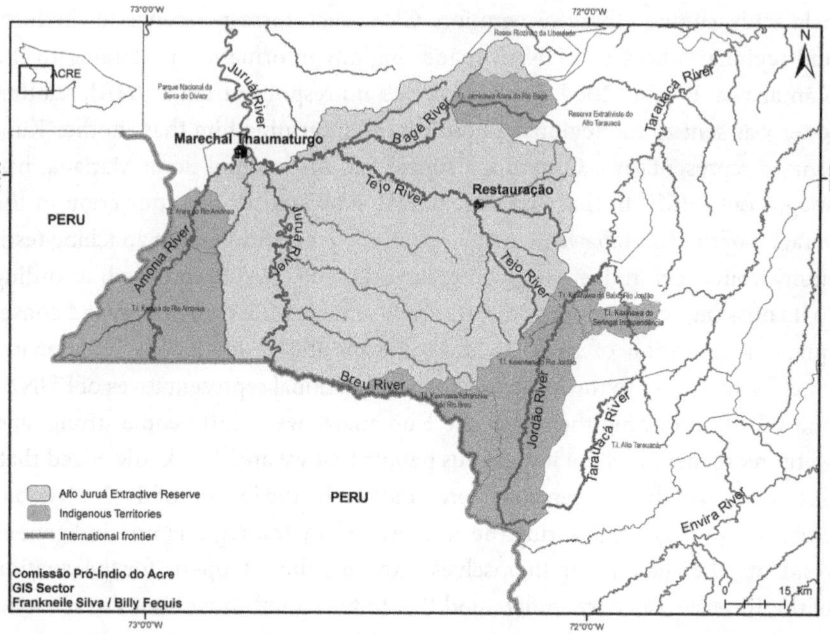

Figure 2.1. Alto Juruá Extractive Reserve. Map reprinted with the permission of Billy Shelby Fequis and Frankneile De Melo Silva.

rubber estates (*seringais*).[17] The rubber estate society that was then forming did so on top of indigenous territory, and in many cases incorporated individuals and even entire ethnic groups.

Dona Mariana and seu Milton, children of Maria Regina da Silva and Pedro Tibúrcio, respectively, grew up on the Jordão River, where they met and were married, in 1953. In 1955, they moved to a neighboring river, the Tejo, where they live today. Together with their ten children, working as rubber tappers for the *patrões*,[18] they were always known as *caboclos*, a term that in Acre designated indigenous or mestizo (with indigenous ancestors) families and that even today has, in interethnic contexts, a pejorative connotation.

At the close of the 1980s, seu Milton and his sons engaged in the social struggle against the *patrão* regime, which resulted in the creation of the Alto Juruá Extractivist Reserve in 1990.[19] During the following decade, they openly supported the reserve establishment process, holding positions in the residents' association and participating in various projects carried out in the area. It was at this time that we met. I was working on research and political consultancy projects for the association, and my proximity to seu Milton, dona Mariana, and the rest of the family ended up leading to a collaborative effort that resulted in my doctoral thesis, which was defended in 2001. In that work, I sought to reconstruct the history of the family, and the theme of ethnic heritage imposed itself with unprecedented force, especially for the sons and daughters of the couple, who never knew their indigenous grandparents.

I recorded various interviews with dona Mariana, an excellent storyteller and guardian of the memory of her Kuntanawa mother. She repeatedly revisited the capture of her mother in the forests of the Envira River and their life together in the rubber estates, their time with other indigenous "relatives," such as the Kaxinawá in the Jordão River, and her mother's midwifery skills. On these occasions, a circle of listeners sometimes formed. All this material was later transcribed and converted into long narratives, preserved in the body of the academic thesis, which was later published as a book to which the whole family had access.[20] An official memory of the group, more or less consensual, was thus produced. The book is cited by many Kuntanawa as one of the historical documents that testifies to their indigenous authenticity. It was also part of a commitment that formed between us, out of which this article has grown.

The twenty-first century began a new phase for the reserve. Out of a conjuncture of political changes at the state level and the arrival of financial resources from international partners, a new political group took over the leadership of the residents' association. This development resulted in the progressive exclusion of seu Milton's extended family from the management of the reserve, an exclusion that began to take on tones of ethnic discrimination. At the association's 2002 assembly, the recently elected leaders were concerned about the threat that the ethnic and territorial demands of the Apolima-Arara already posed to the reserve, and they feared the same thing could happen on the Tejo River.[21] On the same occasion, my colleague Terri Valle de Aquino told me that members of the family headed by seu Milton had sought him out to discuss the possibility of FUNAI's designation of a TI for them on the Tejo River, and said that they felt discriminated against and excluded by the leadership of the association.

Political relations were clearly at play, yet the rupture was expressed in ethnic terms. The family of seu Milton and dona Mariana proclaimed their ancestry publicly, and its members now wanted to be recognized, not as caboclos but as *índios*. In a fashion, they had gone beyond some limit, and this limit, it could be said, spoke to the impossibility of continuing to live on the reserve while classified in a category that was forged in a context of domination, stripped of rights, and devalued. To accept being called caboclo would be, in this sense, to remain symbolically dominated. The self-affirmation as índio would bring, in this context, a movement of liberation and freedom from fear of discrimination, and also, of course, a search for political space in an extremely unfavorable conjuncture for seu Milton and his family in the reserve and in its association.[22] To assume a Kuntanawa identity was both a political strategy to gain visibility and rights and a courageous drawing of a line of flight that confronted the common sense of "whitening" and of "acculturation." And the Kuntanawa were not alone.

In addition to the Arara of the Amônia River, some years before the Nawa of the Moa River presented similar demands on lands in the Serra do Divisor National Park, also in the Acrean Alto Juruá.[23]

Osmildo, a Path in Ayahuasca[24]

It is August 1989, on a moonlit night in the TI of the Amônia River Kampa. A quite heterogeneous group of people—including a famous Brazilian singer, his producer and friends, directors of a renowned NGO, researchers, and Indian and rubber tapper leaders—is visiting the land's owners, Ashaninka Indians, an ethnic group belonging to the Arawak linguistic family, and whose largest settlements are in neighboring Peru.[25] Like many indigenous groups in the Amazon, Brazilian and otherwise, the Ashaninka are familiar with, and make use of ayahuasca, which they call *kamarãpi*. At night, those who were interested in drinking it met together to participate in a ritual led by the Ashaninka *pajés*.[26] Among them was Osmildo.

Born in 1962, on the upper Tejo River—an important affluent of the Juruá—Osmildo is the son of seu Milton and dona Mariana and the grandson, therefore, of Nehanawa and Kuntanawa Indians captured on the Envira River, as we have seen. Having grown up in the Restauração rubber estate on the Tejo River, and having later worked as a rubber tapper, Osmildo says that he has heard talk about the *cipó* (literally, the vine: ayahuasca) and its use by Indians and rubber tappers in the vicinity since he was a boy. Names such as Crispim (a Jaminawa shaman), Sebastião Pereira, and Major (both rubber tappers who used to prepare and drink ayahuasca in the 1980s), live in his memory, but it was only in 1988, when he was twenty-six years old, that he was able to try the drink himself. He did it at the hands of Antonio Macedo, an ex-bush guide for FUNAI who was, at that time, coordinating the revolutionary experiments with cooperatives that, two years later, broke the monopoly and the dominion of the rubber bosses, resulting in the creation of the country's first extractive reserve. Osmildo's entire family, under his father's leadership, was deeply involved in the confrontations that took place at the time.

In those tumultuous and charismatic years, Macedo liked to gift his rubber tapper friends with ayahuasca sessions. He had learned about the drink, and gained respect for it, in his nearly twenty years of work with indigenous groups in Acre, as well as with the Santo Daime churches in the capital.[27] Seu Milton and some of his sons were frequent participants in these ritual meetings promoted by Macedo. In 1988, however, Osmildo's experience was incomplete: he drank the cipó but didn't feel any effect. It was only the next year, on the Amônia River with the Ashaninka, that he was able to convince himself that he was dealing with something capable of opening new paths: there, he relates, he reviewed his whole life under the effects of kamarãpi, and asked permission to work with that "science."[28] He received no reply on that occasion, but it was not long in coming.

In 1991, Osmildo traveled to other TIs, neighbors of the newly created extractive reserve. These travels, like his visit to the Ashaninka, imprinted on him an indelible memory. On the Jordão River, where his parents grew up and met one another, he visited some Kaxinawá, an ethnic group also from the Pano family. From the Breu River he brought strong memories of the pajé Davi Lopes Kampa and of nights of kamarãpi.[29] It was during these years that he learned to appreciate the hymns of the Santo Daime "doctrine," and later he got to know some of the churches and their rituals. Among seu Milton and his children, rituals with ayahuasca slowly became more regular, with the double influence of cipó and daime conferring an eclectic tone on them that was also very much their own, marked by musical expressions from Santo Daime, mestizo ayahuasca practices, popular music, even Evangelical Christianity, and interspersed here and there with musical passages in indigenous languages.

I met Osmildo in that the same year, 1991. He had just returned from those same Jordão and Breu rivers, and my attention was drawn to his undeniably indigenous mien and style of dress, which incorporated indigenous accessories, such as necklaces of wild animal teeth and headbands. In the ayahuasca session that we both participated in on that occasion, he repeatedly sang recently learned indigenous songs, in addition to one or two hymns of Mestre Irineu, the founder of the Santo Daime doctrine. It seems to me that his gifts as a singer and composer, amply recognized with the passage of years, were just emerging at the time. Among the children of seu Milton and dona Mariana whom I was getting to know during those years, Osmildo was, without a shadow of a doubt, the least inhibited in calling on and publicly declaring his indigenous heritage. I believe, moreover, that it was in these first years of Osmildo's contact with ayahuasca that the roots were laid down for a project that would blossom over the next twenty years, one in which he himself would become a pajé.

He recalls those early days:

> So then I went on to drink ayahuasca for three more months, seeing if there was a place for me to work as well. I was following the advice of the indigenous shamans, I didn't want to make a ritual drink that I didn't have the permission to do so. Every time I drank, I was asking to work, but I still didn't have an answer, so I couldn't get into something if I wasn't certain that it was really that, that I wanted to follow. I only came to make this brew when one day I met up with shamans in my vision and they came and showed me what was the type of leaf that was right one to use, how they did it, and what was the cipó.[30]

Figure 2.2. Osmildo preparing ayahuasca in his village in 2007. Photograph by Mariana Ciavatta Pantoja.

In 1993, when my work with the reserve led me practically to live in the Restauração rubber estate where seu Milton's family resided, Osmildo underwent periods of ritual initiation that he conceived of himself, with the aim of building his knowledge as an *ayahuasqueiro* and budding pajé: he drank ayahuasca daily for months, or else scheduled days of the week when he would do it, whether accompanied by his father and brothers, or alone, as he did many times. He himself prepared the ayahuasca he drank, generally with his father's assistance, but also alone, and his ayahuasca was known for being "strong" or "disciplinary." Another brother of his also made his own ayahuasca at the time, but they never established a partnership, although they sometimes participated in the same ritual. At the time, those rubber tappers who wished to try the drink sought seu Milton's family out. On these occasions, Osmildo was the principal singer. During those days, I recorded the repertoire of songs that he would sing during these rituals, several of them composed by him. Along with the song and melody came the guitar.[31]

Osmildo's initiation to ayahuasca, therefore, was marked by direct contact with indigenous groups and their pajés, progressively awakening a shamanic vocation in him that he has followed to this day. From a virtually solitary initiation (albeit one occasionally empowered by shamans), he underwent a significant but never exclusive identification with the doctrine of Santo Daime in the mid-1990s. Then, beginning with the first years of the twenty-first century, a kind of "return to the roots" can be seen: Osmildo, now as a Kuntanawa and leader of his people, once more approached the Ashaninka of the Amônia River, establishing political alliances and work partnerships, and came to be advised and supported in his political and spiritual aims by pajés and leaders from that group. The ayahuasca he prepared began to be recognized for its quality and, little by little, he started to introduce changes in the manner of preparation, notably in the addition of some medicinal plants to the basic mixture of vine and leaf, likely borrowed from the Ashaninka knowledge. His shamanic gifts became known, and he worked to broaden his ethnomedicinal knowledge.

Among the younger Kuntanawa, Osmildo's reputation has grown as a knowledgeable authority on ayahuasca. He began to introduce changes in family rituals with ayahuasca, practically eliminating the place of Santo Daime hymn singing and giving more room to "hearing nature" in long periods of silence, as well as to the songs of those Kuntanawa present, and their indigenous "relatives." It can be said that Osmildo's career trajectory, though not free from divisions and factional groupings, has been repeated by several of his nephews and sons, for whom the initiation into ayahuasca is accompanied by the awakening of ethnic sentiment and a turn toward music. Today, among Kuntanawa belonging to the generation after Osmildo's, virtually all have their own songs, which they play on guitar. Group rituals are marked by the passing around of the instrument, with individual performances backed by the chorus of the others.[32]

"I have no doubt that what I have learned from ayahuasca is with my people," Osmildo told me in 2010. And the lessons have been many, ranging from figures used for body painting to the significance of *cocares* (feather crowns), and to songs and ritual healing procedures. Osmildo has put special effort in one of these areas, that of "medicines" (medicinal plants). Ayahuasca teaches him to recognize plants that heal, but he makes a point of crediting his Kuntanawa grandmother, who was a renowned midwife and very knowledgeable about the forest, who taught his mother, dona Mariana, who in turn teaches him today to be a healer. He also credits his "relatives" from other ethnic groups, themselves ayahuasqueiros, with whom he has exchanged knowledge. To learn the art of healing with plants, he says, is "the strongest thing in the Indian's life." And so it is in the life of Osmildo, Kuntanawa.

In his "twenty-three year career" with ayahuasca, the more contact he has with the drink, he recognizes, the more he learns. He trusts in the ayahuasca that he prepares. With surety he affirms that, whether by song or through recourse to "medicines," he knows how to cure any ill feeling or suffering that a person may experience in an ayahuasca ritual. He adds, "I have never told anyone that I am a pajé; I am learning."

The Kuntanawa and the Others

In the context of the political-institutional struggle for the creation of the Kuntanawa Indigenous Territory, beginning in 2004, various letters began to fly demanding its demarcation and the inclusion of the ethnic group in public programs aimed at indigenous peoples. Among the principal recipients of these letters, besides FUNAI, were the Extraordinary Secretariat of Indigenous Peoples (a state agency) and the National Health Foundation (FUNASA). In the face of delays in obtaining a concrete response to the territorial demands and of pressure from Kuntanawa leaders, in 2008, the Federal Public Ministry filed a Public Civil Action against FUNAI. In November 2010, official correspondence from FUNAI announced the agency's commitment to undertake an "anthropologically grounded preliminary study" in the first half of 2011 to support the process of identifying the Indigenous Territory.

The legal process moves relatively slowly, and the Kuntanawa did not wait for its results. At the events they attended from 2005 on, they were already appearing painted, with cocares and necklaces of *kunta*.[33] In their speech, references to their locales of residence gave way to "my village." They began to adopt Indian names. Visits to, and exchanges with, indigenous "relatives" (such as Ashaninka, Yawanawa, and Puyanawa, among others) became more frequent and represented a way to establish alliances within the indigenous social field. On such occasions, ceremonies with ayahuasca, *rapé* (tobacco snuff), and other "medicines" were held, and aspects of language, material culture, and experiments with political and economic organization were shared.

Also beginning in 2005, Osmildo and a grandson of seu Milton, José Flávio Nascimento (whose indigenous name is Haru Xinã), found roles within the Organization of Indigenous Peoples of the Juruá River (OPIRJ): Haru as secretary and Osmildo, in 2010, as coordinator. In 2006 they participated in Indigenous April, a national demonstration held in Brasília. In 2007, they won the Indigenous Cultures Prize, from the Culture Ministry, for a project of "cultural revitalization and recovery." State government publications on indigenous peoples gave them space, and a prestigious website on Brazil's indigenous people added the term "Kuntanawa."[34] Also during these years, the musical Vukanã Band, composed of Haru and relatives of his generation, all born in the 1980s, produced its first CD and gave presentations within and outside of Acre. Gradually, the Kuntanawa are becoming known, and one can perceive the consolidation of a national and international agenda, with Haru as its principal articulator and the focal point of alliances with people and institutions.[35]

On the other side, in the context of local interethnic relations, a new element has entered into Kuntanawa discourse: opposition to the failure to follow the "laws of the Reserve" on the part of its residents.[36] The conquest of their own land is thus reinforced by environmental justification. According to plans, there will be no "invasions" (predatory exploitation) like those occurring in the reserve; there will be refuge areas for game, and deforestation will be controlled. In 2009, at the start of the New Social Cartography Project of the Amazon, two workshops were held in the Sete Estrelas Village, in the Tejo River (the "heart" of the reserve), and the Kuntanawa who participated in them discussed these and other issues, formulating a first sketch of their future Indigenous Territory and establishing its borders and zoning.[37]

Festival of "Culture"

The First Pano Cultural Festival was held the next year, in August 2010, under the leadership of Haru and in the area requested by the Kuntanawa. The multiethnic encounter, which lasted six days, brought together representatives of nine Pano indigenous ethnic groups (Kuntanawa, Huni Kuin, Yawanawa, Shanenawa, Shawãdawa, Jaminawa, Nukini, Marubo, and Katukina), as well as guests from various Brazilian states and also from other countries (England, Spain, Switzerland, and Germany, among others). The most notable presence was of an Inuit delegation from Greenland and its shaman. An estimated two hundred to three hundred people were present. Non-indigenous neighbors had restricted access to the festival. The entire event and its indigenous participants were intensively filmed and photographed, and their speeches and songs were recorded. The "whites" present there, in an interesting historical inversion of regional interethnic relations, sought ways to become "Indians," whether by painting their bodies, using indigenous accessories (cocares, grass skirts, etc.), or simply participating in the programmed activities. These were principally aimed at fraternization and the strengthening of a pan-ethnic Pano alliance. At the site of the festival—the Kuntamanã village—a large central grounds was prepared specially for the occasion. This village hosted everyone, and the *terreirão*, as the grounds became known, was the main stage for happenings and performances, such as *mariri* circles (indigenous song and dance), games, musical presentations, exchange of presents, and healing ceremonies. "Traditional fishing" took place in the lake to the sides of the grounds and, at a nearby beach on the banks of the Tejo, the Inuit shaman conducted an Eskimo "sweat lodge" ceremony.

Figure 2.3. Danca de mariri: In 2011, the Kuntanawa organized the second edition of the Cultural Pano Festival. Photo reprinted with the permission of Luana Almeida.

Rituals with ayahuasca were held nearly every night, in addition to other healing ceremonies (with chants, rapé snuff, etc.) that took place at various times throughout the festival. On these occasions, Pano, Arawak, and Inuit pajés guided the ceremonies.[38] Among them were Haru Xinã and, less often, Osmildo. Although the latter prepared part of the ayahuasca consumed in the festival, his presence and public participation in it were quite discreet.[39] But there were many pajés at the Festival, and it was possible to observe, as Manuela Carneiro da Cunha has noted, that the shamanic vocation, which was always reserved for few, subject to long initiatory periods, and marked by its high personal cost, is undergoing a real expansion, particularly among young indigenous leaders.[40] Talking with several Brazilian visitors from other states, one could see that many were ayahuasqueiros, whether through the Santo Daime churches or through pajés travelling outside Acre, possibilities that were not mutually exclusive.

In effect, there is an unprecedented and intense movement of young indigenous leaders out of the state of Acre, both permanent and temporary—and their presence in urban centers such as Rio de Janeiro and São Paulo has resulted in an increase in ayahuasca rituals and interchanges with ayahuasca groups, notably the Santo Daime churches. These young pajés return to their lands and their people anointed with a new legitimacy and prestige. To act as translator or mediator between worlds and perspectives is the domain of shamans. In the case discussed here, as in many other cases of ayahuasca shamanism, one can see an interesting inversion in shamanic power: if out there it is their indigenous capital that is valuable, at home their new capital of alliances and resources fortifies their position in the group.[41]

One of the objectives of the festival was the launching of a trans-ethnic and trans-territorial project baptized the "Pano Corridor." The project is the flagship of the recently created Guardians of the Forest Institute (IGF), a civil organization conceived of and led by Haru Xinã, which joins together Pano indigenous representatives and diverse professionals from Brazil's center-south region, a good number of whom are ayahuasqueiros. The festival was, therefore, the first event held by the IGF, and in some measure it reflected Haru's years of effort in search of external alliances using the trump cards of his people's "culture" and the defense of the "environment."

Haru's discourse, like that of the members of IGF, emphasized the cultural fortification of Pano peoples, and their union and mutual solidarity, especially for those who were more weakened culturally. As he himself said:

> Each person who is here is a bead on this great necklace. Let us make a commitment to raise up each nation. Just as you all are coming here from other places to show my people that it is possible to do this, we also want to take on this responsibility to take this same commitment to all the indigenous lands that will have us, that invite us .... Those who are really weak, whose roots have been so trodden upon already...we will go there, and lift up, with our spirit, with our heart, all those people.

In another solemn moment of the festival, in a rite held at the place where the "sacred house of our ancestors" was erected, Haru declared, "for many years our traditions were forgotten, and now we are coming here to unearth them." With that, in a symbolic act, Haru and others actually dug into the ground. And that is what seemed to be happening at the festival: the Kuntanawa were unearthing their "traditions" and retaking their "culture." In all these years of being with them, I never saw them seeming so "Indian." From the patriarch seu Milton and the matriarch dona Mariana to their great-grandchildren, everyone was present. The festival was clearly an extraordinary moment, removed from everyday life: everyone moved to small, improvised houses in the Kuntamanã village, leaving behind their usual residences, meals were eaten collectively (although each ethnic group had created a modest hearth in its "house" for smaller meals), work in the gardens and other day-to-day chores were put aside until the end of the festival. When the end came, it was time to live the "culture." These quote marks contain no irony; they are rather a means of quoting, since it was in this very same fashion that everything that was being "recovered" in the festival—painting, dress, dance, music, games, language, knowledge, sacred rituals—was conceptualized.[42]

Final Considerations

This chapter has sought to characterize and contextualize the ayahuasca shamanism present in the Kuntanawa group by way of two narratives. One is focused on the personal trajectory of a shaman; in it, the culture (in a broad anthropological sense) that informs it is taken for granted (after all, everyone has culture)—diffuse and unsaid, but without a doubt, present. The other narrative is marked by interethnic relations and situations, which is to say, situations where ethnic differences are produced and identities demarcated, where "culture" is visible and named. In both cases, and through the ritual use of ayahuasca, perspectives are being enunciated about oneself, the other, and the world; perspectives that are not necessarily coincidental, but are coexistent. And one of the conclusions to be drawn, within the exploratory purview that marks this chapter, is that it is sometimes not easy to distinguish, or even to separate, these situations and perspectives that, in daily life, exist side by side and do not bother themselves over their inconsistencies.[43]

"Cultural rebirth," "efflorescence," "cultural self-consciousness": there are various forms today by which to describe this contemporary phenomenon of global reach, as Marshall Sahlins ably shows.[44] "Culture" is objectified, displayed ostentatiously, negotiated, and recovered through projects. Is it a political act affirming ethnicity and rights? Yes, of course. But it is also one of appropriation by the native populations for their own benefit, and for their own ends, of what modernity imposes on them and demands of them. To be "Indian" in this sense, in an interethnic context, is for those who "guarantee themselves," as Eduardo Viveiros de Castro has said: those who transform the costs of Indianness into creative opportunities to foment practices, relations, and knowledge that have disappeared, are in decline, or are under threat.[45]

Of course, changes have their place: after all, new contexts impose themselves. Were the ayahuasca ceremonies at the Pano Cultural Festival "traditional" in the sense of "from the origin"? The Kuntanawa are not immune to history and its transformations. They are not the same as they were a century ago, but their ancestors are without doubt present in the cultural invention of today's descendants. I would insist, thus, on the notion of invention. Cited at the start of this article, it points toward a creativity on the part of the Kuntanawa and their leaders in taking "culture," an idea of foreign origin, and imprinting it with, and expressing through it, contents that concern them as an ethnic group, as much for their internal as external fortification.

I shall close this chapter recognizing that the use of ayahuasca among the Kuntanawa, their shamanism, and the processes of subjectivation they experience, demand more ethnography. Said another way, access to Kuntanawa culture (without quotes) requires more time, observation, and conversation about the meanings they attribute to their existence as a people, to the context in which they find themselves, and to what they put in practice. Only thus might a more inviting dialogue between their theories and ours be possible. Ayahuasca shamanism, it has been shown, operates in context of translation between worlds—in short, of cosmological cosmopolitanism.

Notes

1. Philippe Erikson, "Uma singular pluralidade: A etno-história Pano," in Manuela Carneiro da Cunha, ed., *História dos indios do Brasil* (São Paulo: Cia. das Letras, 1992), 239–52.
2. See, for example, Constant Tastevin, "Na Amazônia (viagem ao Alto Juruá e ao rio Tejo), 1914," in Manuela Carneiro da Cunha, ed., *Tastevin, parrisier: Fontes sobre índios e Seringueiros do Alto Juruá* (Rio de Janeiro: Museu do Índio, 2009), 61–71; and Mariana C. Pantoja, *Os Milto: Cem anos de história nos Seringais* (Rio Branco: Edufac, 2008).
3. Max Weber, "Comunidades étnicas," in Economia y sociedad: Esbozo de sociología comprensiva (México: Fondo de Cultura Económica, 1984), 315–27; Fredrik Barth, ed., *Ethnic Groups and Boundaries* (Oslo: Universitetsforlaget, 1969).
4. Manuela Carneiro da Cunha, "Etnicidade: Da cultura residual mas irredutível," in *Antropologia do Brasil: Mito, história e etnicidade* (São Paulo: Brasiliense, 1987), 97–108.
5. Eduardo Viveiros de Castro, "Cosmological Deixis and Amerindian Perspectivism," *Journal of the Royal Anthropological Institute,* nos. 4/3 (1998): 469–88.
6. I assure the reader that I am aware of the difficulties inherent in referring to my interlocutors as "the Kuntanawa," a generic collective term that does little to clarify things, though it serves some function in allowing more general formulations. It should be clear that during the last twenty years, my degree of contact and work with the members and the generations of this ethnic group has not been uniform, and this is certainly reflected in my data and ethnography.
7. Roy Wagner, *The Invention of Culture* (Chicago: University of Chicago Press, 1981).
8. This is what prompted Manuela Carneiro da Cunha to add quote marks to the concept of culture as a way of calling attention to this reflexive quotation and to the relationship between culture (in an anthropological sense) and "culture" (in an interethnic context). Cf. Manuela Carneiro da Cunha, *"Culture" and Culture: Intellectual Rights and Traditional Knowledge* (Chicago: Prickly Paradigm Press, 2009).
9. Mauro Almeida and Manuela Carneiro da Cunha, Preface to *Os Milton: Cem anos de história nos Seringais,* by Mariana C. Pantoja (Rio Branco: Edufac, 2008), 14.
10. See, for example, Michael Taussig, *Shamanism, Colonialism and the Wild Man: A Study in Terror and Healing* (Chicago: University of Chicago Press, 1987); Peter Gow, "River People: Shamanism and History in Western Amazonia," in Caroline Humphrey and Nicholas Thomas, eds., *Shamanism, History and the State* (Ann Arbor: University of Michigan Press, 1996), 90–113; and Manuela Carneiro da Cunha, "Points de vue sur la forêt Amazonienne: Chamanisme et traduction," in Adauto Novaes, ed., *L´autre rive de l´Occident: Dialogues Brésil-France* (Paris: Metailié, 2006), 309–22.
11. I want to thank Marcos de Almeida Matos and Amilton Pelegrino Mattos, with whom I have shared research, study, and reflection.
12. Marshall Sahlins, "'Sentimental Pessimism' and Ethnographic Experience: Or, Why Culture Is Not a Disappearing 'Object'," in L. Daston, ed., *Biographies of Scientific Objects* (Chicago: University of Chicago Press, 2000), 158–202; Carneiro da Cunha, *"Culture" and Culture*; and Wagner, *The Invention of Culture.*
13. CIMI is a pastoral action organization linked to the avowedly progressive National Conference of Brazilian Bishops (CNBB). Cruzeiro do Sul is the second largest municipality in the state of Acre, Brazil, and the largest in the Acrean Juruá Valley. This region has the greatest concentration of Conservation Units and Indigenous Territories in the state.

14. The FUNAI is the agency responsible for government management of issues related to the indigenous presence in the country.
15. Small genus of South American trees yielding latex.
16. See, among others, Taussig, *Shamanism, Colonialism and the Wild Man*; Cristina S. Wolff, *Mulheres da floresta: Uma história* (São Paulo: Hucitec, 1999); Pantoja, *Os Milton*; and Marcelo P. Iglesias, *Os Kaxinawá de Felizardo: Correrias, trabalho e civilização no Alto Juruá* (Brasília: Paralelo 15, 2010).
17. Rubber estates (*seringais*) are territorial units in the forest that mark property, composed primarily of smaller units called *colocações*. These, in turn, are composed of houses inhabited by extractive laborers (*seringueiros*; rubber tappers) and various resource niches, especially *Heveas*.
18. The term by which the owners or administrators of rubber estates were known.
19. The category of extractive reserves was created by presidential decree in January 1990. They are Sustainable Use Conservation Units, that is, areas of recognized ecological value that include human residents whose economic activities are compatible with environmental conservation. The model was the fruit of the struggles of the Amazonian rubber tapper social movement, and it gained international recognition after the murder of Chico Mendes in 1988. On this subject see, among others, Mary H. Allegretti, "Extractive Reserves: An Alternative for Reconciling Development and Environmental Conservation in Amazonia," in Anthony Anderson, ed., *Alternatives to Deforestation: Steps Toward Sustainable Use of the Amazon Rain Forest* (New York: Columbia University Press, 1990), 253–64; and Mauro W. B. de Almeida, "Le statut de la terre et les réserves extractivistes," *Cahiers du Brésil contemporain*, no. 29/30 (1998): 169–89.
20. The first edition was published in 2004; a second edition, revised and updated with a special chapter on the Kuntanawa, was printed in 2008. See Pantoja, *Os Milton*.
21. The Apolima-Arara, as they were initially known, are an ethnic group resulting from the meeting of survivors of several ethnic groups from more than one linguistic family. In 2008, an Arara Indigenous Territory on the Amônia River was recognized, and its demarcation reached areas that belonged, until then, to the reserve, which entailed the resettlement of rubber tapper families.
22. The self-identification as Kuntanawa really represented a significant political rupture in the local relations, and since then the Kuntanawa have had to deal with resistance from residents of the reserve, directors of the association, mayor and aldermen, and even researchers. Describing this very complex historical process was not one of my objectives in this chapter. I did it partially in a nonpublished work presented at a national meeting of the Brazilian Association of Anthropology (Pantoja, 2006) and in a postscript to Pantoja, *Os Milton: Cem anos de história nos Seringais*, 377–93.
23. In fact, cases are becoming ever more common in which indigenous peoples, thought to have disappeared, demand lands superimposed on Conservation Units that have already been established, both within and outside Amazonia. Cf. Fanny Ricardo, ed., *Terras indígenas & unidades de conservação da natureza: O desafio das sobreposições* (São Paulo: ISA, 2004). For critical reflections on the phenomenon of "ethnic emergence" of indigenous groups thought extinct, see João Pacheco de Oliveira, "Uma etnologia dos 'Índios Misturados'? Situação colonial, territorialização e fluxos culturais," *Mana*, no. 4/1 (1998): 47–77.
24. This section leans heavily on my fieldwork, part of which was published in Pantoja, *Os Milton*; and Mariana C. Pantoja and Osmildo S. da Conceição, "The Use of Ayahuasca Among Rubber Tappers of the Alto Juruá," in Beatriz C. Labate and Edward MacRae, eds., *Ayahuasca, Ritual and Religion in Brazil* (London: Equinox, 2010), 21–38.
25. The Ashaninka are sometimes called "Kampa."
26. The term "*pajé*," an equivalent to "shaman," derives from the Tupi spoken by Brazilian Indians on the Atlantic Coast and became common in the context of indigenous social movements. It is the term used by the indigenous groups referred to in this chapter when they communicate among themselves in Portuguese.

27. On ayahuasca and its various cultural and religious uses, see Labate and MacRae, *Ayahuasca, Ritual, and Religion in Brazil.*
28. Meant here in the sense of a system of knowledge.
29. Osmildo visited the Indigenous Territories of the Kaxinawá of the Jordão River and of the Kaxinawá-Ashaninka of the Breu River, both of which were fully established by then.
30. Pantoja and Conceição, "The Use of Ayahuasca among Rubber Tappers of the Alto Juruá," 23.
31. Cf. Beatriz C. Labate and Gustavo Pacheco, *Opening the Portals of Heaven: Brazilian Ayahuasca Music* (Munster: Lit Verlag, 2010). Several writers have pointed out the importance of the musical dimension in rituals with ayahuasca. It is recognized as a vehicle of forms of understanding that are nonverbal, sensory, and intuitive. Even with lyrics, music would seem to have the capacity to send those who perform it, or even who only hear it, to another reality, beyond the objectively perceptible. In this sense, it is a vehicle for subjective, internal exploration.
32. Though the greater part of this young generation of ayahuasqueiros are male, there are also females, some of whom have their own songs.
33. The word *kunta* refers to the fruit of the cocão (*Scheelea phalerata*). "Kuntanawa" could be translated as "people of the cocão" or "of the coconut."
34. http://pib.socioambiental.org/pt/povo/kuntanawa.
35. In 2008, Haru Xinã took part in a Brazilian commission that attended the Ninth Conference of the Parties (COP) of the Convention on Biological Diversity (CBD) in Germany; in 2009, with his father Univu Kuntanawa, he went to Greenland to participate in the Ceremony of the Sacred Fire; in 2010, he visited the Global Country of World Peace in the Netherlands, as well as the Soirée de la Biodiversité, in France. I would call attention, moreover, to the fact that the prestige enjoyed by young indigenous leaders outside their village, state, and country is a general phenomenon in Acre.
36. They were referring here to the Utilization Plan, a management instrument in extractive reserves that establishes rules and penalties with regard to the use of natural resources.
37. On the NSCP, see www.novacartografiasocial.com/. The workshops with the Kuntanawa were organized by Terri Valle de Aquino, with whom I put together the serial "Kuntanawa do Alto Rio Tejo," in which the map was published.
38. One night was reserved for a ceremony led by members of Santo Daime from Rio de Janeiro.
39. An exception was the moment when he presented himself publicly as coordinator of OPIRJ.
40. Carneiro da Cunha, *"Culture" and Culture*, 35.
41. This observation is made in Carneiro da Cunha, "Points de vue sur la forêt Amazonienne," and also in Sahlins, "Sentimental Pessimism and Ethnographic Experience." Michael Taussig and Peter Gow called attention to this same question, the second even questioning whether ayahuasca shamanism, as practiced contemporarily, originated from native peoples or is part of an Amazonian colonial situation. Cf. Taussig, *Shamanism, Colonialism and the Wild Man*; and Gow, "River People."
42. In a work on the role of the school in the strengthening of "culture" among the Kaxinawá, Ingrid Weber called attention to this objectification of "culture." Cf. Ingrid Weber, *Um copo de cultura: Os Huni Kuin (Kaxinawá) do Rio Humaitá e a escola* (Rio Branco: Edufac, 2006).
43. As Manuela Carneiro da Cunha noted so aptly in her 2009 work repeatedly cited here.
44. Sahlins, "'Sentimental Pessimism' and Ethnographic Experience."
45. Viveiros de Castro, Eduardo. "No Brasil, todo mundo é Indio, exceto quem não é," in Renato Sztutman, ed., *Encontros* (Rio de Janeiro: Azougue, 2008), 142.

Bibliography

Allegretti, Mary H. "Extracting Reserves: An Alternative for Reconciling Development and Environmental Conservation in Amazonia." In *Alternatives to Deforestation: Steps Toward Sustainable Use of the Amazon Rain Forest*, edited by Anthony Anderson, 253–64. New York: Columbia University Press, 1990.

Almeida, Mauro W. B. de. "Le statut de la terre et les réserves extractivistes." *Cahiers du Brésil contemporain*. Paris, 1996: 169–89.

Almeida, Mauro W. B. de, and Manuela Carneiro da Cunha. Preface to 2nd edition of *Os Milton: Cem anos de história nos Seringais*, by Mariana C. Pantoja, 13–14. Rio Branco, Brazil: Edufac, 2008.

Barth, Fredrik, ed. *Ethnic Groups and Boundaries*. Oslo: Universitetsforlaget, 1969.

Carneiro da Cunha, Manuela. *Antropologia do Brasil: Mito, história e etnicidade*. São Paulo, Brazil: Brasiliense, 1987.

Carneiro da Cunha, Manuela. "Points de vue sur la forêt Amazonienne: Chamanisme et traduction." In *L'autre rive de l'Occident*. Dialogues Brésil-France series, edited by Adauto Novaes, 309–22. Paris: Metailié, 2006.

Carneiro da Cunha, Manuela. *"Culture" and Culture: Intellectual Rights and Traditional Knowledge*. Chicago: Prickly Paradigm Press, 2009.

Erikson, Philippe. "Uma singular pluralidade: A etno-história Pano." In *História dos índios no Brasil*, edited by Manuela Carneiro da Cunha, 239–52. São Paulo, Brazil: Cia Das Letras, 1992.

Gow, Peter. "River People: Shamanism and History in Western Amazonia." In *Shamanism, History, and the State*, edited by Caroline Humphrey and Nicholas Thomas, 90–113. Ann Arbor: Michigan University Press, 1996.

Iglesias, Marcelo P. *Os Kaxinawá de Felizardo: Correrias, trabalho e civilização no Alto Juruá*. Brasília, Brazil: Paralelo 15, 2010.

Labate, Beatriz C., and Wladimir Araújo, eds. *O uso ritual da ayahuasca*. Campinas, Brazil: Mercado de Letras, 2004, 2nd edition.

Labate, Beatriz C., and Gustavo Pacheco. *Opening the Portals of Heaven: Brazilian Ayahuasca Music*. Munster, Germany, Lit Verlag, 2010.

Oliveira, João Pacheco de. "Uma etnologia dos 'Índios Misturados'? Situação colonial, territorialização e fluxos culturais." *Mana*, no. 4/1 (1998): 47–77.

Pantoja, Mariana C. "Apontamentos sobre a emergência étnica dos Kuntanawa (Alto Juruá, Acre)." Paper presented at the twenty-fifth Brazilian Reunion of Anthropology, Goiânia, Brazil, June 11–14, 2006.

Pantoja, Mariana C. Foreword to *Os Milton: Cem anos de história nos Seringais*, 375–93. Rio Branco, Brazil: Edufac, 2008.

Pantoja, Mariana C. *Os Milton: Cem anos de história nos Seringais*. Rio Branco, Brazil: Edufac, 2008, 2nd edition.

Pantoja, Mariana, and Osmildo S. Conceição. "The Use of Ayahuasca Among Rubber Tappers of the Alto Juruá." In *Ayahuasca, Ritual and Religion in Brazil*, edited by Beatriz C. Labate and Edward MacRae, 21–37. London: Equinox, 2010.

Ricardo, Fany, ed. *Terras indígenas & unidades de conservação da natureza: O desafio das sobreposições*. São Paulo, Brazil: Instituto Socioambiental, 2004.

Sahlins, Marshall. "'Sentimental Pessimism' and Ethnographic Experience: Or, Why Culture Is Not a Disappearing 'Object.'" In *Biographies of Scientific Objects*, edited by L. Daston, 158–202. Chicago: University of Chicago Press, 2000.

Tastevin, Constant. "Na Amazônia (viagem ao Alto Juruá e ao Rio Tejo), 1914." In *Tastevin, parrissier: Fontes sobre índios e Seringueiros do Alto Juruá*, edited by Manuela Carneiro da Cunha, 61–71. Rio de Janeiro, Brazil: Museu do Índio, 2009.

Viveiros de Castro, Eduardo. "Cosmological Deixis and Amerindian Perspectivism." *Journal of the Royal Anthropological Institute*, no. 4/3 (1998): 469–88.

Viveiros de Castro, Eduardo. "No Brasil, todo mundo é índio, exceto quem não é." In *Encontros*, edited by Renato Sztutman, 130–61. Rio de Janeiro, Brazil: Azougue, 2008.

Wagner, Roy. *The Invention of Culture*. Chicago: University of Chicago Press, 1981.

Weber, Ingrid. *Um copo de cultura: Os Huni-Kuin (Kaxinawá) do Rio Humaitá e a escola*. Rio Branco, Brazil: Edufac, 2006.

Weber, Max. "Ethnic Groups." In *Economy and Society: An Outline of Interpretative Sociology*, 385–98. Berkeley: University of California Press, 1978.

3

Materializing Alliances

Ayahuasca Shamanism in and Beyond Western Amazonian Indigenous Communities

PIRJO KRISTIINA VIRTANEN

In Western and Southwestern Amazonia, ayahuasca shamanism constitutes one of the most important forms of shamanism, especially for the Panoan and Arawakan speakers of the region. The expanded contexts for their ayahuasca shamanism in the state of Acre, Brazil, are the evenings of indigenous political meetings in urban areas, cultural festivals, indigenous people's training courses, and ayahuasca rituals practiced in homes by indigenous peoples in cities. They gather together indigenous peoples with diverse shamanic knowledge and their particular animal, plant, nature, and ancestor spirits (nonhumans). Here, my ethnography comes from ayahuasca rituals shared with Manchineri, Cashinahua, Yawanawa, and Ashaninka Indians both in the rainforest and urban environments. The ritual groups were composed in various ways, some with members of only one indigenous community, others with one or more members from an indigenous group together with non-Indians, rituals with various indigenous groups, and groups made up of numerous indigenous groups with non-Indians. Some indigenous people from Acre who practice ayahuasca shamanism have also become famous outside the region, and occasionally travel to other parts of the country and abroad to conduct ayahuasca rituals and other shamanic practices there. The indigenous groups, who prepare and consume the hallucinogenic ayahuasca brew in the region, have differing traditions of its use. Both Arawakan and Panoan shamans drink it in their shamanic healing works, but other community members may also practice ayahuasca shamanism collectively or individually. Through ayahuasca shamanism, the power of the sacred vine and certain nonhumans (animal, plant, nature, and ancestor spirits) can be experienced in controlled contexts, even by "laymen." In many groups, the use of ayahuasca has become more popular and common only recently.[1] Those who are dealing with the ayahuasca plant are relating to a powerful entity, and therefore the question of power is a key issue.

The acknowledged shamans are healers, but sometimes also sorcerers, and they usually know other shamanic practices. They are called by generic names, such as *kahontshi* ("shaman" in Manchineri). In addition, there are also special terms for those people who have specialized shamanic knowledge, such as healing from sorcery, or who know medicinal plants. In many communities, those who have developed their shamanic skills have names for their specialized knowledge. They can also be masters of chanting, and so forth. These people have usually passed a tough shaman training that includes becoming familiar with the effects of various psychoactive plants, isolation, and learning many other shamanic techniques.

I will show that ayahuasca shamanism is an important part of materializing new alliances and relations through ritual openings. First, I look at the ayahuasca rituals I shared in the Manchineri community, as these were, owing to my presence, about a new alliance to be negotiated. Then, I will discuss the shamanic encounters of different indigenous groups in the state of Acre. Lastly, I will look at the shamanic practices introduced recently by the Indians to non-Indians in urban areas. I will argue that ayahuasca shamanism makes indigenous knowledge visible, but the preference is to keep this at a personal level, inside the controllable "cultural borders," as it is closely related to systems of affinity. Thus only certain kinds of intergroup contacts made through shamanism are accepted. The theoretical framework comes from the Amerindian horizontal thinking on multiple entities. Shamanism is a key tool used to deploy that space in order to recreate the world. Anthropologists such as Jonathan Hill, Stephen Hugh-Jones, and Robin Wright have argued in their studies about Northwest Amazonian peoples (Tukanoan and Arawaks) that the vertical lines of the microcosmos in human bodies and horizontal lines of the macrocosmos are connected in the ritual spaces through ritual poetics and chanting.[2] Chanting is a central part of ayahuasca shamanism: it offers the means of communication and vehicle for sharing knowledge and experiences. Moreover, shamanic power and ritual hierarchy are vital to understanding the reinvention and expansion of today's ayahuasca shamanism.

Sharing Shamanic Knowledge

On my very first night of in the Manchineri reserve, a young Manchineri unexpectedly came to the house were I was staying to invite me to the place where they were taking *kamalampi* (ayahuasca). I appreciated the invitation greatly, as the Manchineri rarely let others enter their territory by the River Yaco. I was in one of the downriver villages closer to urban areas, as there was a meeting of the recently established Manchineri association and I was there to introduce my research to the community. Present at the ayahuasca ritual were only a shaman from another village, the association's coordinator, and some younger people. The shaman was chanting, and no one spoke much during the whole evening. In the meeting of the association next day, my research was officially presented, and after a conversation with the community, it was authorized. I could then continue with my official research-permit applications with Brazilian authorities. However, I knew that the real acceptance would come only when I started living with the Manchineri in their community.

After the governmental office for indigenous affairs granted the research permit, I stayed first in Extrema, the farthest upriver village from urban areas, at the home of a young Manchineri family. It was only two days after my arrival in that village that a small boy from a house farther from the central village came to our house to deliver an invitation to go there that night to take ayahuasca. After a while, the young couple of the house, their two kids, and I trekked there with the boy. I was surprised that the invitation to the ritual had again happened so quickly, but also glad, as the best chanters were to be found in that village. That evening, we gathered at the house of another Manchineri family, with about a dozen Manchineris. A young man was still preparing the ayahuasca beverage, and showed me how they do it. He also looked for a special herb (*kamaleji*) to put in the pot, together with *Banisteriopsis caapi* and *Psychotria viridis*. When everything was ready, people had found their places and were quiet, and night had fallen, one of the Manchineris told me, "Now you are going to see what we, the Manchineri, are like."

That night there was no one present who was known as a shaman: only younger people and two elders with experience with the plants. For the Manchineri, ayahuasca shamanism may be led by a shaman who works through kamalampi, for instance to cure a specific person, but anyone can take ayahuasca if he or she wants guidance from this ritual drink and the nonhumans that become present and visible when it is consumed. At dusk, an old woman served a cup of ayahuasca to everyone, according to their familiarity with the plant. The Manchineris were talking in low voices while waiting for the effects of the drink. If there is no special ritual leader, the one who feels the effects of ayahuasca first starts singing the ayahuasca chants and thereby calls the spirit of ayahuasca or certain plant or animal spirits. Various Manchineris sang during the night with the guidance of the elders.

We stayed overnight in a house distant from the village center. In the morning, people were chatting, eating a little, and preparing for their departure. They explained that the chants sung by the elders were about their ancestors who had appeared in the night. For the Manchineri, the chants facilitate the appearance of nonhuman beings and encourage them to share their teachings and protective

Figure 3.1. Ayahuasca being prepared in a Manchineri village. Photograph by Pirjo K. Virtanen.

powers. The ancestors, animals, plants, and natural elements have their own songs and designs that appear in visions. These designs, which are applied on ceramics and in body paintings,[3] are the origin of the artwork of various Arawakan- and Panoan-speaking groups and are said to be protective and carry knowledge. The chants materialize the designs. Consequently, the ritualized space created when ayahuasca is taken is the Manchineri's way of materializing nonhuman worlds. According to the Manchineri man who had prepared the ayahuasca, it was also the additional herb added to the brew that had helped me to experience what kind of people the Manchineri are.

Later, an old man told me that during the same night in his ayahuasca vision he had seen an animal with horns, and he asked if there are such animals in my country. I answered that there are elk, deer, and reindeer, among others. He answered happily that he had, then, seen an animal from my country. He continued by asking if there is a football team where I am from, and so forth.

In fact, later I discovered that I was invited to the ritual because the community wanted to find out what kind of person I was. For them, the ancestors who had appeared had accepted my presence. It had been difficult for the community to understand why I was interested in living with them. Some community members thought that non-Indians' only aim was to become rich by acquiring knowledge of their medicinal plants. By taking ayahuasca they could identify my essence,[4] and discern if their cooperation with me would harm them. The ritual space had enabled the Manchineri to travel in the space of essences, for instance, of my nation. They often asked directly which nation I was from. In the end, I guess the Manchineri thought that we could build up an exchange of knowledge, and many things were told to me and shared with me. For the Manchineri, the most "other" in their social system are the non-Indians, *payri*. The ritualized context in which ayahuasca was taken opened up an opportunity for me to see their past and present, but also for them to get to know distant places (my country, in this case). According to the Manchineri, it had been especially the kamaleji that revealed to me the essence of the Manchineri nation.

For some peoples, the door to see the world differently opens by chanting and the use of psychoactive substances. According to an anthropologist who has been working in northwestern Amazonia, Jonathan D. Hill, "Musicalization is a process of expanding, opening, and augmenting the miniaturized vertical creation into a horizontal dimension of exchange relations among a plurality of peoples from different places."[5] For him, native singing has to be understood within a social space of many beings, which forms horizontal space, and the individual human body, which comprises vertical space in the line of generations. Ritual poetics establishes new relationships to distant peoples, enemies, and alliances in a controlled way. Taking ayahuasca can be understood as a means of establishing generational line in a space through which human bodies can experience their individuality and connection to horizontal space vertically: both lines are always connected.

We can turn now to look at ayahuasca shamanism as it is shared among indigenous people from various backgrounds, and with non-Indians as it relates to unfamiliar subjects and their essences, as well as building recognition as peoples with history, power, and knowledge. Political and cultural meetings, as well as the training courses of indigenous teachers and agro-forestry agents in urban areas, are typical events where some Indians take ayahuasca outside the official program. In the evenings during these encounters, some Cashinahua, Ashaninka, or Yawanawa participants lead ayahuasca rituals and may invite other people to join in. Some indigenous people are afraid of the shamanic rivalries that may occur during these rituals, and thus take ayahuasca only among their own group. Ayahuasca shamanism is also considered a tool for harm, such as through sorcery, as well as for curing.

The leader of the ritual usually personally invites other people to the event, who occasionally invite their friends along. By inviting only certain people, ritual leaders can show their power. The non-Indian participants are usually familiar with ayahuasca from the so-called ayahuasca churches. In this part of Amazonia, a large number of non-Indians visit the Santo Daime, União do Vegetal, or Barquinha churches, and thus the brew is relatively well known in the region.[6] The exchange between the Indians and non-Indians is not recent. Raimundo Irineu Serra, for instance, took ayahuasca for the first time with the Indians in the 1930s, and this led to the foundation of the Santo Daime church.

Ayahuasca rituals in urban areas follow the same form as those among the indigenous communities, and thus they remain different from the ayahuasca churches, which have relatively larger ceremonial groups and set of hymns. In the indigenous communities, chants, visions, and what I call "ritual speeches" are shared besides the substance of the ayahuasca beverage. The person who leads the ritual controls the chanting and determines when the ayahuasca is taken. The chants and the ritual speeches set vertical lines as reflections of times and spaces. These special speech forms usually occur after the first effects of the ayahuasca have vanished and people reflect on their experiences. They concern personal life stories, travels to distant places, reflections on their community's situation today, teachings of the ayahuasca plant, and so on. For instance, an Ashaninka man once explained how he had learned many things about nonhuman beings through the use of *kamarampi* (ayahuasca), such as about *Pawa,* the Great Being of their people. Before or during the ritual, Cashinahuas often talked about *yube,* the powerful boa constrictor who brings the visions through the *nixi pãe* (the brew). Other Panoan speakers, the Yawanawa, talk about *uni,* referring to the vine, interacting with people. We can see these ritual speeches as making history and expanding the world,[7] while indigenous people experience themselves in the vertical line of the generations. For the nonkin, the speeches are presentations of that indigenous group's thinking and lineages.

The ayahuasca plant and brew is regarded as a person, known as the "mother of ayahuasca," who is represented as the vine of *Banisteriopsis* in the form of a female person.[8] She is usually called from the web of relations at the beginning of the ritual by singing. This powerful being of the *Banisteriopsis* works through the drink. She may also appear in the form of the boa constrictor that colors a person's body with designs, making it vivid, appealing, and strong. This female nonhuman being allows the person taking the psychoactive substance into his or her body to assume the point of view of others, such as animals (which actually see themselves as humans), and to learn from this metamorphosis and transcendence.

For indigenous people from different historical and social backgrounds, ayahuasca shamanism provides important spaces to share experiences. They can communicate information about their nonhuman beings, ancestors, and history in an embodied way. For non-Indians, it presents the ways of thinking of other peoples, and highlights their differences, as various indigenous groups use diverse methods, chants, and instruments. The Yawanawa, for instance, often start by cleaning the body with a snuff, *rapé*.

In intergroup encounters, the organization of the ayahuasca ritual sets specific groups in the space in new relationships to other groups, persons, and nonhumans. The presence of a numerous group of people opens the cosmos for multiple beings as the nonhumans from various mythologies and histories may all be present. Indigenous people can relate differently in ritual space than in other situations in villages or with non-Indians. As one example, on the last evening of a course for indigenous teachers organized by the secretary of education, a young Yawanawa man arrived with his Cashinahua and non-Indian musician friends from Rio Branco. He said that his relatives in the course had been waiting for him for many days to conduct the ritual there. Besides people from his indigenous group, he had invited some non-Indians to the ritual. Many of them had been working with indigenous peoples, but had rarely lived with them. Later, in Rio Branco, the young Yawanawa explained which non-Indians had been there, from which indigenous groups people had been singing, and how happy everyone had been thanks to the event. It was as if the multipresence had made the encounter more beautiful, just as many instruments can make a musical performance more sonorous.

Sometimes ayahuasca practices are introduced to the indigenous people who are not in the habit of taking ayahuasca.[9] Once, an Ashaninka participant invited people to take ayahuasca in the evening on the last day of a meeting in Acre of various indigenous associations. Most of the non-Indian and Indian participants were from the states of Brazil where ayahuasca rituals were not common. Everything was first conducted according to the Ashaninka traditions. An Ashaninka man, already known for his shamanic knowledge, was the ritual leader. The venue was the same as for the meeting, in a place distant from Rio Branco, the state capital. The Ashaninka first played a guitar and sang Portuguese songs he made up himself. Then he served the ayahuasca drink for everyone, and the Ashaninka chants started. During the night, the Ashaninka man also healed people personally by blowing smoke from his pipe, removing the essences causing sickness, singing, and other specific acts.

Particular to the night's meeting was that later, when the Ashaninka man was singing in deep communication with the nonhuman beings of the forest, a young Cashinahua man also started to sing a different chant in Cashinahua, and a Yanomami participant joined in with them in Yanomami. An interesting point is that the Yanomami use only a hallucinogenic snuff in their shamanic practices, and not ayahuasca. However, now all three of them were singing at the same time in their own languages, their own chants, and in totally different rhythms. The

Yanomami man was standing and acting typical to the Yanomami shamans' work. The three people were communicating with the various nonhuman beings of their particular sociocosmos. That meant importing three mythic landscapes into the ritual encounter. Then they imitated several animals, accompanied by the Yanomami's theatrical movements, for a good while. It was a very intense and extraordinary moment thanks to the multipresence of beings representing a number of mythic landscapes, aesthetics, and histories. The Yanomami live far away from the state of Acre and have very different traditions of shamanism. I had never seen that kind of shamanic activity previously. The modern encounter between the indigenous associations had allowed this kind of shamanic exchange to happen. The nonhumans with whom the singers interacted brought along their various protections and powers for the participants.

I was especially amazed by the variety of musical tones and the strength of singing of the three performers. Indians from these groups usually quietly chanted the chants of their own groups along with the leader of the ritual. Heterophony in South American Lowlands has earlier been stated to be about affirmation of individuality. I thought that it would be excellent to record the mixture of languages and sounds of this rare moment. But in the darkness of the night, I did not want to look for my recorder, as it could disturb the atmosphere and the shamanic work. Moreover, I never recorded anything if it had not been agreed on previously. The next day, however, when I was with the Ashaninka shaman, who wanted me to listen to some of his new songs in Portuguese on his MP3 player, he mentioned that he could not record the event yesterday because he did not have batteries. I said that I had my equipment there, but explained why I did not dare to use it. He said that of course I should have recorded it. It would have been meaningful for him to listen again to the others' singing. It is essential to note that knowledge is built up participatively and acquired from the others, including from other groups.

On the day following the ritual, I conversed with the Yanomami participant, and he said that in their shamanic work the hallucinogenic snuff they use is much stronger. I knew that, besides being their most important spokesman, he was also a powerful shaman in his community. He said that on the previous night he had been calling the spirits to expel bad entities, as they do in their shamanic work. His methods were different from, but the aims very similar to, those of other groups. The Yanomami continued that he liked non-Indians coming from abroad. He had already met with many cooperative partners, and non-Indians had hosted him abroad, where he had been talking about the Indians' situation. In previous times, the Yanomami had only known non-Indians with other types of interests, such those who brought them many diseases.

For indigenous people from dissimilar backgrounds, the organized ritual encounters are important spaces where they can live their spirituality outside the formal classrooms or political meetings, spaces not fully designed by them. I will return to this question of power later on. Next, I will discuss how shamanism provides healing and cleaning events and works to (re)establish alliances.

Materializing Alliances

For many indigenous groups, taking ayahuasca is about reinforcing social relations and establishing new connections. It is also a manifestation of cooperation between indigenous peoples, as well an expression of their will to establish new relations with non-Indians.[10] The use of ayahuasca induces an extraordinary state of perception that changes the participant's point of view, allowing him or her to see the nonhuman world.[11] Ayahuasca shamanism provides the opportunity to materialize ways of thinking, cosmology, and a holistic worldview. It may not be possible outside the ritualized context for Indians to express their point of view as they want to. The experiences shared in the ritual can create new social relations between the participants.[12] Moreover, it is now important to be recognized as "indigenous" and to show what this means for the indigenous peoples themselves.

Ayahuasca, prepared according to the traditions of specific indigenous groups, is a substance taken into the body that materializes entities of specific indigenous groups, making it possible to adopt their point of view. Different groups know the various types of vines of *Banisteriopsis caapi*, as well as the leaves of the *Psychotria viridis* bush, that are boiled together, occasionally with other plants added, as I previously explained discussing the Manchineri. For the Amerindians, subjective relations are both materialized and represented in bodily social activities and the substances consumed.[13] Substantiality in social bodies changes integration of social relations and subjects.

The singer of shamanic songs relates his views, dialogues, and experiences with other beings.[14] The shaman's chanting refers to a change of perspective, as Eduardo Viveiros de Castro has argued: in the Amerindian context, shamans adopt the perspective of animals and see the world from the animal's or spirit's intentionality and the animal's normally invisible "human" viewpoint.[15] In the ayahuasca ritual, this is possible for many participants.[16] The participants are guided by the singing of one lead singer. Singing is an important way to materialize knowledge.

For indigenous peoples, music is about imagining mythic places and actors.[17] Ayahuasca shamanism generates an intersubjective field in which things that are normally invisible (the nonhuman world) become visible and materialized, and music is one of the methods to visualize that. Chanting encourages nonhuman agents to share their knowledge and protective powers. In the words of Anthony

Seeger: "Music transcends time, space, and existential levels of reality. It affects humans, spirits, animals, and those hard-to-imagine beings in between."[18] According to Manchineris, through the chants, a person's body can receive elements that cure, defend the person, or animate the person at the time of the festivity, even if the person is not aware of this. I was told many times how some children became lively or tall, or received some other quality because their elders had sung of a certain animal for them, for instance of a lively species. The Manchineri chant lyrics are about the qualities of animals or natural elements that were presented as humans, for instance, how they play musical instruments, or their way of moving. They were also addressed in kinship terms, such as "grandfather" (*tote*) or "uncle" (*patu*: brother of father). Overall, we can see that ayahuasca chants deal with materializing nonhumans, each with its own habitus. They enable the embodiment of the "viewpoints" of these nonhumans and help to create special bonds between the participants.

Sometimes the leader of the ritual may ask the participants to accompany his singing. Participants might also be asked to sing individually. If non-Indians have an active part, they usually sing hymns from the ayahuasca churches, as many were frequent visitors there. I have also heard that non-Indians who have been asked to sing have even presented songs from capoeira, part of the Afro-Brazilian tradition. The numerous ways to sing are learned from various sources, not just from nonhumans. The Manchineri shaman also used secular or religious songs of the dominant society, for which he had provided Manchineri lyrics. For instance, he sang, in Manchineri and with a very slow melody, "Happy Birthday to You." This song he probably knew to be sung by non-Indians at one of their most important celebrations, individual birthdays. Indigenous participants could also sing in Portuguese, but I never heard anyone sing in the language of another indigenous group, even if their rhythms would fit the musical repertoire. Moreover, the young generation especially is introducing new musical instruments, such as the guitar. All this shows how relations are established with new actors, as new types of knowledge are appropriated, and an attempt is made to understand the new points of view. Viveiros de Castro has depicted how learning enemies' songs changes the point of view of the singer.[19] For the Manchineri, the chants are usually about particular animals or natural elements that have played a central role in their mythology. The new songs can be regarded as materializing new agents in sociocosmology. A young Manchineri man told me that once, when he had taken ayahuasca and I was not even present in the place, he had "received" my song, which was about protecting the forests (which I thought was very nice).

Ayahuasca has typically been used to analyze people through examination of their bodies in the ayahuasca rituals. It can show evil spirits and people's motivations, and it is used to identify true political alliances.[20] Ayahuasca brew guides political practices and formation of alliances. For instance, I was once in an ayahuasca ritual at a Manchineri family's house in Rio Branco a few days before a meeting of indigenous groups at three national frontiers. After the hallucinogenic effects had passed, an older shaman spoke to a younger man who was active in a leadership position in the local indigenous movement, and explained what could happen in the upcoming political meeting. He advised the younger man to choose his partners carefully and take care in how he dealt with them. Later, the old shaman explained to me that everything had been fine in the meeting because of the guidance of the ayahuasca, and the younger Manchineri man had stayed in the leadership position without any arguments from others.

The ritual space "brings" normally invisible beings into interactive relations with people taking ayahuasca. Its effects can rarely be ignored. The non-Indians who had, for the first time, experienced indigenous spirituality in this ritual space usually talked about the ayahuasca ritual as something unforgettable. They become very sensitive and say that they have connected with the natural environment. Indigenous traditions were often positioned as the "other," opposed to Western cultures. The feelings they expressed having can be compared to sensations experienced after other indigenous rituals, which usually take days and occur in the distant communities. As an example, the comments of non-Indians about the Yawa festival (festivities of the Yawanawa community lasting several days in their territory) were very similar to ones I heard after ayahuasca rituals. In a documentary about the Yawa festival to which a small number of nonnatives come, two white women comment: "They [the Yawanawa] . . . are very humble people, but with a lot to teach"; "Everything has a meaning; you're connected to all the forces"; and "If everyone had the opportunity to be here only for one day, in one of those festivals, the world would be completely different."[21] These non-Indians usually live close to urban consumer cultures and distant from the things the rituals are about. Shamanic practices may also help non-Indians in relationship or health troubles for which Western science does not have cures.

Questions of Power

Outside their territories, indigenous people rarely have dominant or leadership positions. Political and cultural events or training courses involving Indians in urban areas are usually designed by non-Indians, who organize transport, create timetables, and provide technology. They have to be consulted, even if discourses made by Indians and their manifestations, songs, and ritual dances are embodied during the days of the meetings. In contrast, ayahuasca shamanism allows a dominant position for indigenous peoples, who have long been marginalized by the dominant society, and allows them to demonstrate how knowledgeable they, in fact, are.

When I wrote a popular article about indigenous youth in the local newspaper in Acre, I mentioned that the ayahuasca ritual is an ancient Amazonian ritual and is very important to the indigenous population in urban areas.[22] I also wrote that it is undertaken with families and other people in private houses. Thus young people learn their traditions and can live their indigenous identity. When I asked a Manchineri man, who was involved in indigenous politics and was aware of the rights of the Indians, for his opinion on my text, he said that the readers of the newspaper might get an impression that the homes of indigenous people in urban areas are popular places of ayahuasca rites open to anyone. He told me that I should not write about everything that I learnt, because for his people, some things, such as the details of their shamanism, are private and sacred. "That is ours," as the Manchineri man said. In my research publications, I have opted not to present a detailed description of the rituals, chants, or nonhumans.

Shamanic practices have become important carriers of indigenous identity in Amazonia. Evangelical missionaries, for instance, forbade the use of ayahuasca as an act of the devil. The continuation of the use of ayahuasca shows the control the Indians maintain over their traditions. Today, ayahuasca shamanism is also part of the expression of the shamanic fame of indigenous groups. Shamans are specialists in ayahuasca songs, since they know dozens of chants. They have learned these songs and how to use them from other people or directly from

Figure 3.2. Young Manchineri man's drawing of an ayahuasca ritual in Rio Branco.

nonhuman beings. The visions produced depend closely on the chant leader of the ritual. Taking ayahuasca allows a shaman or ritual leader to control encounters with the nonhuman world through music, by singing chants that either invigorate or calm the participant's visions. As Graham Townsley says, "Songs are a shaman's most highly prized possessions, the vehicles of his powers and the repositories of his knowledge."[23] The language of singing can, he argues, be metaphorical and include unusual words. The Manchineri shamans sometimes use chant language that is incomprehensible to others; it is said to be the language of the ancients. Thus it does not matter if the participant does not speak the indigenous language, because the sounds in themselves will have an influence, as will the other ritual substances, such as the brew. It depends on human knowledge, control of the behavior before and after the ritual, the quality of the ayahuasca, and so forth, but in the end the nonhuman beings determine whether the ritual has any effect.

In the indigenous communities, old people especially have questioned young people's direct interaction with the vital nonhuman forces. For instance, elders will say that the young people learning the songs do not really know how to use them. Each song has its specific meaning, and it is important to know in which situations it is used and in what order the songs are chanted. One young indigenous teacher even had to stop working on the research of ayahuasca chants for teaching purposes, because the elders of his community had told him not to get involved with things he had not enough knowledge or experience of. As Viveiros de Castro argues, singing is corporal activity and can harm the singer.[24]

Musicality has been an important bridge builder with non-Indians, as singing in the ritual offers a special participative form. As indigenous groups have their own myths, they have corresponding chants picturing their ancestors, nonhumans, and the rhythms that conjure them. When people from different backgrounds meet, the materialization of new agents in sociocosmology becomes possible through chanting. Music is a bridge between the people, and it is also an agent of communication. The participants from ayahuasca churches, however, usually stick to their own hymns, and other types of chants are used as only a vehicle to interact with those nonhuman beings they are already familiar with. Participants can use bodily expressions, emphasize certain sounds and words, and employ their voices differently. Individuals can create new lyrics and compositions. Even if the chants come from the nonhumans, they can be identified with the singer and his or her type of knowledge. Some of the songs are narrated in the singular first person present form. Ayahuasca shamanism thus produces a space to share personal life histories, which can be a very confidential context between new alliances.

A number of musically talented indigenous persons who have memorized many chants or produced new ones have become known outside their communities. Indigenous groups, particularly the Ashaninka, Cashinahua, and Yawanawa, have recorded albums of their chants in Portuguese and in their own language. Their musicians also lead ayahuasca sessions in intergroup contexts, making them known among non-Indians and Indians from other groups. Those groups who reproduce and re-create their traditions using new technology and combining it with knowledge of the dominant society are often looked on highly by both other indigenous groups and non-Indians.

Some indigenous people from Acre have been invited over state borders and to foreign countries to conduct ayahuasca rituals. For instance, a Yawanawa man told me about his trip to France and Russia, invited by a group of people interested in unfamiliar forms of shamanism. He was pleased with his trip and said that the people were very interested in the work he did there. Those who engage in these travels are rarely older shamans, but ones from the younger generation who have learned shamanic skills from their own people to pursue their own interests. This has surely been motivated by the positive feedback from the non-Indians who have shared the rituals. These non-Indians are from very diverse backgrounds. Those who have taken the initiative to organize the travels abroad are usually alternative therapists, members of ayahuasca churches, and New Age movement members. Recently, Cashinahua and Yawanawa Indians made a trip to a Brazilian metropolis. Their shamanic sessions have been advertised in the networks of people interested in neo-shamanism, meditation, and alternative healing.

In 2003, some Cashinahuas started to lead ayahuasca sessions in São Paulo and Rio de Janeiro. Three brothers, who had learned various shamanic techniques from people in their community, got to know many people through their father, who was a well-known leader and had many contacts, although he was no longer present in the village. They were originally from the Jordão area and had moved to Rio Branco because of their father's work and travels as a Cashinahua spokesman. The oldest brother was already in São Paulo when I started my research in 2003.[25] Two younger ones lived in Rio Branco. One of them had a Cashinahua wife and stayed in Rio Branco. The contacts of the youngest brother led him to Rio de Janeiro in 2005. When I met the youngest brother, he explained that he was already trying to learn as much as he could in the city, and wanted to continue to study in the biggest cities of Brazil.

Once, in Rio Branco in 2005, the younger of the two then living in Rio Branco invited me along to where he was about to go to conduct an ayahuasca ceremony at the home of their family friend, a non-Indian. I had never before seen him taking the leadership position in such events. Despite his young age, he explained very well for everyone the meaning of the ritual for his people, *Huni kuin* (the Cashinahuas' autonomination). However, at the end of the night, one non-Indian man started to lead the ritual with methods derived from ayahuasca churches. When I discussed this later with the young Cashinahua man, he said that it had been OK, as "it was their territory." He said he was rather disappointed because he had "called" his (nonhuman) spiritual master and tried to build a space for relations in this way, but then everything had changed because other beings became involved. He had wanted me to see the shamanic event conducted solely by him. In fact, he did so later outside of Acre, in Rio de Janeiro, where he had become known as a shaman and leader of the space of the ayahuasca rituals and many other shamanic practices offered for non-Indians. This was a space where Indians were received as authentic ayahuasca teachers.

A lively discussion in the local media started later in 2005 when *Cerimônia Nixi Pãe* in the São Paulo area was advertised with an entrance fee of 100 reals. The involvement of economic resources is always a sensitive issue for indigenous communities, but Indians from the other groups in the region were more worried about the capacity of young Cashinahuas to properly conduct the rituals and that non-Indians would not understand indigenous spirituality correctly. Ayahuasca's authenticity was also questioned. The issue received numerous comments in the social media at that time, especially in the blog of a local journalist.[26] The young Cashinahua brothers organizing it were seen as slipping into the neo-shamanic movement of the Southern cities. One person from São Paulo said that he would very much like to participate in the ritual with "real Indians" without any Judeo-Christian influences, if he had an opportunity. Other persons argued that, especially in cities, people were deprived of contact with nature and therefore the sacred plant would be welcome there. Several non-Indians expressed the benefits the plant has for humans. The differences in Amerindian and Western epistemology can be seen in how "nature" was objectified in the comments. In contrast, for Amerindians, animals and plants are humans whose different corporal behaviors constitute their own cultures. Therefore, "nature" is human and has its "cultural" elements.[27]

There was also much discussion of whether ayahuasca was the property of Indians or the whole of humanity. Those non-Indians who had tried it regarded the plant as something that represented truth, universal knowledge, equality, brotherhood, liberty, and the experience of nature. Someone defended the idea that it was the Indians', saying that they have more knowledge of the plant thanks to a longer relationship with it.

In regard to the economic criticism, some tried to explain that travel from Acre is very expensive, and the ritual had its costs, and nobody would make a profit. It was also added that in Western society everything has its commercial price, and the Indians also needed money in the city.

There is a great controversy over the expansion of the use of the ayahuasca. The blog criticized the urban environment for the ritual as being unbeneficial; the Cashinahua brothers leading the ritual were criticized for having been raised in an urban environment, for not having enough knowledge of the use of the plant, and for being called shamans. The Cashinahua brothers answered that the Indians in the city are not less Indian,[28] and that they had not called themselves shamans.

Today, two of these Cashinahua brothers continue practicing shamanic rituals, and they say that they are raising funds for their people. Both brothers have non-Indian spouses, live in the two biggest cities of Brazil, Rio de Janeiro and São Paulo, and have become fathers. Even if learning to live in the urban jungle has not been without difficulties, their indigenous immaterial traditions have given them pride and a life with dignity. The ayahuasca ritual has also opened doors to upper-class homes for them. This ritual is promoted as a sacred and ancient ritual, but the form in which it is conducted by Cashinahuas in urban spaces has already been infused with many new elements, such as ritual assistants, the use of maracas, and fire, that are alien to their original context.[29]

When ayahuasca rituals are advertised outside the Amazon, the concepts of "shaman" and "sacred" are used. The rituals are marketed as "Ritual nixi pae with Cashinahua shaman," "Ritual uni with Yawanawa shaman," or shamanic practices with Yawanawa shaman ("pajelança com Yawanawa pajé"). The Indians who lead the ceremonies are rarely considered shamans in their communities, even if in the dominant society they are named as such.[30] Many community members learn shamanic skills in order to achieve a healthy body, for instance, or for success in hunting, agriculture, or love affairs. The "real" shamans are usually only those who deal with illnesses, sorcery, and the health of the community as a whole, since they have the broadest knowledge of the cosmos and its nonhuman beings. I was told by one of the Yawanawa leaders that the Yawanawa man who taught about the shamanism of his people in southern Brazil for non-Indians had never been known in his community as a shaman. At his return to his village, everyone made jokes about him, because he had appeared in the South as a shaman. He was very embarrassed, but he also defended himself by saying that he had told only the stupid non-Indians that he was a shaman.

The fame of certain indigenous groups' shamanic work among urban high-class Brazilians brings acknowledgment for them as they become known. This has also been a learning experience for indigenous peoples, as they observe urban dwellers looking for shamanic experience and knowledge, and realize that this is what indigenous peoples can offer them at a considerably good economic return. Today, ayahuasca rituals are also accompanied by opportunities to take frog vaccinations (*Phyllomedusa bicolor*),[31] and lessons in body painting and dancing are also proffered. These types of packages have increased the economic value Indians can realize from contact with urban environments.

The same hybridity can be seen to some extent in Acre as ayahuasca ritual groups become more diverse. Indians are increasingly opening their ritual spaces to non-Indians interested in their spirituality. This has been noted particularly

Figure 3.3. Diversity of body paintings in Yawa festival, a Yawanawa village. Photograph by Pirjo K. Virtanen.

among non-Indians who work closely with Indians. In 2009, a phone belonging to the coordinator of a pro-indigenous association rang and someone asked, "What time do the Indians start to take ayahuasca at their training place?" The coordinator did not know anyone went there for this purpose: for her it was as if, in the eyes of the dominant society, the Indians' training center were becoming a place to take ayahuasca, while other issues affecting the Indians, such as illegal logging or drug trafficking, were of no interest to outside society. Later, she found out that the phone call had been from a young indigenous man who had invited some people to take ayahuasca that night. Ayahuasca is becoming more popular and, at the same time, ayahuasca churches in Acre are controlling their visitors more, and the leaders of the churches must approve participation in the events. The younger indigenous generation especially likes to share the ayahuasca ritual with friends and acquaintances, but they are also key actors in deciding how and with whom the ritual will be reproduced.

Expansion of the Web of Relations

Even if the expansion of ayahuasca shamanism is not a recent phenomenon, the new forms it takes are worthy of note. It is introduced in new contexts with new actors, mediating how they relate. The expansion and reinvention of Amazonian shamanism reveals indigenous peoples' concern with establishing alliances within the changing power relations between other indigenous peoples and the dominant non-Indian society. Through ayahuasca shamanism, new horizontal openings between new actors, beings, and entities are created. It can also be used as a tool to relate to the common opposite of numerous indigenous groups: the non-Indians, who have themselves become more diverse and open for partnerships and collaborations. In the meantime, it produces new hierarchies as some indigenous people and individuals become known as possessing more shamanic power than others and cultural differences are looked at anew. Furthermore, modern ayahuasca ritual leaders establish contacts with new actors that can be beneficial at the communal and individual levels.

Janet Hendricks noted in 1988 that the Shuar aspired to power in indigenous politics, in technology, and in regard to knowledge of whites very similarly to how they had searched for power through shamanism. She looked at the discourses used in both contexts and noted their similarities.[32] Today, they do not just take the same form; they are increasingly combined and are part of the same phenomenon. Indians have noted that the healing skills and environmental practices that differ from those of Westerners are becoming acknowledged. Those who lack them are often ready to pay considerably to know more about them. Since non-Indians created the ayahuasca churches, for some people it is more authentic to take kamalampi/kamarampi and nixi pãe with Amazonian Indians. This also has a circular effect on the indigenous people's own interest in reproducing the ritual and trying to translate their ways of thinking and acting in culturally new contexts. This is also reminiscent of the environmentalists' interest in Amazonian shamans as protectors of the natural environment and native traditions that resulted in a resurgence of traditional dress in the 1990s and made shamans into spokespeople.[33] Shamanism is especially known for its capacity to reshape and renew.

The empowering of shamanism and the materializing of alliances all relate to the new positions of non-Indians and Indians of other groups in affinity systems of Amazonian Indians. The new allies are addressed as *txai*, the Panoan term for brother-in-law or potential marriage partners. The term was first used by indigenists to address both male and female Cashinahuas, but it was then also used by Cashinahuas themselves to address certain whites.[34] The term has become so popular that even Arawakan speakers use it, although they have their own term for brothers-in-law. However, they have also adopted its use not as meaning "potential marriage partner" but as "potential ally." Today "txai" is used for both male and female non-Indians, and for Indians of other groups. Non-Indians are sources of many material resources, know how to master them, and may make the laws, but they also destroy the natural environment of indigenous peoples, and consequently their health and elements that they consider sacred. The non-Indians are important partners in indigenous politics. Their knowledge and practices can be embodied temporarily.

The contact with powerful shamanic plants that, for the natives, are persons, must be done in a controlled way, as the horizontal space of essences must not be kept open. Besides the ritual setting, the intentions set when using powerful teacher plants are important. A native filmmaker, for instance, told me in another native group's festival that he had taken a small bit of ayahuasca in order to open his vision for better filming there. He had ayahuasca with him and had taken it before boarding a propeller plane transporting him to the village of the festival. He followed the diet rules for the use of ayahuasca and had had long experience with the plant that followed the controlled ritualized cultural template for its use. According to many indigenous groups, for instance, it is considered a bad thing if a person has visions outside the ritual context. The authenticity issues relating to elders and to certain groups are part of reproducing and maintaining indigenous identities and the vertical lines of generations. Ayahuasca shamanism may offer an experience of power at the individual level.

In the controlled spaces of these gatherings, new allies try to reach mutual understanding. Increasingly, ayahuasca shamanism is introduced together with other elements of indigenous practices and aesthetics, such as medicines, and body paintings that create distinctive embodiments and changes bodies. For Amerindians, if the body varies, it also effects a change in subjectivity. Through embodied ayahuasca rituals in new territories, such as in Rio Branco, São Paulo, and Rio de Janeiro, knowledge of previous native generations, forest environments, and memories of them become materialized. The sharing of indigenous knowledge offers the opportunity to learn from enemies and turn them into allies, but also to learn different indigenous views of the world. Ayahuasca shamanism makes native spirituality and thinking more visible.

Notes

1. See Shepard's Chapter 1 in this volume.
2. Jonathan D. Hill, *Keepers of the Sacred Chants: The Poetics of Ritual Power in an Amazonian Society* (Tucson: University Press of Arizona, 1993); Jonathan D. Hill, "Social Equality and Ritual Hierarchy: The Arawakan Wakuénai of Venezuela," *American Ethnologist* 11, no. 3 (1984): 528–44; Robin M. Wright, *Cosmos, Self, and History in Baniwa Religion: For Those Unborn* (Austin: University of Texas Press, 1998), 287–89; Stephen Hugh-Jones, "Shamans, Prophets, Priests and Pastors," in Nicholas Thomas and Caroline Humphreys, eds., *Shamanism, History, and the State* (Ann Arbor: University of Michigan Press, 1994), 32–75.
3. Peter Gow, *An Amazonian Myth and Its History* (Oxford: Oxford University Press, 2001), 103–29; Elsje M. Lagrou, *A fluidez da forma: Arte, alteridade e agência em uma sociedade Amazônica* (Rio de Janeiro: Topbooks, 2007); Angelika Gebhart-Sayer, "The Geometric Designs of the Shipibo-Conibo in Ritual Context," *Journal of Latin American Lore* 11, no. 2 (1985): 143–75.

4. See the Panoans identifying *yoshis* or *yuxins* (essences, spirits).
5. Hill, *Keepers of the Sacred Chants*, 202–3.
6. See Beatriz Caiuby Labate and Wladimyr Sena Araújo, eds., *O uso ritual da ayahuasca* (Campinas, Brazil: Mercado de Letras, 2004).
7. Hill, *Keepers of the Sacred Chants*, 202–3; Wright, *Cosmos, Self, and History in Baniwa Religion*, 287–89.
8. Gow, *An Amazonian Myth and Its History*, 138–44.
9. See also Shepard's Chapter 1 in this volume.
10. Carlos Fausto and Michael Heckenberger, "Introduction: Indigenous History and the History of the 'Indians,'" in Carlos Fausto and Michael Heckenberger, eds., *Time and Memory in Indigenous Amazonia: Anthropological Perspectives* (Gainesville: University Press of Florida, 2007), 1–46.
11. Elsje Lagrou, "Identidade e alteridade a partir da perspectiva Kaxinawa," in Neide Esterci, Peter Fry and Mirian Goldenberg, eds., *Fazendo antropologia no Brasil* (Rio de Janeiro: DP&A Editora, 2001), 93–128; Cecilia McCallum, *Gender and Sociability in Amazonia: How Real People Are Made* (Oxford: Berg, 2001), 93–128.
12. Pirjo Kristiina Virtanen, "Shamanism and Indigenous Youthhood in the Brazilian Amazon," *Amazônica. Revista de Antropologia* 1, no. 1 (2009): 152–77; Pirjo Kristiina Virtanen, "Shamanic Practices and Social Capital Among Native Youths in the Brazilian Amazon," in Sylvia Collins-Mayo and Pink Dandelion, eds., *Religion and Youth* (London: Ashgate, 2010), 96–116.
13. Terence Turner, "Social Body and Embodied Subject: Bodiliness, Subjectivity, and Sociality Among the Kayapo," *Cultural Anthropology* 10, no. 2 (1995): 166–68.
14. Eduardo Viveiros de Castro, *A inconstância da alma selvagem: E outros ensaios de antropologia* (São Paulo: Cosac & Naify, 2002), 274–78; Graham Townsley, "The Song Paths: The Ways and Means of Yaminahua Shamanic Knowledge," *L'Homme* 33, nos. 126/128 (1993): 449–68.
15. Eduardo Viveiros de Castro, "Os prononomes cosmológicos e o perspectivismo Ameríndio," *Mana: Estudos de Antropologia Social* 2, no. 2 (1996): 115–44.
16. Laura Pérez Gil, "Chamanismo y modernidad: Fundamentos etnográficos de un proceso histórico," in Oscar Calavia Sáez, Marc Lenaerts, and Ana Maria Spadafora, eds., *Paraíso abierto, jardines cerrados: Pueblos indígenas y biodiversidad* (Quito, Ecuador: Abya-Yala, 2004), 179–99.
17. Hill, *Keepers of the Sacred Chants*, 202.
18. Anthony Seeger, *Why Suyá Sing: A Musical Anthropology of an Amazonian People* (Cambridge: Cambridge University Press, 1987).
19. Viveiros de Castro, *A inconstância da alma selvagem*, 274–78.
20. Fernando Santos Granero, "Power, Ideology and the Ritual Production in Lowland South America," *Man* 21, no. 4 (1986): 657–79; Gow, *An Amazonian Myth and Its History*, 139.
21. Marcos Lopes and Claudio Quartilho, "*In the Heart of the World*," http://youtu.be/bNw_M6bvjsg?hd=1.
22. Virtanen, Pirjo Kristiina, "A presença de jovens indígenas em Rio Branco," *Jornal Página 20*, Sep. 21, 2005: 17–18.
23. Townsley, "The Song Paths," 457.
24. Viveiros de Castro, *A inconstância da alma selvagem*, 274–78.
25. The first fieldwork periods was in 2003 and series of later fieldworks resulted in the publication of the book Pirjo Kristiina Virtanen, "*Indigenous Youth in Brazilian Amazonia: Changing Lived Worlds*" (New York: Palgrave Macmillan, 2012). That was followed by postdoctoral research in the same area on indigenous leadership and chiefdoms.
26. Altino Machado, "Nishi Pay dá Grana," http://altino.blogspot.com/2005/10/nishi-pay-d-grana.html.
27. For Amerindians, animals and plants are humans, but they are beings whose corporal behaviors (and therefore different cultures) differ from those of humans. See e.g., Viveiros de Castro, "Os prononomes cosmológicos e o perspectivismo Ameríndio," 115–44.

28. Pirjo Kristiina Virtanen, "Amazonian Native Youths and Notions of Indigeneity in Urban Areas," *Identities: Global Studies in Culture and Power* 17, nos. 2/3 (2010): 154–75.
29. See Esther Jean Langdon and Isabel Santana de Rose, Chapter 4, in this volume.
30. Pérez Gil, "Chamanismo y modernidad," 179–99.
31. See Edilene Coffaci Lima and Beatriz Caiuby Labate, "A expansão urbana do *kampo* (*Phyllomedusa bicolor*): Notas etnográficas," in Beatriz Caiuby Labate et al., eds., *Drogas e cultura: Novas perspectivas* (Salvador: EDUFBA, 2008): 315–44.
32. Janet W. Hendricks, "Power and Knowledge: Discourse and Ideological Transformation Among the Shuar," *American Ethnologist* 15, no. 2 (1988): 216–38.
33. See Beth Conklin, "Body Paint, Feathers, and VCRs: Aesthetics and Authenticity in Amazonian Activism," *American Ethnologist* 24, no. 4 (1997): 711–37; Beth Conklin, "Shamans versus Pirates in the Amazonian Treasure Chest," *American Anthropologist* 104, no. 4 (2002): 1050–61.
34. Cecilia McCallum, "Comendo com txai, comendo como txai: A sexualização de relações étnicas na Amazônia contemporânea," *Revista de Antropologia* 40, no. 1 (1997): 110–47.

Bibliography

Conklin, Beth. "Body Paint, Feathers, and VCRs: Aesthetics and Authenticity in Amazonian Activism." *American Ethnologist* 24, no. 4 (1997): 711–37.

Conklin, Beth. "Shamans versus Pirates in the Amazonian Treasure Chest." *American Anthropologist* 104, no. 4 (2002): 1050–61.

Fausto, Carlos, and Michael Heckenberger. "Introduction: Indigenous History and the History of the 'Indians.'" In *Time and Memory in Indigenous Amazonia: Anthropological Perspectives*, edited by Carlos Fausto and Michael Heckenberger, 1–46. Gainesville: University Press of Florida, 2007.

Gebhart-Sayer, Angelika. "The Geometric Designs of the Shipibo-Conibo in Ritual Context." *Journal of Latin American Lore* 11, no. 2. (1985): 143–75.

Gow, Peter. *An Amazonian Myth and Its History*. Oxford: Oxford University Press, 2001.

Hendricks, Janet W. "Power and Knowledge: Discourse and Ideological Transformation Among the Shuar." *American Ethnologist* 15, no. 2 (1988): 216–38.

Hill, Jonathan D. "Social Equality and Ritual Hierarchy: The Arawakan Wakuénai of Venezuela." *American Ethnologist* 11, no. 3 (1984): 528–44.

Hill, Jonathan D. *Keepers of the Sacred Chants: The Poetics of Ritual Power in an Amazonian Society*. Tucson: University Press of Arizona, 1993.

Hugh-Jones, Stephen. "Shamans, Prophets, Priests, and Pastors." In *Shamanism, History, and the State*, edited by Nicholas Thomas and Caroline Humphreys, 32–75. Ann Arbor: University of Michigan Press, 1994.

Labate, Beatriz Caiuby, and Wladimyr Sena Araújo, eds. *O uso ritual da ayahuasca*. Campinas, Brazil: Mercado de Letras, 2004 [2002].

Lagrou, Elsje M. "Identidade e alteridade a partir da perspectiva Kaxinawa." In *Fazendo antropologia no Brasil*, edited by Neide Esterci, Peter Fry and Mirian Goldenberg, 93–128. Rio de Janeiro: DP&A Editora, 2001.

Lagrou, Elsje M. *A fluidez da forma: Arte, alteridade e agência em uma sociedade Amazônica*. Rio de Janeiro: Topbooks, 2007.

Lima, Edilene Coffaci, and Beatriz Caiuby Labate, "A expansão urbana do *Kampo* (*Phyllomedusa bicolor*): Notas etnográficas." In *Drogas e cultura: Novas perspectivas*. Edited by Beatriz Caiuby Labate, Sandra Lúcia Goulart, Mauricio Fiore, Edward MacRae and Henrique Carneiro, 315–44. Salvador: EDUFBA, 2008.

Lopes Marcos and Claudio Quartilho. "*In the Heart of the World*." http://youtu.be/bNw_M6bvjsg?hd=1 (accessed Feb. 16, 2011).

Machado, Altino. "Nishi Pay dá Grana." *Blog do Altino Machado*. June 10, 2005. 6. http://altino.blogspot.com/2005/10/nishi-pay-d-grana.html (accessed Feb. 9, 2010).

McCallum, Cecilia. "Comendo com txai, comendo como txai: A sexualização de relações étnicas na Amazônia contemporânea," *Revista de Antropologia* 40, no. 1 (1997): 110–47.

McCallum, Cecilia. *Gender and Sociability in Amazonia: How Real People Are Made*. Oxford: Berg, 2001.

Pérez Gil, Laura. "Chamanismo y modernidad: Fundamentos etnográficos de un proceso histórico." In *Paraíso abierto, jardines cerrados: Pueblos indígenas y biodiversidad*, edited by Oscar Calavia Sáez, Marc Lenaerts, and Ana Maria Spadafora, 179–99. Quito: Abya-Yala, 2004.

Santos Granero, Fernando. "Power, Ideology and the Ritual Production in Lowland South America." *Mana* 21, no. 4 (1986): 657–79.

Seeger, Anthony. *Why Suyá Sing: A Musical Anthropology of an Amazonian people*. Cambridge: Cambridge University Press, 1987.

Townsley, Graham. "The Song Paths: The Ways and means of Yaminahua Shamanic Knowledge." *L'Homme* 33, nos. 126/128 (1993): 449–68.

Turner, Terence. "Social Body and Embodied Subject: Bodiliness, Subjectivity, and Sociality Among the Kayapo." *Cultural Anthropology* 10, no. 2 (1995): 143–70.

Virtanen Pirjo Kristiina. "A presença de jovens indígenas em Rio Branco." *Jornal Página* 20, Sep. 21, 2005.

Virtanen, Pirjo Kristiina. "Shamanism and Indigenous Youthhood in the Brazilian Amazon." *Amazônica. Revista de Antropologia* 1, no. 1 (2009): 152–77.

Virtanen, Pirjo Kristiina. "Amazonian Native Youths and Notions of Indigeneity in Urban Areas." *Identities: Global Studies in Culture and Power* 17, no. 2/3 (2010): 154–75.

Virtanen, Pirjo Kristiina. "Shamanic Practices and Social Capital Among Native Youths in the Brazilian Amazon." In *Religion and Youth*, edited by Sylvia Collins-Mayo and Pink Dandelion, 96–116. London: Ashgate, 2010.

Virtanen, Pirjo Kristiina. *Indigenous Youth in Brazilian Amazonia: Changing Lived Worlds*. New York: Palgrave Macmillan, 2012.

Viveiros de Castro, Eduardo. "Os prononomes cosmológicos e o perspectivismo Ameríndio." *Mana: Estudos e Antropologia Social* 2, no. 2 (1996): 115–44.

Viveiros de Castro, Eduardo. *A inconstância da alma selvagem: E outros ensaios de antropologia*. São Paulo: Cosac & Naify, 2002.

Wright, Robin M. *Cosmos, Self, and History in Baniwa Religion: For Those Unborn*. Austin: University of Texas Press, 1998.

4

Medicine Alliance

Contemporary Shamanic Networks in Brazil

ESTHER JEAN LANGDON AND ISABEL SANTANA DE ROSE

This chapter focuses on the emergence of a contemporary shamanic network called *Aliança das Medicinas,* or Medicine Alliance, formed during the first decade of the twenty-first century in the state of Santa Catarina in Southern Brazil. It started originally out of collaboration between representatives of three groups: the Guarani Indian village of Mbiguaçu, the international contemporary shamanic group called Sacred Fire of Itzachilatlan, and the local Santo Daime community of Céu do Patriarca São José. More recently, the ceremonies of this alliance have benefited from ever-expanding inclusion of new participants, such as the Cashinahua and Yawanawa from the Brazilian Amazon, the Shuar and lowland Quechua from Ecuador, and members of *Sangoma,* a shamanic and healing tradition from South Africa. Currently, this network extends beyond the borders of Santa Catarina and Brazil, joining a larger transnational movement. This case study of the Medicine Alliance documents the growing circulation of actors associated with shamanic practices among urban populations. Moreover, this circulation of people, rituals, knowledge, substances, and aesthetic elements involves a variety of emergent networks between indigenous and non-indigenous groups in which the interchange of knowledge flows simultaneously in several directions.[1]

The exchange of shamanic knowledge along trading networks in South America is not new, and indigenous shamans have long been in dialogue with other groups.[2] Studies of the interchange between Indians and their mestizo neighbors, or "mixed blood shamanisms," argue that the flow of influences has never been unidirectional.[3] This is even more evident as international tourists flock to the Amazonian jungles to learn shamanic practices,[4] and indigenous shamans circulate in countries far from their homelands. As the analysis of the Medicine Alliance shows here, shamanism is reinvented inside as well as outside native communities.

Shamans and shamanisms have been the object of speculations regarding magic, primitive mentality, and madness for centuries.[5] Early anthropological analyses viewed shamanism as a survival of archaic practices doomed to disappear in the face of modernity. Contrary to such a view, shamans today circulate in large cities throughout the world, their practices perceived as offering primordial truths to resolve afflictions of contemporary society. In Brazil, shamanic practices are regarded as the essence of indigenous traditional medicine, an image that is held by medical personnel working in Indian health programs as well as by many New Age therapists and clients. From our study of the Medicine Alliance, we suggest that shamanism emerges out of historical and political contexts and is more adequately comprehended as a dialogical category resulting from the interaction between actors with diverse origins, discourses, and interests. In many cases, shamanism is best understood today as an emergent dialogical practice, rather than as a philosophy, logic, or spiritual consciousness independent of social, political, or historical contexts.

Shamanic Networks and Contemporary Shamanisms

Studies in Peru, Colombia, and Ecuador have documented shamanic networks that, since pre-Columbian times, have accompanied vast trade routes, linking different lowland indigenous groups between themselves[6] and also to groups from the Andean highlands.[7] Authors such as Jean-Pierre Chaumeil[8] argue that interethnic borders are extremely permeable on account of shamanic interchanges, which even occur between indigenous groups at war. Such permeability is evident today in the popular medical practices of the rural and urban poor in the countries sharing the Amazon basin. These folk medicines include various kinds of shamanic practices and specialists that attend to the afflictions of both the mestizo and indigenous populations.

Since the 1980s, new shamanic networks have connected indigenous shamans to contemporary circuits. Different from those of popular medicine, these new circuits involve the urban middle and professional classes. The motivations of the participants diverge from those of the popular classes that seek shamanic healers or *curandeiros* to help with problems of employment, love, luck, or illness. A good example is found in Colombia, where indigenous shamans conduct *yagé* (*Banisteriopsis* sp.) rituals in the highland cities for students, journalists, anthropologists, and others. Frequently organized by psychologists, the sessions are directed to the participants' individual interests and goals and to the restoration of personal equilibrium or balance.[9] These urban participants respect the lowland Amazonian shamans, known as *taitas*, as the most authentic sources of shamanic substances[10] and as counselors and sages.[11]

Pajelança, the term used to refer to popular medical practices of the *caboclo* or mestizo population, is found throughout the Brazilian Amazon. Healing specialists known as *pajés, curadores,* or *rezadores*[12] conduct rituals called pajelança using herbs, prayers, and ecstatic techniques. Sharing characteristics with indigenous shamanisms, their rituals also have roots in popular Catholicism and in Afro-Brazilian religious practices, reflecting the region's multifaceted ethnic panorama.[13] Currently pajelança is blossoming in Amazonian cities as a healing resource. To some extent, these caboclo practices show similarities to the dynamics of the mixed blood and popular shamanisms found in Colombia and Peru.[14] However, beyond the Amazon, there is little documentation of pajelança connecting indigenous practices to popular classes in urban centers of Brazil, or of the circulation of healing practices between indigenous populations and their neighbors.

Brazil is recognized as a fertile environment for the development of nonorthodox religious movements that combine Catholic, African, and esoteric traditions.[15] Brazilian ayahuasca religions, which originated as charismatic cults among the caboclo population and spread to urban areas throughout Brazil beginning in the 1980s, are a good example of this phenomenon. The most well-known of these religions, Santo Daime and União do Vegetal, have expanded over the last few decades to other countries in South America, as well as to North America, Europe, and Asia.[16] Although they have common origins in Amazonian caboclo culture, each group takes on its own characteristics owing to their differing incorporation of elements from other spiritual traditions. Moreover, each center takes on expressions specific to its leader's interpretation of practices and cosmology, making it difficult to generalize about these groups. Nevertheless, for both religions, ayahuasca represents the core element orienting a set of ritual practices and cosmologic visions that differ significantly from those of indigenous cultures.

These religions have had an important role in ayahuasca's dissemination beyond the Amazon in Brazil. Currently, the beverage is ingested at countless gatherings of friends and colleagues for leisure and healing purposes. Psychologists and other professionals have adopted its use as a therapeutic tool in major Brazilian cities.[17] Also common are shamanic workshops similar to those of Michael Harner[18] and ayahuasca centers directed at foreign tourists. Furthermore, globalized ceremonies influenced by North American indigenous groups, such as the Temazcal, are found throughout the country. These new contexts are more closely related to what Guilherme Magnani[19] has called "urban shamanism," defined as a market of alternative and mystical practices. Sonia Maluf's studies of New Age therapies in Rio Grande do Sul and Santa Catarina also place neo-shamanic practices within this market.[20] All of these practices share a closer relation to the global heterogeneous phenomenon of post-enlightenment religiosity[21] than to pajelança from Amazonian cities.[22]

The growing expansion of contemporary shamanisms among urban classes makes it evident that shamanism is no longer primarily an indigenous phenomenon originating in groups sharing a common culture, geographical region, and history. The concept "shaman" has disseminated beyond academia and is widely referenced by contemporary groups. Indians who circulate outside their communities have also adopted this term to refer to their practices. "Shaman" and "shamanism" have replaced diverse native terms formally used to refer to indigenous ritual practitioners.

The roots of contemporary shamanic movements are linked to a broader context in which the Indian is objectified as the "primitive Other" who possesses an ancestral and primordial knowledge.[23] This generic Indian is represented as having a special ability to access the secrets of the natural and supernatural universe. Studies of practices identified as neo-shamanic or New Age—from Siberia to South and North America—point out certain shared characteristics, among them promotion of a universal primordial shamanism independent of cultural and historical context, modern individualism, and psychological and therapeutic goals. Such characteristics differ greatly from those described by the classical studies of indigenous shamanism, which emphasize the collective aspects of the shamanic role and community ritual practices simultaneously with ambiguous, predatory, and aggressive characteristics in a multinatural universe.[24]

Ethnographic studies of contemporary shamanic movements tend to locate their origins in radical modernity and not in indigenous logic and cosmologies. However, evidence indicates that these conclusions are not adequate to comprehend the dialogical encounter between indigenous groups and contemporary spiritual movements. "Shamanisms today" do not represent a homogeneous universal phenomena or a cosmologic system that can be considered as exclusively "native" or "traditional." On the contrary, the emergence of these contemporary shamanisms, especially among urban and privileged classes, cannot be explained as the historical development of local indigenous cultures.

The Medicine Alliance

The Medicine Alliance[25] emerged at the beginning of the twenty-first century in the metropolitan area of Florianópolis, the capital of Santa Catarina. The participants in this network are from the Santo Daime community Céu do Patriarca São José, the Brazilian Sacred Fire of Itzachilatlan, and the Guarani village Yynn Morothi Wherá, or Mbiguaçu.

Céu do Patriarca, founded in 1987 in Florianópolis, is associated with the Igreja do Culto Eclético da Fluente Luz Universal (ICEFLU, previously known as CEFLURIS), the most well-known branch of Santo Daime. It is located in an environmental preservation area in the northern part of the Island of Santa Catarina and has approximately two hundred affiliates, many of whom reside in the community full-time. Its role is central to the Medicine Alliance, since it supplies the network with ayahuasca, which is produced in collective ritualized events called *feitios*. Since 2007, the community has also hosted annual Medicine Gatherings (*Encontros de Medicinas*), in which members from all these groups assemble to share knowledge and ritual substances. The Medicine Gatherings last for approximately two weeks, during which sacred substances from around the world are employed in rituals with participants from many places and traditions. As will become clearer below, this event is characteristic of the circulation of substances, symbolic values, and peoples in the Medicine Alliance.

Sacred Fire of Itzachilatlan, also known as Red Path, was founded in the United States by a Mexican artist and since then has spread to several Latin American countries as well as to Europe. Its rituals are inspired by the Native American Church, a pan-indigenous religion that started in the nineteenth century and is known for ritual use of peyote[26] and other North American Indian practices, especially those of the Lakota.[27] In addition, Sacred Fire rituals include elements originating from non-indigenous traditions. For the group, these eclectic practices are both inspired by, and expressions of, the ancestral or primordial roots of humanity.

In Brazil, the group began its activities at the end of the 1990s, directed by the young doctor and psychiatrist Haroldo Evangelista Vargas. Currently, their rituals are held in cities throughout southern Brazil in various locations. Leaders of the ceremonies are known as "medicine men" or "medicine women" and have attained this status by passing through a series of prescribed rituals that authorize their role as specialists. Sacred Fire's national headquarters, Segualquia, is located in the highlands of Santa Catarina. Since 1999, the group has hosted an Annual Ceremony of Indigenous Nations of America in this center. This month-long event attracts people from many parts of the world to take part in the Vision Quest and Sun Dance ceremonies, the principal rituals of Sacred Fire. The Vision Quest is a retreat in which the apprentice spends a prescribed period of isolation in the mountains fasting and meditating in order to seek contact with the Great Spirit. Those who participate in the Sun Dance, a rite dedicated to life's continuity, fast and dance unceasingly from dawn until sunset during four days.

Other rituals characteristic of the group are the Medicine Ceremony, the *Shanoopa* (Sacred Pipe Ritual), and the Temazcal (sweat lodge). The Medicine Ceremony is a ritual that involves the use of sacred plants. It is held around a fire built out of wood arranged in the form of an arrow within a low half-moon clay altar. The principal function of the Medicine Ceremony is that of holistic healing, which is accomplished through recognizing the "true nature" or "essence" of a transcendental reality. The website of the group describes the nature of this healing ritual: "All that is unreal disappears when exposed to the 'Fire of Truth.' Through the search for your true nature, for who you really are, only the real remains, eternally."[28]

The Medicine Ceremony exhibits the sacred elements present in most of the group's rituals: fire, psychoactive plants, spring water, and aromatic herbs. Most ceremonies have a circular disposition and are oriented by the four cardinal directions: north, south, east, and west. With the air charged with tobacco smoke and expectation, the ritual performances are punctuated by extensive spiritual discourses, chants, and music. They are designed with special attention to highly elaborated aesthetic and symbolic details expressed in formal ritual structure and process to enhance or intensify the experience. Many of the aesthetic and symbolic elements reference an indigenous origin: the arrangement of the fire, psychoactive plants as medicines, shamanic drums, eagle feathers, flowers, woven cloth with Indian designs, animal pelts, etc. Graphic representations of the condor and American eagle are found in the middle of the half-moon fire altar, signifying the union of the native peoples from North and South America. The participants in the rituals tend to use clothing and personal adornment that reference indigenous or ethnic groups.

The Shanoopa, or Sacred Pipe ritual, has a central role in the group's tradition. Known for its ritual use among indigenous peoples of the New World, tobacco is one of the sacred plants used by Sacred Fire's members, who smoke it to establish connection with the Divine. The Temazcal is a version of the globally known sweat bath performed in an enclosed space in which steam is made by pouring water mixed with aromatic herbs over red-hot stones. Although "temazcal" is a Nahuatl name from Mexico, the inspiration for this healing ceremony for spiritual development comes primarily from the sweat lodge of North America's Plains Indians. In the symbolic universe of Sacred Fire, the plants and the rituals described above represent practices that access pan-indigenous ancestral knowledge.

The Guarani are a large Indian population numbering approximately 145,000. Composed of several subgroups speaking languages belonging to the Tupi-Guarani family, they migrate across a transnational territory of approximately 1.2 million square kilometers, encompassing Brazil, Argentina, and Paraguay.[29] Traveling in small groups, the Mbya and Chiripá subgroups from southern Brazil circulate between the settlements dispersed throughout their ancestral territory, which today is populated and controlled by non-Indians and includes a number of large urban areas.[30] Because of constant mobility in extended family groups, they form a large network of relatives whose migrations contribute to communication, reciprocal exchange, and transformations between settlements.

The maintenance of the native language and traditional religious practices has functioned as an important strategy of resistance to the Spanish and Portuguese presence in Guarani territory since early colonial times. Although unable to isolate themselves from non-Indians in many situations, a large number of the Guarani remain monolingual in their native language. In the presence of non-Indians, they are characterized as extremely silent and closed and are known for the secrecy of their ritual practices. In Southern Brazil, many Guarani villages are located on the periphery of large metropolitan regions and are confined to small and nonproductive lands. A great number of communities suffer from poverty and its consequences, such as disease, violence, and alcohol abuse. Like most Indians in this part of the country, the Guarani are often marginalized and labeled as ignorant and lazy.

The Guarani village of Mbiguaçu is located near Florianópolis, a metropolitan area with more than seven hundred thousand people. Created in 2003 as a *Terra Indígena* with 59 hectares, it was the first officially recognized Guarani reserve in Santa Catarina. Although it is part of their traditional territory, the actual village was reoccupied in the 1980s with the arrival of an extended family originating from the south. Today, Mbiguaçu holds an important position in the exchange network of the Guarani villages along Brazil's southern coast. Different from many of the other Guarani villages, it has demonstrated an unusual openness in its recent interactions with non-Indians. Because of changes in the Federal Constitution of 1988, which recognizes the multiethnic nature of Brazil, Indian communities have been the focus of public service projects, such as schools, health centers, and agricultural assistance. The Guarani settlements in general have experienced increasing interaction with the surrounding society over the last twenty years.[31] However, Mbiguaçu appears to be assuming leadership in the mediation of ritual practices with non-Indians.

Over the last twenty years, the inhabitants of this community have engaged in a broad cultural revitalization process that encompasses initiatives such as the formation of the *Yvychy Ovy* (Blue Clouds) chorus in 1996, the construction of a bilingual school inside the Indigenous Land in 1998, and the building of an *opy* or prayer house in this same year.[32] The incorporation of ayahuasca approximately ten years ago in their traditional prayer and chanting ceremonies can be seen as part of this cultural revitalization process, and the Guarani of Mbiguaçu claim that this Amazonian shamanic drink is part of their ancestral culture and tradition.[33] Adoption of its use and reference to it as "tradition" has resulted from interaction with Vargas, the leader of Brazilian Sacred Fire, which led to the establishment of the Medicine Alliance.

In 1999 a seriously ill Guarani was a patient in the hospital where Vargas was serving his medical internship. Vargas slowly befriended this Guarani and learned of Alcindo Wherá Tupã and Rosa Poty Djá, the *karaikuery* (spiritual leaders) who led their extended family to Mbiguaçu in the 1980s. *Karaí* and *cunha karaí* designate respectively the male and female sacred leaders who

Figure 4.1. External view of Mbiguaçu's prayer house. Photograph by Isabel Santana de Rose.

mediate with the spiritual world through collective prayer ceremonies involving dancing, singing, and performance of healing rituals. The ethnological literature on the Guarani identifies the karaí with the anthropological concept "shaman." Currently, Alcindo and Rosa, the founding couple of the community, are recognized by many Guarani as the eldest and most powerful karaikuery in southern Brazil thanks to their well-known healing and prayer capacities.

Once he had gained the confidence of the Guarani patient, Vargas was invited to Mbiguaçu to meet the couple and was received with special consideration. As recalled by several members of the community, Vargas's arrival in the village had been foretold to Alcindo in a prophetic dream. Hyral Moreira, the *cacique* (political leader) of Mbiguaçu and Alcindo's grandson, highlights this in the following narrative:

> When I was younger, *tcheramoi* (grandfather; old person) Alcindo and my own great-grandfather, his father, always told us: "There will be a moment in which the Guarani culture will be in danger; after this, it will

> grow strong again." They said they didn't know if this would happen in this generation or in the next, but they always told us that our culture would be in danger and someone would help it to live again. This happened more than thirty years ago, when my great-grandfather was still alive. After he died my grandfather, Alcindo, became our spiritual leader, but we didn't respect him much at that time. One day he said: "Nobody cares about our culture and tradition anymore, but I had a vision. In this vision, I saw someone that is not Guarani; someone that isn't part of our culture. It is this person who is going to help the Guarani culture to rise again." We didn't pay attention to what he said. But eight years ago, this person showed up. His name was Haroldo. We didn't know who he was. He said he had come from Mexico and he wanted to speak to grandfather Alcindo. This happened because Haroldo had met a man from our community at the hospital where he worked as a doctor. Haroldo asked this man if his community had a spiritual leader or shaman. Then the man told him about Alcindo. One day Haroldo came to our village and talked to Alcindo. We see this as something magical: you can't explain why it happened. When Haroldo arrived at our village, Alcindo ran to him, saying, "That is the person I was waiting for!" People thought he must be crazy to say this to someone he had never seen. Then the relationship between them started. They started to talk about spiritual things and their friendship began.
>
> —(Hyral Moreira, *interview Aug. 19, 2008*)

Vargas began visiting Mbiguaçu periodically, taking part in Guarani ceremonies held in Alcindo's house. At one point, he resided in the village for a number of months; he was baptized with a Guarani name and invited to help in healing rituals.

The idea of conducting a ceremony with ayahuasca at Mbiguaçu village resulted from the dialogues between Alcindo's family and Vargas. The narratives of their first rituals with ayahuasca express how Alcindo's family experienced contact with their ancestors and other spiritual beings. The consumption of ayahuasca has become associated with the ancestral past and Guarani tradition. Mbiguaçu's inhabitants affirm that its use represents a revival of past practices that have contributed to their cultural revitalization process. According to Celita Antunes, Hyral Moreira's wife and an important cunha karaí in the village:

> Since we started to use the ayahuasca medicine, grandfather Alcindo is remembering forgotten things. Every ceremony he tells us something new. His own grandchildren had never entered a prayer house. He is remembering what the Guarani people were forgetting: prayers, customs. He always says that the Guarani are the guardians of fire, earth, and

> nature. If we forget the knowledge about the plants and the spirits, and how to talk and listen to nature, our culture will end. The day our culture ends, our people also will end. We will no longer be the Guarani people. Alcindo says this knowledge is very ancient. He tells us it was taught by Fire, the oldest grandfather. All this knowledge is passed on along the generations. It is hard to explain the Guarani spiritual way of seeing things. What Alcindo says about the importance of keeping this spiritual knowledge is the same thing my great-grandfather already said. When we take the ayahuasca medicine, we are ingesting knowledge itself. It is the knowledge of our grandparents; the blood of our grandparents. This is how we learn. I didn't understand why elder people cry when they pray. Now I understand. They are praying for our ancestors. And in their prayers our grandparents always remember the Guarani people.
>
> —(Celita Antunes, *interview Oct. 1, 2008*)

In a proposal for health services that respected and incorporated traditional Guarani medicine, Vargas argued that efforts to strengthen their spiritual leaders and traditional ritual practices were necessary to resolve the social and health problems facing many of the Guarani villages. He gained the support of the nongovernmental organization contracted by the National Foundation of Health (*Fundação Nacional da Saúde,* FUNASA) for the provision of primary health services in the Indian communities. Together, a project was elaborated, with Vargas as coordinator, for reviving traditional healing rituals through the construction of a new and larger prayer house and Temazcal, both defined as traditional healing centers, and for identifying potential spiritual leaders to participate in the annual gatherings held at Sacred Fire's headquarters in the mountains.

The project aimed to "promote the health of the Guarani people, recovering and strengthening the spiritual/mystical aspects based on ancient traditional ceremonies."[34] With funding approval, ayahuasca and Temazcal ceremonies were conducted in at least ten Guarani villages during four years. Vargas's closest association was with the Guarani of Mbiguaçu, where the project had its greatest impact. A large traditional prayer house was constructed to replace the existing one. The number of community members participating in the nightly collective prayer ceremonies increased, and the karaikuery, including Alcindo and his sons, incorporated ayahuasca into their traditional rituals.

Stimulated by Vargas's health project to revitalize the community's spiritual practices, the Guarani at Mbiguaçu also constructed their Temazcal igloo-like ritual space. Located beside the village prayer house (*opy*), its name *opydjere,* or "round prayer house," is derived from their traditional prayer house, so important for Guarani collectivity. Mbiguaçu's inhabitants affirm that the performance of the sweat bath is another revival of their tradition. Often, the sweat bath ritual, also called opydjere, is held before the nightly chanting and dancing ceremonies in the opy for purification and ritual preparation. For them, the rite has healing properties that contribute to the cures performed in the prayer house.

By the time the four-year project financed by FUNASA had ended, the Guarani from Mbiguaçu were regularly incorporating ayahuasca into their community rituals and had achieved a certain independence from Sacred Fire in the organization of their rituals and in contacts and negotiations with representatives of Santo Daime, their source of ayahuasca. Currently, they continue to conduct regular ayahuasca ceremonies in their village. They also continue to take part in Sacred Fire's Vision Quest and Sun Dance and in events sponsored in the Santo Daime community. Moreover, they occasionally perform ayahuasca ceremonies or Temazcals for urban middle-class groups in spiritual and New Age centers in the Florianópolis metropolitan area.

It is possible that the adoption of ayahuasca in Mbiguaçu has contributed to the larger political process of strengthening the Guarani spiritual practices and values. However, there are many important elements in this process besides the use of ayahuasca itself. Among these factors, it is important to highlight the increasing value that non-Indians give to indigenous culture. In Brazil, public policies in health and education call for the respect of indigenous culture. These two factors have had a central role in stimulating the Guarani from Mbiguaçu to

Figure 4.2. Eastern altar of prayer house with *Banisteriopsis caapi* vine. Photograph by Isabel Santana de Rose.

engage in this broad cultural revitalization movement and to adopt a more active role than is usually seen in interactions between the Guarani and the members of the larger society.

Dialogues between leaders of Sacred Fire and Santo Daime began in the year 2000, shortly after Vargas initiated contact with the Guarani, because of the need to find a dependable source of ayahuasca for their rituals. Although Amazonian indigenous groups have employed ayahuasca for centuries, neither the plants nor their ritual use is documented for southern Brazil, where local ayahuasca religious groups introduced cultivation of the *Banisteriopsis* vine in the final decades of the twentieth century. When invited to furnish ayahuasca for the Guarani ceremonies, the leaders from Céu do Patriarca responded positively and joined the network forming between Sacred Fire and Mbiguaçu. In 2003, the leader or "padrinho" of Céu do Patriarca traveled to Mexico to mediate an agreement between Santo Daime and the international group of Sacred Fire.

Figure 4.3. Prayer house central half-moon altar with arrow-shaped fire. Photograph by Isabel Santana de Rose.

Over the past decade, these three groups have frequently participated in each other's rituals and gatherings held throughout the year. The Guarani participate in important ceremonial activities sponsored by both Sacred Fire and Santo Daime; in turn members from these groups attend rituals and other activities performed in Mbiguaçu. In sum, members from Brazilian Sacred Fire, *Daimistas* of Céu do Patriarca community, and Guarani of Mbiguaçu are connected through relations of mutual influence, forming a network with a constant circulation of people, ideas, concepts, metaphors, plants, substances, practices, rites, and aesthetics. The circulation of these symbols and practices flows in many directions, simultaneously creating exchanges and innovation in ritual events in a multidirected dialogue between the various actors.

Networks, Flows, and Circulations

One of the unifying principles of the Medicine Alliance and its participants is the ritual employment of plants and substances, such as ayahuasca and tobacco, considered sacred and designated as medicines. From the native point of view, this is a fundamental point, although each group employs and interprets these substances in culturally specific ways.

Of the three groups, Santo Daime is the only one with a foundation based on the ritual use of ayahuasca. The beverage, commonly called *Daime* (a Portuguese verbal inflection from the verb *dar,* "to give," that can be translated as "give me") is intrinsic to Daimista rites and cosmology.[35] Its incorporation in Sacred Fire rituals, however, is an innovation specific to Brazil, justified as a Brazilian indigenous tradition that reveals the essence of the pan-indigenous universal spirituality. Ayahuasca is classified along with their other plant medicines that possess ancestral knowledge. The Guarani of Mbiguaçu are the most recent group to adopt systematic use of ayahuasca, and they privilege its capacity to enhance aspects that are central to their shamanism: vision, audition, perception, and concentration. They affirm that ayahuasca helps the karaikuery to perform the ritual responsibilities of healing, communication with the deities, and mediation with the beings and worlds that compose the cosmos. Like dreams, experiences with ayahuasca are interpreted as messages from the ancestors or as the presence of *Nhanderu* ("Our Father").[36] It is evident that the adoption of ayahuasca was facilitated by their existing shamanic cosmology, which allowed the village inhabitants to interpret the intense experiences produced by its ingestion as reifying their shamanic tradition.[37]

Native tobacco, on the other hand, has historically occupied a central role in Guarani rites. Their clay pipe, *petynguá,* is a conduit for communication with deities and spirits.[38] Sacred Fire's symbolic associations and use of the shanoopa were an inspiration from North American Indian practices. On the other hand, Santo Daime did not include tobacco in its rituals nor consider it a sacred substance. Since the formation of the Alliance, the Céu do Patriarca community has regularly performed rituals that include tobacco as a sacred plant, including the Medicine Ceremony and Shanoopa rituals. In the Medicine Alliance ceremonies performed by both Sacred Fire and Santo Daime, the Guarani petynguá often is used side by side with the shanoopa pipe, at times substituting it. People who circulate in the Alliance network consider these two instruments equivalent, since both kinds of pipes are used to establish a connection with the Divine.

In short, rituals using sacred substances circulate among the groups in the Medicine Alliance; each one incorporating new elements in their traditional ritual practices as well as adopting new ritual forms learned from the others. The Medicine Ceremony, Shanoopa, Temazcal, Vision Quest, and Sun Dance are performed by the specialists authorized to lead them, be they Guarani karaikuery, Sacred Fire's medicine men and women, or Santo Daime's padrinhos. The performances vary with the context of the group conducting them. For example, Medicine Ceremonies are part of the Annual Ceremony of Indigenous Nations of America held in Segualquia, where Sacred Fire medicine men and women conduct them. At Céu do Patriarca, these ceremonies are led by authorized padrinhos and are usually a part of the program of the annual Medicine Gatherings and the ritualized production of ayahuasca. Although Medicine Ceremonies held at Céu do Patriarca have the same structure and symbolism as those of the Sacred Fire, more references to the Daimista symbolic universe are present.

In the same way, rituals held in Mbiguaçu by the karaikuery reflect Guarani ritual structure and ethos; contrary to Sacred Fire ceremonies, concern with detail and elaborate verbal explanations is secondary to aesthetic and sensorial experiences. The preoccupation with long discourses and solemnity characteristic of Sacred Fire events is absent in the rituals conducted in Mbiguaçu's opy, which are marked by informality and humorous moments. Guarani shamanism is typically ambiguous, with the potential for evil and witchcraft as a possible manifestation. Sacred Fire's representations lack the ambiguous and evil symbolic references found in indigenous shamanism. Their practices are directed primarily to restoration of a holistic self and personal transformation, with more focus on the individual participants and less on the collective group.

Sacred Fire was responsible for the introduction of the Temazcal to the Medicine Alliance. As a central ritual, it is an inherent part of many other ceremonies, either preceding them or performed between major phases of the ritual process. For instance, in the Vision Quest, the Temazcal is performed before and after the period of isolation and fasting. During the Sun Dance, the Temazcal is held daily at the beginning and ending of the dance. Since 2003, Céu do Patriarca's padrinho has incorporated the Temazcal in his community, where an *inipi* (place where the temazcal is held)[39] has been built beside the Daimista church. The Temazcal often follows traditional Santo Daime rituals and is part of the many activities of the Medicine Gatherings held there. The Guarani ritual performance of the sweat bath, like their other rituals, tends to be more informal and flexible than the Temazcals conducted by other members of the Alliance, and it also has become a source of revenue for them when held in spiritual and New Age centers in Florianópolis, adding to their autonomy within the Alliance.

Like the Temazcal, the Vision Quest is no longer only performed in Sacred Fire's highland center. In October 2009, it was held for the first time in Mbiguaçu especially for the Guarani of this community and others along the Santa Catarina coast. Members of Céu do Patriarca, who have taken part in the events at Segualquia since 2003, also held a Vision Quest in their community in 2011 and 2012.

Along with ayahuasca and tobacco, other ritual objects are part of alliance ceremonies, independent of where they occur. Cedar, copal, and *palo santo* (aromatic wood used as an incense),[40] as well as the Peruvian *água florida* (water perfumed with herbal essences), are valued for their aromas, which evoke memories and generate typical moods and dispositions. The ethnic dress characteristic of Sacred Fire members has been adopted in various ways by the others in the Medicine Alliance, and both Daimistas and Guarani Indians commonly wear dresses and tunics embroidered with indigenous motifs, Andean *ponchos* and shawls, braided hair, feather earrings, and necklaces made of seeds or colorful beads. Many of the chants sung in the Medicine Ceremonies are in Lakota and may include words in other languages, such as Quechua, Nahuatl, or Spanish. Eventually, one may hear a Daimista hymn or a Guarani prayer song. These chants are accompanied by the water-drum, a kind of membranophone common in Native American music that has a chamber filled with water creating a unique sound, and the *sonaja*, a special kind of indigenous Mexican rattle. Guarani baskets of *taquara* (a native kind of bamboo) are found among the various ceremonial objects, which may be placed on animal pelts from wolves, felines, and bears.

Spiritual concepts and metaphors also circulate in the Medicine Alliance, forming dialogues that are multidirectional in character. Not only have the Guarani and Daimistas constructed their Temazcal shelters, but the central ceremonial house in the Segualquia was also built with the help of the Indians from Mbiguaçu, who employed wood and taquara, materials typical of their village prayer house. In addition, the Guarani term "opy," used for their prayer house, now also refers to this the central ceremonial dwelling at Sacred Fire's headquarters.

These examples show the nature of mutual influence in the dialogue between network participants. The impact of the Guarani on the transformations and adaptations incorporated by the other groups is manifest in the adoption of other spiritual concepts that now circulate in the Alliance's discourse. The Guarani name for its principal deity, *Nhanderu Tenonde*, the "first" or "principal" *Nhanderu*, is used to refer to the Great Spirit of the Sacred Fire. The Guarani perceive a semblance of meaning between their concept of *aguydjevete* and the Sacred Fire's salutation *aho mitakuye oyas'i*. The first comes from the Guarani concept of *aguydje*, which can be translated as "perfection," "completeness," or "immortality."[41] The second is a traditional Sioux Lakota expression used as a refrain in many Lakota prayers and songs, which was appropriated by Sacred Fire. Commonly translated as "all my relatives," "we are all related," or "all my relations," this expression reflects the perception that everything is connected. Although there might be no apparent similarity between these two concepts, they are often used by Guarani Indians, Sacred Fire members, or Daimistas as equivalent expressions, punctuating the beginning and end of ritual speeches, chants, and prayers. Moreover, the Guarani use of the expression *aho mitakuye oyas'i* to explain to non-Indians what *aguydjevete* means indicates an effort to translate Guarani concepts to a language that can be comprehended by those who circulate in the Medicine Alliance.

The analogies drawn between the symbolic concepts of the two groups are manifested even more clearly when the Guarani refer to Sacred Fire as *Tata Endy Rekoe*. The expression derives from the concepts of *teko* or *reko*, commonly translated as "system," "ethos," or "Guarani way of life," and more recently used by the Guarani to refer to their "culture." According to Hyral Moreira, cacique from Mbiguaçu, the translation of the expression *Tata Endy Rekoe* as Sacred Fire aligns and identifies Sacred Fire with Guarani tradition and memory. This idea is clearly expressed in the School Plan, elaborated in 2008 by the indigenous teachers of the Mbiguaçu School, in which Hyral also participated. The name of this document is "Guarani Knowledge and Wisdom *Tata Endy Rekoe*."

> *Tata Endy Rekoe* is one of the most ancient indigenous traditions of South America. It exists since immemorial times. We call *Tata Endy Rekoe* as Sacred Fire because it represents the center of life itself, the source of light and heat, and the true Knowledge, which comes from the Guarani language. In our vision, we comprehend that this spiritual indigenous tradition from South America, called *Tapé Marã'ey* (Red Path), has in its roots the same foundations of all the spiritual traditions from the four human races that inhabit this planet (red, yellow, black and white). We understand that the foundation of the Spirit of Life is only one, although we may have diverse names and interpretations for this same Spirit.

In this document, *Tata Endy Rekoe* is translated into Portuguese as "Sacred Fire" to designate an ancient indigenous tradition existing since immemorial times.

Originating in True Knowledge, the Sacred Fire tradition represents the "center of life itself." The text also creates an analogy between Guarani tradition expressed as *Tapé Marã'ey*, translated literally as "path without evil," and Red Path, a synonym for Sacred Fire. The influence of Sacred Fire's discourse is evident. This document highlights how the Guarani place themselves within the larger dialogue of shared spiritual traditions and primordial wisdom.

In sum, symbols and meanings circulate in the Medicine Alliance network; they encompass sacred plants, rituals, and aesthetic and organizational aspects of the ritual environment, including objects, clothing, chants, and instruments. The circulation of these elements points to the construction of an ethos and ideology characteristic of the activities and locations belonging to the Medicine Alliance. Actors circulate in this network, elaborating analogies and joining concepts and notions that come from a number of symbolic universes.

The flow of exchanges in the Alliance is evidence of reciprocal appropriations and multidirectional dialogues. Sacred Fire elements and concepts are now present in Guarani as well as Daimista rites. As we have seen, the Guarani adapt and reinvent these elements in their ritual practices. When translating the concepts circulating in this network, they interpret them according to their own cosmology. The Medicine Alliance rites that happen in the Céu do Patriarca community are led by padrinhos and influenced by Daimista ethos and cosmology, assuming specific characteristics. Here we have shown how concepts and ritual elements originating both from Guarani and Daimista settings are interwoven with the Sacred Fire's ritual structure, creating an intricate and complex pattern, colored by the mutual dialogues that form the Medicine Alliance.

Final Comments

In this chapter we have employed terms such as *flow*, *network*, *circuit*, and *circulation*, and now we wish to reflect on them. In a discussion about the role of globalization in the history of ideas, anthropologist Ulf Hannerz argues that flow, mobility, recombination, and emergence are the key words of transnational anthropology. "Flow" and "emergence" are the most important for our present reflection. According to Hannerz, the concept of flow remits to something moving in time and space; it has an essentially temporal meaning. Furthermore, the concept of cultural flow implies the constant reorganization of culture in space, as opposed to a static view of culture. To speak in terms of cultural flow suggests continuity and transformation, and indicates "a broader conception according to which cultural acquisition is constantly happening."[42]

Emergence is related to the notion of dialogue and to a vision of culture as dialogical. Cultures are continuously produced and reproduced; they emerge in the dialogues between the people that are a part of them, and they are in a continuous state of creation and recreation, negotiation and renegotiation.[43] The perspective of language as dialogical is closely connected to that of culture as emergent. Both perspectives highlight culture's heterogeneous nature and the discursive character of its constitution, as well as the social character of interaction. According to Bakhtin, dialogue emerges through socially situated action. Therefore, social and cultural worlds are constantly built and rebuilt through specific discourses and historical contexts.[44]

A static conception of culture portrays native cosmologies as closed and internally coherent systems, and they are described according to an ideal and naturalized image.[45] On the other hand, a historically oriented anthropology considers the cultures of both the indigenous and the ethnographer to be contemporary, and all societies to be polyphonic, complex, heterogeneous, and diverse.[46] The task of a historically and contextually oriented anthropology is to understand the "processes of circulation of meanings, emphasizing that the nonstructural and dynamic character is constitutive of culture."[47]

Western perceptions of shamanism tend to seek the primordial shaman, emphasizing an essential connection with the past. This past, constructed as timeless, primordial, and mythical, represents shamanism as a stagnated cultural form. However, modern ethnographies show that shamanisms today must be understood in light of the interethnic context in which indigenous peoples are inserted. Shamanisms are situated historically and constitute dynamic systems of knowledge and practices that are negotiated and renegotiated in contexts where diverse cultural actors are in dialogue.[48] This approach emphasizes indigenous agency, negotiation, and dialogue as constitutive aspects in the construction of shamanisms today. At the same time, it highlights the importance of the inclusion of history and context in order to perceive the dynamic and emergent character of culture.

Research on the Medicine Alliance demonstrates how dialogue contributes to a constant re-creation of shamanism through interactions between actors in a postcolonial and postmodern world. Various actors are interested in the global revival of this phenomenon: anthropologists, journalists, environmental organizations, health care professionals, Indians, and neo-shamans, among countless others.[49] The contemporary emphasis on the shaman and shamanic knowledge is present inside indigenous activism as well as in public policy. This emphasis is related to international policies that unite diverse issues and interests, such as environmental laws and the postcolonial politics of pan-indigenous movements. Furthermore, although Western New Agers appropriate shamanic practices, indigenous peoples prove to be equally capable of appropriating elements from a variety of cultural traditions. Shamanism manifests dynamic and unexpected dimensions present in the contemporary world.[50]

On the one hand, the formation of the Medicine Alliance network is part of the praxis of a Guarani population that is related to the dialogues and negotiations between indigenous peoples and larger society. On the other hand, it is a reflection of local, national, and international processes involving ahistorical images of the shaman and indigenous therapeutic practices.

The various flows and negotiations and the multidirectional character that constitute the Medicine Alliance network bring into question the idea of homogeneous cultures with clear and well-defined boundaries.[51] Furthermore, this case study calls attention to the relationship between the local and the global, making it evident that today it is no longer possible to think about native shamanisms without considering the broader dialogical contexts into which these are inserted. Finally, it can be seen that native shamanisms also play an active role in the very construction of these dialogical contexts.

Notes

1. Anne-Marie Losonczy and Silvia Mesturini Cappo, "La selva viajera: Etnografia de las rutas del chamanismo ayahuasquero entre Europa y America," *Religião e Sociedade* 30, no. 2 (2011): 164–83.
2. Esther Jean Langdon, "Social Bases for Trading of Visions and Spiritual Knowledge in the Colombian and Ecuadorian Montaña," *Networks of the Past, Proceedings of the Twelfth Annual Conference*, Archaeological Association of the University of Calgary, Canada, 101–16; Jean-Pierre Chaumeil, "Varieties of Amazonian Shamanism," *Diogenes* 158 (1992): 101–13; Laura Pérez Gil, "Chamanismo y modernidade: Fundamentos etnográficos de un processo histórico," in Óscar Calavia Sáes, Marc Lenaerts, and Ana María Spadafora, eds., *Paraíso abierto, jardines cerrados: Pueblos indígenas, saberes y biodiversidad* (Quito, Ecuador: ABYA-YALA, 2004), 179–99.
3. Peter Gow, "River People: Shamanism and History in Western Amazonia," in Nicholas Thomas and Caroline Humphrey, eds., *Shamanism, History, and the State* (Ann Arbor: University of Michigan Press, 1994), 90–114; Pérez Gil, "Chamanismo y modernidade," 179–99. María Clemencia Ramírez, "El chamanismo, un campo de articulación de colonizadores y colonizados en la región Amazónica de Colombia," *Revista Colombiana de Antropología* 33 (1996–1997): 165–84.
4. Silvia Mesturini Cappo, "Espaces chamaniques en movement: Itinéraires vécus et géographies multiples entre Europe et Amérique du Sud." (Ph.D. diss., Faculté des Sciences Sociales et Politiques, Solvay, Brussels, 2010).
5. See Jeremy Narby and Francis Huxley, eds., *Shamans Through Time: 500 Years on the Path of Knowledge* (New York: Tarcher/Putnam, 2001) for the reproduction of classic articles by travelers and others describing encounters with shamanism.
6. Donald W. Lathrap, "The Antiquity and Importance of Long-Distance Trade Relationships in the Moist Tropics of Pre-Columbian South America," *World Archaeology* 5, no. 2 (1973): 170–86.
7. Jean-Pierre Chaumeil, "'Le huambisa défenseur': La figure de l'Indien dans le chamanisme populaire," *Recherches Amérindiennes au Québec* 23 no. 2–3 (1988): 115–26; Langdon, "Social Bases for Trading," 101–16.

8. Chaumeil, "Varieties of Amazonian Shamanism," 101–13.
9. Alhena Caicedo Fernández, "Neochamanismos y modernidad. Lecturas sobre la emancipación," *Revista Nómadas* 26 (2007): 114–47; Caicedo Fernándes, "Neochamanismo yajecero en contextos urbanos Colombianos" (paper presented at the Fifty-Third International Congress of Americanists, Mexico City, Mexico, July 19–24, 2009).
10. Jorge Ronderos Valderrama, "Rituales del yagé en zonas urbanas del eje cafetero: Practicas y dinâmicas de interculturalidad y mentalidades emergentes," *Cultura y Droga* 14, no. 16 (2009): 119–40.
11. Alhena Caicedo Fernández, "Buena pinta. Dynamiques d'une tradition indigène dans la modernité: Les cãs dês séances de yajé à Bogotá, Colombie" (Master's thesis, École Des Hautes Études en Sciences Sociales, 2004).
12. Chaumeil, "Varieties of Amazonian Shamanism," 101–13.
13. Raymundo Heraldo Maués and Maria Angelica Motta, "O modelo da 'Reima': representações alimentares em uma comunidade Amazónica," *Anuário Antropológico* 77 (1978): 120–47; Raymundo Heraldo Maués, "Um aspecto da diversidade cultural do caboclo Amazônico: A religião," *Estudos Avançados* 19, no. 53 (2005): 259–74; João Valentin Wawzyniak, "Engerar: Uma categoria cosmológica sobre pessoa, saúde e corpo," *Ilha* 5, no. 2 (2003): 33–55.
14. Chaumeil, "Varieties of Amazonian Shamanism," 101–13; Gow, "River People," 90–114; Ramírez, "El chamanismo, un campo de articulación," 165–84.
15. Sidney M. Greenfield, "Pilgrimage, Therapy and the Relationship Between Healing and Imagination," *Discussion Paper* 82 (Madison: University of Wisconsin, Center for Latin America, 1989); Edward MacRae, "The Ritual and Religious Use of Ayahuasca in Contemporary Brazil," in Whitney A. Taylor, Rob Stewart, Kerry Hopkins, and Scott Ehlers, eds., *DPF 12 Policy Manual* (Washington, DC: Drug Policy Foundation Press, 1999), 47–50.
16. Beatriz C. Labate, Isabel S. Rose, and Rafael G. Santos, *Ayahuasca Religions: A Comprehensive Bibliography & Critical Essays* (Santa Cruz, CA: Multidisciplinary Association for Psychedelic Studies, 2010).
17. Beatriz Caiuby Labate, *A reinvenção do uso da ayahuasca nos centros urbanos* (Campinas, Brazil: Mercado de Letras, 2004).
18. Michael Harner, *The Way of the Shaman* (San Francisco: HarperCollins, 1980); Merete Demant Jakobsen, *Shamanism: Traditional and Contemporary Approaches to the Mastery of Spirits and Healing* (New York: Berghahn Books, 1999); Paul C. Johnson, "Shamanism from Ecuador to Chicago: A Case Study in New Age Ritual Appropriation," *Religion* 25, no. 2 (1995): 163–78.
19. José G. C. Magnani, "O xamanismo urbano e a religiosidade contemporânea," *Religião & Sociedade* 20, no. 2 (2000): 113–40; Magnani, "Xamãs na cidade," *Dossiê 67—Religiosidade no Brasil. Revista da USP* no. 67 (2005): 218–27.
20. Sônia Maluf, "Os filhos de aquário no país dos terreiros: Novas vivências espirituais no Sul do Brasil," *Ciências Sociais e Religião* 5, no. 5 (2003): 153–72; Sônia Maluf, "Mitos coletivos, narrativas pessoais: Cura ritual, trabalho terapêutico e emergência do sujeito nas culturas da 'Nova Era,'" *Mana* 11, no. 2 (2005): 499–528.
21. Olav Hammer, introduction to *Claiming Knowledge: Strategies of Epistemology from Theosophy to the New Age* (Leiden, Holland: Brill, 2001), 2–25.
22. Kenneth W. Tupper, "Ayahuasca Healing Beyond the Amazon: The Globalization of a Traditional Indigenous Entheogenic Practice," *Global Networks* 9, no. 1 (2009): 117–36.
23. June Macklin, Victor A. Martinez, and Elizabeth Gonzalez Torres, "New Religious Movements and Ritual Transformations of the Modern Self," *Scripta Ethnologica* 21 (1999): 35–58.
24. Eduardo B. Viveiros de Castro, "Os pronomes cosmológicos e o perspectivismo Ameríndio," *Mana* 2, no. 2 (1996): 145–62.
25. From 2006 to 2009, Isabel S. de Rose conducted fieldwork among the groups that are part of the Medicine Alliance. The information in this text about the emergence of this network text is based on her fieldwork. The interviews quoted here are part of the research for her Ph.D. and were carried out at the Guarani village *Yynn Morothi Wherá*, Santa Catarina,

Brazil (see Isabel Santana de Rose, "*Tata Endy Rekoe*—Fogo Sagrado: Encontros entre os Guarani, a ayahuasca e o Caminho Vermelho," Ph.D. diss., Universidade Federal de Santa Catarina, Florianópolis, Brazil, 2010).

26. Weston La Barre, *The Peyote Cult* (New York: Schocken Books, 1969).
27. Macklin et al., "New Religious Movements."
28. www.fogosagrado.org.br; translation by the authors, accessed in March 2011.
29. In the 1950s, Egon Schaden suggested a division of the Guarani in three main subgroups: Kaiowa, Nhandeva, and Mbya (Egon Schaden, *Aspectos fundamentais da cultura Guarani*, São Paulo, Brazil: Edusp, 1974). This classification, based centrally on linguistic differences, has influenced most of the ethnographic literature on the Guarani written in the last five decades. However, contemporary ethnographers point to the complexity of the divisions of the Guarani subgroups, and argue that these are not consensual (see Valéria de Assis and Ivori José Garlet, "Análise sobre as populações Guarani contemporâneas: Demografia, espacialidade e questões fundiárias," *Revista de Indias* 64, no. 230, 2004: 35–54).
30. De Assis and Garlet, "Análise sobre as populações Guarani Contemporâneas," 35–54.
31. See Valéria Mendonça de Macedo, "Nexos da diferença. cultura e afecção em uma aldeia Guarani na Serra do Mar" (Ph.D. diss., Universidade de São Paulo, São Paulo, Brazil, 2010).
32. Melissa Santana de Oliveira, "*Kiringué i Kuery* Guarani: Infância, educação e religião entre os Guarani de M'Biguaçu, SC" (Master's thesis, Universidade Federal de Santa Catarina, Florianópolis, Brazil, 2004).
33. Rose, "*Tata Endy Rekoe*—Fogo Sagrado."
34. Haroldo Evangelista Vargas, "Fortalecimento das lideranças espirituais da Nação Guarani" (Project presented by the NGO Rondon Brazil to FUNASA, 2002), 11.
35. See Alberto Groisman, *Eu venho da floresta: Um estudo sobre o contexto simbólico do uso do Santo Daime* (Florianópolis, Brazil: Editora da UFSC, 1999); and Edward MacRae, *Guaido pela lua: Xamanismo e uso ritual da ayahuasca no culto do Santo Daime* (São Paulo, Brazil: Editora Brasiliense, 1992).
36. The Guarani recognize and invoke in their prayers a variety of deities, which are associated with the celestial directions. However, when they speak about the divine, it is common to refer to *Nhanderu* or "our Father" in a unified manner (see Elizabeth Pissolato, *A Duração da pessoa: Mobilidade, parentesco e xamanismo Mbya Guarani*, São Paulo, Brazil: Editora da UNESP, 2007, 58).
37. Rose, "*Tata Endy Rekoe*—Fogo Sagrado."
38. See Flávia Cristina de Mello, "*Aetchá Nhanderukuery Karai Retarã*: Entre deuses e animais: Xamanismo, parentesco e transformação entre os Chiripá e Mbyá Guarani" (Ph.D. diss., Universidade Federal de Santa Catarina, Florianópolis, Brazil, 2006); and Pissolato, *A duração da pessoa*, among others.
39. According to Sacred Fire's members, the name *inipi* given to the place where the Temazcal happens means "Mother Earth's womb." Thus the ceremony is connected with the moment of conception and birth, with life's real purpose, and with rebirth.
40. This Spanish expression means "holy wood." It refers to the plant *Bursera graveolens*, commonly found in Argentina, Paraguay, Bolivia, and some parts of Brazil. The wood from this tree is often used as incense because it exudes a strong and sweet smell when burned.
41. Mello, "*Aetchá Nhanderukuery Karai Retarã*."
42. Ulf Hannerz, "Fluxos, fronteiras, híbridos: Palavras-chave da antropologia transnacional," *Mana* 3, no. 1 (1997): 18.
43. Dennis Tedlock and Bruce Mannhein, eds., *The Dialogic Emergence of Culture* (Urbana: University of Illinois Press, 1995).
44. Ibid.
45. João Pacheco de Oliveira, "A problemática dos 'Índios Misturados' e os limites dos estudos Americanistas: Um encontro entre antropologia e história," in *Ensaios de antropologia eistórica* (Rio de Janeiro, Brazil: Editora da UFRJ, 1999), 99–123.
46. Pacheco de Oliveira, "Uma Etnologia dos 'Índios Misturados'? Situação colonial, territorialização e fluxos culturais," *Mana* 4, no. 1 (1998): 47–77.

47. Ibid., 69.
48. Shane Greene, "The Shaman's Needle: Development, Shamanic Agency and Intermedicality in Aguaruna Lands, Peru," *American Ethnologist* 25, no. 4 (1998): 634–58.
49. Isabel Santana de Rose and Esther Jean Langdon, "Diálogos (neo)xamânicos: Encontros entre os Guarani e a ayahuasca," *Revista Tellus* year 10, no. 18 (2010): 84–113.
50. Esther Jean Langdon, Shamanisms and Neo-Shamanisms as Dialogical Categories: Case Studies from Colombia and Brazil. *Civilizations: Revue internationale d'anthropologie et de sciences humaines* 61, no. 2 (2013): 19–35.
51. Langdon, "Shamans and Shamanisms," "Shamans and Shamanisms: Reflections on Anthropological Dilemmas of Modernity," *Vibrant* 4, no. 2 (2007): 27–48. http://www.vibrant.org.br/downloads/v4n2_langdon.pdf.

Bibliography

Caicedo Fernández, Alhena. "Buena pinta: Dynamiques d'une tradition indigène dans la modernité; Les cãs dês séances de yajé à Bogotá, Colombie." Master's thesis. Ecole Des Hautes Etudes En Sciences Sociales, 2004.

Caicedo Fernández, Alhena. "Neochamanismos y modernidad: Lecturas sobre la emancipación." *Revista Nómadas*, no. 26 (2007): 114–47.

Caicedo Fernándes, Alhena. "Neochamanismo yajecero en contextos urbanos Colombianos." Paper presented at the Fifty-Third International Congress of Americanists, Mexico City, Mexico, July 19–24, 2009.

Chaumeil, Jean-Pierre. "'Le huambisa défenseur: La figure de l'Indien dans le chamanisme populaire." *Recherches Amérindiennes au Québec* 23, no. 2–3 (1988): 115–26.

Chaumeil, Jean-Pierre. "Varieties of Amazonian Shamanism." *Diogenes* 158 (1992): 101–13.

Greene, Shane. "The Shaman's Needle: Development, Shamanic Agency and Intermedicality in Aguaruna Lands, Peru." *American Ethnologist* 25, no. 4 (1998): 634–58.

Greenfield, Sidney M. "Pilgrimage, Therapy, and the Relationship Between Healing and Imagination." *Discussion Paper* 82. Madison: University of Wisconsin, Center for Latin America, 1989.

Groisman, Alberto. *Eu venho da floresta: Um estudo sobre o contexto simbólico do uso do Santo Daime.* Florianópolis, Brazil: Editora da UFSC, 1999.

Gow, Peter. "River People: Shamanism and History in Western Amazonia." In *Shamanism, History, and the State*, edited by Nicholas Thomas and Caroline Humphrey, 90–114. Ann Arbor: University of Michigan Press, 1994.

Hammer, Olav. Introduction. In *Claiming Knowledge: Strategies of Epistemology from Theosophy to the New Age*, 2–25. Leiden, Holland: Brill, 2001.

Hannerz, Ulf. "Fluxos, fronteiras, híbridos: Palavras-chave da antropologia transnacional." *Mana* 3, no. 1 (1997): 7–39.

Harner, Michael. *The Way of the Shaman*. San Francisco: HarperCollins, 1980.

Jakobsen, Merete Demant. *Shamanism: Traditional and Contemporary Approaches to the Mastery of Spirits and Healing*. New York: Berghahn Books, 1999.

Johnson, Paul C. "Shamanism from Ecuador to Chicago: A Case Study in New Age Ritual Appropriation." *Religion* 25, no. 2 (1995): 163–78.

La Barre, Weston. *The Peyote Cult*. New York: Schocken Books, 1969.

Labate, Beatriz Caiuby. *A reinvenção do uso da ayahuasca nos centros urbanos*. Campinas, Brazil: Mercado de Letras, 2004.

Labate, Beatriz C., Isabel S. Rose, and Rafael G. Santos. *Ayahuasca Religions: A Comprehensive Bibliography & Critical Essays*. Santa Cruz, CA: Multidisciplinary Association for Psychedelic Studies, 2010.

Langdon, Esther Jean. "Social Bases for Trading of Visions and Spiritual Knowledge in the Colombian and Ecuadorian Montaña." *Networks of the Past, Proceedings of the Twelfth Annual Conference*, 101–16. Archaeological Association of the University of Calgary, Canada, 1981.

Langdon, Esther Jean. "Shamans and Shamanisms: Reflections on Anthropological Dilemmas of Modernity." *Vibrant* 4, no. 2 (2007): 27–48. http://www.vibrant.org.br/downloads/v4n2_langdon.pdf.

Langdon, Esther Jean. "Shamanisms and Neo-Shamanisms as Dialogical Categories: Case Studies from Colombia and Brazil." *Civilizations: Revue internationale d'anthropologie et de sciences humaines* 61, no. 2 (2013): 19–35.

Lathrap, Donald W. "The Antiquity and Importance of Long-Distance Trade Relationships in the Moist Tropics of Pre-Columbian South America." *World Archaeology* 5, no. 2 (1973): 170–86.

Losonczy, Anne-Marie, and Silvia Mesturini Cappo. "La selva viajera: Etnografia de las rutas del chamanismo ayahuasquero entre Europa y America." *Religião e Sociedade* 30, no. 2 (2011): 164–83.

Macedo, Valéria Mendonça de. "Nexos da diferença: Cultura e afecção em uma aldeia Guarani na Serra do Mar." Ph.D. diss., Universidade de São Paulo, São Paulo, Brazil, 2010.

Macklin, June, Victor A. Martinez, and Elizabeth Gonzalez Torres. "New Religious Movements and Ritual Transformations of the Modern Self." *Scripta Ethnologica* 21 (1999): 35–58.

MacRae, Edward. *Guaido pela lua: Xamanismo e uso ritual da ayahuasca no culto do Santo Daime*. São Paulo, Brazil: Editora Brasiliense, 1992.

MacRae, Edward. "The Ritual and Religious Use of Ayahuasca in Contemporary Brazil." In *DPF 12 Policy Manual*, edited by Whitney A. Taylor, Rob Stewart, Kerry Hopkins, and Scott Ehlers, 47–50. Washington, DC: Drug Policy Foundation Press, 1999.

Magnani, José G. C. "O xamanismo urbano e a religiosidade contemporânea." *Religião & Sociedade* 20, no. 2 (2000): 113–40.

Magnani, José G. C. "Xamãs na cidade." *Dossiê 67—Religiosidade no Brasil. Revista da USP* no. 67 (2005): 218–27.

Maluf, Sônia. "Os filhos de aquário no país dos terreiros: Novas vivências espirituais no Sul do Brasil." *Ciências Sociais e Religião* 5, no. 5 (2003): 153–72.

Maluf, Sônia. "Mitos coletivos, narrativas pessoais: Cura ritual, trabalho terapêutico e emergência do sujeito nas culturas da 'Nova Era.'" *Mana* 11, no. 2 (2005): 499–528.

Maués, Raymundo Heraldo. "Um aspecto da diversidade cultural do caboclo Amazônico: ArReligião." *Estudos Avançados* 19, no. 53 (2005): 259–74.

Maués, Raymundo Heraldo, and Maria Angelica Motta. "O modelo da 'Reima': Representações alimentares em uma comunidade Amazônica." *Anuário Antropológico* 77 (1978): 120–47.

Mello, Flávia Cristina de. "*Aetchá Nhanderukuery Karai Retarã*: Entre deuses e animais. xamanismo, parentesco e transformação entre os Chiripá e Mbyá Guarani." Ph.D. diss., Universidade Federal de Santa Catarina, Florianópolis, Brazil, 2006.

Mesturini Cappo, Silvia. "Espaces chamaniques en mouvement: Itinéraires vécus et géographies multiples entre Europe et Amérique du Sud." Ph.D. diss., Faculté des Sciences Sociales et Politiques, Solvay Brussels, 2010.

Narby, Jeremy, and Francis Huxley, eds. *Shamans Through Time: 500 Years on the Path of Knowledge*. New York: Tarcher/Putnam, 2001.

Pacheco de Oliveira, João. "Uma etnologia dos 'Índios Misturados'? Situação colonial, territorialização e fluxos culturais." *Mana* 4, no. 1 (1998): 47–77.

Pacheco de Oliveira, João. "A problemática dos 'Índios Misturados' e os limites dos estudos Americanistas: Um encontro entre antropologia e história." In *Ensaios de antropologia histórica*, 99–123. Rio de Janeiro: Editora da UFRJ, 1999.

Pérez Gil, Laura. "Chamanismo y modernidade: Fundamentos etnográficos de un processo histórico." In *Paraíso abierto, jardines cerrados: Pueblos indígenas, saberes y biodiversidad*. Edited by Óscar Calavia Sáes, Marc Lenaerts and Ana María Spadafora, 179–99. Quito, Ecuador: ABYA-YALA, 2004.

Pissolato, Elizabeth. *A duração da pessoa: Mobilidade, parentesco e xamanismo Mbya (Guarani)*. São Paulo, Brazil: Editora da UNESP, 2007.

Ramírez, María Clemencia. "El Chamanismo, un Campo de Articulación de Colonizadores y Colonizados en la Región Amazónica de Colombia." *Revista Colombiana de Antropología* 33 (1996–1997): 165–84.

Rose, Isabel Santana de. "*Tata Endy Rekoe—Fogo Sagrado*: Encontros entre os Guarani, a ayahuasca e o Caminho Vermelho." Ph.D. diss., Universidade Federal de Santa Catarina, Florianópolis, Brazil, 2010.

Rose, Isabel Santana, and Esther Jean Langdon. "Diálogos (neo)xamânicos: Encontros entre os Guarani e a ayahuasca." *Revista Tellus* year 10, no. 18 (2010): 84–113.

Santana de Oliveira, Melissa. "*Kiringué i Kuery* Guarani: Infância, educação e religião entre os Guarani de M'Biguaçu, SC." Master's thesis, Universidade Federal de Santa Catarina, Florianópolis, Brazil, 2004.

Schaden, Egon. *Aspectos fundamentais da cultura Guarani*. São Paulo, Brazil: Edusp, 1974.

Tedlock, Dennis, and Bruce Mannhein, eds. *The Dialogic Emergence of Culture*. Urbana: University of Illinois Press, 1995.

Tupper, Kenneth W. "Ayahuasca Healing Beyond the Amazon: The Globalization of a Traditional Indigenous Entheogenic Practice." *Global Networks* 9, no. 1 (2009): 117–36.

Valderrama, Jorge Ronderos. "Rituales del yagé en zonas urbanas del eje cafetero: Practicas y dinâmicas de interculturalidad y mentalidades emergentes." *Cultura y Droga* 14, no. 16 (2009): 119–40.

Vargas, Haroldo Evangelista. "Fortalecimento das lideranças espirituais da Nação Guarani." Project presented by the NGO Rondon Brazil to FUNASA, 2002.

Wawzyniak, João Valentin. "Engerar: Uma categoria cosmológica sobre pessoa, saúde e corpo." *Ilha* 5, no. 2 (2003): 33–55.

5

Ritualized Misunderstanding Between Uncertainty, Agreement, and Rupture

Communication Patterns in Euro-American Ayahuasca Ritual Interactions

ANNE-MARIE LOSONCZY AND
SILVIA MESTURINI CAPPO

The purpose of this chapter is to present a hypothesis that can shed some light on the nature of the interactions supporting and feeding a particular relational field resulting from the internationalization of rituals and discourses labeled as "shamanic," particularly those centered around the ritualized consumption of ayahuasca. Confronted with the bipolarity of discursive categories such as "Occidental" and "Indigenous," we shall suggest an analysis elucidating the patterns at work in many successful intercultural communication settings that we have observed during fieldwork. Our argumentation is rooted in the classic thought of Marshall Sahlins concerning "working misunderstanding" between cultural systems.[1] It is also inspired by the innovative work of Veronique and Christine Servais[2] that has illuminated a particular communication pattern by challenging the classical definition of "good" or "successful" communication as the exact decoding of a transmitted message through the study of interpersonal interactions between humans and dolphins.

By tracing the networks and the places where the internationalization of the discourse and practice of shamanic reference accompanies the consumption of ayahuasca, we will present three settings in which the search and reproduction of interaction between Amazonian ritual experts and Western public rests on a communication model based on misunderstanding. We shall thereby address the pertinence of Servais and Servais' model[3] within our own field observations. This model shows how "misunderstanding" can sometimes be the central mechanism of a successful communication, and through the presentation of ethnographic settings, we shall argue that misunderstanding is what allows communication between a multiplicity of actors and ritual contexts across the contemporary shamanic landscape. As an extension of this model, we shall investigate the manner in which ritualized interactions centered on the collective consumption of ayahuasca become "stabilized metalinguistic devices." In fact, together with the metalinguistic effect of ritual action, the content of the communication itself may also contribute to the production or consolidation of misunderstanding. In this case, misunderstanding would arise from, and rest on, explicit verbal exchanges concerning what it is possible to agree on and what not, and what is translatable, omissible, or synonymous and what is not. These ritualized devices, both metalinguistic and verbal, permit the joint construction of a third category of conversational partners, which may be referred to as "spirits" or "inner selves." The misunderstanding that emerges from our ethnographical material stands exclusively around and within a ritualization process and is inscribed and framed by larger cultural and social codes whose restraints can push the partners' misunderstanding beyond acceptable limits and therefore lead to a communication breaking point. These cultural and social codes, which reproduce historical inequalities and asymmetries, constitute what we shall analyze here as "context." Unlike Servais and Servais, who consider the context as an inherent part of the interaction, our ethnography leads us to believe, following Sahlins, that if the context is an inherent part of the ritual interaction, it remains at the same time external to this same interaction and it therefore overlooks and frames the situations of communication.

Ritualized misunderstanding stages an historical "working misunderstanding"[4] between "Occidentals" and "Natives" and therefore creates new intercultural contexts. It is, at the same time, the means by which an agreement is made concerning the content of ritual action. It is also what allows ritual action to take place and what constructs and establishes its effectiveness. Because of what it allows to create and to legitimate, the type of misunderstanding we will be treating here is not entirely a "working misunderstanding" in Sahlins' manner, nor a structural misunderstanding as it appears in Servais and Servais' model, but a *performative* one, both ritually co-constructed and verbally negotiated, between partners who find their own benefit in misunderstanding one another in order to agree with one another.

Ayahuasca Shamanism Itineraries Between Europe and South America

The ethnographic theme developed in this article concerns the international ayahuasca itineraries that connect Europe and South America. It rests on the analysis of interactional and communicative processes that produce, support, and feed the discourses, practices, and rituals that connect the ritualized consumption of ayahuasca to the activation of the category of "shamanism." Within this frame, ayahuasca and its rituals have become one of the most prominent shamanic practices linking Europe and South America.

Our approach is based on multi-sited fieldwork conducted by Mesturini Cappo in shamanic localities representative of Western shamanic tourism in both Europe and South America from 2004 to 2010, and on the fieldwork conducted by Losonczy in Medellin (Colombia) in 2006.[5] It incorporates a theoretical thought-in-progress that longs to understand the articulation of representation, discourse, and ritual in different settings and situations where ethnical, *mestizo,* and international ritual experts meet each other and offer services to those who belong to these equally different cultural and social backgrounds.

The search for authentic shamanic practice in Europe typically looks to faraway places; distant in either time or in space. According to the definition of *shamanism* defended by Mircea Eliade in his famous book,[6] each set of practices finds a legitimized place within a universal idea of individual spiritual contact with another world—"a world of spirits"—which becomes accessible through an induced state of body and mind that this author has called "trance." Within this framework, the notions of "altered states of consciousness" or "shamanic states of consciousness," as Michael Harner[7] would put it, carries the idea that the differences between various ritual practices is merely of ritual tools, with all practices leading to one commonly shared universal experience.

Within this widespread and universalized interpretation of spirituality and experience, ayahuasca has gained the reputation of being a particularly powerful ritual and spiritual tool, one that is capable of inducing a profound spiritual experience even among the most skeptical participants.

This interpretation of ayahuasca, spread through websites, literature, documentaries, and even movies, has supported the rise of an expanding, organized shamanic tourism, bringing more and more groups from Europe and North America to the South American continent—specifically to the Amazonian region—in order to allow them to drink the substance in its original environment under the guidance of local *ayahuasqueros*. Increasingly, more shamanic centers are being built in the Amazonian region—mainly in the Peruvian Amazon—in the areas around the cities of Iquitos and Pucallpa, and also in the region stretching between these two cities. These centers are designed to accommodate large groups of Occidental travelers looking for an authentic experience with ayahuasca.

Our fieldwork has revealed several types of roaming activity within this Occidental "spiritual" and "therapeutic" search, sometimes labeled "New Age." The most salient manifestations of this type of traveling are the organized charter groups that fly into the Amazon for a week or two of prebooked ayahuasca ritual sessions. These groups may be organized and led by a shaman, sometimes an ayahuasquero and sometimes not, who usually officiates as a ritual expert in their country of origin. These groups may also constitute themselves casually via common booking dates on the website of a shamanic workshop center. A second type of traveling consists of a central figure officiating as a shaman in the tourists' country of origin. This person leads the tourists from one local Amazonian expert to another in order for them to try a number of ways of working with the substance, or sometimes even different substances. In this case, the foreign travelers might experiment with ayahuasca in the Amazon, and, less frequently, with the *San Pedro* hallucinogen in the Andes or in the Peruvian coast deserts, or possibly with a ritual offering to Mother Earth performed by an Andean *paco* (healer). Another potential, but less common, way of traveling involves solitary European or North American individuals who visit the South American continent, specifically the Amazon, to follow a long-term initiation and apprenticeship with either a single shaman or a relatively small number of local experts.

These long-term initiated travelers may return to their homelands where they might then officiate as ayahuasqueros, and as such they might regularly bring additional groups to their former teachers. Others might stay in the Amazon, most likely alongside their current or former teachers. They might then help organize regular incoming groups who could provide regular income for themselves and their teachers. This income could also contribute to the construction of hosting facilities, which are often associated with private botanical gardens focused on cultivating medicinal plants.

Concurrently, the international interest in ayahuasca has allowed more and more South American practitioners to travel to either Europe or North America, often invited by former clients or apprentices, to lead collective ayahuasca sessions. Sometimes these South American ayahuasqueros choose to remain abroad and work permanently with European or North American clientele.

In Colombia, Brazil, and Ecuador, a national urban middle-to-high class of ayahuasca sympathizers is participating in and supporting the spread of this contemporary international use of ayahuasca, along with its experts. This tendency relates to a more general policy of revalorization and promotion of indigenous culture and defense of minority rights within those countries. These uses of ayahuasca generate the opening of new "ritual spaces," such as local universities, cultural centers, and private homes.

With this in mind, the existence of international ayahuasca networks should be understood as a constant circulation of practitioners and practices, and as a constant adaptation of both to the groups and the contexts that frame and support the circulation itself. Nevertheless, linguistic borders mark these itineraries.

Most research related to these discursive and ritualized interfaces—led by the association of the category of shamanism with the reference to the ayahuasca practice—is interdisciplinary (anthropology, botany, psychiatry, and law). It tends to put forward the physical and psycho-emotional effects that result from the ingestion of the plant and to minimize the history of the expansion of ayahuasca and the consequences of the increasing ayahuasca tourism within the context of the Amazon and its local communities. This makes it possible to understand the interest surrounding ayahuasca and the works that it has inspired as the continuation of a wider countercultural intellectual current, one that started in the sixties, was based on personal experimentation, focused on hallucinogens and their therapeutic potential, and presented indigenous knowledge as the last repository of a primordial ecological vision.[8]

Brazilian syncretic religions such as Santo Daime, União do Vegetal, and Barquinha, which are focused on the use of ayahuasca, have inspired numerous anthropological essays in the last fifteen years. These essays have served to integrate an analysis of ritual modalities, their evolution, and their association with representations related to the ritual use of ayahuasca.[9] Corresponding ethnographies and analyses of the itineraries, the localities, and the actors of the contemporary networks linked to shamanism and ayahuasca are far less evident. Mesturini Cappo's Ph.D. thesis[10] and our previous common writings[11] all contribute to shedding new light on the relation between shamanism and ayahuasca.

The centrality of ritual action, produced and legitimized by the ritual expert, constitutes one of the convergence points between the various ethnic and mestizo shamanic practices of the Amazon and those adapted to the demands of an urban Occidental clientele.

From an Amazonian point of view, Peter Gow,[12] Miguel Alexiades,[13] and Anne-Marie Losonczy[14] have shown how ayahuasca, and shamanic expertise in general, has been a catalyst for regional traveling and interethnic exchange long before the recent international interest in this substance and its specialists. Michael Taussig[15] and, later, Peter Gow, among others, have argued that the use of ayahuasca followed the same paths as the social reorganizations caused first by colonial policies and later by the politics of massive extraction campaigns, which were local manifestations reflecting the impact of the global capitalistic economy. Within this context, ayahuasca has appeared as a set of ritual practices fully capable of leaving behind its strictly ethnic usage, one that can be readily adapted to the needs of a more urban, mixed-blood population. Thanks to the interest of many white colonizers, among others, ayahuasca has progressively gained the reputation of being a powerful healing substance for a very mixed local clientele.

The mestizo shamanic system consists of an association with, on the one hand, references to the forest and ethnical shamanic practices and associated representations and, on the other hand, the mobilization of tutelary entities borrowed from the ontology of the Christian religion. This association implies the manipulation of both speech and ritual practices in which Christian naming is used to unify certain aspects of ethnical spirit profiles with those of Christian entities, such as angels, demons, saints, and devils. In another article,[16] subsequent to Gow's analysis,[17] we have shown the essential mediation role played by speech, practices, and experts belonging to the mestizo milieu in the management of local ritual interactions between urban Occidentals and indigenous specialists. The mestizo practice that we have named "interface shamanism" offers a semantic compromise between the representational codes of the partners.

The recent international concern for ayahuasca can therefore be understood as a recent development of an ongoing historical process. During this process, ayahuasca has come out of the forest and gradually been integrated into a set of popular ritual practices, where it has mingled with popular Christian rituality, and later been confronted with the arrival of biomedicine and the installation of medical centers in many local areas and villages.

Within this locally bound urbanization process, the power of ayahuasca has been legitimized by its savage origins: it has donned a halo of mystery, and facilitated a metaphor of an inviolate and nourishing nature. Ayahuasca and its

Figure 5.1. Pasaje Paquito Market. Stand with typical Amazonian remedies used in urban mestizo shamanism: Iquitos, Peru. Photograph by Ana Gretel Echazú Böschemeier.

Figure 5.2. Mestizo shamanism ritual kit: Andean and Amazonian objects, manufactured and homemade perfumed essences, Cuenca, Ecuador. Photograph by Claude Guislain.

ritual guardians have construed a complex constellation, the power of which is rooted in the association with the wild potent forest. Little by little, the set of ayahuasca, ayahuasqueros, the ritual songs (called *icaros* in Peru), the rattles made of dried leaves, and the perfumed essences have become an increasingly standardized ritual set that is the emblem of an ancestral indigenous power.

Rethinking the Model: Toward Ritualized Misunderstanding and the Emergence of a Third Party

Our approach is based on both a finding and a question. As far as the finding is concerned, the ritualized drinking of ayahuasca by Occidental individuals—directed by indigenous or mestizo ritual specialists coming from a background strongly marked by its "otherness"—takes place in a manner that furthers mutual fulfillment, and thus reiteration of such ritual encounters. The question, issued from this finding, wonders what permits this mutual fulfillment and the perception of a successful communication between urban Occidentals searching for answers to their perceived lack of well-being and the indigenous or mestizo local experts.

In analyzing the divinization of Captain Cook by the Hawaiian people, Sahlins writes: "I do not mean to suggest that the Hawaiian concept of Cook's divinity was a simple assimilation of European belief. We have to deal rather with a parallel encoding... as a 'working misunderstanding.' It is a sort of symbolic serendipity, or at least a congruent attribution from two different cultural orders of a special meaningful value to the same event, so as to give it a privileged and determining position in history."[18] Conceiving misunderstanding in this manner makes two different social and cultural logics appear as diverging interpretations of the same event that culminate in the same result: its inscription as a relevant event in both collective cultural memories. From theses two logics emerge, in turn, the cognitive and social commitments that condition the pragmatic communication situations between individuals on both sides.

Similarly, the model presented by Servais and Servais takes as its starting point the work of Catherine Coquio, Franco La Cecla, and Jacques Derrida,[19] and queries classic communication theory. This theory, based on a model called "telegraphic," rests on the idea that there are such things as "good" communication and "bad" communication, the "good" being an integral and complete transmission of the sender's message to his receptor, and the "bad" being a particular interpretation of the receptor, divergent from the transmitter's message. Coquio stresses that "the ignored conflict, the 'misunderstanding,' is an exchange setting which protects the unthought-of from divergence in order to let a false agreement last," similar to the adage "it is far better to agree than to understand each other."[20] In his essay on misunderstanding, the anthropologist Franco La Cecla insists on the fact that *agreeing* with each other does not absolutely mean *understanding* each other.[21] Therefore, the notion of misunderstanding implies that sharing a common language does not exclude the possibility that even though people might actually believe they are understanding each other, they may instead be speaking of greatly different things.[22]

Servais and Servais' communication model, based on misunderstanding, creates a space of interpretative freedom for the receptor. Going beyond the information transported by the sign itself, their model equally stresses the importance of the metalinguistic tools supporting communication, such as gestures, looks, and all such signs belonging to nonverbal communication. The communicational unity, so defined, no longer applies to a "telegraphic" and mechanical definition of "sign"; it corresponds to what Derrida calls a "mark."[23] Alterations can take place when the interpretation of the receptor contrasts with the cultural code of the transmitter, and if all acts of communication necessarily involve a certain amount of misunderstanding, the degree of misunderstanding—i.e., the possible divergence of interpretation—increases as the cultural codes of the social actors communicating only partially overlap. We therefore defend the centrality of ritual space and action in the establishment of such successful misunderstanding dynamics.

Within the ritualization process, let's first observe how the ritual expert is perceived by the Occidental-urban audience. Culturally, he is "Other," and therefore his spiritual power and knowledge are part of his Otherness. In order to comprehend this communicational frame, we propose, together with Houseman's analysis of New Age rituals,[24] that, if vernacular rituality (which exists when cultural intimacy links all the participants) consists of generating complex acts through the ritual condensation of relationships that would be considered incompatible in ordinary life,[25] intercultural forms of shamanism will produce instead a "ritual refraction."[26] This implies that the ritual participants follow the shaman's instructions and procedures in order to integrate emblematic qualities and emotions attributed to exotic or pre-Christian figures, which are considered exemplary. The shaman himself is one of these figures and therefore an object of mimesis, as he is asked to incarnate exemplarity and exoticism. Through the belief that he is reproducing the mental disposition from which the Other's actions supposedly proceed, the participant experiences himself as transforming into an exceptional entity (shaman, spirit, etc.) and develops then, next to his "real self," an "emblematic self." This partial identification with emblematic and exemplary figures, supported by the ritual, seems to produce two concomitant effects. In the first place, we observed a strong emotional state supported by the impression of an abolished distance between the participant and the shaman, who is then progressively transformed and integrated by the participant as part of himself. In the second place, the very emotion that radiates among the participants reinforces the perception of a metacultural collective agreement.

The psychoactive ayahuasca also possesses powerful purgative effects accompanied by important changes of perception, and often by the emergence of hallucinogenic visions. The ritualization of the collective consumption then gives visibility to superhuman entities, third-party interlocutors who become both subjects and objects of communication for both shaman and participants. The words, gestures, and expressions of this third party—reported and rendered in the exchanges taking place between human partners—continuously influence verbal interaction and thereby transform this third party into an "indirect speech" communicational partner.[27]

Visual, as well as auditory, and even olfactory, perceptions of these entities validate their existence in the eyes of the Occidental audience. Conversely, from the shaman's point of view, these same entities tend to belong to the realm of cultural evidence. Therefore, these entities become figures condensing the agreement within a misunderstanding. Meanwhile, they also allow various divergent interpretations, mostly latent, concerning their identity and intentionality.

The Occidentals' perception articulates three representations related to ayahuasca. The first one, linked to the biomedical point of view, sees ayahuasca as a powerful psychoactive substance. The second one seems linked to the idea of ayahuasca being a natural spiritual beverage capable of "opening the way" toward superhuman interlocutors belonging to "another world." The third sees it as a tutelary feminine spirit, often called "mother ayahuasca" or "spirit of ayahuasca" (*la madre de la ayahuasca* or *el espiritu de la ayahuasca*), who communicates with humans in order to heal and teach. Indigenous and mestizo shamans lean closer to the last two representations, more strongly related to more complex and extensive vernacular cosmologies.

The emergence of such superhuman partners within the ritual frame widens the model of Servais and Servais by adding a third party. The latter is literally produced by the effects of ritualization related to ayahuasca consumption, namely the interdependence between the agreement (existence and presence of invisible partners) and the divergence of interpretation concerning their identities and intentions. These superhuman actors manifest themselves in the shaman's speech and in the participants' visions and physical perceptions. They thus communicate through verbal speech and through gestural and acoustic metalinguistic means.

In this ritualized misunderstanding with superhuman third-party intervention, a specific use of verbal exchange appears where a representation shared by both shaman and participants localizes the spirits' speech within dreams and in ayahuasca-induced visions. The spirits' speech constitutes one of the major subjects in the verbal exchanges between the shaman and the participants, outside the ayahuasca drinking ceremony. First, the spirits' words perceived by the participants in their vision are immediately present in the conversations after the ceremony. The use and interpretation of the spirits' speech is then picked up by the shaman and sent back to the participants. Some observations[28] have shown that a sort of echo effect makes each speech act about superhuman entities bounce back and forth between the shaman and the participants, allowing, with each bounce, either a slight modification leading to more precision or a simple repetition. These repetitions and slight modifications serve to both validate and complete the narrative and the interpretation of a vision. This reciprocal adjustment and accordance of simple speech acts, which prevents mutual contradiction, leads to the co-construction of knowledge,[29] a type of "circular discourse" validated through the ritual action. There, the complexities of both Indigenous and Occidental cosmologies are put aside by an action, always contextual, and by a communicational fumble aiming at agreement, mutual legitimacy, and the reproduction of an ambiguity and blurriness that stabilizes and perpetuates the ritualized misunderstanding. We will test the relevance of this theoretical framework through the description of three primary settings of repeated misunderstandings.

The first type of situation involves the preliminary conditions for the construction of a ritualized misunderstanding and stresses the importance of the third party within the interaction. There, the existence of superhuman partners becomes a primary agreement point for the repetition of the ritual consumption of ayahuasca. If the first misunderstanding setting emerges from different uncertainty registers surrounding the presence of superhuman partners, the second setting finds its specific place within the modalities that support the co-construction of knowledge, leading to progressive agreements concerning the nature, identity, and intentionality of the superhuman third parties.

Ultimately, the third misunderstanding setting concerns the inscription of these ritualized third-party exchanges within external sociocultural contexts that constrain the interpretation of the relationship between shaman and clients. The key role played by the mechanism of legitimation of the shaman, grounded either in his native milieu or in Occidental values, will appear clearly, thanks to this misunderstanding setting. This third setting also touches the limits of a communication based on ritualized misunderstanding and shows when agreement becomes impossible.

A First Misunderstanding Setting: The Emergence of Uncertainty and the Interface Between Ontological Doubt and Epistemic Doubt

What drives diverse populations to approach ayahuasqueros and to drink ayahuasca? Beyond the various expressions of these motivations in the international landscape of shamanism, a common quest seems to underlie and bind ayahuasca drinkers despite their social and cultural differences. Studying this quest leads us to consider the notion of "uncertainty," and the "search for a way out of uncertainty," as central for the comprehension of the communication dynamics that permit an ethnical and traditional version of ayahuasca rituality and an internationalized one to coexist. The common search for a way out of uncertainty reveals the existence of two main cultural logics.

Numerous Amazonian shamanic systems are based on an implicit theory of metamorphosis relating all beings evoked in myths and cosmogonies: humans, spirits, animals, and plants. The possibility of "reversible transformation" is part of this metamorphosis and translates into a temporary change of bodily form and appearance. This capacity is consubstantial to the spirits and, through apprenticeship, becomes a skill of the initiated shaman. The sharing of this competence between the shaman and the spirits is an essential part of the shamanic identity and its specificity.[30] It also permits the emergence of narratives concerning the multiple encounters, casual or wished for, with beings whose identities have yet to be determined.

Animal tutelary spirits are likely to appear to hunters and fishers during the daytime, particularly in wild places within the local geography, and in either animal or human form. Experienced shamans can, during ritual celebrations or after their death, leave their human appearance and take on that of various predatory animals. In the nocturnal dreamtime of the non-shamans, unidentified living forms, spirits, or shamans appear. Their encounters are often loaded with danger for the dreamer's life and soul. In this manner, narratives belonging to ordinary everyday conversations may evoke daytime or dreamtime encounters with beings whose identities and intentions are uncertain, and which often predict illness for the individual and misfortune for the family. Thus, a permanent uncertainty emerges regarding the meaning of those encounters as well as the identity and intentions of the encountered beings. If the being has predatory features, the physical and psychological impact left by the encounter can turn into something called "the fright"[31] in vernacular languages.

Identification of the encountered figures, clarification of their intentions, and a diagnosis of their impact, together with the management of the interactions taking place between the person and those beings, are primordial motives for the solicitation of shamanic competences, and also for the ritual drinking of ayahuasca. Thus, the task falls on the shaman to offer a way out of the uncertainty by assigning a specific identity to the encountered form, elucidating its purposes and effects, and determining how to appropriately restore the well-being. In Amazonian societies where ayahuasca consumption has long been a local custom, or where it may have only recently become such, the shaman fulfills his task through the interpretation of physical symptoms and of the visions induced by the consumption of the substance.

In the context of the international itineraries binding Europe and South America through the circulation of a commercial supply and demand of ayahuasca rituality, the primary approach of the users tends to include an initial phase involving consultation of testimonial literature or shamanic websites and forums. We have argued in previous writings that this discursive approach to the ayahuasca experience creates a set of preformatted expectations that the ritual experts must manage and that will influence the actual lived experiences.[32] Within the frame of this seemingly formatted and homogeneous discourse, the most evoked themes concern a personal unwellness connected with past experiences, or with what are regarded as the consequences of a fundamentally damaging Occidental urban lifestyle. In this context, the search that leads to ayahuasca and its experts binds individual physical, psycho-emotional, or relational issues with an underlying existentialist ontological uncertainty concerning the possibility of believing that "there is something out there," that spirits may actually be "real," or that there could be such thing as a "soul" or as a "spiritual world." Such are the uncertainties with which this particular public approaches the ayahuasca milieu and for which the consumption of the beverage and the participation in the ritual space must represent some kind of a "way out." The visions achieved during the sessions, the physical effects that appear as a purge and purification, the interpretations of shamans and those of other participants: all contribute to the construction of a new ontological and existentialist certitude.

As presented previously, the uncertainty characterizing the ethnical search for ayahuasca rituality emerges from a certainty background that concerns the existence of spirits, the potential impact of their powers, and the control that the shaman can have over them. Unlike the Occidental adepts, their doubt is related to the identities of those who are seen in dreamlike states—in savage zones, or during ayahuasca sessions—and the impact of these encounters on the resources, the relationships, and the health of those meeting them. All these elements suggest the existence of an underlying *epistemic doubt.*

On the contrary, in the second logic, the primary uncertainty concerns the existence and the "reality" of beings and entities that cannot be perceived through ordinary perception. This doubt leads to the quest for an *ontological certainty*. Within this logic, once this basic certainty is constructed and validated by both the individual and the collective, visionary ayahuasca experience and the spirits are represented as having stable forms, identities, purposes, and appearances. These entities are often seen as closely related to typical Christian figures—such as the devil, or demons and angels—which reactivates the binary logic dividing "good" from "evil." When the spirits are seen as animal spirits or plant spirits inspired by the Amazonian cosmogonies, the identity and the intentions of these entities are described as totally stable, exclusively positive, fully certain, and far more powerful than any shaman.

In these two sociologically and culturally different frames, ayahuasca appears as a ritualized, mobile apparatus that is likely to offer a way out of uncertainty. This occurs even though, in the first case, it represents a powerful means of handling the possible relationship between humans and spirits, and in the second case, it becomes a primary means of validating their existence. Nevertheless, this common cognitive function related to uncertainty opens the communication between Amazonian shamans and Occidental clients. This gets condensed in the sharing of common images, such as those of plant and animal spirits, although the meaning given to these terms is different. The misunderstanding setting materializes each time an indigenous or mestizo shaman holds an ayahuasca session for the Occidental urban public. Thanks to shared emotions and common speech, they can both interact, thereby creating an agreement whose condition of performance rests on the fact that the actors involved do not actually understand each other.

The divergences in the agencies of doubt within the two logics pointed out above do not exclude the idea that the existence of doubt itself can create a conduit between the two, a bridge made of common speech items and similar sentiment of doubt and anguish. We might then conclude that each partner reads the other's doubts in the light of his own.

"Epistemic doubt"—proper to ethnical and mestizo milieus—rests on a tacit knowledge of myths that narrate the birth of those entities, and also on the numerous narratives that belong to everyday conversation about casual encounters with them. Since such encounters are considered common, the epistemic doubt that they awaken goes together with everyday life events. Time and time again, it leads to consulting the shaman, thus producing and validating the ritual and the shamanic interpretative system. "Ontological doubt"—what we have also called "existential doubt"—is what pushes the Occidental audience toward shamanic rituals and ayahuasca drinking. The visionary experience and its shamanic interpretation in terms of "spirit presence" imply, for participants, the validation of an ontological system and the emergence of a certainty that is not partial, but global. Because of this, the Occidental public shows a common tendency to look for a renewed experience of transcendence, through "spirits" who represent an alternative to the divine entity of the monotheist religions of their cultures of origin, an entity in whom, it seems, they no longer manage to "believe" and who is fundamentally characterized by a sort of "speechlessness," or at least, by the absence of relational competence and discursive exchange.

For the Occidental audience, as well as for the ethnical and *mestizo* milieus, those doubts, always renewed, form a sort of ritual residue that leads both parties to a periodical repetition of ritual action.[33] Doubt and certainty function as interdependent partners assessing the reproduction of ritual interaction. Even so, the reappearance of ontological doubt among the Occidental audience can cause for them an invalidation of the shamanic system as a whole, and eventually the abandonment of the ayahuasca networks. For those who witness such an exit and for the shamans themselves who "stay behind," the invalidation of the whole system leads to a type of interpretation in which evil spirits or dark forces are accused of misleading the person, an interpretation that preserves the validity of the system as a whole.

A Second Misunderstanding Setting: Misfortune and "Malady" Between Sorcery and Psychology

Seeking recourse to ayahuasca or to shamanic ritual work in ethnical, mestizo, or Occidental milieus is almost always prompted by the emergence of a disorder in daily life of the individual, the family, or the collective. This disorder often appears in the ethnical and mestizo milieus as an accumulation of negative events regarding the body and possessions of individuals and of their close family members. This sequence of negative events, which classical British ethnology has united under the concept of "misfortune,"[34] has become the foundation for a sorcery-based interpretation that points to human malevolence as the origin of such sequences. The discourse of Occidental urban users often evokes a diffuse unwellness as a recourse motivation, one that is often described in psycho-emotional terms even when it includes physical symptoms. Therefore, this interpretation situates the source of malady inside everyone's interior individual realm.

Fieldwork has shown how local Amazonian ayahuasqueros do not separate their comprehension and use of ayahuasca from the task of protecting their local clients and family members from magical or supernatural attacks originating in the malevolence of spirits who wander in the surrounding environment or are sent by another ayahuasquero acting in the interest of a rival social group or individual. In a more strictly Amazonian ethnic context, the collective and periodical ingestion of the substance, along with the visions that it generates, is used by the group members to learn how to master the fear caused by forest encounters with unidentified entities whose intentions are unclear, or how to handle the confrontation with animal protector spirits during hunting expeditions. However, in both these contexts, the power of the shaman and the power of the spirits—including the power of the ayahuasca—are represented as being as much at the service of protection and misfortune reparation as they are of malevolent aggression.

On the contrary, the Occidental audience tends to refuse to interpret any feeling of unwellness as the result of a voluntary malevolence of others, and longs instead for an interpretation of ayahuasca rituality based on individual experience and on the possibility of transcending individual psychological blocks or emotional traumas due to negative past experiences.

This confronts two different causality frameworks and interpretations of ayahuasca usage: On the one hand, there is a sorcery-based interpretation in which ayahuasca is a means of looking beyond that which is ordinarily visible in order to evacuate malevolent spirits from the person's body or environment through a dream-state magical combat led exclusively by the shaman. On the other hand, this same dream-state is evoked as a field of experimentation, as a search for personal psychological issues, and as a field of transcendence and resolution of those same issues. This search appears as an exercise led individually by each participant, during which the shaman is asked to perform the mere role of guide and counselor.

These two interpretations seem to have found a translation compromise owing to the idea, or the image, that each person must lead his own combat against his own issues. These images are sometimes interpreted, or translated, as malevolent spirits inhabiting the person's body and mind. Thanks to a "synonymy effect," full of ambiguity and blurriness, which puts spirits and sorcery on the same plane as psychological and emotional states, a metaphorical continuum seems to be created between those two frameworks, which are then able to communicate. The visions that emerge during the ayahuasca session, often preformatted by the recent literature and the numerous websites on the subject, confront Occidental users with entities interpreted by the shaman as either figures that incarnate psycho-emotional states such as fear, sadness, sorrow, and guilt or as custodial entities of "good" and "evil" inspired by Christianity such as angels, demons, devils, etc.

Within this process, psychological states often related to traumatic past experiences become "third party communicational partners" against whom the battle can be fought, with the help of the shaman and of the ayahuasca. In this frame, ayahuasca plays the role of an exclusively benevolent entity that is collaborating in a process of psychological and physical purging conducted under the surveillance of a shaman, who tends to be perceived as a transcended and enlightened human being.

However, if this shifting of meaning and interpretation seems functional as far as the encounter and sharing between local ayahuasqueros and foreigners is concerned, it refers to the permanence of fundamentally divergent ways of conceiving the social environment as well as one's place and role within this environment. The sorcery-based interpretation reveals itself as highly competent at handling long-term genealogical and social relations within a context of relatively steady and settled communities. On the contrary, the psychologically based framework seems particularly well adapted to handle socially isolated individuals coming from a highly urbanized context.

The designation of third-party disorder "agents," which are incarnated in figures that the Western public manages to treat as "real" thanks to the experience of ayahuasca drinking and to the shamanic discourse surrounding it, is a point of convergence between these two logics. The notion of "spirits"—a Spanish and Portuguese term (*espiritus*) commonly adopted by the regional mestizo shamanism—is used by Occidental, mestizo, and indigenous experts and users alike. The shared usage of this notion helps to conceal divergence regarding, on the one hand, the profiles of indigenous supernatural entities belonging to a realm co-extensive with humans and, on the other hand, those belonging to the individual's psycho-emotional realm, which nevertheless persist as part of everyone's psychic space.

In both interpretations, the ayahuasca appears as an entity enabling those who drink it to see other entities, and to interact with them. Nonetheless, what is being perceived, and the answers that the visions and the experience are supposed to bring about, are additional manifestations of divergence and misunderstanding. In the Occidental conception, experimentation with this substance is supposed to deliver an answer to an ontological quest that ultimately concerns what is "real" and what is "beyond" the commonly perceived reality. Once again, a divergence appears when we compare this type of fundamental search for a unique, universal reality with the local request for solutions to pragmatic everyday life problems.

This divergence is followed by another regarding the temporality of reference evoked in the explanation of malady and misfortune. In indigenous and mestizo interpretation, the causes for disorder are commonly linked with conflicting interests and hostilities associated with the current local, social, and relational context. On the contrary, the Occidental discourse that underlies the quest for ayahuasca drinking frames the causes of the present situation of being or feeling unwell within the realm of past experience.

Therefore, the preservation of a communicational blur concerning the nature of spirits, their possible or impossible ambivalence, and the regimes of causality that can be evoked to explain and justify each individual life situation effectively produces a permanent misunderstanding that makes interaction possible and preserves the freedom of interpretation and the core of each individual's cultural code. Nevertheless, mestizo shamanic practice and its intertwining with popular Christian practices creates an interfacing set of representations that enables a ritualized transformation of "angels" and "demons" into "spirits," as well as opening the way to the transformation of "fears" and "traumas" into "spirits." The permanent shifting, typical of mestizo practice, between these entities constructs a space of mediation between indigenous representations and those underlying Occidental expectations. The verbal dimension of the ritualized misunderstanding, which rests on the management of these synonymy effects, obeys the "circular discourse" logic. Therefore, the verbal exchanges also become ritualized devices, which progressively construct potentially shared and ritually functional meanings and legitimate the enunciating and acting position of both parties.

A Third Misunderstanding Setting: Legitimation Modes and Misunderstanding Limits

As the tourism linked with ayahuasca represents a direct access to cash money for the local experts, those experts who are already involved with the ayahuasca business act as professional ritual experts within the context of the local towns.

The increasing foreign demand for ayahuasqueros, however, along with the wish of most travelers and tourists to meet with authentic indigenous ritual experts, seems to accentuate an ethnic migration toward the urban centers. In turn, this migration is provoking an increase in the number of experts present in the local towns. Furthermore, some ethnographers, among them Jean Langdon, Oscar Calavia Saez, Peter Gow, and Glenn Shepard,[35] have reported a tendency of certain indigenous populations who did not traditionally use ayahuasca to show a new interest in this substance because of its regional urban success, and because of the international connections and cash flows it makes possible.

A more visible consequence of the local conscription of ayahuasca into the world market economy is the transformation of the status of local healers within their local communities and towns. If, on the one hand, a certain prestige seems associated with those working with tourists, their international fame is most often interpreted locally as a "temptation" that will eventually corrupt the powers and the benevolence of the healer. Money that is not controlled by the community appears as antagonistic to healing powers, and the admiration with which foreigners often treat shamans is interpreted as an attack on the healer's modesty and on his loyalty to the community. Furthermore, a shaman of good reputation should be able not only to heal but also to counterattack the malevolent aggressions coming from rival shamans or wandering spirits. Given the fact that tourists are a generous source of income, the shaman might maintain a good reputation locally if he continues to perform for a local clientele at a reduced price and, more particularly, if he redistributes the suddenly acquired wealth. On the contrary, a local expert who does not redistribute his wealth within his local social network in one manner or another will acquire the reputation of being a "sorcerer."

As a consequence, the tourism phenomenon and the access to foreign clientele has become one of the main reasons for magical combat among local practitioners. Jealousy related to working with tourists has become a common explanation for misfortune among the practitioners, their families, and their protégés. This is reminiscent of the close association, often mentioned by anthropologists, between the sorcery accusation and the lack of wealth redistribution within the community. Avoiding redistribution implies bypassing the customary exchange networks that not only regulate the local social life but also appear in numerous indigenous myths as the key condition for a culturally "humanized" social life. Accumulating wealth without redistributing among a community reveals the complementary danger of illegitimately taking what rightfully belongs to another. It outlines the visage of the predator as a liminal figure of the human condition, building a case for the sorcerer figure as the dark, threatening side of shamanic power, which is inextricably bound to his shamanic healing competence.

Therefore, the third misunderstanding scene is built on the legitimacy of the shaman. For the nonlocal public, the shaman's reputation and trustworthiness depends primarily on his local origin, preferably indigenous, or on his local or indigenous initiation. Secondarily, it is linked to the presence in his discourse of a moral and spiritual motivation—one deemed contrary to any commercial or financial preoccupation—that would justify the interaction with the Western audience. A first modality of vindicatory speech moves the center of decision toward the ayahuasca entity, who would then order the interaction with the foreigners because "she wants to travel." In a second modality of speech, the shaman presents himself as the carrier of an ancestral and indigenous culture revalorization inspired by the recent national and international political acknowledgment of minorities, or by the ecological discourse of many NGOs who defend ancestral indigenous knowledge because they deem this knowledge likely to help remedy the threatened balance between man and nature.

In spite of this, the primary exchange means between the Western public and the local ayahuasqueros is cash money. The permanent swap of ritual sessions and knowledge for cash dollars creates a tension over and over again in the minds of the Western clientele because of the perceived conflict between the factual exchange of money and the moral values defending a purely spiritual exchange. Thus, we observe a tension between the indigenous and mestizo's legitimization criteria—based on remunerated access to shamanic power—and the Occidental one.

Considering the increase of ayahuasca sessions, it is pertinent to question which communication and interaction patterns absorb those tensions and facilitate conflict resolution. In order to answer this question, we may contrast the profile of a shaman who has a widely recognized international reputation, but is profoundly discredited in the local milieu, with that of a local expert who has not managed to become legitimate in the Western milieu, but is recognized and respected by his local community. Most shamans who work with both Westerners and locals present, in varying ways and degrees, some of the elements present in these two rare, opposite, and extreme profiles.

Don Vicente (a pseudonym) is a middle-aged man who has numerous descendants from various wives. Proceeding from a prestigious dynasty of Shipibo shamans based in the city of Pucallpa in the central Peruvian Amazon, he has become internationally known as a result of his participation in movies and documentaries produced by a famous European *cinéaste,* and thanks to his travels to Europe. On the other hand, according to local rumors, he had to flee from Pucallpa because of sexual abuse and sorcery accusations emanating from his community as he started to work with foreigners. On his arrival in Iquitos, he built one of the first and largest hosting facilities for ayahuasca tourism on the Iquitos-Nauta road. Very present on shamanic websites, he has developed a model of self-advertising coupled with a discourse that fully responds to the expectations of the Western public. According to local rumors, he possesses great personal wealth that he redistributes only within his immediate family. Today, his great reputation among the European clientele goes hand in hand with a severe local mistrust that considers him to be a powerful and aggressive sorcerer.

The elements constituting his international reputation are a discourse that stresses his mission as a teacher of an indigenous ancestral knowledge, beyond all economic interest; the spread of this message through the media; his Shipibo origin, his place in a dynasty of shamans; and the presence of Occidental apprentices working alongside him in a shamanic center. These factors, ascribed to another interpretation frame, are the same ones that support his locally discredited reputation and lead to the accusations of violence and sorcery. He embodies a figure of extreme excess: his ethnic origins and his kinship are locally interpreted as a source of power, a power now perceived as totally malevolent because of an accumulation of wealth that is not redistributed and that includes permanent coexistence with foreigners. His local image echoes the Amazonian trans-ethnical representation, which originated in the colonial period, where the "white man" is seen as a "predator," grasping all the resources, goods, and knowledge that the Indians possess.[36]

Don Gabriel (a pseudonym), also a middle-aged man, was born in a riverside community on the Ucayali River. Reputed as a healer in his home community, he regularly comes to Iquitos because he longs for a shamanic career with the increasing number of foreign tourists—like many of his congeners—in order to gain access to foreign cash. His contact with the city and the foreign tourists is a travel-guide friend who comes from the same village. Don Gabriel must meet the tourists in the local hotels where they stay because he does not have any hosting facilities of his own, and also because he has neither a reputation in Iquitos nor a presence on the web that would lead the tourists to him.

By observing his interactions with certain foreigners, we have been able to watch him present his competencies and stress his expertise in undoing bewitchment, which he achieves by sending the witchcraft back to the senders thanks to the help of spirits of the dead that he picks up during his travels in the underworld. While doing this, he enunciates the price of his services and the modalities of payment with insistence. The reactions of the tourists seem to oscillate among dismay, disquiet, apprehension, and fright. His reference to bewitchment, to aggressive counterattacks, and to the dead clearly frightens the Westerners. Furthermore, besides the fact that his shamanic competency isn't locally referenced and doesn't appear on the web, he talks about money in an explicit and insisting manner. The Westerners perceive neither in his discourse nor in his attitude any of the marks that would justify the legitimacy of a shaman. On the contrary, the explicit presentation of a triptych of bewitchment, death, and money condenses into all that must be obliterated in order to let an interaction labeled as "shamanic" take place. Thus, it appears that Don Gabriel was incapable, at least at that point in time, of earning a clientele among the Westerners

Figure 5.3. Touristic options offered by travel agency in the Main Square in Iquitos, Peru. Photograph by Claude Guislain.

visiting Iquitos, although it is equally plausible to suppose that the local inhabitants of the city would solicit his competence.

Don Gabriel's case shows that when a shaman trespasses, because of speech and presentation of practice, the limits of the unspoken and the implicit that create the possibility of misunderstanding, his or her legitimacy becomes impossible for the Occidental public, despite an ethnical or mestizo origin and the reputation possessed within the home community. As such, this marks the limit of possible misunderstanding: the blur and the polyphonic, which normally furthers useful misunderstandings, give way to undisputed divergences, which, in turn, lead to impossible agreements.

Conclusions

Multi-sited ethnography has shown that, no matter how different the speech and practices surrounding ayahuasca may be, this beverage seems to function as a ritual device capable of opening a relational field that allows people who were previously spatially separated to meet and interact in a common ritual frame while remaining culturally and socially distinct. This meeting stimulates a process of communication and exchange that rests on ritually framed mutual misunderstandings that create, time and time again, the perception of a mutual agreement, expressed in shared ritual action.

The three interaction settings show that it is precisely the existence of incomprehension regarding various aspects of the cultural patterns at stake that creates concatenated misunderstandings. These misunderstandings—fed by the obliteration, the unspoken, and the blurriness caused by synonymy effects, or, additionally, by the intervention of superhuman partners—are at the core of the mutual satisfaction of the communication partners and lead to the reproduction of ritual interaction.

The blur that enables a shifting between the categories of "spirits," "traumas," "psychic states," and "psychic entities" leads to a constant creation and redefinition of third-party partners who are available for interaction during the ritual sessions. These interactions always take place through the management of emotion, and this represents, once again, a communicational field where different cultural logics are at stake.

It is possible to demonstrate that, although "misunderstanding" as a communicational structure can be detected in most human interactions,[37] the intercultural encounter settings—hosting practices, objects, or discourses related to shamanic ayahuasca rituality—construct certain specific patterns of misunderstanding. These patterns all contribute to the *performativity of ritualized misunderstanding*, pertinent for the analysis of other modalities of intercultural encounter. In this sense, this text offers only a preliminary illustration of the utility of this approach.

We have argued that these three settings show how misunderstanding disperses onto various complementary registers. Starting from a cosmological misunderstanding between two types of uncertainty as preliminary conditions for the ritual encounter, we have shown that ritualization functions as a stabilizer for misunderstanding by opening up a number of expressive dimensions. First there is the emergence of a third-party interlocutor, who is superhuman and articulates both the agreement and the divergence. Second, the "psychologization of spirits," together with the "spiritualization of psycho-emotional states," creates the necessary blur that permits a successful communication and permeability between different logics.

The misunderstanding, shaped by this particular language, leads to two divergent representations of misfortune, of its causes and of its relations with the society of origin. This differential affiliation within the social network appears quite clearly in the local and foreign representation of what composes and supports shamanic legitimacy. Therefore, it stands as a point of rupture and as a limit of misunderstanding, pointing to impossible agreements.

This misunderstanding approach, based on ritualization and three-party communication, also considers that the actors may talk explicitly, outside the ritual space, about misunderstanding itself. Finally, this communication model is articulated to a particular treatment of otherness through Houseman's ritual refraction and its consequences to both the individual and collective emotional field.

We believe that a future challenge in the same direction of research and analysis would be to consider the implications of these ritualized misunderstanding patterns in the interpretation and communication of emotions between the users and the ritual leaders. Observing and addressing the emotional responses of the shaman to the Occidental ritual refraction could achieve this.

Notes

1. Marshall Sahlins, "The Apotheosis of Captain Cook," in Izard Michel and Smith Pierre, eds., *Between Belief and Transgression: Structuralist Essays in Religion, History and Myth* (Chicago: University of Chicago Press, Chicago Original, 1982): 73–102.
2. Christine Servais and Véronique Servais, "Le malentendu comme structure de la communication," *Questions de Communication* 15 (2009): 21–49.
3. Ibid., 21–49.
4. Sahlins, "The Apotheosis of Captain Cook," 73–102.
5. Most localities in Europe were linked to a middle-high-class population residing in the capital cities of Belgium, France, Holland, and Spain. As far as South America is concerned, following the shamanic label led to two main hot spots of the "shamanic"-ayahuasca rituality: Iquitos and Cusco (Peru). Nevertheless, the triple frontier of Northern Peru, Brazil, and Colombia, the Amazonian border zone between Peru and Ecuador, and capital cities such as Lima (Peru), Medellin (Colombia), and Buenos Aires (Argentina) have also permitted pertinent fieldwork.
6. Eliade Mircea, *Le Chamanisme et les techniques archaïques de l'extase* (Paris: Bibliothèque Historique Payot, 1951).
7. Harner, Michael, *The Way of the Shaman: A Guide to Power and Healing* (New York: Bantam New Age Books, Harper and Row, 1980).
8. See on this matter Esther Jean Langdon, preface to Beatriz Caiuby Labate and Sandra Goulart, eds., *O uso ritual das plantas de poder* (Campinas, Brazil: Mercado das Letras, 2005), 13–57; and Anne-Marie Losonczy and Silvia Mesturini Cappo, "Pourquoi l'ayahuasca? De l'internationalisation d'une pratique rituelle Amérindienne," *Archives des Sciences Sociales des Religions* 153 (2011): 207–28.
9. Beatriz Caiuby Labate, Isabel Santana de Rose, and Rafael Guimarães dos Santos, *Ayahuasca Religions: A Comprehensive Bibliography and Critical Essays* (Santa Cruz, CA: Multidisciplinary Association for Psychedelic Studies, 2009).
10. Silvia Mesturini, *Espaces chamaniques en movement: Itinéraires vécus et géographies multiples entre Europe et Amérique Latine,* (Ph.D. diss., Université Libre de Bruxelles, 2010).
11. Anne-Marie Losonczy and Silvia Mesturini Cappo, "La selva viajera: Etnografía de las rutas del chamanismo ayahuasquero entre Europa y América," *Religiâo e Sociedade* 30, no. 2 (2010): 164–83.
12. Peter Gow, "River People: Shamanism and History in Western Amazonia," in Nicholas Thomas and Caroline Humphrey, eds. *"Shamanism, History, and the State"* (Ann Arbor: University of Michigan Press, 1999).
13. Miguel N. Alexiades, ed., *Mobility and Migration in Indigenous Amazonia: Contemporary Ethnoecological Perspectives* (Oxford, UK: Berghahn Books, 2009).
14. Anne Marie Losonczy, "De l'énigme réciproque au co-savoir et au silence: Figures de la relation ethnographique," in *De l'ethnographie à l'anthropologie reflexive: Nouveaux terrains, nouvelles pratiques, nouveaux enjeux* (Paris: Armand Colin, 2002), 91–103.

15. Michael Taussig, *Shamanism, Colonialism and the Wild Man: A Study in Terror and Healing* (Chicago: University of Chicago Press, 1986).
16. Losonczy and Mesturini Cappo, "Pourquoi l'ayahuasca?" 207–28.
17. Gow, "River People."
18. Sahlins, "The Apotheosis of Captain Cook," 81.
19. Servais and Servais, "Le malentendu comme structure de la communication," 26–28, 38.
20. Catherine Coquio, "Du malentendu," in *Parler des camps, penser les génocides*, ed. Catherine Coquio (Paris: Albin Michel, 1999), 21–22, quoted by Servais and Servais, "Le malentendu comme structure de la communication," 21–49.
21. Franco La Cecla, quoted by Servais and Servais, "Le malentendu comme structure de la communication," 21–49.
22. Servais and Servais, "Le malentendu comme structure de la communication," 28.
23. Ibid., 38.
24. Michael Houseman, "Relationality," in Jens Kreinath, Jan Snoek, and Michael Stausberg, eds., *Theorizing Rituals: Issues, Topics, Approaches, Concepts* (Leiden, Netherlands: Brill, 2006), 413–28.
25. Michael Houseman and Carlo Severi, *Naven or the Other Self: A Relational Approach to Ritual Action* (Leiden: Brill, 1998).
26. Houseman, "Relationality," 413–28.
27. The consequences of what we may call a "mediated agency" of the "spirits" within this type of ritual will be the object of further investigation and analysis by the authors.
28. Katarzina Zajda, *L'analyse relationnelle des dialogues rituels entre les chamans Shuars (Amazonie équatorienne) et les néochamans occidentaux* (master's thesis, École Pratique des Hautes Études, 2011).
29. Losonczy, "De l'énigme réciproque au co-savoir et au silence," 91–103.
30. See on this matter Jean Pierre Chaumeil, "Le Huambisa défenseur: La figure de l'Indien dans le chamanisme populaire," *Recherches Amérindiennes au Québec* 23, no. 2–3 (1988): 115–26; and Anne-Marie Losonczy, *Viaje y violencia: La paradoja chamánica emberá* (Bogota: Universidad Externado de Colombia, 2006).
31. Patrick Deshayes, "L'ayawaska n'est pas un hallucinogène," *Psychotropes* 8, no.1 (2002): 65–78.
32. See on this matter Silvia Mesturini Cappo, "Espaces chamaniques en movement: Itinéraires vécus et géographies multiples entre Europe et Amérique Latine" (Ph.D. diss., Université Libre de Bruxelles, 2010); and Anne-Marie Losonczy and Silvia Mesturini Cappo, "Pourquoi l'ayahuasca? De l'internationalisation d'une pratique rituelle Amérindienne," *Archives des Sciences Sociales des Religions* 153 (2011): 207–28.
33. Anne-Marie Losonczy, "Cadrage rituel et improvisation: Le chamanisme embera du Choco (Colombie)," in *Essai sur le rituel II* (Louvain-Paris: Peters, EPHE, 1988).
34. Eduard Evan Evans-Pritchard, *Theories of Primitive Religion* (Oxford, UK: Oxford University Press, 1965).
35. See Shepard's Chapter 1 in this volume.
36. Michael Taussig, *Shamanism, Colonialism, and the Wild Man: A Study in Terror and* Healing (Chicago: University of Chicago Press, 1986).
37. Servais and Servais, "Le malentendu comme structure de la communication," 21–49.

Bibliography

Alexiades, Miguel N. ed. *Mobility and Migration in Indigenous Amazonia: Contemporary Ethnoecological Perspectives.* Oxford, UK: Berghahn Books, 2009.

Calavia Sáez, Oscar. "A Vine Network." In *The Internationalization of Ayahuasca*, edited by Beatriz C. Labate and Henrik Jungaberle, 131–50. Zurich: Lit Verlag, 2011.

Chaumeil, Jean-Pierre. "Le Huambisa défenseur: La figure de l'Indien dans le chamanisme populaire." *Recherches Amérindiennes au Québec* 23, no. 2–3 (1988): 115–26.

Chaumeil, Jean-Pierre. "Chasse aux idoles et philosophie du contact." In *Politique des esprits. chamanisme et religions universalistes,* edited by Denise Aigle, Bénédicte Brac de la Perrière, and Jean-Pierre Chaumeil, 151–64. Paris: Nanterre, Société d'Ethnologie, 2000.

Deshayes, Patrick. "L'ayawaska n'est pas un hallucinogène." *Psychotropes* 8, no. 1 (2002): 65–78.

Eliade, Mircea. *Le Chamanisme et les techniques archaïques de l'extase.* Paris: Bibliothèque Historique Payot, 1951.

Evans-Pritchard, Eduard Evan. *Theories of Primitive Religion.* Oxford, UK: Oxford University Press, 1965.

Gow, Peter. "Gringos and Wild Indians: Images of History in Western Amazonian Culture." *L'Homme* 33, no. 126–128 (1993): 327–47.

Gow, Peter. "River People: Shamanism and History in Western Amazonia." In *Shamanism, History, and the State,* edited by Nicholas Thomas and Caroline Humphrey, 90–114. Ann Arbor: University of Michigan Press, 1999.

Harner, Michael. *The Way of the Shaman: A Guide to Power and Healing.* New York: Bantam New Age Books, Harper and Row, 1980.

Houseman, Michael. "Relationality." In *Theorizing Rituals: Issues, Topics, Approaches, Concepts,* edited by Jens Kreinath, Jan Snoek, and Michael Stausberg, 413–28. Leiden, Netherlands: Brill, 2006.

Houseman, Michael, and Carlo Severi. *Naven or the Other Self: A Relational Approach to Ritual Action.* Leiden, Netherlands: Brill, 1998.

Labate, Beatriz Caiuby, Isabel Santana de Rose, and Rafael Guimarães dos Santos. *Ayahuasca Religions: A Comprehensive Bibliography and Critical Essays.* Santa Cruz, CA: MAPS, 2009.

Langdon, Ester Jean. Preface to *O uso ritual das plantas de poder,* edited by Beatriz Caiuby Labate and Sandra Goulart, 13–27. Campinas, Brazil: Mercado das Letras, 2005.

Losonczy, Anne-Marie. "Cadrage rituel et improvisation: Le chamanisme embera du Choco (Colombie)." In *Essai sur le rituel II, EPHE.* Louvain-Paris: Peters, 1988.

Losonczy, Anne-Marie. "De l'énigme réciproque au co-savoir et au silence: Figures de la relation ethnographique." In *De l'ethnographie à l'anthropologie reflexive: Nouveaux terrains, nouvelles pratiques, nouveaux enjeux,* 91–103. Paris: Armand Colin, 2002.

Losonczy, Anne-Marie. *Viaje y violencia: La paradoja chamánica emberá.* Bogota: Universidad Externado de Colombia, 2006.

Losonczy, Anne-Marie, and Silvia Mesturini Cappo. "La selva viajera: Etnografía de las rutas del chamanismo ayahuasquero entre Europa y América." *Religião e Sociedade* 30, no. 2 (2010): 164–83.

Losonczy, Anne-Marie, and Silvia Mesturini Cappo. "Pourquoi l'ayahuasca? De l'internationalisation d'une pratique rituelle Amérindienne." *Archives des Sciences Sociales des Religions* 153 (2011): 207–28.

Mesturini Cappo, Silvia. "Espaces chamaniques en movement: Itinéraires vécus et géographies multiples entre Europe et Amérique Latine." Ph.D. diss., Université Libre de Bruxelles, 2010.

Sahlins, Marshall. "The Apotheosis of Captain Cook." In *Between Belief and Transgression: Structuralist Essays in Religion, History and Myth,* edited by Michel Izard and Pierre Smith, 73–102. Chicago: University of Chicago Press, Chicago Original, 1982.

Servais, Christine, and Véronique Servais. "Le malentendu comme structure de la communication." *Questions de Communication* 15 (2009): 21–49.

Shepard, Glenn H., Jr. "A Sensory Ecology of Illness and Therapy in Two Amazonian Societies." *American Anthropologist* 106, no. 2 (2004): 252–66.

Taussig, Michael. *Shamanism, Colonialism and the Wild Man: A Study in Terror and Healing.* Chicago: University of Chicago Press, 1986.

Zajda Katarzina. *L'analyse relationnelle des dialogues rituels entre les chamans Shuars (Amazonie équatorienne) et les néochamans occidentaux.* Master's thesis, École Pratique des Hautes Études, 2011.

6

Shamans' Networks in Western Amazonia

The Iquitos-Nauta Road

FRANÇOISE BARBIRA FREEDMAN

In conjunction with ecotourism, the recent expansion of ayahuasca shamanism in western Amazonia, most particularly in Peru and Ecuador, has transnationalized shamanic practice in an unprecedented way. Since colonial times, a complex meshwork of ties has interlinked shamans from indigenous and mixed backgrounds, resulting in the syncretic popular medicine-cum-shamanism known as *vegetalismo* in Peru. Since the 1970s, however, the contours of shamanic practice in western Amazonia have become increasingly shaped by distant sponsors and clients in a process centered on the use of ayahuasca.[1]

Western Amazonian shamanism can best be comprehended through a model of polarities of power between upstream and downstream, uplands and lowlands, town and forest, indigenous and cosmopolitan Western (*gringo*). Relations of exteriority are primary. Outsiders, whether potential enemies turned trade partners or oppressors turned grateful clients, have always played an important role in the historical transformation of both the ideologies and the forms of shamanism. Yet a remarkable continuity in both ontology and praxis since pre-Hispanic times, in the Andes and in the Amazon region, also needs to be accounted for.

One aspect of Amazonian shamanism that has been little researched, due to the academic tradition of situated ethnographies and the analytic divide between indigenous and non-indigenous people in contact zones, is the extent to which shamans have traveled and continue to travel over long distances in the region to exchange and trade knowledge and to gain personal power. The social networks constituted during geographical travels that double as astral or out-of-body travels under the effect of psychotropic plants are crucial for activating the polarities of power that shamans operate with.

In this chapter, I look at a particular site in Peruvian Amazonia, the Iquitos-Nauta road, as a "transformer node" in the recent historical evolution of ayahuasca shamanism over the decade 2000–2010. As an artificial frontier, the road offers many possible analytical perspectives. With an interest in discussing the current reinvention of ayahuasca shamanism in a comparative perspective within Amazonia, I have selected two aspects: One is related to the continuities and discontinuities in the topology of shamanic encounters and "transformer nodes" in shamans' networks. The other aspect is concerned with the aesthetics of shamanism. Two emergent forms, the *maloca,* or round temple, and the shaman's ethnobotanical garden, underpin and enable the recent expansion of ayahuasca shamanism in western Amazonian regions of Peru and Ecuador.[2]

My interest is to document at a particular point in time, in the decade 2000–2010, an instance of the historical transformations and/or reinvention of shamanism in the region. In particular, I look at continuities and discontinuities in the topology of contact zones, where shamans interact intensely with outsiders as well as with one another.

The contact zone I am considering is the Iquitos-Nauta road, an anomalous 75 kilometer stretch of road between two Amazonian ports with no other road links. This is a showpiece of recent development policies, albeit one that exposes familiar contradictions in the region. Finally completed in 2004, after nearly a decade of roadworks that made it the most expensive road in the world per kilometer, the Iquitos-Nauta road exemplifies the gap between the rhetoric of colonization and sustainable exploitation of forest resources, on the one hand, and the reality of an extractive economy that depends on day laborers for commercial logging and on imports of cheap subsistence crops for growing urban markets on the other. Admittedly, the road saves long hours of navigation along two meanders of the Amazon River, and it links more effectively the eastern port of Iquitos with the port of Nauta, bypassing the older silted western port of Iquitos now occupied by the floating district of Belén. Beyond its pragmatic purposes, the road is also part of a centuries-old ambitious geopolitical plan of transcontinental connections that was first conceived of as railways and waterways.[3]

The traffic intensifies every year along the Iquitos-Nauta road. Incessantly, day and night, besides vans transporting people and produce, large Volvo trucks take timber out and bring in goods more cheaply than by air freight. Within a decade, the nonchalant outposts of earlier settlers attracted by abundant game have been hemmed in and then pushed back to the hinterland by the opening of cattle ranches, cane plantations, and colonization projects in the inevitable property boom that moved ahead with the tractors along the old hunting trail. The space of forward-looking negotiation, which brought together biodiversity conservation advocates, government officials, and development experts to conflate environmental, social, and economic agendas along the road at the turn of the millennium, did not include shamans. In the jamboree of colonization, however, the high density of shamans in Western Amazonia was rapidly replicated: In 2010

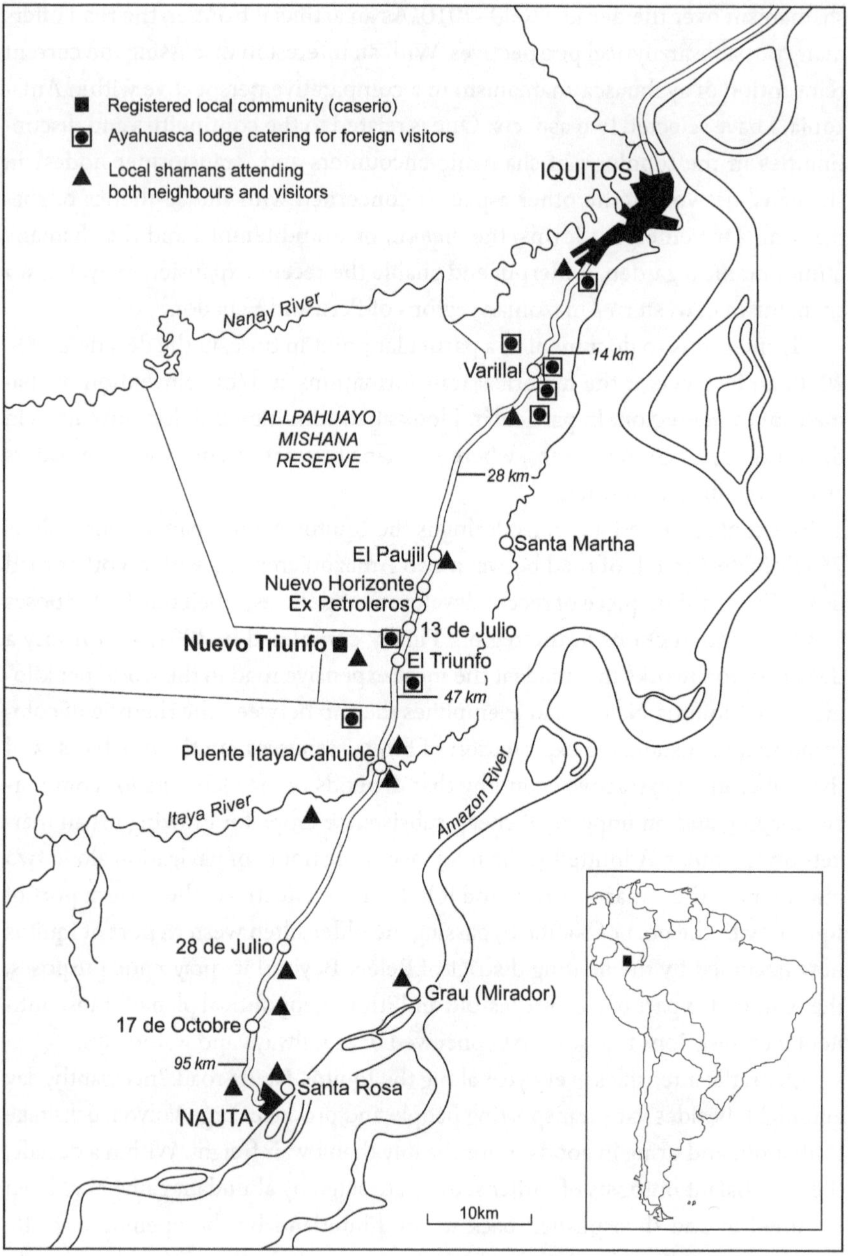

Figure 6.1. Shamans along the Iquitos-Nauta Road. Designed by Françoise Barbira Freedman with the help of the University of Cambridge Cartographic Unit.

there were twenty-eight self-identified shamans along the Iquitos-Nauta road, and possibly twice as many covert ones, with sites ranging from international centers on the roadside to small huts in the new colonies of the road hinterland.

As often in colonization stories in the New World, road shamans have reclaimed their role as primary interlocutors, mediators, and intercultural agents in relation to the "outside." Besides blazing its brutal trail of neocolonialism, the Iquitos-Nauta road also constitutes a "spherical frontier" on which shamans take it on themselves to articulate difference and sameness within the dynamics of globalization.[4] Their strategies of extensive networks could be plausibly analyzed within the historical dialectics of subversion and subaltern illusory resistance to external forces. Unlike the situation on which Taussig based his analysis in 1986, however, road shamans do not merely operate through symbolic inversions, but actively negotiate multilayered and multifaceted power bases in relation to one another through interactions with both local and international clienteles.

Like other shamans in western Amazonia, the shamans settled along the road "grow" their networks heterogeneously in the unplanned directions of their lives like rhizomes,[5] following opportunities and obstacles encountered. Totalities are not possible in these rhizomatic assemblages that always remain contingent and open-ended. Attempts at systematic ordering are made elusive as the effects of new interactions are felt along rhizomes in unpredictable ways that exclude any possible illusion of center and periphery the observer might have. In this flat ontology, subjective perspectives can be exchanged, and dimensions of the real and the imaginary collapse onto one another as the dream ancestor time collapses onto the present. The values that are negotiated along shamans' networks are invariably associated with indigeneity. Although the modus operandi of road shamans appears to be little different from that of ayahuasca sessions described in chronicles or by travelers, their main interlocution is no longer with Christianity or Medicine, but closer to home and more complex, with Western notions of "consciousness" and the fabric of the self as ambiguous and constantly recreated. As Walsh has argued, indigenous people—including mixed Amazonian forest people—operate within an overall relational and post-representational dynamic.[6] Consciously or not, shamans define themselves along the road as bordering between exotic Indians and real forest people, and between places of power in real time and in dream time; as a hub of local, national, and international associations; as a space for the exchange of knowledge and skills; and between local experiences and generalizing points of view.

How does the road, as a linear artificial artery that cuts strangely through the forest in aerial views, sit with shamans' agential arena as a landscape cosmically and historically determined by waterways? "The road," an artifact of development at the turn of the twenty-first century, conjures up other concentrations of shamanic activity in contact zones in the region. Like other logging roads elsewhere in the world, the Iquitos-Nauta road has resulted in "separating off- and on-road sites and creating obstacles between once-connected forest places," but it has also unexpectedly conjured up past connections.[7] Can ancient contact zones in the region throw light on the aggregation of road shamans?

Waterways and Portals

Shamans' networks in western Amazonia have been steeped in the history of colonization since the Hispanic conquest and even earlier. They can already be traced on the borderlands between pre-Inca chiefdoms and forest peoples. This is part of local collective memories as a set of intersecting pathways that are superimposed on one another in space and time and activated with reference to the acquisition and trade of shamanic knowledge. The Huallaga River, the second southern main tributary to the Marañon, as the Upper Amazon is known above Nauta, was the eastern boundary of the Inca Empire on the forested lower slopes of the Andes.[8] The Spanish military and missionaries followed the trails of the Incas and took over their trade posts. The discovery of burial sites, as well as archaeological evidence of long-distance trade in stone axes and later metal axes, shells from the Pacific coast, and forest slaves (Q. *shungo*)[9] point to a continuity of exchange linked with shamanism to this day (for instance, at the archaeological site of Chazuta).[10]

Huallaga shamans attribute special symbolic value to two categories of sites: the meeting of waterways (Q. *urmana*) and the river rapids in which the flow of water is restricted in a narrow passage that then opens out (Q. *pongo,* or door, gateway). The availability of natural resources such as rock salt to ensure supplies of salt fish, or plants for making strong poisons for arrows and fishing near one type of site or the other, reinforces a congruence of symbolic and economic trade that is not systematically documented historically but that shamans give importance to. The Pongo de Cainarachi and Pongo de Aguirre, on the Huallaga River, both abound in small stone axes. This is the point at which the river is about to enter the Amazonian floodplain, where stone is no longer available. Whetting stones and stone mortars are still important trade items with people who live in the lowlands. Renard-Casevitz describes the Pongo de Mainike as "the highest locus of shamanism and the meeting point of dreamlike or narcotic trips" among the Matsiguenka.[11] Throughout western Amazonia, anthropologists have collected information about long-distance trade networks that endured until recently. Trade partnerships between the Keshwa Lamas and the Shuar and curare trade from the Huallaga to the Canelos Quechua in Ecuador and to the Urarina involved annual trips over several hundred miles of rough terrain and the crossing of major rivers. Lakes, mostly those with outflows in rivers, and pongos (Pongo de Manseriche) served as meeting points documented in narratives of Keshwa Lamas shamans in the early 1980s as they followed these ancient trade routes to seek partners in trade and shamanism among less Christianized forest people on the "forest or wild" end of the ethnic continuum. Long-distance travel seems to have always combined walking along trails linking rivers across hinterlands and canoe navigation, as in the case of the Piro, who traveled from the Ucayali River to the Huallaga in annual trade expeditions.[12]

I was told that, no matter how the inner knowledge (Q. *yachay*) is acquired, once a shaman has it he or she needs to honor it by settling near a place with urmana, that is, a connection with the waterways. Through urmana, a Keshwa Lamas shaman who lives near a small tributary of the Huallaga River is connected with people and places throughout western Amazonia, and can travel to them in ayahuasca journeys. The distance of travels is an indication of his or her shamanic power ("I traveled down to or up to this place, no further"). Waterways include underground streams, water tunnels, and secret channels that join rivers, ox bow lakes, and the most valued hinterland lakes. One's relative position within the fluvial network becomes a metaphor for one's position relative to the generalizing degree of a particular polarity of power between upstream and downstream, forest and town. This geographical code gathered importance with steam navigation and river trade posts, but preceded them as an indication of convergence between local experience and more encompassing points of view with command over a wider set of relations.

Huallaga people negotiated the crossing of the Amazon River with Cocama people (Tupi) who were settled on both banks. Then, they continued on foot along the old trail to Iquitos that would later be retraced to plan the Iquitos-Nauta road. In contrast with meetings of waters and gateways that are dangerous but also powerful, open crossings and fords are considered as mere places of danger; they are not relational spaces where one can mediate, either physically or metaphorically, in time or space, between other spaces.

Urmana and pongo, as meeting points for exchange with long-distance "partners" who may be shamans, invite the questioning of relationships that differ from that with "potential affine" or "enemy," neither including nor excluding them. The widespread shamanic concept of hinge/bridge/bow, epitomized by the rainbow-anaconda, may serve to explore these relationships that bring together members of separate, distant, and disjointed social units. Rather than concentric circles from ego to arch enemies, rhizomatic networks cut across ethnic divides to create pathways that link normally separate domains and, in so doing, generate power that can be harnessed. People from differing language groups and culture areas within western Amazonia had—and possibly still have—common understandings of the powerful places where trade partners and shamans met. With an awareness of common and differentiated values attributed to animals and elements among group members and others with a shared animist outlook, shamans are able live with and in both "place" and network creatively.[13] Dynamic cosmic spaces for the meeting of different people within wide trade areas were also probably instrumental to the colonial social continuum linking pacified Indians (Q. *runa*) from rebel (pagan or wild) Indians (Q. *auka*) throughout the colonial period. In Taussig's words, "Underlying the accretion of added elements and transformations, something essential in the pre-colonial structure of ideas continues, not as a mere survival or relic from an irretrievable past but as an active force mediating history."[14]

The training trajectories I have collected from Upper Amazonian shamans since the 1980s show the extent and ease with which they travel afar in their formative years, combining trade in stones, coconuts, and water pots downstream, and sale of pelts and animal teeth to finance their trips back. Tales of distant travel traced patterns of long-standing paths of interaction: Lamista and Cocamas, both partners and rivals; Lamista and Candoshi/Shapra/Huambisa, partners and allies against Achuales (local ethnic categories); Lamista and Shipibo, for dangerous yet attractive trade related to love magic and sorcery. These ancestral patterns of interaction still hold along the Iquitos-Nauta road today.

Colonial and Post-Colonial Urban Melting Pots

Little is known about the early incidence of urban shamans of mixed blood that belonged to the local mestizo elite rather than to the social no-man's land between diacritically opposed "Indios" and "Mestizos-Blancos" of colonial missions and frontier outposts. Andean sources and narratives of urban shamans who attended clients with ayahuasca in the first half of the twentieth century indicate that the number of Mestizo shamans may have been underestimated. This poetic statement by Griffiths applies to the early colonized areas of the Amazon as much as to the colonial Andes: "The two religious systems were like two streams, constantly converging, intermingling and crisscrossing down to the present day without ever flowing into one large river; the elements of each system folding over one another incessantly until there was no part of one that had not been touched by the other."[15]

Quechua, the language of trade and colonization deliberately selected by the Spanish for colonial articulation with pacified Amazonian forest people, remains to this day the idiom of reference, if not usage, among urban ayahuasca shamans, even those originating from populations contacted after Quechua ceased to be dominant as a lingua franca in western Amazonia. A third generation of urban shamans who do not speak Quechua still sing Quechua *icaros,* spirit songs, during their ayahuasca ceremonies.[16] Although visitors to Lamas seek in vain powerful shamans such as those they have heard about in Iquitos, Pucallpa, or Madre de Dios, the Huallaga area (San Martín) continues to have a hold on popular imagination in the lowlands. Former mission sites, like Lagunas, and colonial towns like Jeberos and Balsapuerto are still held in collective memory as prestigious meeting points for translocal shamanic exchanges.

The idea that ayahuasca shamanism in western Amazonia was developed in missions and then made its way along rivers through patron-client ties of the "*habilitación*" debt system of the rubber boom is appealing, but only partly right.[17] Although the use of ayahuasca spread upstream among forest people who did not previously use it, or did not use it predominantly, in their shamanic practices,[18] the relative attribution of greater power to lowland shamans on the part of upstream forest people was tempered by enduring and significant translocal interactions between upland and lowland shamans. Throughout the twentieth century, the diacritical opposition between forest (with connotations of cosmos, wilderness, and indianity) and urban (with connotations of national political power and international political economy) sources of shamanic power became conflated in an idealized memory of the former colonial melting pots where mixed shamanism had emerged. In their quest for knowledge, shamans continued to travel back and forth between former and current contact zones, both in the Upper Amazon and in the Lowlands. Even if they did not personally travel, they integrated the travel experience of others in their shamanic practice in the form of learned incantations, imported plants, and novel practices.

Rapport between Amazonian shamans and the outsiders that have facilitated their networks since colonial times is mentioned in many sources, albeit in passing rather than as significant information. Whether they are truthful or confabulated, or both, the bio-narratives of shamans along the Iquitos-Nauta road reveal an experiential convergence of intimacy with gringos in the form of early education in mission schools or under local priests, patronage from influential foreign residents, work with foreign companies in a wide range of capacities,[19] and, recently, familiarity with foreign visitors interested in shamanism ("pasajeros," as they are called to distinguish them from mere "turistas").[20] This acquired intimacy, as a way to carefully evaluate the habitus of persons in order to engage in relations of seduction or predation with them, provides the basis for establishing shamans' networks that incorporate the power of archetypal outsiders. The frequent transmission of shamanic substances and skills along ties of kinship may also widen "trails" first opened by ancestors into common pathways for the extension of networks.

Traders in lesser towns of western Amazonia, particularly those who supplied rum or meat down the fertile Huallaga valley to the lowlands, traveled frequently to Iquitos and Nauta and were keen to develop social ties with foreigners. The Liverpool-Iquitos Booth line had a monthly service to Iquitos, and local elite families favored English nannies. Mixed marriages with gringos still convey social prestige. Models of social networks linking mestizo urban residents to gringos were therefore widely available in western Amazonia early in the twentieth century. Shamans applied these models to warrant their mobility in the margins of a postcolonial society that tolerated, but did not sanction, their activities.

Since the nineteenth century, and perhaps earlier, prestigious European doctors and spiritual leaders have figured among the tutelary spirits of western Amazonian urban shamans. The travels of road shamans such as Francisco Montes and Guillermo Arévalo to capital cities in America, Europe, and Asia manifest through actual personal networks the worldwide connections that shamans pursue in their ayahuasca visions: Pablo Amaringo, Francisco's cousin, included yogi masters from India in his paintings of Ayahuasca visions.[21] In popular Amazonian culture, gringos are the ultimate seducers, the appearance that dolphins or sirens take to lure forest people to the underwater realm, where they lose their human subjectivities. The gringos that are involved in road shamans' networks include mythical characters, historical figures with hero stature in religion or medicine, and also actual gringos who act as cultural agents. These mediators play a crucial role in linking the operational sphere of shamanism, in which perspectives can be exchanged and subjectivities appropriated, with local, national, and international Western associations catering to audiences receptive to the ideas and practice of Amazonian shamanism. The nonrelevance of scale fits shamanism well and differentiates it from missions and even NGOs, which articulate local and international connections within and outside Amazonia through frameworks in which scale is a main organizing principle. Amazonian shamans' lives, to an even greater extent than the lives of other Amazonians, point to experiences of miscegenation, and geographical and social mobility, that are obfuscated both in Western perceptions and in ethnographies.

Who Are the Road Shamans? The Road as Convergence of Local and Transnational Shamanism

Like its colonial antecedents, the Iquitos-Nauta road, as a transformative mixed-contact zone, suggests a continuity of convergence as well as displacement. The Iquitos-Nauta road is a site of convergence for local Huallaga shamans who migrated with the successive waves of colonists, and who continue to settle among them and cater to them. Other shamans chose this location preferentially for their purpose of incrementing their local-global networks on the basis of this convergence. Within the last decade, the road has brought a wide range of shamans together, including foreign neo-shamans, in a process that is gathering momentum of its own near Iquitos.

On the periphery of Iquitos and Nauta, urban mestizo shamans, with a variety of affiliations, had already opened forest sites along the trail to host ayahuasca ceremonies out of town and also to care for residential patients who required isolation in order to follow the shamanic diet (Q. *sasiku*). This pattern corresponds to widespread adoption of dual residences of a town, village, or riverine house, where social interaction is open, and a forest house, relatively protected from outsiders' intrusions in communities of western Amazonia. Shamans use their forest residential sites to maintain and renew their relationships in the spirit world. The urban shamans studied by Luis Eduardo Luna followed this pattern. After working with foreign companies in Iquitos, they offered consultations, for mixed urban clienteles spanning the social spectrum, at their town houses but held ayahuasca ceremonies out of town.[22]

Migrant colonists along the trail, and later in new communities off the road, reflect the local social continuum, from shamanizing activities of individuals in households or neighborhoods to publicly recognized shaman status. This status, either as "wounded healer" or following initiation, involves a temporary distancing from one's community and the activation of a personal network in shamanic practice. Most "local shamans" along the road serve co-residents in mixed communities where their ethnic origin is acknowledged: Quechua-speaking people or people holding identifiable Quechua names from the middle and lower Huallaga valley are mainly represented, together with Cocama and Cocamilla from the lower Huallaga. Road shamans, however, include most of the ethnic identities present in the past western Amazonian trading area (except for the Matsis, who migrated eastward). These local shamans have not cut their ties with their places of origin: they maintain active networks of kin and affines, eliciting ties as relevant to needs that can be pragmatic or symbolic. There is a constant coming and going of people visiting relatives along the road on their way to Iquitos or beyond; they visit shamans for treatment or training, and they pay their way with trade items. They bring plants and animals for exchange; they, and their hosts, share news and assess opportunities. This is consistent with the historical pattern of the urban-forest continuum in western Amazonia.

There is fluidity between categories as local shamans may access or create new identities and "international shamans" may lose their clientele through wrong actions and be demoted to marginal locality again (as has been the case with two shamans along the road).

Gilber Chufandama, like his Huallaga ancestors, was familiar with the old Iquitos-Nauta trail, and founded a pioneering local community in what was then, in the 1960s, a distant hunting territory with abundant game and roaming jaguars. He helped me draw up a list of road shamans in 2010. Settled off kilometer 47, halfway along the road, and with a command of the historical process, he was well placed to trace the spread of self-proclaimed road shamans. Of the twenty-eight

Figure 6.2. Don Gilber Chufandama displaying his shamanic outfit, which we won as a prize at the 2004 Iquitos city council's shamans' competition. Photograph by Stephen Hugh-Jones.

shamans listed as "curanderos legítimos" (true healing shamans, as opposed to covert sorcerers), he categorized twenty-four, including himself, as "curanderos nativos," indigenous shamans, in spite of the fact that two of them are gringos (U.S. nationals). In contrast, he saw Francisco Montes and Guillermo Arévalo, two shamans whose ethnic background is no more or less mixed than that of most of the other road shamans, as other, non-indigenous in the sense of nonlocal, catering mainly to an international, foreign clientele. Eight of the "local" road shamans had worked either for Montes or for Iquitos tourist operators who include ayahuasca sessions in their "jungle packages," before settling on their own along the road, usually with the help of a foreign mediator who supplied initial capital and access to clients, and two more gringo shamans were listed as outsiders.

Ayahuasca Tourism and Its Impact on Shamanic Practices

The increasing coupling of ecotourism and ayahuasca shamanism in what amounts to a mini economic boom in both the Peruvian and the Ecuadorian Amazon regions lies outside the scope of this chapter, yet it provides a backdrop to new standardized styles of shamanic performance among road shamans and more widely in western Amazonia. *The Yaje Letters*, published in 1963, served as a blueprint for "psychonauts" following in the footprints of American poets William Burroughs and Allen Ginsberg. The present-day commodification of ayahuasca ceremonies in jungle lodges makes little allowance for the contextualization of the plant-induced visions in terms of a western Amazonian shamanic cosmos. Amazonian river lodges, where tourists could "experience the jungle" or "contact the rainforest," were initiated in the 1960s, but did not reach their full development until the 1980s, when ayahuasca sessions were first offered routinely in tour packages. Circles of people attracted by forms of spirituality outside mainstream religions and by alternative paths to well-being outside of biomedicine are favored milieus for the recruitment of visitors to "ayahuasca retreats," as opposed to ad hoc ceremonies. Some of these visitors then became mediators who promote the shamans' activities in their countries and arrange tours to Iquitos as well as shamans' visits to their home countries. In 1999, after taking ayahuasca at Sacha Mama, the site of Francisco Montes off kilometer 18 of the road, the curator of the October Gallery in London invited him to London for a conference and exhibition. Exhibitions followed in Tokyo, and later, in 2003, Francisco and his wife were invited to contribute shamanic paintings of plant spirits to the Eden Project[23] in Cornwall.

Before the expansion of a mass market for ayahuasca shamanism in the late 1990s, shamans contracted to work in the jungle lodges designed by gringo entrepreneurs to welcome gringo tourists were in their majority non-indigenous, second-generation mestizo-trained, who nonetheless maintained strong links with shamans from the Huallaga and Ucayali rivers. Their initiation journeys, typically confabulations of real and imagined trips, all included some contact with remote tribal forest people constituting their "wild" pole of power.

Whether shamans who settled along the Iquitos-Nauta road were contracted to work in jungle lodges or not, they sought instrumental contacts with gringos that could help them access new, more encompassing poles of power from the point of view of their contact zone. Recent trends of shamans' invitations by foreign sponsors indicate the relation between these invitations and the changing global political economy that impinges on the lives of ordinary people in Amazonia. Though the United States and Europe are still primary destinations, Beijing, Sydney, and Moscow are now attracting shamans along the Iquitos-Nauta road. Guillermo Arévalo, who relocated his center of ayahuasca shamanism from Pucallpa to the road in 2003, has honored invitations from American and European universities. The respect he enjoys at the Peruvian Amazonian Research Institute singles him out among other road shamans. The divide between shamans who have been invited abroad and those who operate at the local level is one that all road shamans aspire to cross. Young shamans, mostly those from families of shamans, seek opportunities to work with prestigious shamans' international clienteles and to foster ties with them that will help consolidate their own power base. Access to an international network does not necessarily conflate with recognition as a powerful shaman, but it is one of several factors that may lead to recognition. The negotiation of appropriate fees and also of gender codes has been, and continues to be, the most delicate aspect of encounters between local shamans and their Western clienteles, resulting in a number of cultural misunderstandings and problems, including rape accusations.[24] Znamenski reviews the hazards of the "spiritual industry" around ayahuasca and the disenchantment of spiritual seekers turned foreign agents who are used as "geese supplying the golden nest eggs" for local shaman operators in the Iquitos area.[25]

Shamans' foreign agents are instrumental in the dual transmission of concepts and operating modes. Road shamans internalize and adapt imported notions within the popular cultural framework that sustains a shared culture of shamanism: understandings about illness, fortune and misfortune, intrusion of the spirit world into ordinary reality, and possibilities to act on these connections. All road shamans are also aware of new developments in the jungle lodges. To various extents, they strive to replicate the invented archetypal Indian forest spaces of the lodges on their sites, particularly if they have to learn to "act out" the exotic wisdom and guidance that their agents advertise.

Translations of visitors' expectations have resulted in the emergence of two "forms" of ayahuasca shamanism that became standardized over the last decade throughout western Amazonia in both Peru and Ecuador: the maloca and the "shaman's garden." Rather than the modalities of relationship with plant spirits and of healing agency, these new forms affect the performance aspect of shamanism. In contrast, the postcolonial reinvention of shamanism as vegetalismo did not target performance, but instead focused on the codification of shamanic plants used for healing purposes as opposed to sorcery, on diagnostic methods, and on distinctive medicinal preparations by differentiated categories of shamans.[26]

Emerging New Forms of Ayahuasca Shamanism

The Iquitos-Nauta road provides a living laboratory in which local shamans engage with their practice through the indexical and iconic features of ayahuasca shamanism developed in response to the global popularity of ayahuasca. The standardization of brews in response to outsiders' demands, the spread of round lodges or temples as sites for ayahuasca "ceremonies," and the expectation of shamans' gardens for plant display have emerged as salient features that all new shamans elaborate in their practice of ayahuasca shamanism.

The Brew

The urbanization of vegetalismo (mestizo urban shamanism in western Amazonia) consistently called for stronger ayahuasca brews that would have marked purging effects on consumers. More recently, in the face of increasing demand from lodges for brews that would guarantee effects without requiring that people follow the traditional dietary rules before and after sessions, more concentrated brews have apparently become the norm in urban settings. Tourists expect to have visions rather than purge. Until recently, each shaman had brews made up according to locally available plants, local traditions, and also methods learned from their trainings away with distant shamans. A large variety of *Psychotrias* and also other plant species were also used as Q. *chacruna,* or activators for ayahuasca, together with a variety of *Banisteriopsis* and *Brugmansia* species.[27] The recent trend for standardization of the brew has called for restricted use of plants that formerly individualized shamans' brews with their particular compositions and modes of preparation. *Psychotria viridis* has been the admixture plant of choice described by ethnobotanists for its high tryptamine content.[28] *Psychotria viridis,* however, does not thrive in flooded forest areas and needs to be imported to Iquitos from increasingly distant areas. Spiritual seekers' demands for beautiful visions have resulted in the further selection of Cielo ayahuasca (a particular variety of *Banisteriopsis*) for use in ceremonies held for international clientele, while the formerly frequent addition of *Brugmansias* has been reduced or eliminated.

Tobacco remains an essential tool of shamanic agency and the main companion plant used with ayahuasca, but its use has been muted with foreign participants in ceremonies; this is possibly due to negative associations with smoking as a health threat. However, there is a new trend, simultaneous with a resurgence in local production of tobacco, of returning to the traditional use of pipes that fell into disuse in the late twentieth century. The expansion of ayahuasca shamanism has stimulated renewed production of local Amazonian tobacco (*Nicotiana tabacum*) for shamanic activities in the particular form of cigars (Q. S. *mapachos*). Rolls of pipe tobacco (Q. S. *masos*) could not be found in Iquitos in the 1990s, but they are now commonly sold in local markets.[29]

After a period of reducing time in the preparation of ayahuasca brews to the point of using ready-made brews sold at the Iquitos market, new modes of preparation adhere to pseudo-"traditional" codes regarding the fire (even the wood used matters), the use of clay rather than metal pots, the blowing of tobacco smoke and chanting by the shaman to ensure healing efficacy, and strict gender codes excluding the participation of women from the procedures. Preparing ayahuasca is becoming an overtly ritualized process displayed for visitors, but both local shamans and cosmopolitan shamans alike may use brews that are not produced to these specifications if this is expedient for them. Road shamans may commission other shamans or local residents related to them—including women—to prepare brews if they need large quantities over consecutive days. The supply of component plants implies sustained ties with chains of reliable plant collectors and transporters over considerable distances from the road. The people involved in these supply chains are paid very little, but their possible role as cultural mediators is significant in shamans' networks that extend into hinterland areas.

In keeping with the continuity of shamanic trade described earlier, road shamans engage in personal expeditions for sourcing plants that increase their competitive edge as healers and also enable them to expand their connections with spirit allies in the cosmos. Chufandama was keen to recover the ancestor *Banisteriopsis* plant stem (Q. *mallki*) of his shaman grandfather from an abandoned site in the Huallaga. He also sent a nephew to collect a medicinal orchid known to him from a specific location on the Yavari River on the Peru-Brazil border. Montes contracted local collectors from all over western Amazonia to bring shamanic plants that he had studied in his youth and wanted to cultivate and use in his Sacha Mama site. Plant exchange is an important currency among shamans who wish to establish or consolidate partnerships, while plant theft signals enmity. Road shamans widely share the belief that plants sourced closer to "the wild" are more potent, but wilderness can be located either upstream or downstream.

In contrast with the new ayahuasca-based religions in Brazil, the spread of ayahuasca shamanism in western Amazonia has prompted not just renewed use of tobacco, but also a revitalization of shamanic plant medicine. The marketing and use of "master plants" associated with ayahuasca under the guidance of shamans toward the treatment of psychosomatic disorders and addictions is expanding. There is also a spread of "fusion shamanism," mixing ayahuasca with San Pedro cactus and hallucinogenic mushrooms. Following new trends started in the jungle lodges, shamans play down dietary restrictions but add ritual purifications to their ayahuasca ceremonies. Rather than innovations, these trends consist in gradual substitutions of imported products such as commercial cheap cologne (*agua florida*) and creosote (*creolina*) with "natural" colognes that are more pleasing to gringo tastes, or in additions such as flower baths (*baños de florecimiento*), now standardized among all shamans, and the less popular "nettle flogging" or purging.

Maloca

Vegetalismo moved ayahuasca shamanism away from the clandestinity of the previous colonial and early independence period into a more open social arena where it could be presented as popular medicine and popular religion. Many shamans of mixed blood operating in towns or in forest colonization areas made conspicuous use of crosses, Catholic icons, and stethoscopes and camphor to signal their legitimacy as bona fide healers. In dialectics of inversion such as those described by Taussig, the figure of the Indian redeemer healing colonizers was actually represented by mestizo shamans, with minimal indicators of indianity: bare torso, bare feet, and the use of leaf rattles and shamanic pipes. Around the 1950s, a few mestizo shamans in Iquitos started to refer to direct contact with "remote forest Indians" and to use more indigenous insignia, such as tooth necklaces and seed bandoliers. The renewed appeal to a putatively universal indigenous subjectivity in shamanism is rooted in the relation between shamanism and hunting that all western Amazonians, even urban mestizos, are aware of: breast bands, arm bands, and animal teeth are simultaneously talismans against threats of evil and public insignia of a hunter's courage and a shaman's power. Road shamans respect injunctions about respectful hunting and even more about the trading of bush meat, which is thought to bring forth cosmic retaliation. Although road shamans at the more indigenous end of the ethnic continuum are excellent hunters and have a vast knowledge of the forest that is beyond the reach of their mestizo or gringo fellow shamans, they do not seem to value or even reckon their advantage in claiming a positive indigenous identity.

The consumption of ayahuasca seems to have always been more or less ritualized in time depending on circumstances, from divinatory purposes in intimate shaman-patient interaction to collective ayahuasca sessions involving either therapy groups or shamans partaking in a common experience. The traditional locus of ayahuasca is a forest site, with a temporary shelter (S. Q. *tambo*) erected for protection from rain. This site is often specially selected in accordance with cosmic criteria personal to the shaman: a tree spirit ally; convergence between domains of water, earth, and sky; or the site of a vision. Road shamans who operate mostly with local clientele still use humble shelters or the raised wooden platform floors of their houses to hold ayahuasca sessions (S. *tomas*). Any shaman aspiring to a clientele of "visitors," in contrast, has adopted the implicit norm of an imagined generic indigenous round hut maloca, inspired from the large collective houses of Northern and Central Amazonia, for their ayahuasca "ceremonies." The ritualization of sessions as "ceremonies" has also prompted a secondary model of a rectangular temple (S. *templo*). Typical malocas are open or closed circular buildings with traditional woven palm roofs supported by hardwood posts. Individual mats or mattresses for participants to lie down on are a recent addition, since traditionally ayahuasca is taken in an upright position. Individual buckets to vomit in are also a recent substitution to communal pits dug outside.

Local Huallaga shamans still use a shaman's bag (Q. *shikra*), which has common features with hunters' bags, to keep their magic stones, charms, pipe,

Figure 6.3. Maloca for ayahuasca rituals. Photograph by Françoise Barbira Freedman.

cup, other personal objects of power, and perhaps a cloth to arrange them on, during ayahuasca sessions. Fixed "altars," however, now tend to replace ephemeral cloth displays in both templos and malocas. Ritual objects arranged in a symbolic order on these altars reproduce the shaman's mastery of the spirit world.[30]

Shamans officiating in malocas increasingly don borrowed "Indian" garb that mixes elements from contrasting cultural backgrounds. A common mix is a Shipibo tunic and a Shuar/Achuar feather crown, both of which can be purchased in tourists' markets. In 2004, Chufandama won the shamanic display and performance competition organized by the Iquitos city council with this costume, to which he added a large pipe and a Huallaga shaman's nut rattle. Some tourists request items that they have seen in DVDs about Amazonian shamanism. The use of musical instruments such as panpipes and three-string lutes besides the leaf rattle (Q. *shakapa*) to complement the whistling and chanting of shamanic songs (S. Q. *icaros*), both in ordinary voice and in falsetto overtones by western Amazonian shamans, is part of the recent ritualization of ayahuasca ceremonies everywhere in the world. Music is played before the onset of visions to help guide them. Incantations sung at the beginning of ayahuasca sessions to invite spirits, and assumed to be personal to each shaman, have also been adapted to suit the gentler, natural-harmony seeking of visitors.[31] Already in 1991, a shaman named Don Julio, in Tamshiyaku, near Iquitos, sang the same atypically Amazonian native incantation that Manuel Córdoba claimed to have learnt from Honi Xuma, the headman of the remote and legendary Amahuaca Indians who captured him as a young man. Did this spread as a favorite incantation for gringo consumption?

Shamans' Gardens

Keshwa Lamas shamans keep secluded areas of clearings where they tend the plants with which they have a cathectic connection for accessing vital spirits conceived of as plant mothers (Q. *mama*, S. *madre*). These spirits confer tutelary sources of protection and power to male shamans. Seclusion is required on account of the possible pollution and danger caused by contact with women, most particularly menstruating women or women after childbirth.[32] Shamanic plants are described as "jealous" and possessive. The proximity of spirit plants (S. *plantas con madre*) is of great importance to a shaman as he or she draws strength from them and identifies with them. Western Amazonian forest people have a continuum of house gardens, nearby gardens, distant gardens, previously abandoned gardens, and also forest areas such as swamps or high grounds in which they tend significant plants along a continuum from wild tending to semi-domestication. Shamans have the same continuum, but each of the plants that are nurtured has its place in a crisscrossing set of symbolic connections that potentiate individual shamanic agency.

Shamans' sites along the Iquitos-Nauta road nearly all include a conspicuous "shaman's garden," which has features of the traditional tending of personal power plants in combination with features of a "botanical garden," inspired from ecotourism and conservation projects. As a large or small area of cultivated shamanic plants around the maloca or temple, the "shaman's garden" is now part of the architecture of ayahuasca shamanism not only in Iquitos but also throughout western Amazonia. It would now be unthinkable for any shaman to install a new site without including a shaman's garden. Some shamans also have private small areas where they cultivate special power plants, or hide their power plants among other cultivated species, or keep a symbolic control over particular trees or clumps of palms, which may be secret or shared with people in their entourage.

Sacha Mama, the site of shaman Francisco Montes, has a large shaman's garden deliberately created to illustrate Pablo Amaringo's plant visions in a forest environment that was no longer easily accessible near the Peruvian Amazonian town of Pucallpa, where Pablo was based in the 1980s. Sacha Mama was created under the umbrella of the rainforest Conservation Alliance, with the intent to ensure the documentation and conservation of both plant species diversity and shamanic plant knowledge. Systematic collections of plant species were displayed with labels according to a Linnaean classification, rather than on the basis of local understandings. Other gardens vary in their organization of plants, but the Western botanical garden model has had a clear overall influence. Besides images of Western botanical gardens created in South America since the eighteenth century, the botanical garden developed by Jim Duke in his Napo river concession provides a concrete model for shamans' gardens. The shamanic garden of the Yakumamay forest reserve off kilometer 47, designed by Chufandama with initial input from Montes, but without any specific guidance about how to arrange the plants, displays a combination of Western categories (ideas about beds) with associations of plants on the basis of relatedness (families of plants), purpose (plants for treating misfortune or plants related to love magic), and pragmatic concerns about plant requirements for sun, shade, humidity, and soil qualities. Shamans' gardens, even as botanical gardens, continue to encode the strong color symbolism with which shamans operate (black, red, and white; red and black; red and white). Gender associations and hot-cold opposites, which may be pre-Hispanic, are also respected.

From their contact zone, road shamans are taking ownership of the image of Indian guardianship of the forest, in contrast to how past shamans owned the devil. Forest people who visit road shamans take back these new parameters of ayahuasca shamanism with them to their areas of residence. Following visits, they may be inspired to access relevant websites, which are increasingly available even in remote Amazonian locations. As part of a general concern with a re-Indianization of shamanism linked with forest conservation and ecology, the shamans aim, ironically, is to develop malocas and gardens that are more authentically close to the essentialized image of forest Indians that tourists have. Simultaneously in Peruvian and Ecuadorian Amazonia, since the millennium, new ecolodges doubling as shamans' sites are being developed by young indigenous entrepreneurs for an international clientele who seek direct contact with indigenous "guardians of the forest" and their knowledge, rather than with the urban mestizo shamans who, until recently, controlled ayahuasca shamanism in western Amazonia.[33]

Figure 6.4. "Road shaman" teaching his gringo partner/apprentice about plants in his newly planted shaman's garden. Photograph by Françoise Barbira Freedman.

Transformation or Reinvention?

In the seventeenth century, the postconquest subversive tactics of Amerindians involved a readjustment of concepts; Q. *hucha*, "disharmony," was equated with the Catholic notion of "sin," and shamans' spirits to this day are sometimes called devils (Q. "*llablonguna*" for S. "diablos"). This required a prior remobilization of native religion.[34] In western Amazonia, as well as in the Andes, this remobilization was effected through the healing, and, subsequently, the training, of Spanish patients by indigenous shamans in zones where ethnic interaction was most intense. During therapeutic encounters between healers and patients, and through the interpretation of patients' plant-induced dreams, visions, and multisensorial experiences, the ideas immanent in shamanism were actively elaborated and brought to the consciousness of non-Indians. In contradistinction to the folk healing of envy and social strife (S. Q. *envidia*) and personal harm (S. *daño*) among the mixed Hispanic, Andean, and Christianized Indians who colonized the wild forest people (Q. *auka*), shamans, both Indian and mestizo, taught local populations about encounters and symbolic exchanges between humans, animals, plants, and their animated essences. *Envidia* was mediated not just by the return of disease and lethal shamanic arrows (Q. *chonta*) to identified perpetrators but also through myths, narratives of journeys into the cosmos to retrieve souls, and ideas of personal power that are anathema to Christians involving transfers of substance and osmosis with inanimate natural elements. Animistic concepts central to shamanism made practice precarious even for shamans as famous as Manuel Córdoba, who was called to heal regional and national dignitaries in the first half of the twentieth century. To this day, no road shaman, even those with millionaire gringo sponsors, has become rich. Not only are shamans' lives threatened, but all shamans need to show their local communities tangible signs of their beneficence and redistribute gains instantly.

The most contested aspect of shamanism, the ambivalent agency of good and evil that it implies, has been superficially suppressed in the ayahuasca shamanism developed for international clientele. This is perhaps the most questionable and intractable feature that has come to the fore in this process; one that may invite future comparisons with developments of shamanism in other parts of Amazonia.[35] In the treatment of gringos, *daño* (pathology) is now removed from bodies as a manifestation of generalized harm rather malevolent agency.

The social recognition of shamanism as a beneficial cultural resource to be promoted rather than kept underground has been manifested in unprecedented ways in main Amazonian towns since the turn of the millennium. In Iquitos, the Catholic Church opened its doors to gatherings of shamans, promoting an ontological dialogue in the face of radical rejection by Evangelical Churches; the Peruvian Amazonian research institute organized colloquia for the discussion of shamanic knowledge and seminars for "training" local shamans in ecology. The Iquitos office of tourism displays posters of "chamanes." The multifaceted activities of shamans as naturopaths, owners of ecological knowledge, and ritual performers allow sufficient ambiguity for other, less acceptable aspects of shamanic ontologies and epistemologies to be temporarily discarded in sanitized and exotic idealized representations. Znamenski sees neo-shamanism as corresponding to the aesthetics of non-Judeo-Christian "nature spiritualities."[36] Western Amazonian shamans signal their alignment with this interpretation by the use of the term *chamán* (rather than "curandero" or "vegetalista") at the antipode of the negative label *brujo* (sorcerer) that is still used locally to refer pejoratively to shamans in popular parlance. In the words of Hamilton Souther, a gringo shaman who manages a road site with two mestizo shaman partners (kilometer 52), "Universal Shamanism no longer focuses on, or even recognizes, duality. It is based in universal philosophy and uses the traditional shamanic practices like the ayahuasca ceremony as a way of training in the philosophy.... The spirits are no longer considered to be separate from the participant but rather part of the wholeness of the participant. There is no philosophical separation and no opposites, no opposing forces. Life is experienced as a great singular manifestation."[37]

The muting of sorcery accusations and retaliations (S. *venganzas*) in transnational ayahuasca shamanism is strongly resisted in local shamanic practice. Most afflictions are attributed to malevolent agents (Q. S. *brujos, maleros*) or subjectivized elements in the cosmos. Along the Iquitos-Nauta road, or even in jungle lodges, shamans are always preoccupied with protecting themselves from enemies virtual and actual, direct and indirect. The classic feuds, vendettas, and rife that characterize shamanism throughout western Amazonia are visible along the road in spectacular attacks: various attempts to gun down Francisco Montes and rumors that Norma Panduro, the only cosmopolitan female road shaman, was murdered during an ayahuasca ceremony in 2008 stand out as dramatic events, but tales of sorcery-induced accidents or pathologies are frequent along the road. The agents who mediate between shamans and their foreign clientele are well aware of, if not involved in, the contradictions between local "shamans' wars" and the idealized understandings of spiritual seekers.

Given that the ambivalence of shamanic practice has not been erased, or may even have been exacerbated by superficial idealized representations,[38] the transformative impact of the emergent forms of ayahuasca shamanism can be questioned. Western Amazonian shamans who profess to be exclusively healers are inevitably labeling themselves as low-grade, incomplete shamans vulnerable to malevolent attackers. To be a strong shaman (Q. *sinchiruna, sinchiyachak*) is to have a double-edged knowledge and ability to heal and harm others.

Recent shared narratives (blogs, articles about personal experiences) articulate Western visitors' encounters with the dark side of western Amazonian shamanism in ways that promote acceptance and understanding of the dilemmas involved. Steve Beyer's account of the death of his female shaman teacher from a sorcery attack in a jungle lodge near Iquitos in 2008 is particularly moving. Some gringo shamans seek to help visitors to demystify shamanic practice. In 1997, Alan Shoemaker offered his "Lessons in Mestizo Shamanism" to this purpose. Once visitors start receiving "substance" from Amazonian shamans in the form of chants, spells, body seals, knowledge, phlegm, and ingested animal spirits, they enter the shamans' extended networks that confer power to shamans in their agential arena. The necessary involvement of apprentices in the mesh of alliances and enmities of teacher shamans, both in mundane day-to-day living and in the cosmos, explains how gringos can be classified as "native shamans."

For Western visitors, ayahuasca ceremonies articulate the role of experience, feelings, intuition, and embodied knowledge through questioning generally held assumptions about perception, reality, and self-identity. The new forms of ayahuasca shamanism sit with perceptions of Eden or jungle hell. Its objects are evocative and open-ended.[39] Whether visitors are already familiar with mind-altering substances or not, reports concur to describe ayahuasca experiences as making their current personal concerns present to their awareness in ways that they can neither easily dismiss nor explain rationally. As keen observers, western Amazonian shamans working with international clienteles seek to identify and address observed cultural patterns of affliction, both national and international, that are expressed during their ayahuasca ceremonies.[40]

International demand for ecology-conscious, authentically Amerindian shamans that meet exemplary criteria for moral virtue has prompted a renegotiation of the staging of encounters between shamans and their foreign clients. Road shamans are well aware that their international clientele has an exoticized view of shamanism and perceive them as "Indian," even though most are clearly of mixed race. Along the Iquitos-Nauta road, all shamans, from the most local to the most cosmopolitan, are constantly engaging with indigeneity, whether they have carefully constructed an image in the course of their shamanic career or are unsure of proclaiming an indigenous identity that is still stigmatized in their area of origin. Along the road, the "curanderos nativos legítimos," true native shamans, are now expressing their indigeneity as a performed identity not devoid of irony and self-irony about being really Indian but putting on an act as fantasized Indian shamans.

Young local shaman entrepreneurs who are developing their websites and who own mobile phones are able to communicate directly with "friends" in Europe, America, and now also in China to organize tours and ayahuasca sessions (which may be illegal). Pristine images of their environment, their local communities, and themselves are part of a carefully developed essentialized construct that some have actually embraced as a lifestyle with a refined aesthetic sense, excluding symbols of artificial wild indianity, Christian iconography, or wise doctor spirits. The forest, its spirits, and the symbols they provide are the only alleged sources of power with reference to their distant urban clients in other continents, in a quasi-perfect extended polarity that bypasses former networks mediated by urban shamans.

Conclusion

My intention has been to draw more attention to the relatively scant attention given to shamans' networks and the multidimensional communications they imply for creating a culture of shamanism in western Amazonia. In a cosmos where geography, history, and myths intertwine and overlap, road shamans mediate the social contradictions of colonization in continuity with past contact zones in the region. Their alliances with outsiders play a major transformative role. Shamans who have aggregated along the Iquitos-Nauta road use their networks to mediate across and between the analytical divides that partition local and global, past and present, materiality and meaning making, affect and rationality, human and nonhuman. Their resistance is not a social or political one, but a subversive exposure of entanglements and the personal dramas associated with them.

Originally presented as a new arena of social relations that aimed to mitigate difference and inequality, the Iquitos-Nauta road negated conjunctural assemblages of cosmic and historical relations among people and between people and the forest. In the margins of the politics of colonization and market forces and in response to them, however, the "road shamans," individually and together, have activated these assemblages creatively. Engaging, or at times grappling, with changing perceptions of indigeneity in Amazonia and elsewhere in South America, western Amazonian healer-sorcerers have become Q. S "chamanes," a new category of shamans that distances them from vegetalismo. To them, this term displaces their agency from the colonial and postcolonial inverted dialectics of folk healing to a global arena of shamanic culture. In this arena, they continue to operate through polarities of power that imply connections with both urban and forest poles. These relationships are still established through actual networks that are developed individually and contingently, albeit with distinctive local patterns, as rhizomatic pathways during shamans' lives.

As different assemblages of shamanic practice coalesce in time, with their distinctive icons and codes that both adjust to and resist the totalizing visions imposed at any one time, none of them ever completely displaces another. Each new assemblage is actualized within an evolving, yet perennial, mixed Amazonian popular culture that resonates with and supports shared perceptions of the cosmos, of an etiology of illness rooted in subjective malevolence, and of curing practices involving diagnosis based on plant-induced visions and dreams. Looking at shamans' networks as both individual and collective cultural devices to increase differentials of (illusory) power between historically determined polarities can highlight the importance of mobility and exchange in an enduring dynamic process of transformation of shamanism. Rainbows, fault lines, or gringos turned local shamans invite a focus shift from categorical opposites to mediation and to the historical contours of perspectival agency.

Notes

1. For the purpose of this chapter, I assume that readers are familiar with ayahuasca.
2. This argument was developed with Stephen Hugh-Jones in conversations over many years and particularly during our joint fieldwork along the Iquitos-Nauta road in 2004. I am very grateful to Stephen not only for supporting my interest in the mobility of shamans across all borders but also for making the emergence of cultural forms more visible to me when we traveled to the Huallaga river.
3. Fernando Santos Granero and Federica Barclay, *Tamed Frontiers: Economy, Society and Civil Rights in Upper Amazonia* (Boulder, CO: Westview Press, 2000).

4. Arturo Escobar, *Territories of Difference: Place, Movements, Life, Redes* (Durham, NC: Duke University Press, 2008).
5. Gilles Deleuze and Félix Guattari, *A Thousand Plateaus* (Minneapolis: University of Minnesota Press, 1987).
6. Catherine Walsh, "Shifting the Geopolitics of Critical Knowledge: Decolonial Thought and Cultural Studies of 'Others' in the Andes," *Cultural Studies* 21, nos. 2–3 (2007): 224–30.
7. See Manuel De Landa, *A Thousand Years of Non-Linear History* (New York: Zone Books, 1997); and Anna Lowenhaupt Tsing, *Friction: An Ethnography of Global Connection* (Princeton: Princeton University Press, 2005).
8. When Ursúa and Aguirre led their 1560 expedition from Lamas down to the mouth of the Putumayo River, this route was already known to the natives of Lamas. In 1806, Father Bousquet led his expedition from the Urubamba to the Ucayali via the Huallaga and Cainarachi rivers. In 1851 Herndon confirmed Maw's 1827 report that there was only one settlement on the right bank of the Huallaga; this was due to the fear of the infidel savages living on that side. See Henry Lister Maw, *Journal of a Passage from the Pacific to the Atlantic: Crossing the Andes in the Northern Provinces of Peru, and Descending the River Marañon or Amazon* (London: J. Murray, 1829); William Lewis Herndon, *Exploration of the Valley of the Amazon:* 1851–1852, edited and with a foreword by Gary Kinder (New York: Grove Press, 2000 [1854]); and Christopher Sandeman, *Forgotten River: A Book of Peruvian Travel and Botanical Notes* (London: Oxford University Press, 1939), 99–105.
9. In this text I index Quechua idioms widely used in western Amazonia with reference to shamanism with the prefix *Q* and Spanish terms with the prefix *S*. I signal Spanish imports in the Amazonian Quechua dialects with the prefix *S. Q.*
10. Donald Lathrap, *The Upper Amazon* (London: Thames & Hudson, 1970), and recent excavations in Chazuta.
11. France-Marie Renard-Casevitz, "Guerriers du sel, sauniers de la paix," *L'Homme* 33 (1993): 2–4. See also Manuela Carneiro da Cunha, "Pontos de vista sobre a floresta amazônica: Xamanismo e tradução," *Mana* 4, no. 1 (1998): 7–22.
12. For trade relations between the Kechwa Lamas and the Shuar, see Philippe Descola, *In the Society of Nature: A Native Ecology in Amazonia* (Cambridge: Cambridge University Press, 1994); between the Kechwa Lamas and the Canelos Quechua, see Françoise Barbira Freedman (Scazzocchio), "Curare Kills, Cures and Binds: Change and Persistence of Indian Trade in Response to the Contact Situation in North-Western Montaña," *Cambridge Anthropology* 4, no. 3 (1978): 30–57, and Norman Whitten, *Sacha Runa: Ethnicity and Adaptation of Ecuadorian Jungle Quichua* (Urbana: University of Illinois Press, 1976); between the Kechwa Lamas and the Urarina, see Bartholomew Dean, *Urarina Society: Cosmology and History in Peruvian Amazonia* (Gainesville: University Press of Florida, 2009). For annual trade expeditions by people living along the Ucayali River to the Huallaga River, see Alejandro Camino, "Trueque, correrías e intercambios entre los Quechuas Andinos y los Piro y Machiguenga de la Montaña Peruana," *Amazonia Peruana* 1, no. 2 (1977): 123–42; and T. P. Myers, "Redes de intercambio tempranas en la Hoya Amazónica," *Amazonia Peruana* 4, no. 8 (1983): 61–76.
13. Escobar, *Territories of Difference*, 208.
14. Michael Taussig, *Shamanism, Colonialism and the Wild Man: A Study in Terror and Healing* (Chicago: University of Chicago Press, 1986), 221–36.
15. Nicholas Griffiths, *The Cross and the Serpent: Religious Repression and Resurgence in Colonial Peru* (Norman: University of Oklahoma Press, 1996), 19.
16. See Stephan V. Beyer, *Singing to the Plants: A Guide to Mestizo Shamanism in the Upper Amazon* (Albuquerque: University of New Mexico Press, 2010).
17. Peter Gow, "River People: Shamanism and History in Western Amazonia," in Nicholas Thomas and Caroline Humphrey, eds., *Shamanism, History and the State* (Ann Arbor: University of Michigan Press, 1994).
18. See Shepard's Chapter 1 in this volume.

19. Native shamans' widespread experience of schools or mission schools is exemplified by the Shuar shaman Tsakimp: he went to Salesian school, trained as a carpenter in the Andean region, and then worked in the lab of a North American scientist working with medicinal plants. Steven Rubenstein, *Alejandro Tsakimp: A Shuar Healer in the Margins of History* (Lincoln: University of Nebraska Press, 2002), pp. 103–9.
20. "Pasajero," the Spanish term for passenger, is mostly familiar to Amazonian people from plane travel when they are addressed as "señores pasajeros"; its current common use to denote foreign visitors who attend ayahuasca ceremonies in the Iquitos area may originate from the fact that they were picked up from the airport to be taken to lodges, with a possible connotation of shamanic travel for vision seeking.
21. Luis Eduardo Luna, *Ayahuasca Visions: The Religious Iconography of a Peruvian Shaman* (Berkeley, CA: North Atlantic Books, 1993).
22. Luis Eduardo Luna, *Vegetalismo: Shamanism Among the Mestizo Population of the Peruvian Amazon; Stockholm Studies in Comparative Religion 22* (Stockholm: Almqvist & Wiksell, 1986).
23. The Eden Project, set up in 2001, is an innovative educational nonprofit organization based in Cornwall that includes Rainforest and Mediterranean Biomes.
24. See Peluso's Chapter 10 in this volume.
25. Andrei A. Znamenski, *Beauty of the Primitive: Shamanism and the Western Imagination* (New York: Oxford University Press, 2007), 155–64.
26. The previous colonial reinvention, which is not easy to trace in the absence of written sources, appears to have revolved around the enduring distinction between shamanic preparations that were boiled in water and those macerated in alcohol after sugar cane cultivation and mills were introduced in Amazonia.
27. J. C. Callaway et al., "Various Alkaloid Profiles in Decoctions of *Banisteriopsis caapi*," *Journal of Psychoactive Drugs* 37, no. 2 (2005): 151–55.
28. Richard Evans Schultes and Robert F Raffauf, *Vine of the Soul: Medicine Men, Their Plants and Rituals in the Colombian Amazonia* (Oracle, AZ: Synergetic Press 1992).
29. In 2000, shamans in Iquitos had to send for tobacco from distant local producers known to them. In 2004, one small stall in the Iquitos market offered hand-rolled cigarettes of home-grown tobacco for shamanic use. In 2010, tobacco stalls occupied a dedicated area in the market and some offered tobacco rolls made in the traditional style.
30. The new Amazonian shamanic altars may have a relation to the North Andean Altars, but their symbolic displays are not described in terms of Manichaeism and the struggle of good against evil. For North Andean shamanic altars, see Douglas Sharon, *Wizard of the Four Winds: A Shaman's Story* (New York: Free Press, 1978).
31. For an influential example of new musical styles in ayahuasca ceremonies, see Jaya Bear, *Amazon Magic: The Life Story of Ayahuasquero and Shaman Don Agustin Rivas Vasquez* (Taos, NM: Calibri, 2000).
32. On this point see Françoise Barbira Freedman, "Shamanic Plants and Gender in the Peruvian Upper Amazon," in Elizabeth Hsu and Stephen Harris, eds., *Plants, Health and Healing: On the Interface Between Ethnobotany and Medical Anthropology* (New York: Berghahn Books, 2010).
33. See Znamenski, *Beauty of the Primitive*, note 40, for reports exposing questionable and disingenuous objectives of local operators. A Peruvian Andean shaman with a Ph.D. in medical anthropology from Berkeley, Alberto Villoldo, was offering Western spiritual seekers a "rebirthing" as "the new caretakers and healers of the earth" at a cost of $30,000 for a three-week tour of sacred sites including an Amazonian lodge near Iquitos. But, as Furst pointed out long ago, what's wrong with exploiting Western romance with shamanism and tribal spirituality?
34. In the colonial period, his (the curandero's) ability to both accept and design and effect changes in the categories of the sacred conferred a dynamic flexibility on the native religious system. See Griffiths, *The Cross and the Serpent*, 200–201, 247, 265–66.

35. See Françoise Barbira Freedman, "The Jaguar Who Would Not Say Her Prayers: Changing Polarities in Upper Amazon Shamanism," in Luis Eduardo Luna and Steven F. White, eds., *Ayahuasca Reader: Encounters with the Amazon's Sacred Vine* (Santa Fe, NM: Synergetic Press, 2000); Michael F. Brown, "Dark Side of the Shaman: The Traditional Healer's Art Has Its Perils," *Natural History* 98 (1989): 8–10; Michael F. Brown, Michael F. "Beyond Resistance: Comparative Study of Utopian Renewal in Amazonia," in Anna Curtenius Roosevelt, ed., *Amazonian Indians from Prehistory to the Present: Anthropological Perspectives* (Tucson: University of Arizona Press, 1994), 287–311; and Neil L. Whitehead, *Dark Shamans: Kanaima and the Poetics of Violent Death* (Durham, NC: Duke University Press, 2002).
36. Znamenski, *Beauty of the Primitive*, 368–70.
37. Blue Morpho Shamanic Center and Jungle Lodge, at kilometer 53 along the Iquitos-Nauta Road; <http://www.bluemorphotours.com> (Accessed August 26, 2011).
38. Jungle lodges, cosmopolitan shamanic sites, and healing centers in western Amazonia may have unexpectedly stimulated conflicts associated with the positioning of local shamans in relation to outsiders.
39. For a perceptive analysis of evocative objects, see Marilyn Strathern, "Entangled Objects: Detached Metaphors," *Social Analysis* 34 (1993): 88–98.
40. A discussion of these identified patterns lies outside the scope of this chapter, but personal problems that road shamans perceive as afflicting Western visitors from various nations are related to the use of drugs, self-blame, depression, and failed relationships with parents and sexual partners.

Bibliography

Arévalo, Guillermo V. "El ayahuasca y el curandero Shipibo-Conibo del Ucayali, Perú." *America Indígena* 46, no. 1 (1986):147–61.

Barbira Freedman, Françoise (Scazzocchio). "Curare Kills, Cures and Binds: Change and Persistence of Indian Trade in Response to the Contact Situation in North-Western Montaña." *Cambridge Anthropology* 4, no. 3 (1978): 30–57.

Barbira Freedman, Françoise. "The Jaguar Who Would Not Say Her Prayers: Changing Polarities in Upper Amazon Shamanism." In *Ayahuasca Reader: Encounters with the Amazon's Sacred Vine,* edited by Luis Eduardo Luna and Steven F. White. Santa Fe, NM: Synergetic Press, 2000.

Barbira Freedman, Françoise. "Tobacco and Curing Agency in Western Amazonian Shamanism." In *New Advances in Archaeology*, edited by P. A. Baker and G. Carr, 136–60. Oxford: Oxbow Books, 2002.

Barbira Freedman, Françoise. "Shamanic Plants and Gender in the Peruvian Upper Amazon." In *Plants, Health and Healing: On the Interface Between Ethnobotany and Medical Anthropology,* edited by Elizabeth Hsu and Stephen Harris. New York: Berghahn Books, 2010.

Bear, Jaya. *Amazon Magic: The Life Story of Ayahuasquero and Shaman Don Agustin Rivas Vasquez.* Taos, NM: Calibri, 2000.

Beyer, Stephan V. *Singing to the Plants: A Guide to Mestizo Shamanism in the Upper Amazon*. Albuquerque: University of New Mexico Press, 2010.

Blue Morpho Tours. <http://www.bluemorphotours.com> (accessed Aug. 26, 2011).

Brown, Michael F. "Dark Side of the Shaman: The Traditional Healer's Art Has Its Perils." *Natural History* 98 (1989): 8–10.

Brown, Michael F. "Beyond Resistance: Comparative Study of Utopian Renewal in Amazonia." In *Amazonian Indians from Prehistory to the Present: Anthropological Perspectives,* edited by Anna Curtenius Roosevelt, 287–311. Tucson: University of Arizona Press, 1994.

Burroughs, William, and Allen Ginsberg. *The Yage Letters: Redux.* Edited and with an introduction by Oliver C. G. Harris. San Francisco: City Lights Books, 2006 (1963).

Callaway, J. C. "Various Alkaloid Profiles in Decoctions of *Banisteriopsis caapi*." *Journal of Psychoactive Drugs* 37, no. 2 (2005): 151–55.
Callaway, J. C., Brito, G. S., and Neves, E. S. "Phytochemical Analyses of *Banisteriopsis caapi* and *Psychotria viridis*." *Journal of Psychoactive Drugs* 37, no. 2 (2005): 147–50.
Camino, Alejandro. "Trueque, correrías e intercambios entre los Quechuas Andinos y los Piro y Machiguenga de la Montaña Peruana." *Amazonia Peruana* 1, no. 2 (1977): 123–42.
Carneiro da Cunha, Manuela. "Pontos de vista sobre a floresta amazônica: Xamanismo e tradução." *Mana* 4, no. 1 (1998): 7–22.
Csordas, Thomas. *Body/Meaning/Healing*. Hampshire, UK: Palgrave Macmillan, 2002.
De Landa, Manuel. *A Thousand Years of Non-Linear History*. New York: Zone Books, 1997.
Dean, Bartholomew. *Urarina Society: Cosmology and History in Peruvian Amazonia*. Gainesville: University Press of Florida, 2009.
Deleuze, Gilles, and Félix Guattari. *A Thousand Plateaus*. Minneapolis: University of Minnesota Press, 1987.
Descola, Philippe. *In the Society of Nature: A Native Ecology in Amazonia*. Cambridge: Cambridge University Press, 1994.
Edwards, Jeanette, Penelope Harvey, and Peter Wade, eds. *Anthropology and Science: Epistemologies in Practice*. Oxford: Berg, 2007.
Escobar, Arturo. *Territories of Difference: Place, Movements, Life, Redes*. Durham, NC: Duke University Press, 2008.
Fausto, Carlos, and Michael Heckenberger, eds. *Time and Memory in Indigenous Amazonia: Anthropological Perspectives*. Gainesville: University Press of Florida, 2007.
Gow, Peter. *Of Mixed Blood: Kinship and History in Peruvian Amazonia*. Oxford: Clarendon Press, 1991.
Gow, Peter. "River People: Shamanism and History in Western Amazonia." In *Shamanism, History and the State*, edited by Caroline Humphrey and Nick Thomas. Ann Arbor: University of Michigan Press, 1994.
Gow, Peter. *Amazonian Myth and its History*. Oxford: Oxford University Press, 2001.
Griffiths, Nicholas. *The Cross and the Serpent: Religious Repression and Resurgence in Colonial Peru*. Norman: University of Oklahoma Press, 1996.
Herndon, William Lewis. *Exploration of the Valley of the Amazon:* 1851–1852. Edited and with a foreword by Gary Kinder. New York: Grove Press, 2000 (1854).
Lathrap, Donald W. *The Upper Amazon*. London: Thames & Hudson, 1970.
Luna, Luis Eduardo. *Vegetalismo: Shamanism Among the Mestizo Population of the Peruvian Amazon. Stockholm Studies in Comparative Religion* 22. Stockholm: Almqvist & Wiksell, 1986.
Luna, Luis Eduardo. *Ayahuasca Visions: The Religious Iconography of a Peruvian Shaman*. Berkeley, CA: North Atlantic Books, 1993.
Luna, Luis Eduardo, and Stephen F. White, eds. *Ayahuasca Reader: Encounters with the Amazon's Sacred Vine*. Santa Fe, NM: Synergetic Press, 2000.
Matteson Langdon, Jean, and Gerhard Baer, eds. *Portals of Power: Shamanism in South America*. Albuquerque: University of New Mexico Press, 1992.
Mauss, Marcel. *The Gift: Forms and Functions of Exchange in Archaic Societies*. Translated by Ian Cunnison with an introduction of E. E. Evans Pritchard. London: Cohen & West, 1966.
Mauss, Marcel. *General Theory of Magic*. Translated by Robert Brain with a foreword by D. F. Pocock. London: Routledge, 2001 (1950).
Maw, Henry Lister. *Journal of a Passage from the Pacific to the Atlantic: Crossing the Andes in the Northern Provinces of Peru, and Descending the River Marañon or Amazon*. London: J. Murray, 1829.
McKenna, Terence. *True Hallucinations: Being an Account of the Author's Extraordinary Adventures in the Devil's Paradise*. London: Rider, 1994.
Myers, T. P. "Redes de intercambio tempranas en la Hoya Amazónica." *Amazonia Peruana* 4, no. 8 (1983): 61–76.
Renard-Casevitz, France-Marie. "Guerriers du sel, sauniers de la paix." *L'Homme* 33 (1993): 2–4.

Renard-Casevitz, France Marie, Thierry Saignes, and Anne Christine Taylor, eds. *L'Inca, l'Espagnol et les sauvages: Rapports entre les sociétés Amazoniennes et Andines du XVe au XVIIe siècle*. Paris: Recherche sur les Civilisations, 1986.

Roosevelt, Anna. "Maritime, Highland, Forest Dynamic." Vol. 3, part 1, of *The Cambridge History of the Native Peoples of the Americas*, edited by Frank Salomon and Stuart Schwartz. Cambridge: Cambridge University Press, 1999.

Rubenstein, Steven. *Alejandro Tsakimp: A Shuar Healer in the Margins of History*. Lincoln: University of Nebraska Press, 2002.

Sandeman, Christopher. *Forgotten River: A Book of Peruvian Travel and Botanical Notes*. London: Oxford University Press, 1939.

Santos Granero, Fernando, and Frederica Barclay. *Tamed Frontiers: Economy, Society and Civil Rights in Upper Amazonia*. Boulder, CO: Westview Press, 2000.

Schultes, Richard Evans, and Robert F. Raffauf. *Vine of the Soul: Medicine Men, Their Plants and Rituals in the Colombian Amazonia*. Oracle, AZ: Synergetic Press, 1992.

Sharon, Douglas. *Wizard of the Four Winds: A Shaman's Story*. New York: Free Press, 1978.

Shoemaker, Alan. "The Magic of Curanderismo: Lessons in Mestizo Ayahuasca Healing." *Shaman's Drum* 46 (1997): 39–42.

Slater, Candice. *Entangled Edens: Visions of the Amazon*. Berkeley: University of California Press, 2002.

Strathern, Marilyn. "Entangled Objects: Detached Metaphors." *Social Analysis* 34 (1993): 88–98.

Taussig, Michael. "Folk Healing and the Structure of Conquest in South America." *Journal of American Lore* 6 (1980): 217–78.

Taussig, Michael. *Shamanism, Colonialism and the Wild Man: A Study in Terror and Healing*. Chicago: University of Chicago Press, 1986.

Taylor, Anne-Christine. "The Soul's Body and Its States: An Amazonian Perspective on the Nature of Being Human." *Journal of the Royal Anthropological Institute* 2 (1996): 201–15.

Tsing, Anna Lowenhaupt. *Friction: An Ethnography of Global Connection*. Princeton, NJ: Princeton University Press, 2005.

Walsh, Catherine. "Shifting the Geopolitics of Critical Knowledge: Decolonial Thought and Cultural Studies of 'Others' in the Andes." *Cultural Studies* 21 nos. 2–3 (2007): 224–30.

Whitehead, Neil L. *Dark Shamans: Kanaima and the Poetics of Violent Death*. Durham, NC: Duke University Press, 2002.

Whitten, Norman. *Sacha Runa: Ethnicity and Adaptation of Ecuadorian Jungle Quichua*. Urbana: University of Illinois Press, 1976.

Znamenski, Andrei A. *Beauty of the Primitive: Shamanism and the Western Imagination*. New York: Oxford University Press, 2007.

7

On the Uneasiness of Tourism

Considerations on Shamanic Tourism in Western Amazonia

EVGENIA FOTIOU

Tourism as a research subject causes anthropologists great uneasiness, possibly because of the commonalities between anthropologists and tourists. Anthropologists have considered themselves the experts on culture who can legitimately tell stories about the "other." With the increasing access of tourists to the "other," however, anthropologists do not own the discourse anymore. Much of the anthropological discourse on tourism has focused on the effects of tourism rather than the motives and experiences of tourists. In this chapter, I will address some of the motives of shamanic tourists, as well as how they perceive the phenomenon they participate in, using data collected in Iquitos, Peru, between 2003 and 2007.

The phenomenon of "drug tourism"[1] in Amazonia appeared in academic discourse in the 1990s. The term *ayahuasca tourism* appeared around the same time.[2] I chose to use the term *shamanic tourism* as opposed to the more often used *drug tourism* to refer to this phenomenon, because I see a substantial difference between the two. The latter tends to be used to describe recreational consumption of drugs as well as travel to exotic places (popular destinations are Amsterdam, Southeast Asia, and South America) with the intention to smuggle illegal drugs. This is not the case with ayahuasca shamanism, and at least one other researcher has pointed this out.[3] Even though some tourists are motivated by curiosity—because ayahuasca is so widely talked about in Iquitos—most people will begin their quest with more complex motives. The unpleasantness of the experience, physical and psychological, for some makes recreational use of ayahuasca unlikely. Finally, the experience often involves the participation in a shamanic *dieta* that, in addition to ayahuasca ceremonies, involves fasting and the ingestion of both nonhallucinogenic and hallucinogenic plants, with the purpose of learning directly from the plants.[4]

I have come across the term *mystical tourism* (*turismo místico*) at least once in a short article in a Peruvian newspaper discussing ayahuasca and in two scholarly works,[5] but it seems to include a variety of activities that do not apply to this context; "spiritual tourism" has also been used for similar phenomena,[6] but it encompasses a wider range of activities. I have also encountered "entheogen tourism,"[7] which is closer to ayahuasca tourism but does not necessarily account for the aspects of the shamanic experience I mention above. For these reasons, in this context "shamanic tourism" is more appropriate.

Many of my consultants[8] would not be comfortable with the word *tourist* because of its negative connotations; anthropologists themselves have been ambivalent about studying tourists.[9] Tourism is often associated with superficial and detrimental activities, and there is a hint of judgment when classifying someone as a tourist. A lot has been written about the negative effects of tourism.[10] It is no surprise that I was treated with distrust when I told people I was studying tourists. For these reasons, I have to clarify that I do not use the word with any value judgment attached to it; rather I use "tourism" to signify any travel for any purpose or duration when the traveler has the intention of returning home.

Even though the ayahuasca experience is possible throughout the world, through the use of "ayahuasca analogues" and the visits of shamans to Europe and the United States, people still take expensive trips to South America with the expectation of having an "authentic" experience. There is some shamanic tourism activity in Ecuador and countries such as Brazil and Colombia, but Peru, especially the Iquitos area, seems to attract the majority of it. There are a few reasons Iquitos is such a hot spot for ayahuasca tourism. Even though Pucallpa, a town in central Peru, also has a reputation for shamanism (mainly Shipibo), tourism there has not developed as much as in Iquitos. The reason is that Pucallpa is a smaller town with fewer amenities to offer to Western tourists and does not have a permanent port, which makes transportation more difficult. Iquitos is much more urbanized and is considered safer. In addition, it has a fairly large expatriate community. Many people still consider Pucallpa a better place to get a more authentic experience, but some successful shamans have moved from Pucallpa to Iquitos because of safety and accessibility concerns. The increase of access to ayahuasca ceremonies in Peru has also been attributed to the collapse of the Shining Path rebels, which has made it safer to travel in the Peruvian Amazon since the 1990s.[11]

For a long time, Iquitos was the ecotourism gateway to the Amazon. It is surrounded by a number of jungle lodges and is relatively close to the Pacaya Samiria Reserve. As interest in ayahuasca among Westerners increased in the 1990s, lodges started offering ayahuasca ceremonies as part of their ecotourism packages. One source states that "ayahuasca ceremonies can be purchased in most major tourist destinations in Peru, and numerous jungle lodges now offer ceremonies or retreats, the latter costing in the neighborhood of $700–$1,500 a week."[12] Today, there are an increasing number of lodges that specialize in ayahuasca retreats. Most places focusing on ayahuasca ceremonies and catering to Westerners are on the road that leads from Iquitos to Nauta, which is the only road connecting Iquitos to other towns.[13] A few experienced ayahuasca drinkers will often participate in ceremonies held in the city in the house of a curandero.

Most of the lodges have websites and bring groups directly from the United States or Europe through established contacts there. They also have offices in the city for the tourists that come to Iquitos looking for a tour. Most of these offices have representatives who walk around Iquitos looking for tourists and get paid on commission. Most hotels and some restaurants will refer clients to these offices on commission as well. Consequently, there is great competition for tourists, and often rivalries arise between locals that take the form of spreading rumors about competitors. Because of this, most companies prefer bringing groups directly from abroad.

During my dissertation fieldwork between 2003 and 2005, there was a small but steady flow of visitors who came to Iquitos specifically for ayahuasca. In 2005, an employee of the municipal tourist office estimated the number of ayahuasca tourists to be about two hundred a year, a number that at the time seemed realistic from my observations. In the following years, this number has probably doubled. One reason is that in the summer of 2005, an American living in Iquitos started organizing an annual conference on shamanism, bringing scientists and shamans together and providing a safe environment for first-time users to learn about ayahuasca and participate in ceremonies with local shamans between conference sessions. The first conference had two hundred attendees, with similar numbers in the following years. This means that hundreds of new visitors started coming to Iquitos every summer specifically for ayahuasca. Another event that spiked interest in ayahuasca shamanism in the area was an article published in *National Geographic Travel,*[14] which was widely read and attracted a great number of visitors.

The first question that comes to mind when discussing shamanic tourism is, Who are the participants? A close look at the population I researched reveals no patterns in age, class, education, or social status. The only disparity I found was one of gender, with more than twice as many men as women in my sample. Given the challenges of traveling in South America for women, and the fact that consuming psychoactive plants might be considered risky behavior by most, this gender discrepancy makes sense. People interested in ayahuasca come from a variety of backgrounds. Some of my interviewees were middle-class professionals, and even though many of them were pursuing unconventional careers, for the most part they were people with regular jobs and commitments. Even though about half had no college education, all were well-read. Many traveled to Iquitos specifically to take ayahuasca, while others found out about it while traveling and decided to try it. If the trip was made for the purpose of taking ayahuasca, then some reading on ayahuasca and shamanism usually preceded. Contrary to what I expected, many of these participants had never tried other hallucinogens. In the larger scheme of things, this sacramental use of ayahuasca is embraced by only a small, though increasing, part of Western society and accounts for a fraction of the tourist flow to Iquitos.

More specifically, among the people I interviewed there were sixty males and twenty-two females. Their ages ranged from twenty to sixty-one years. Thirty-six, almost half, were from the United States and Canada; thirteen were Peruvian and the remaining were mostly from Europe. At least twenty-three said they had never tried other hallucinogens before ayahuasca, and more than half did not travel to South America or Iquitos specifically to try it. Most were raised Christian but did not consider themselves religious; rather they preferred the term *spiritual* or used some other word. The vast majority found out about ayahuasca either from friends or relatives or from books. Experience with ayahuasca also varied among my sample; I interviewed people who had been in only a couple of ceremonies and others who had been in hundreds. I need to caution that even though some of my findings and numbers might be typical for ayahuasca drinkers, others are not. Some of these numbers would change considerably depending on the context in which they were collected. For example, if I had worked only with people in one of the lodges that specialize in ayahuasca retreats, then I suspect I would have gotten more people with no previous experience with hallucinogens, because inexperienced users tend to feel safer in the more structured environment of the lodge.

Some critics of drug tourism and the introduction of therapeutic milieus to Amazonia express concern about outsiders interacting with what they consider unenculturated indigenous groups. Some of these critiques suffer from naïve notions of authenticity. With the commercialization of ayahuasca, some proponents of "traditionally" constructed use argue that ayahuasca is in danger of being profaned.[15] They caution that, as many South Americans realize its moneymaking potential, they "come to adopt a New Age vocabulary of shamanic healer/spiritual voyager."[16] Some warn of the impact this "industry" might have on the environment. Others warn that this commercialization can have negative effects on healthcare in Amazonian communities, as a lot of shamans are interested more in tourism than in healing members of the community, and that shamans are adapting to the expectations of the tourists, a fact that greatly distorts indigenous shamanism.[17]

I did not approach tourism from the perspective of it being an exogenous force to local society, as early anthropological studies have done, and my study is not of the one-way impact of tourism (whether negative or positive). Instead, this was a study on interculturality. South American shamanism has always thrived on intercultural exchange and has drawn symbols and power from a variety of sources. More than sharing sociocultural content, ayahuasca shamanism provides an intercultural space for Westerners and locals to dialogue. Just as shamans cross boundaries between worlds, tourists cross cultural and geographical boundaries with a variety of motivations and often find common humanity beyond the particularity of their lives. Tourists, in this case, take a journey both literally and metaphorically. And, similar to shamanism, tourist activities are often ambiguous themselves, as they can have at the same time positive as well as negative effects on local society. In the case of Iquitos, for example, something that most critics fail to acknowledge is that despite the problems associated with tourism, it does bring much-needed income into an impoverished area, not to mention renewed interest in indigenous knowledge.

Motives of Shamanic Tourists

The question that guided my research is, What are the motives of Westerners pursuing shamanic experiences? I will summarize their motives, some of which I have discussed in great ethnographic detail elsewhere.[18] Some authors[19] attribute Western interest in ayahuasca to the fact that Westerners seek novel experiences not offered by their culture. Dobkin de Rios emphasizes "the empty self of the post-World War II period, a self which is soothed and made cohesive by becoming filled up by consuming food, consumer products, and experiences."[20] This perspective does not leave any room for the possibility that Westerners might engage meaningfully in their ayahuasca experiences. Kristensen found four main reasons people became ayahuasca tourists: self-exploration and spiritual growth, curiosity, physical and emotional healing, and the desire for a vacation in an exotic location.[21] Some of these have been quoted as motives for pilgrimage as well.[22] The common theme that one can discern in what follows is the attractiveness of anything that is perceived as the antithesis of Western civilization: pre-industrial, premodern, natural, exotic, spiritual, sacred, traditional, and timeless—a yearning that runs deep in Western culture.

For many, participating in shamanic ceremonies fulfills a need to connect to an archaic past, or a desire for continuity of consciousness from ancient times. The past is thought to hold what the modern lacks, and that is located in cultural others and is consumable by moderns in their search for self-fulfillment.[23] In seeking an explanation for why there is such rising interest in ayahuasca worldwide, Ralph Metzner sees an attempt to bridge the gap between the sacred and the natural that Western civilization has brought about with the rise of the mechanistic paradigms in science. Shamanism is seen as timeless and universal, and according to neoshamanism,[24] every person has the ability to "remember" what Christianity has caused the West to lose.

This idea is not entirely new but was previously expressed by scholars and artists such as the romantic poets; Antonin Artaud, Aldous Huxley, and Walter Benjamin all expressed the yearning to recover the sense of sacred that European culture had lost and pursued altered states of consciousness as a form of rebellion against industrialization and to facilitate personal transformation. Carl Jung and Mircea Eliade, who lamented the loss of magic in European culture, have expressed similar ideas. Western culture is perceived as deficient in this respect, and the remedy is sought among the traditions and beliefs of indigenous peoples. There is a yearning to connect to a "tribal past," the wisdom of the ancestors, a wisdom that is not culturally specific but rather is perceived as "universal." Ritual is fundamental in this process, and most of my consultants have stressed the importance of context in the ingestion of ayahuasca and to the positive effects of the ritual itself. This is one of the reasons they take the expensive trips to Peru. According to them, the structure of the ritual provides a framework for healing and spiritual work, something that Western culture lacks.

Shamanism becomes the "embodiment of pre-Westernness" and "premodernness," what Greene calls "the West's historically and temporally subordinated *ante-self*, that perennial prior self doomed to the temporal stasis of primitivity."[25] Shamanism, like all traditional medicine, has been viewed as "epistemologically and practically static"[26] in the West. These misconceptions have evolved over years, and it is no surprise that they prevail among tourists. After all, one reason that Amazonia is so attractive to this type of tourist is that, apart from its ecological importance, it is considered to be the home to some of the last primordial peoples of this planet. Occasional articles in the press warn of the rapid disappearance of the knowledge and lore of indigenous tribes and of shamans in particular.[27]

Earlier scholarly work has presented the indigenous peoples of the area as culturally intact; for example, Lewis and Lewis, who presented traditional Shuar medicine as a static body of knowledge, stated that "they use plants now as they have for perhaps thousands of years."[28] Similar comments were made by most of my consultants, who believed that the ceremonies in which they participated were identical to the ceremonies that indigenous peoples led "for thousands of years." This point of view ignores the obvious influence of the West on these cultures, as well as the cultures' response to that influence. In this discourse, the figure of the shaman becomes mythologized and is presented as the preserver of ancient tradition. This perspective is not particularly concerned with the reality of the present, but is more likely looking for traces of the primordial in present shamanic practices. Shamanism is therefore essentialized and removed from its historical and cultural context.

As was already mentioned, a discourse lamenting the loss of magic runs deep in Western traditions. In 1934, Jung argued that the decline of magic and religion in our society is harmful because it hinders individuation. Eliade also argued that sacred experience predominates in oral societies and that "modern man has desacralized his world."[29] Like Jung, he argued that hierophanies, or manifestations of the sacred in nature, can help one resolve life's critical situations.[30] Some might relate this to the increasing popularity of ayahuasca and other entheogens among Westerners, since it provides the much-needed spiritual experiences of which people feel deprived. Many of my consultants have reported spiritual experiences with ayahuasca, and some admit to having become more spiritual because of it. As one person put it, "It gave me a new perspective on life, on what it all is about. It resulted in enhanced meaningfulness for me in many, many aspects of my personal life. It caused me to believe in spirit and God for the first time in my life." Others have shared that they met and talked to historical spiritual figures in their visions, such as the Buddha, Jesus, and even God.

Ayahuasca experiences are attractive to Westerners because, in a way, they provide direct access to the spiritual and the "divine within," since there is no intermediary as in organized religions. For some, this is an act of resistance, rejecting organized religion and seeking out a more democratic way to spirituality. They feel that traditionally religious authorities of every form laid claim to and monopolized access to the divine, and priests became the mediators between the people and the divine. Alternative spirituality movements find these mediators unnecessary and look for ways for individuals to tap directly into the divine. Most of my consultants declared themselves "spiritual but not religious." In addition, they drew material from diverse cultural sources such as Buddhism and yogic traditions.

A majority of participants in ayahuasca ceremonies are motivated by a desire to be healed and have reported successful healing from both psychological and physical ailments. Shamanism is seen as the most radically other to Western biomedicine compared to other traditional ethnomedical practices.[31] It is no surprise that people frustrated with biomedicine turn to shamanism, seeking a more holistic healing that is enhanced by greater contact with nature. Thus, their quest for healing also contains a critique of Western medical knowledge.

Ayahuasca is reported to be especially effective in healing psychological trauma and depression. Cleansing or purging is very important in the healing process and is perceived as spiritual, as well as physical, cleansing. When purging during the ceremony, an indispensable part of the ayahuasca experience, many have reported the feeling of purging negative things accumulated in their bodies over years, often referred to as "psychic garbage." In the healing process, the idea that individuals are responsible for their own healing or nonhealing is very important: characteristically, people would say that "everyone is their own shaman." Healing by intervention of spirits is reported quite often as well.

Shamanic ceremonies also provide the ideal setting for the personal transformation of the participants. For some, the ayahuasca experience poses a challenge and offers a significant spiritual experience as well as a way to connect to their "inner self." One consultant said that he was attracted by the fact that ayahuasca forces one to face one's "demons." Many (notably Grof) have stressed the fact that psychedelic experience causes dissolution of the ego and is a catalyst for personal transformation, and they note that substances such as LSD have been used successfully in psychotherapy.[32]

On the other hand, lack of context or a framework for Western people for interpreting the visionary experience can cause misconceptions. In indigenous cultures, there is a very specific geography and structure of the other worlds shamans visit in their trance, a structure that is learned during their apprenticeship. Some Westerners may interpret their visions more personally or psychologically, using Jungian archetypes. If this is the case, they interpret the beings or demons in their visions as manifestations of conflicts in their subconscious mind. Although traditionally shamanism was a healing force for the community, in this context it is about healing the individual. I encountered what has been called "psychologizing the religious," using the cosmos as a tool for "therapizing the psyche,"[33] very often in my fieldwork. Kleinman[34] speaks of a "psychologizing process" that has affected American culture since World War I, and forms part of a "cultural transformation in which the self has been culturally constituted as the now-dominant Western ethnopsychology." Thus the psyche replaces religion. With this movement from the cosmological to the psychological, the shamanic journey becomes not a journey to other worlds but a journey of the mind to the subconscious.

However, in the context of shamanic tourism, this is not a one-way process. Many Westerners who engage with Amazonian shamanism for an extended time end up interpreting what we would perceive as psychological processes in the West using "spirit" vocabulary.[35]

Authenticity and Interculturality

An issue that comes up often in this type of tourism, as in ethnic tourism, is authenticity. Shamanic tourism brings Westerners into contact not only with the "divine other," but with the "*exotic* other" as well. The shamans embody this exotic other, and often tourists have preconceived notions of what constitutes the authentic. However, as has been shown in the case of ethnic tourism, when natives try to conform to tourists' expectations of authenticity, this authenticity is immediately lost.[36] People, including shamans, adapt constantly to new circumstances, and as anthropologists have stressed, culture constantly takes new forms and should never be viewed as static. Bruner[37] has argued that the dichotomy of authenticity versus inauthenticity may be a false one, and one must regard culture as always alive and changing. Since cultures constantly reinvent themselves, every cultural act, including shamanism, should be considered authentic.

However, intercultural exchange in the context of shamanic tourism has been heavily criticized. Joralemon[38] initially expresses his indignation toward the commercialization of shamanism. He is critical of both Westerners who naïvely perceive the performance of shamans as authentic and the shaman himself who is transformed into a "clown in a New Age circus."[39] He compares Villoldo (the neoshaman/psychologist who commercialized the Peruvian shaman Calderón) to himself, expressing a sort of superiority for having more of a sense of what is truly authentic and implying that a shaman who works with Westerners is not authentic. This reveals an issue that has no black-or-white answer. Joralemon himself argues that neoshamanism can be of ethnographic value and that "anthropologists might well study the choices of these culture consumers and the way the resulting mosaics reformulate local traditions to express the shopper's implicit premise."[40]

Despite the fact that most Westerners pursuing ayahuasca experiences have read about it and have access to the literature, misconceptions about shamanism abound. In addition to believing that this form of shamanism has been practiced exactly in this way for thousands of years, they tend to overlook the historical and cultural context of shamanism; for example, Amazonian cosmology is ignored, because it does not fit life in the West. They also overlook the ambiguous aspects of shamanism, such as sorcery, even though they are starting to take them into account, as more and more have been involved in cases of sorcery. In addition, tourists have unrealistic perceptions of indigenous and local people. They romanticize them, only to be disappointed in their first few days in Peru. Dobkin de Rios also addresses this issue when she argues that drug tourists "see the Noble Savage in the visage of the urban poor carpenter, tradesman, or day laborer. They see exotic people of color untouched by civilization, who are close to nature . . . drug tourists perceive the natives as timeless and ahistoric."[41]

An ethnographic example that pertains to this is the reaction of some Westerners to a plant dieta, as discussed by one of the shamans:

> The spirits will come to you during your dream time and will teach you. But many Westerners come and think that they will have what they consider stereotypical, or Indian, or native, tribal dreams and that is supposed to describe to them that something shamanic is taking place, but they are filled with great doubt. Really, the spirits will come and teach you through the metaphors and dreams that you know well.

> So, a lot of the time Westerners find themselves in dreams like mountainous areas that they know, or cities that they know or things like that. And they think this is not shamanic; this diet is not working.

One aspect of shamanic tourism that is criticized is the introduction of foreign concepts to the vocabulary of the curanderos. Joralemon[42] discussed the case of Eduardo Calderón, whose involvement with neoshamans has had the effect of blending traditional healing with New Age terminology. I observed the same phenomenon in Iquitos. Foreign concepts from Asian traditions are often adopted by the shamans to accommodate tourist expectations and needs. Notably, a mestizo shaman with whom I worked for two months would often refer to the body's chakras, or energy centers, a concept borrowed from Eastern spirituality. Although cultural exchange has always been part of shamanism and curanderos have been eager to adopt powerful foreign elements—for example, biomedical symbolism has been part of curanderismo for a long time[43]—tourism might speed this process up. As a result, the shamans who understand the expectations of the tourists about what is authentic attract more people.

Some aspects that tourists consider authentic are the dress of the curanderos, exclusion of Christian elements, and their location. For example, they consider being in a retreat near Iquitos the authentic experience, because they are in the jungle just a few kilometers outside of the city. Some would argue that since most locals drink ayahuasca in dark rooms in the city, this setting is far from authentic. The clothes that some of these shamans wear during ceremonies are a mixture of attire from a variety of ethnic groups, mainly Shipibo, who sell their crafts in the streets of Iquitos. Most curanderos who choose this attire wear a long robe with Shipibo imagery and usually some sort of headdress made of feathers and other jungle products. I have seen tourists impressed by these shamans.

Mestizo shamans who cater to locals wear Western clothes and are Christian. For example, an older shaman, who works from his house in Iquitos and has no lodge in the jungle, always has a picture of Jesus in front of him during ceremonies. Some tourists might initially be put off by the fact that these shamans are Christian, because they do not identify with Christianity themselves; others just accept it as part of the culture. However, these elements of the culture are constantly renegotiated in the context of tourism. I have observed a shaman adjust her attitude according to the group she had on a particular night. She would remove the Christian images and symbols from the ceremonial space when she realized they were offensive to visitors and put them back when she had groups of Peruvians attending a ceremony. She would also try to distance herself from institutionalized Christianity in discussions with the tourists and openly criticized the Catholic Church. Curanderos will also decorate

Figure 7.1. Blessing the brew. Photograph by Evgenia Fotiou.

ceremonial spaces with indigenous handicrafts bought at the market to convey a more traditional feel.

However, not all local curanderos partake in this performance of "authenticity." Some will do it only in ceremony, while others, as in the case of the conference, will dress up to appear more authentic or attractive to potential clients. There is an increasing number of curanderos who are critical of this trend, refuse to dress up, and insist on wearing Western clothing at all times. They are few, but it is clear that they want to differentiate themselves from the rest and maintain some sort of integrity. I was surprised to see that in one of the most well-known ayahuasca retreats near Iquitos the maestro and apprentices wore Western clothes at all times and never tried to appear more "authentic." Even more surprisingly, guests did not seem to mind, and I heard no one complain that they were not getting an authentic experience.

Another controversy, which for some might compromise authenticity, is the issue of payment of shamans. As has already been noted, most shamans who work with tourists charge steep amounts for ceremonies. Many people are uneasy with this, wondering whether someone should charge such amounts for spiritual knowledge. Wallis[44] mentions similar critiques among Native Americans. Payment of various kinds is normal in the context of South American shamanism, so the fact itself should not be considered to compromise authenticity. Besides, these shamans are part of a capitalist economy; therefore it is appropriate that they be rewarded monetarily. What is alarming, though, is that the more secure shamans feel about their position in the market, the larger amounts they charge, which in turn creates hostility and resentment in local society. Tourists, depending on their background and their financial situation, will either consider that expensive shamans exploit indigenous knowledge, or that the price is fair for what they are receiving.

In terms of interculturality, ayahuasca is perceived to provide access to the "other," in this case not a cultural other but a global, universal, timeless, and even divine other. Many accounts stress the transcendence of time and space in ayahuasca experience, and sometimes this translates into transcendence of cultural boundaries as well. In the Psychoactivity III Conference held in Amsterdam in 2002, Westerners expressed the view that they had every right to use it, since these powerful plants give access to universal knowledge and are there for all humanity to use. Characteristically, an Ecuadorian shaman said that ayahuasca is "the universal science of the universe" ("la ciencia universal del universo").

I hope that the preceding observations have shown that the contact with the "other" can be problematic. Chaumeil[45] explores how indigenous and Western cultures relate to otherness through shamanism. He argues that the relationship with the other is ambivalent and, depending on familiarity with it, can be perceived as suprahuman or subhuman. This expresses the spatial, social, political, and technological, as well as ontological, distance between the self and the other. The other can be monstrous because it represents values opposite to ours or fascinating because it is mysterious and difficult to grasp. These "other" experiences, of course, embody historic experience. According to Gow,[46] ayahuasca shamanism in its present form is not as "authentic" (locally endogenous, unchanging) as it is commonly thought to be and is, in fact, a result of contact with the Western "other" in western Amazonia and the relationships that developed through this.[47]

Whereas this intercultural process today is very different from a few hundred years ago, it would not have been possible without the contribution of individuals who serve as mediators and play a vital role in bringing together Western seekers and Peruvian shamans. These mediators are often Westerners. A couple of the shamans I worked with were Westerners who had apprenticed with local shamans and either led ceremonies on their own or accompanied their teacher. There are a few Westerners in Iquitos practicing shamanism, some of whom have created local businesses. They invest in land, build a lodge, and hire local shamans and staff. More recently, Westerners have acquired such preexisting establishments. These Western shamans, or Peruvian shamans working with a Western partner, have a marked advantage with the tourists because they can communicate better with them in two aspects: language, and the fact that they can convey certain concepts more easily to them. These centers usually combine other healing methods with shamanism, such as visualization and meditation, and offer shamanic dietas.

In addition to these "gringo"[48] shamans, there are a number of people who serve as mediators between local shamans and tourists. Even though some of them have been criticized for capitalizing on indigenous knowledge and for taking advantage of both healers and tourists, reality is much more complex than that. These mediators serve some important functions. Some of these mediators are Americans and have become naturalized Peruvian citizens. One of them owns a restaurant for tourists, while another owns a travel agency and earns money from mediating between healers and tourists. He organizes the Amazonian Shamanism Conference held in Iquitos since 2005. The first helps to bring together tourists who frequent his restaurant and ask for advice about who the good shamans are. He introduced me to one of the shamans with whom I worked, and in such cases he receives part of the fee. The other mediator does more than introduce tourists to shamans: He usually works with a couple of shamans and arranges everything for the tourists including bringing them to the site. He also owns a small piece of land near Iquitos where he had some facilities built that he usually makes available to people attending the conference for free, and to others who want to conduct ceremonies but do not have a space for them.

And let's not forget the role of the anthropologist in this story (myself) who often played the role of the translator between shamans and tourists and was at times considered the "expert" in local shamanism. Although I do not believe that objectivity is possible, or that distance from our subject of study is desirable, I did strive to not "interfere" with the tourist activities going on. However, this last part proved to be very difficult, as both shamans and tourists often solicited my services as translator and asked me for my advice and recommendations.

The Feminization of Ayahuasca

I will close this chapter with an example from my fieldwork that illustrates the transformation of discourse that can occur when outsiders appropriate ayahuasca shamanism. I call this phenomenon the "feminization of ayahuasca." Within my research population, among mestizo shamans and tourists alike, ayahuasca was generally perceived as a female and maternal spirit. For example, the plant spirit was often described as being a "tough" but loving mother. Other qualities, traditionally related to femininity, were also attributed to ayahuasca.

It was thought to develop intuition and connection to nature and all things spiritual and sacred.

This gendered perception of the plant spirit was complicated by the fact that not all shamans shared this viewpoint and Amazonian shamanism is heavily dominated by men and considered to be a "male domain." That ayahuasca has been used and is still used in sorcery and sorcery-related violence, such as shamanic warfare, further challenges this feminized view of ayahuasca. I started looking into this because, during my fieldwork, at least one shaman and his apprentice argued that the ayahuasca spirit is male and frequently shared stories of involvement in shamanic warfare. Even though I will be touching on several issues that warrant deeper discussion (such as gender) only in passing, my goal here is to raise some very important questions about how Westerners perceive indigenous knowledge.

Most early ethnographies we have on Amazonian cultures were written by men. Thus the perspective we have is a male one, for two reasons. First, these ethnographers were focused on male activities, such as hunting and warfare (this might have something to do with preconceived notions of the "savage" perpetuated by popular culture). Second, the ethnographers' gender no doubt posed limitations to how much access they had to women's activities and women's perspectives. Thus, the image we have in the West through these ethnographies is the image glorifying "Man the Hunter" and undervaluing "Woman the Gatherer." Amazonian societies have also been portrayed as highly gendered and even segregated, overemphasizing gender differences and interpreting them from a Western perspective. An example of this gender bias can be seen in a quote from Schultes and Hofmann:

> The famous Yuruparí ceremony of the Tukanoans is an ancestor-communication ritual, the basis of a man's tribal society and an adolescent male initiation rite. Its sacred bark trumpet, which calls the Yuruparí spirit, is taboo to the sight of women; it symbolizes the forces to whom the ceremony is holy, favorably influencing fertility spirits, effecting cures of prevalent illnesses, and improving the male prestige and power over women.[49]

In traditional Amazonian shamanism, ayahuasca had many uses that are not found in mestizo shamanism. Among various ethnic groups it was used in communal rituals of men, singing and dancing, for locating game animals and divination, in warfare and conflict, to see faraway places, and for healing by communicating with spirits. It was also important in native art, cosmology and ethnoastronomy, and in the Jaguar complex.[50] Ayahuasca traditionally was consumed by shamans (who were mostly men) and by male members of the group. Because the ayahuasca experience is challenging, men learned bravery through taking ayahuasca,[51] a quality they need since they hunt and kill and are warriors. Thus, in some ethnic groups women do not need to take ayahuasca since they do not do these things. If a woman wishes to try ayahuasca, however, she can, as is the case among the Cashinaua.

I hope this has provided some background against which we can compare how ayahuasca and Amazonian shamanism are perceived in the context of shamanic tourism. The vast majority of the shamans with whom I worked and the people I interviewed referred to ayahuasca as a female entity. I observed the same pattern while browsing online discussion forums. For example, these are some things that people have said:

> "She is a female energy. She is very strong, very powerful."
>
> "I had a very beautiful experience with grandmother ayahuasca."
>
> "La Madrecita is a Teacher."
>
> "Lately, I've been thinking about how demanding yet nurturing she is. How she can scold you like a stern mother and soothe you to total bliss."
>
> "Meeting Mother Ayahuasca is an intense, immense experience that will change who you are."
>
> "Aya is the mother and Grandma, gentle and nurturing at times, and Kali-like at times when your ego needs to be cut down."
>
> "When I met ayahuasca, she came to me as a young girl, not too much younger than me.... At other times though, she seemed like she had no gender, and just appeared as a voice without a form.... Just a presence... an essence."

An issue that came up a lot during my fieldwork, and that was perceived by Westerners as underlying sexism in indigenous shamanism, was the exclusion of menstruating women from ceremonies. Despite my best efforts, I never got a consensus from shamans on the reasoning behind this prohibition; nor could I confirm sexism as a cause for the exclusion. However, according to several ethnographies, women are more visible to spirits when they menstruate, and therefore they are in greater danger from spirit attacks involving seduction, rape, and jealousy from female spirits.[52] Another perspective is that menstruating women both attract and repel the physical manifestation of spirits.[53] One of the shamans with whom I worked said:

> The understanding is that the energetic scent of the menstruation is repugnant to medicine spirits. So they don't want to come around. The

> medicine spirits don't like gore, they don't really like blood, they don't like all the things that are traditionally, typically human. They don't particularly like sex, they don't like spices; they don't like any of that stuff, unless it's energetically right for your body.

In my dissertation[54] I discuss the prevalence of sorcery and shamanic warfare among shamans, and it seems that there has been a backlash in the ayahuasca community against this. Amazonian shamanism is perceived as sexist and having undesirable traits, all related to maleness. The reaction to this is to seek out female shamans, who are few and far between in the area. A very recent development that I found was the creation of an ayahuasca retreat that specializes in female shamanism, honoring the "Divine Feminine" and working with "Female Energy." When I asked the owners about their choice they responded:

> The reason we chose to work with female shamans exclusively is because traditionally Amazonian shamanism is a very male-dominated domain and the ayahuasca machismo does not come from the heart and is very much ego-driven. We just finished our first workshop with 30 participants and the feedback was mind-blowing!... The participants are relatively experienced (they had worked with several other centers before) and said this was more than they ever dreamed of.

This is what the proprietors state on their website[55]:

> Shamanic practices and the ancients from around the world have long revered the Mother (along and in balance with the Father) for millennia—the Earth, the Great Mother, Pachamama. It is believed by many scholars that it was the eruption of violence as perpetrated by the newer, male dominated cultures that obliterated the peaceful, earth-honouring ways of Goddess worship and paved the way for the strong hold of Christianity and eventually the obliteration of the Goddess from religion, religious texts and teachings.
>
> It became clear to us at the Temple that by offering ceremonies exclusively run by female healers-curanderas (working with Mother Ayahuasca, connecting to Mother Earth) that we would be connecting with Divine Feminine Energy. We believe that the spiritual awakening that we see all over the planet is an effect of the Divine Feminine being reborn in each of us again. As we were each starved from the Divine Feminine energy, it is now being craved from every angle.
>
> Divine feminine energy is comprised of qualities such as love, understanding, compassion, nurturing, and helpfulness to others. It includes

> tenderness, gentleness, kindness and these are the qualities that we help you to reconnect with and are the true nature of the female Shipibo healers (*onanya ainbobo*) who hold ayahuasca ceremonies at the Temple of the Way of Light; ceremonies that are truly lead from the heart, not from the head.

Many will find no problem with this type of statement; they might even find it empowering. The problem that many gender scholars[56] would point out is that even with its good intentions, this kind of discourse perpetuates stereotypes of gender dualism and promotes an essentialist discourse. In addition, it makes certain assumptions about the nature of indigenous shamanism that are overly simplistic.

Looking at indigenous discourse, we note these things appearing more complex. First, it is very important to remember that the ayahuasca brew consists of at least two plants, ayahuasca and chacruna. One of the shamans with whom I worked in Iquitos told me that ayahuasca is most definitely a male spirit, while the spirit of chacruna is female. This reflects the findings of other researchers as well. For example, Bustos[57] mentions that the ayahuasca spirit is perceived by the Asháninka as male and the spirit of chacruna as female.

Feminist anthropologists[58] have discarded dualisms of gender and moved to more nuanced analyses. It would be simplistic, and would impose Western frameworks on indigenous worldviews, to assume that because women did not participate in shamanism, they had less power or were less valued. In addition, the presence of women in shamanism might have been underestimated in the literature, as Colpron has argued.[59] Several scholars[60] have shown that Amazonian cultures have a division of labor, one based on egalitarian complementarity.[61] In addition, many have mechanisms to ensure that no one has more power than anyone else in the group, achieving this through very complex kinship systems and marriage arrangements. In reality, any sort of authority comes with more responsibility than privilege; we should not forget the ambiguity of the shaman figure and the fact that shamans have been killed in the past as a result of sorcery accusations.[62]

Western intellectual thought's association of "nature" with femininity is linked to women's marginalization and classification as second to or lesser than men. Women have been defined in opposition to men and, much like nature, have been perceived as something to be conquered and dominated by "man." However, I argue that the new discourse I described earlier promotes an unrealistic and romanticized view of indigenous knowledge and worldview. Although it attempts to reverse essentialist gender discourse and bring "feminine" qualities into the mainstream by perceiving them as positive, it risks perpetuating the same essentialist discourses and creates the danger of further marginalization of indigenous knowledge. It is my assessment that certain ways of gendering the spirit world, as the case of ayahuasca shows, only affirm ideologies of separate gender spheres and the obvious power relations between them—effects that might not have been there previously or might even be the result of Western influence.

Given the fact that the ayahuasca brew consists of at least two plants creating the synergistic effect, and that without the presence of both the brew would not be effective, it is safe to say that an approach focusing more on the *complementarity* of genders might be closer to the indigenous worldview, something that has been adequately argued for Andean cultures. Even though women did not participate in ayahuasca ceremonies or become shamans in most Amazonian cultures, this should not immediately lead to the conclusion that women were not valued or were powerless. Looking more closely at Amazonian ethnographies shows that even the symbolism, myths, and rituals separating female and male spheres actually reinforce the idea that men and women cannot exist without one another. We also need to entertain the possibility that what today is perceived as machismo is a Western import. Thus I propose a more nuanced interpretation, which focuses not only on the female component of the ayahuasca brew but on the complementarity of the two plant spirits, which not only will reveal the wisdom and complexity of indigenous knowledge and medicine but might provide us with a more nuanced framework of looking at how gender is constructed in indigenous cultures.

Conclusion

To sum up, I do not see shamanic tourism as an anomaly; it is consistent with the nature of shamanic knowledge, which has always been exchanged across and between cultures. Traditionally, in South American shamanism power and symbolism has been sought outside a particular cultural milieu. Moreover, in the West, esoteric knowledge has often been sought in faraway places; thus, this intercultural exchange is also consistent with Western traditions.

However, the way indigenous peoples and their knowledge are perceived in the context of shamanic tourism can be highly problematic. Some have criticized ayahuasca tourism for marketing native spirituality and degrading Amazonian traditions. Others believe that it can help preserve indigenous cultures, especially in the context of ecotourism managed by indigenous people. The truth depends on the context and falls somewhere in between. Neither of the two extremes is true for Iquitos because we are dealing with mestizo shamans who might have apprenticed with Indians, who have introduced Christian elements to shamanism, and who marketed ayahuasca to urban populations before tourism was a major factor. Even though many of the people in the population I studied do show a remarkable engagement with Amazonian shamanism, for the majority the relationship is still superficial and transient, leading to misconceptions.

This might contribute to the further marginalization of indigenous knowledge—something that should be taken seriously.

Notes

1. Marlene Dobkin de Rios, "Drug Tourism in the Amazon," *Anthropology of Consciousness* 5, no. 1 (1994): 16–19.
2. John N Grunwell, "Ayahuasca Tourism in South America," *MAPS* 8, no. 3 (1998): 59–62.
3. Michael Winkelman, "Drug Tourism or Spiritual Healing? Ayahuasca Seekers in Amazonia," *Journal of Psychoactive drugs* 37, no. 2 (2005): 209–18.
4. See Evgenia Fotiou, "From Medicine Men to Day Trippers: Shamanic Tourism in Iquitos, Peru," (Ph.D. diss., University of Wisconsin-Madison, 2010) for a detailed discussion of dietas.
5. Michael Hill, "New Age in the Andes: Mystical Tourism and Cultural Politics in Cusco, Peru" (Ph.D. diss., Emory University, 2005); Jorge Flores Ochoa, "Buscando los espiritus del Ande: Turismo místico en el Qosqo" in Hiroyasu Tomoeda and Luis Millones, eds., *La tradición Andina en tiempos modernos*, 9–29 (Osaka: Ethnological Reports 5, 1996).
6. Bonnie Jean Owen, "Marketing Mysticism and the Purchase of Pilgrimage: The Rise of Spiritual Tourism in Cusco and Iquitos, Peru," (Ph.D. diss., University of Arizona, 2006).
7. Graham Harvey and Robert J. Wallis, *Historical Dictionary of Shamanism* (Lanham, MD: Scarecrow Press. 2007).
8. I prefer to use the term *consultants* to refer to my "subjects" or "informants" because it implies a more equitable relationship. I view them not as people I "studied" but as people with whom I worked and consulted about their experiences and motivations.
9. Tim Wallace, "Tourism, Tourists, and Anthropologists at Work," *NAPA Bulletin* 23, no. 1 (2005): 1–26.
10. Dennison Nash, *Anthropology of Tourism* (Tarrytown, NY: Pergamon/Elsevier Science, 1996).
11. Catherine Elton, "Day Trippers," *Outside* 24, no. 10 (1999): 34.
12. Rachel Proctor, "Tourism Opens New Doors, Creates New Challenges, for Traditional Healers in Peru," *Cultural Survival Quarterly* 24, no. 4 (2001): 14.
13. See also Chapter 6 by Françoise Barbira Freedman in this volume.
14. Kira Salak, "Hell and Back," *National Geographic Adventure* 58 (2006).
15. Marlene Dobkin de Rios, "Mea Culpa: Drug Tourism and the Anthropologist's Responsibility," *Anthropology News* 47, no. 7 (2006): 20.
16. Dobkin de Rios, "Drug Tourism in the Amazon," 18.
17. Proctor, "Tourism Opens New Doors."
18. Fotiou, "From Medicine Men to Day Trippers."
19. Dobkin de Rios, "Drug Tourism in the Amazon"; Grunwell, "Ayahuasca Tourism in South America."
20. Dobkin de Rios, "Drug Tourism in the Amazon."
21. Kim Kristensen, "The Ayahuasca Phenomenon: Jungle Pilgrims: North Americans Participating in Amazon Ayahuasca Ceremonies," Multidisciplinary Association for Psychedelic Studies, 1998. http://www.maps.org/research/kristensen.html
22. Jill Dubisch and Michael Winkelman, *Pilgrimage and Healing* (Tucson: University of Arizona Press, 2005).
23. Johannes Fabian, *Time and the Other: How Anthropology Makes Its Object* (New York: Columbia University Press, 1983).
24. Neoshamanism, sometimes called New Shamanism, refers to the revived forms of shamanism in the West. Jakobsen (1999: xi) defines it as "a form of shamanism that has been created at the end of this century to re-establish a link for modern man to his spiritual roots,

to re-introduce shamanic behavior into the lives of westerners in search of spirituality and, thereby, renew contact with Nature."

25. Shane Greene, "The Shaman's Needle: Development, Shamanic Agency, and Intermedicality in Aguaruna Lands, Peru," *American Ethnologist* 25, no. 4 (1998): 642.
26. Ibid., 634.
27. Ibid., 641.
28. W. H. Lewis and M. Elvin-Lewis, "Basic Quantitative and Experimental Research Phases of Future Ethnobotany with Reference to the Medicinal Plants of South America," in Ghillean T. Prance, Derek Chadwick, and Joan Marsh, eds., *Ethnobotany and the Search for New Drugs*, (New York: Wiley, 1994), 61.
29. Mircea Eliade, *The Sacred and the Profane: The Nature of Religion* (New York: Harcourt, Brace, 1959), 13.
30. Mircea Eliade, *Patterns in Comparative Religion* (London: Sheed and Ward, 1979).
31. Joseph W. Bastien, *Drum and Stethoscope: Integrating Ethnomedicine and Biomedicine in Bolivia* (Salt Lake City: University of Utah Press, 1992), 93.
32. Lester Grinspoon and James B. Bakalar, "The Psychedelic Drug Therapies," *Current Psychiatric Therapies* 20 (1981): 275–83.
33. Piers Vitebsky, "From Cosmology to Environmentalism: Shamanism as Local Knowledge in a Global Setting," in Richard Fardon, ed., *Counterworks: Managing the Diversity of Knowledge* (London: Routledge, 1995), 287.
34. Arthur Kleinman, *Social Origins of Distress and Disease: Depression, Neurasthenia and Pain in Modern China* (New Haven: Yale University Press, 1986), 55–56.
35. Fotiou, "From Medicine Men to Day Trippers."
36. Pierre L. Van den Berghe, *The Quest for the Other: Ethnic Tourism in San Cristóbal, Mexico* (Seattle: University of Washington Press. 1994).
37. Edward M Bruner, *Culture on Tour: Ethnographies of Travel* (Chicago: University of Chicago Press, 2005).
38. Donald Joralemon, "The Selling of the Shaman and the Problem of Informant Legitimacy," *Journal of Anthropological Research* 46, no. 2 (1990).
39. Ibid., 109.
40. Ibid., 112.
41. Dobkin de Rios, "Drug Tourism in the Amazon," 17.
42. Joralemon, "The Selling of the Shaman."
43. Greene, "The Shaman's Needle."
44. Robert J. Wallis, *Shamans/Neo-Shamans: Ecstasy, Alternative Archaeologies, and Contemporary Pagans* (London: Routledge, 2003).
45. Jean Pierre Chaumeil, Jean Pierre, "El otro salvaje: Chamanismo y alteridad," *Amazonía Peruana* 13, no. 26 (1999).
46. Peter Gow, "River People: Shamanism and History in Western Amazonia," in Nicholas Thomas and Caroline Humphrey, eds., *Shamanism, History, and the State* (Ann Arbor: University of Michigan Press, 1994), 90–113.
47. See also the discussion of this by Glenn H. Shepard, Jr., in Chapter 1 of this volume.
48. "Gringo" means foreigner, especially from the United States.
49. Richard Evans Schultes and Albert Hofmann, *Plants of the Gods: Their Sacred, Healing, and Hallucinogenic Powers* (Rochester, VT: Healing Arts Press. 1992), 123.
50. Gerardo Reichel-Dolmatoff, *The Shaman and the Jaguar: A Study of Narcotic Drugs Among the Indians of Colombia* (Philadelphia: Temple University Press, 1975).
51. Cecilia McCallum, *Gender and Sociality in Amazonia: How Real People are Made* (New York: Berg, 2001).
52. Kenneth Kensinger, *How Real People Ought to Live: The Cashinahua of Eastern Peru* (Prospect Heights, IL: Waveland Press, 1995).
53. McCallum, *Gender and Sociality in Amazonia.*
54. Fotiou, "From Medicine Men to Day Trippers."

55. http://www.templeofthewayoflight.org/
56. Judith Butler, *Gender Trouble: Feminism and the Subversion of Identity* (New York: Routledge, 1990).
57. Susana Bustos, "The Healing Power of the Icaros: A Phenomenological Study of Ayahuasca Experiences" (Ph.D. diss., California Institute of Integral Studies, 2008).
58. Pamela Geller and Miranda Stockett, *Feminist Anthropology: Past, Present, and Future* (Philadelphia: University of Pennsylvania Press. 2006).
59. Anne-Marie Colpron, "Monopólio masculino do xamanismo Amazonico: O contra-exemplo das mulheres xamã Shipibo-Conibo," *Mana* 11, no. 1 (2005).
60. Cecilia McCallum, "Gender, Personhood and Social Organization Among the Cashinahua of Western Amazonia," (Ph.D. diss., University of London, 1989); Johanna Overing, "Elementary Structures of Reciprocity: A Comparative Note on Guianese, Central Brazilian, and North West Amazon Socio-Political Thought," in Audrey Butt Colson and H. Dieter Heinen, eds., *Themes in Political Organization the Caribs and Their Neighbours* (Caracas: Fundación La Salle, 1984), 331–48; Fernando Santos Granero, "The Moral and Social Aspects of Equality Amongst the Amuesha of Central Peru," *Journal de la Société des Américanistes* 72 (1986): 107–31.
61. For a discussion on gender complementarity in Upper Amazonian shamanism see Françoise Barbira Freedman, "Shamanic Plants and Gender in the Peruvian Upper Amazon," in Elizabeth Hsu and Stephen Harris, eds., *Plants, Health, and Healing: On the Interface of Ethnobotany and Medical Anthropology* (New York: Berghahn Books, 2010), 135–78.
62. Michael F. Brown, "Shamanism and Its Discontents," *Medical Anthropology Quarterly* 2, no. 3 (1985): 102–20; Michael F. Brown, "Dark Side of the Shaman," *Natural History* 98, no. 11 (1989): 8–10.

Bibliography

Barbira Freedman, Francoise. "Shamanic Plants and Gender in the Peruvian Upper Amazon." In *Plants, Health and Healing: On the Interface of Ethnobotany and Medical Anthropology*, edited by Elisabeth Hsu and Stephen Harris 135–78. New York: Berghahn Books, 2010.

Bastien, Joseph W. *Drum and Stethoscope: Integrating Ethnomedicine and Biomedicine in Bolivia*. Salt Lake City: University of Utah Press, 1992.

Brown, Michael F. "Shamanism and Its Discontents." *Medical Anthropology Quarterly* 2, no. 3 (1985): 102–20.

Brown, Michael F. "Dark Side of the Shaman." *Natural History* 98, no. 11 (1989): 8–10.

Bruner, Edward M. *Culture on Tour: Ethnographies of Travel*. Chicago: University of Chicago Press, 2005.

Bustos, Susana. "The Healing Power of the Icaros: A Phenomenological Study of Ayahuasca Experiences." Ph.D. diss., California Institute of Integral Studies, 2008.

Butler, Judith. *Gender Trouble: Feminism and the Subversion of Identity*. New York: Routledge, 1990.

Chaumeil, Jean Pierre. "El otro salvaje: Chamanismo y alteridad." *Amazonía Peruana* 13, no. 26 (1999): 7–30.

Colpron, Anne-Marie. "Monopólio masculino do xamanismo Amazonico: O contra-exemplo das mulheres xamã Shipibo-Conibo." *Mana* 11, no. 1 (2005): 95–128.

Dobkin de Rios, Marlene. "Drug Tourism in the Amazon." *Anthropology of Consciousness* 5, no. 1 (1994): 16–19.

Dobkin de Rios, Marlene. "Mea Culpa: Drug Tourism and the Anthropologist's Responsibility." *Anthropology News* 47, no. 7 (2006): 20.

Dubisch, Jill, and Michael Winkelman. *Pilgrimage and Healing*. Tucson: University of Arizona Press, 2005.

Eliade, Mircea. *The Sacred and the Profane: The Nature of Religion*. New York: Harcourt, Brace, 1959.

Eliade, Mircea. *Patterns in Comparative Religion*. London: Sheed and Ward, 1979.
Elton, Catherine. "Day Trippers." *Outside* 24, no. 10 (1999): 34.
Fabian, Johannes. *Time and the Other: How Anthropology Makes Its Object*. New York: Columbia University Press, 1983.
Feinberg, Benjamin. *The Devil's Book of Culture: History, Mushrooms, and Caves in Southern Mexico*. Austin: University of Texas Press, 2003.
Flores Ochoa, Jorge. "Buscando los espiritus del Ande: Turismo místico en el Qosqo." In *La tradición Andina en tiempos modernos*, edited by Hiroyasu Tomoeda and Luis Millones, 9–29. Osaka: Ethnological Reports 5, 1996.
Fotiou, Evgenia. "From Medicine Men to Day Trippers: Shamanic Tourism in Iquitos, Peru." Ph.D. diss., University of Wisconsin-Madison, 2010.
Geller, Pamela, and Miranda Stockett. *Feminist Anthropology: Past, Present, and Future*. Philadelphia: University of Pennsylvania Press. 2006.
Gow, Peter. "River People: Shamanism and History in Western Amazonia." In *Shamanism, History, and the State*, edited by Nicholas Thomas and Caroline Humphrey, 90–113. Ann Arbor: University of Michigan Press, 1994.
Greene, Shane. "The Shaman's Needle: Development, Shamanic Agency, and Intermedicality in Aguaruna Lands, Peru." *American Ethnologist* 25, no. 4 (1998): 634–58.
Grinspoon, L., and J. B. Bakalar. "The Psychedelic Drug Therapies." *Current Psychiatric Therapies* 20 (1981): 275–83.
Grunwell, John N. "Ayahuasca Tourism in South America." *Multidisciplinary Association for Psychedelic Studies* 8, no. 3 (1998): 59–62.
Harvey, Graham, and Robert J. Wallis. *Historical Dictionary of Shamanism*. Lanham, MD: Scarecrow Press, 2007.
Hill, Michael. "New Age in the Andes: Mystical Tourism and Cultural Politics in Cusco, Peru." Ph.D. diss., Emory University, 2005.
Joralemon, Donald. "The Selling of the Shaman and the Problem of Informant Legitimacy." *Journal of Anthropological Research* 46, no. 2 (1990): 105–18.
Jung, Carl Gustav. *Modern Man in Search of a Soul*. London: Routledge, 2001.
Kensinger, Kenneth. *How Real People Ought to Live: The Cashinahua of Eastern Peru*. Prospect Heights, IL: Waveland Press, 1995.
Kleinman, Arthur. *Social Origins of Distress and Disease: Depression, Neurasthenia and Pain in Modern China*. New Haven, CT: Yale University Press, 1986.
Kristensen, Kim. "The Ayahuasca Phenomenon/Jungle Pilgrims: North Americans Participating in Amazon Ayahuasca Ceremonies." Multidisciplinary Association for Psychedelic Studies, 1998. http://www.maps.org/research/kristensen.html.
Lewis, W. H., and M. Elvin-Lewis. "Basic Quantitative and Experimental Research Phases of Future Ethnobotany with Reference to the Medicinal Plants of South America." In *Ethnobotany and the Search for New Drugs*, edited by Ghillean T. Prance, Derek Chadwick, and Joan Marsh, 60–76. Chichester, NY: Wiley, 1994.
McCallum, Cecilia. "Gender, Personhood and Social Organization Among the Cashinahua of Western Amazonia." Ph.D. diss., University of London, 1989.
McCallum, Cecilia. *Gender and Sociality in Amazonia: How Real People are Made*. New York: Berg, 2001.
Metzner, Ralph. *Ayahuasca: Human Consciousness, and the Spirits of Nature*. New York: Thunder's Mouth Press, 1999.
Nash, Dennison. *Anthropology of Tourism*. Tarrytown, NY: Pergamon, 1996.
Overing, Johanna. "Elementary Structures of Reciprocity: A Comparative Note on Guianese, Central Brazilian and North West Amazon Socio-political Thought." In *Themes in Political Organization the Caribs and Their Neighbours*, edited by Audrey Butt Colson and H. Dieter Heinen, 331–48. Caracas: Fundación La Salle, 1983/4.
Owen, Bonnie Jean. "Marketing Mysticism and the Purchase of Pilgrimage: The Rise of Spiritual Tourism in Cusco and Iquitos, Peru." Ph.D. diss., University of Arizona, 2006.

Proctor, Rachel. "Tourism Opens New Doors, Creates New Challenges, for Traditional Healers in Peru." *Cultural Survival Quarterly* 24, no. 4 (2001): 14.

Reichel-Dolmatoff, Gerardo. *The Shaman and the Jaguar: A Study of Narcotic Drugs Among the Indians of Colombia*. Philadelphia: Temple University Press, 1975.

Salak, Kira. "Hell and Back." *National Geographic Adventure* (March 2006): 54–58, 88–92.

Santos, Granero Fernando. "The Moral and Social Aspects of Equality Amongst the Amuesha of Central Peru." *Journal de la Société des Américanistes* 72 (1986): 107–31.

Schultes, Richard Evans, and Albert Hofmann. *Plants of the Gods: Their Sacred, Healing, and Hallucinogenic Powers*. Rochester, VT: Healing Arts Press. 1992.

Van den Berghe, Pierre L. *The Quest for the Other: Ethnic Tourism in San Cristóbal, Mexico*. Seattle: University of Washington Press, 1994.

Vitebsky, Piers. "From Cosmology to Environmentalism: Shamanism as Local Knowledge in a Global Setting." In *Counterworks: Managing the Diversity of Knowledge*, edited by Richard Fardon, 276–98. London: Routledge, 1995.

Wallace, Tim. "Tourism, Tourists, and Anthropologists at Work." *NAPA Bulletin*. 23, no. 1 (2005): 1–26.

Wallis, Robert J. *Shamans/Neo-Shamans: Ecstasy, Alternative Archaeologies, and Contemporary Pagans*. London: Routledge, 2003.

Winkelman, Michael. "Drug Tourism or Spiritual Healing? Ayahuasca Seekers in Amazonia." *Journal of Psychoactive Drugs* 37, no. 2 (2005): 209–18.

8

The Internationalization of Peruvian Vegetalismo

BEATRIZ CAIUBY LABATE

This chapter identifies the main processes of transformation that are currently affecting the Peruvian ayahuasca tradition known as *vegetalismo* as a result of increasing interest from nonlocal peoples, mostly international visitors. Although I do not reject such interactions as a priori illegitimate, I do consider the hazards and quandaries that might result from them. I argue that Peruvian vegetalismo can no longer be treated as a phenomenon apart from its dynamics of interaction with new subjects, discourses, substances, and images that now circulate on a global scale. The focus will not be on questions of authenticity, purity, or tradition, but rather on continuities and discontinuities present in the global expansion of vegetalismo.

For my present discussion, I include in the category "vegetalismo" not only Peruvian *mestizo* ayahuasca practices,[1] but also diverse indigenous shamanic traditions, including, among others, those of the Ashaninka, Quechua-Lamas, and especially the Shipibo. In the first place, it is difficult to distinguish between indigenous and mestizo ayahuasca practices, since their origins are frequently historically intermingled, and both remain in constant mutual dialog through the present. Indeed, the term *vegetalismo* itself, though emerging in the academic literature about mainly mestizo traditions, has been adopted in circles by both international and Peruvian adepts and practitioners, taking precedence over the term *traditional medicine*, which might more comfortably accommodate both indigenous and mestizo practices. Moreover, this choice to conflate indigenous and mestizo traditions reflects the fact that Shipibo traditional healers, as much as mestizo *vegetalistas*, have been primary agents involved in the international expansion of ayahuasca consumption from Peru. In this sense, the discussion takes on the international perspective, in which vegetalismo assumes a generic or universal character in relation to local particulars.

This chapter draws on data from a multi-sited ethnography[2] that was the basis of my doctoral dissertation.[3] Fieldwork was initiated in 1996, including six field trips to Peru and Colombia between 1998 and 2009. Between 2002 and 2010, I made systematic observations of an itinerant Peruvian vegetalista based in São Paulo, and from 2007 to 2012, I visited various ayahuasca drinking groups or practitioners active in the United States, Canada, and Europe (Holland, Germany, Spain, UK, Portugal, and Switzerland). In these various contexts, I participated in rituals and interviewed Shipibo healers, mestizo vegetalistas, and "gringo" ayahuasca ceremonial leaders,[4] as well as participants of various backgrounds and some entrepreneurs involved in the promotion of what some authors have labeled as "ayahuasca tourism." I also interviewed some researchers whose academic publications have played a role in the international expansion of vegetalismo and analyzed their work.

Reflecting on general processes occurring in the transnational circuit of ayahuasca, I will nevertheless focus on a particular group: the less commercial and more "initiatic" branches within the ayahuasca expansion movement, mostly based in the town of Pucallpa in the Peruvian Amazon. For this reason, the conclusions here may not apply equally to all of the various ramifications of vegetalismo's international expansion. Moreover, this scenario is highly dynamic, with intense transformations still under way. Thus, the perspectives presented here are already, in some sense, outdated.

A detailed description of the varied ceremonies and other activities performed by indigenous, mestizo, and gringo ayahuasqueros will not be provided here. In general, the sessions are held in the dark, in a circular formation, with a few common central elements considered "traditional" to vegetalismo: pre-session dietary and behavioral taboos; the singing of ritual chants, or *icaros*; *sopladas* or "blowing"—using perfumed water (*agua florida*) or smoke of rustic tobacco (*mapacho, Nicotiana ssp.*)—on patients and other participants to protect, clean and dispel negative forces; and, sometimes, floral or herbal baths. These ritual techniques performed during the session itself are often supplemented with other specific practices before and afterward, which may or may not involve elements from the sphere of Peruvian vegetalismo. These include consumption of other "master plants" (*plantas maestras*), participation in the process of preparation of ayahuasca, and activities involving local traditions. A wide gamut of nontraditional activities that may occur in conjunction with ayahuasca drinking include energy therapy, *reiki*, massage, holotropic respiration, music therapy, meditation, yoga, mantras, sweat lodge or *temazcal* saunas, group conversations or "sharing" of expectations and experiences, and art or poetry workshops. Ayahuasca tourism packages in Iquitos often include jungle walks, observation of flora and fauna, boat rides, visits to native communities, fishing, and adventure sports.

In this chapter, I will concentrate on the transnational as well as local processes involved in the expansion of vegetalismo to a global consumer public.

Figure 8.1. Flowers of the ayahuasca vine. Photograph by Thiago Martins e Silva.

In conclusion, I will examine some of the conflicts and dilemmas that this expansion process has produced, including legal problems and various efforts to formally sanction and regulate these practices.

Significant Processes in the Course of Vegetalismo's Expansion: Psychologization

One of the most evident features in the process of expansion and internationalization of Peruvian vegetalismo is "psychologization." Historically, the category of "shaman" emerged as a kind of "primitive peoples' psychiatrist" and the figure of the shaman has been compared to that of the psychiatrist of our society.[5] With the internationalization of ayahuasca, such implicit parallels between psychiatry and shamanism, or shamanism and altered states of consciousness, have been further developed and established as a central paradigm. Ayahuasca experience is interpreted as a form of reflexive self-knowledge and a technique for constructing the modern self. According to Giddens,[6] there is a deep relationship between modernity and radical doubt. Modernity, which produces a surfeit of choices, hyperspecialization, and emergence of a variety of experts, imposes on day-to-day affairs the urgent question, "How am I to live my life?" This stimulates a need for each person to "find" himself or herself and establish a sense of individual identity. The reflexivity of the modern self is most evident in the growth of all modes of self-help, consultation, and therapy. In this context, ayahuasca becomes one among an array of possible modalities for apprehending the reflexive modern self.

"Neo-vegetalismo," as these practices can perhaps also be called, is obsessed with the necessity of "establishing one's intention" for participating in an ayahuasca session and afterward "integrating the content"; which is to say, a psychological instrumentalization of the experience, albeit with spiritual nuances. The language of trauma, abuse, loss, and so on is commonly evoked. Psychologization is related to a broader trend whereby taking ayahuasca is naturalized as a therapeutic activity.[7] Often, *curanderos*, vegetalistas, and other ayahuasca "facilitators" are equated with psychiatrists or psychologists and are expected to guide participants through their personal questions or issues. Likewise, psychologists and other kinds of therapists are considered pre-adapted for taking on the role of shaman or ayahuasca session guide. Thus, there is a juxtaposition and fusion of roles that, even though not necessarily explicit, is usually accepted and understood.

This recasting of contemporary vegetalismo results in greater emphasis on the visionary elements of the experience in relation to other physiological effects of ayahuasca, such as nausea, vomiting, chills, diarrhea, and so on; the latter are often seen as less important or minor side effects, necessary initial stages required for the nobler, visionary end. Visions may be attributed mystical value as spiritual revelations, but they may also be read as expressing unconscious or subconscious content that needs to be deciphered, like dream interpretation. Interest in the visionary dimension of ayahuasca experience also reflects the somewhat simplistic notion that drinkers tend to see similar things in their visions independent of their sociocultural context and prior experiences. These notions reflect, among other factors, a popularization of the work of the cognitive psychologist Benny Shanon,[8] who interviewed a wide range of subjects from different cultural backgrounds and noted certain common visionary elements, such as reptiles (especially snakes), palaces and temples, magical or artistic objects, divine beings, and fantastical worlds full of marvels and enchantments. This approach is heir to earlier work on supposed universal elements of psychedelic experience by Aldous Huxley and others. Without going into further detail about the ethnographic limitations of Shanon's study, it is worth noting that Westerners' fixation on the centrality of visions in the use of psychedelics is related to a deep-rooted Western sensory valorization of sight over the other senses. It is no coincidence that such substances are known as "visionary plants," and visual hallucinations are emphasized over auditory ones or others. This approach contrasts with local perspectives, where ayahuasca visions are not taken as "things unto themselves" (either psychological or universal) but placed within certain cosmologies and values that have culturally specific attributes. In native experiences, the act of *purgar* (to purge) is considered as fundamental as visions; these physical effects are frequently attributed a positive value.[9]

Psychologization of vegetalismo is in turn linked to a "moralization" of the system.[10] This tendency is most evident in the minimization or repression of the significance of witchcraft and sorcery, which are fundamental in native practices.[11] Negative experiences and other problems that occur to participants during sessions are reinterpreted as symptoms of energetic blockage or psychological resistance, rather than, per typical native interpretations, as signs of attacks by rival shamans or sorcerers or on behalf of spirit agents. Instead of treating vomiting as a process of bodily cleaning, purging in neo-vegetalismo is reinterpreted as a way of processing dark aspects of the subconscious, or as a way of expiating immoral behaviors. In the Santo Daime and União do Vegetal ayahuasca religions of Brazil, this process of moralization takes on overtly Christian tones; the influence of folk Christianity on vegetalismo concepts is variable.

There is, through all of this, a curious process of mutual cross-contagion between the psychological sphere and the spirit world; in other words, psychological processes may be interpreted using the language of the spirits, while spirits can be interpreted through a psychological idiom.[12] By the same token, it is commonly suggested that certain kinds of behaviors or psychological traits result from malevolent spiritual forces and require shamanic mediation through ayahuasca.

Shamanization and Retraditionalization

A process that has been called the "shamanization" or "indigenization" of vegetalismo advances in a somewhat contrary direction.[13] Ayahuasca's origin is typically assumed to be traceable to Amazonian indigenous shamanism. The Internet abounds with generic sources affirming "Ayahuasca is an ancestral, age-old practice of native Amazonian peoples." Classic studies such as those of Mircea Eliade and Joseph Campbell are often cited, identifying shamanism as a "universal phenomenon" and "the world's oldest religion." However, some authors have demonstrated the relatively recent introduction of ayahuasca to some indigenous groups in the western Amazon.[14] The Shipibo people of the Ucayali (or, more recently, the Shipibo immigrants to Iquitos who work in tourists lodges), in particular, are viewed as emblematic of indigenous ayahuasca shamanism: a quick Internet search finds descriptions of the Shipibo as "ayahuasca masters" and "sacred guardians of the ayahuasca ceremony." Because of this particular fame of the Shipibo, mestizo shamans, foreign practitioners, and even native healers from other indigenous groups "shipibize" themselves by using Shipibo-style painted tunics, necklaces, paintings, and other trappings.[15]

In this trend, we also observe a process of "aesthetization," which is to say, the appearance of a common, shared set of aesthetic references throughout transnational networks. Tied to this development is the increasing commercial sale of ayahuasca-related objects on the Internet, alongside popular visionary paintings, often recreated by new digital technologies. At the same time, ayahuasca has become a metonymy with Peruvian vegetalismo, with its use as the central feature, while diverse other elements have become secondary, even dispensable. Basic words in Quechua or Shipibo are frequently used as ceremonial names for apprentice gringo shamans and ayahuasca centers; these centers become associated with "Amazonian indigenous cultures."

All of this reflects a general process of "re-traditionalization," or even "hyper-traditionalization."[16] Foreign ayahuasca converts or new South American urban practitioners tend to place a strong emphasis on the "traditional" rules of vegetalismo, while native and mestizo practitioners sometimes relax or relativize aspects of tradition and criticize such orthodoxy. Those seeking a more orthodox identity purge folk Catholic elements present in some variants of vegetalismo, such as saints' images or references to the Virgin Mary or Christ in the icaros. In some icaros, Spanish-language words are replaced by terms in Quechua or other native languages. Some foreign apprentices regard the Quechua icaros as less valuable, since they are more widely known and thus less esoteric and distinctive. One can

Figure 8.2. Banisteriopsis caapi vine. Photograph by Lou Gold.

hear comments such as "In my work, I sing only in Shipibo." In any case, it seems that the otherness of the foreign language creates a sense of enchantment, and adds to the psychological otherness created by the effects of the brew.

There is an ironic circularity to these developments. As more foreigners have become interested and involved in vegetalismo, and various ritual modalities have multiplied and become available, an emphasis on tradition and authenticity is increasingly stressed. In fact, this happens precisely because the fascination with alterity exists among all participants: just as gringo shamans want to go native and reinvent themselves as traditional healers, so do indigenous and mestizo healers from within the vegetalismo tradition seek to incorporate elements from the "Other" cultural universe of transnational shamanism and New Age spirituality, whether to better arm themselves in their own shamanic battles or to widen their social networks. This follows a typical trend in Amazonian shamanism, where power comes from outside and far away.[17]

Formalization and Ritualization

Vegetalismo is also passing through a phase of formalization and professionalization. The practice of curanderos has come to be represented and understood as a specific kind of knowledge system and valued as such. Orally transmitted traditional knowledge such as songs, ayahuasca brewing, and the preparation of perfumes and special plants, is increasingly systematized and formalized. "Ayahuasca seminars" are organized in modules and separated according to hierarchical levels. Shamanic schools, programs, and associations have appeared; in some cases, even distance-learning mentorship is available. Ayahuasca chants or icaros have been recorded in professional studios and mass-produced for sale on CDs or downloaded from Internet sites. A new generation of practitioners has learned by listening to these recordings and reading notebooks with transcribed melodies, lyrics, and explanations of the symbolism. One particularly important Shipibo curandero has developed a songbook with icaros composed especially for international apprentices, with translations in Spanish and other languages. Adepts can take "courses" or purchase instructional videos explaining how to prepare the ayahuasca brew. Others have taken detailed notes in the field on the brewing process, and their recipes and commentaries have proliferated on the Internet. Apprenticeship and socialization of new generations have thus been transformed.

All of this has also resulted in a growing ritualization of ayahuasca use. Ayahuasca sessions are considered "ceremonies": in the United States and Canada, the phrase "sit in ceremony" is widespread in underground ayahuasca circles. "Prayer" and "meditation circles" are other common synonyms that appear to have migrated from Eastern religions and Native North American shamanism, as popularized by the New Age movement. Local assistants of traveling native or gringo vegetalistas will help "hold the space," evoking a combination of spiritual and psychological care within the "ritual circle." Their ceremonies begin and end at specific times and maintain a solemn atmosphere, sometimes requiring special clothing. Certain aspects of traditional ayahuasca use that were previously looser and less formal have become progressively more rigid and ritualized, including the preparation of the ayahuasca brew itself, or its simple recooking to concentrate it. Common practices include promoting two or three ceremonies in a row, or offering ceremonies devoted just to women. These options combine underlying economic reasons with justifications such as to be able to "deepen the process"; in any case, these innovations are embedded with "ritual formality." Individual eccentricities of a particular curandero can be come invested with a high symbolic value and understood as signs of "tradition." This view brings native vegetalismo practices in line with Western notions about ritual and the sacred; in short, this is the idiom that Westerners have for understanding such experiences.

Professionalization and Market Specialization

Growing numbers of international visitors to ayahuasca sessions in Peru entail various forms of institutionalization. Where ceremonies were once held in forest clearings or in the healer's or the patient's house, one now finds constructions or entire centers built especially for this purpose. Larger centers contain a ritual space for the ceremony along with other facilities such as dormitories, cafeterias, administration, library, and meditation rooms accessorized with imported mattresses, stylized buckets, electric lighting, lamps that project psychedelic colors, and so on. A professional staff mans the larger centers. Such institutions have become both a sign of social, economic, and spiritual prestige and a source of criticism and envy. A number of bureaucratic procedures have become common, such as requiring visitors to fill out forms detailing personal information, medical history, expectations and intentions, and, in some cases formal waivers and releases of liability regarding health risks to avoid possible lawsuits.

Peruvian vegetalismo has remodeled itself and become a kind of network of professional services. At the same time, traditional themes involving sorcery, shamanic rivalry, spirit attack and so on are brought into play in order to interpret the development of these new activities—again, a reverse process of colonizing the gringo's world. However, in the opposite and complementary direction, one finds a fascinating new tendency toward legal adjudication of shamanic conflicts.

Disputes once worked out entirely in the shamanic sphere may wind up in front of a judge. For example, one curandero in a Peruvian jungle town filed a lawsuit against another who had accused him of witchcraft. Others have made claims that their salaries as curanderos in the retreat centers were not properly paid.

As a result of competition for new clients, there has been a tendency toward specialization and market diversification, inspiring new offerings and options. These include workshops on tobacco or San Pedro (*Echinopsis pachanoi*), vision quests and sweat lodges (again, borrowing from Native North American shamanism) alongside ceremonies and *dietas* (diets: certain dietary and behavioral restrictions performed during a period of isolation) in Peru and abroad. New programs have been created in Peru focused on less-well-known plants such as sanango (*Brunfelsia*), ajo sacha (*Mansoa*), camalonga (*Strychnos*), and toé (*Brugmansia*).[18] These additions imply both transformation and continuity; for example, shamans and their clients abroad might "diet" plants local to those environs, such as mistletoe (*Phoradendron flavescens*) in California.

Even the widespread term *ayahuasca,* of Quechua language origin, has become somewhat overused, so some practitioners substitute less-well-known indigenous words such as *yage* (a term used in Colombia), *nixi-pae* (in Cashinahua), or other ethnic terms in order to differentiate their product and gain a competitive edge in the international market. There has also been diversification in the kinds of seminars offered on various subjects such as chants (with or without ayahuasca consumption), preparing the brew, identifying rainforest plants, body painting, traditional weaving, or learning about indigenous worldviews. All of this diversification creatively reinvigorates vegetalismo. However, there are legitimate concerns that this process might also result in the fragmentation of aspects integrated in a specific cosmology, whose various components are decontextualized and reappropriated as mere technique.[19]

Scientization and Medicalization

Another important process is the "scientization" of the ayahuasca experience; which is to say, the appropriation, by the field, of scientific research on the subject. Nonnative drinkers form expectations and then understand, relate, and narrate their experiences in part through their contact with anthropological, biomedical, and psychological literature on ayahuasca.[20] Such appropriations can take curious turns. For example, a foreign drinker might interpret a certain negative experience as evidence of sorcery, having learned the concept through anthropological readings; or, in a different vein, the drinker might describe his or her mystical experience using terms such as pineal gland, serotonin, or tryptamines. Conversely, native and mestizo ayahuasca practitioners appropriate scientific literature in their own ways to promote and legitimate their activities. Most retreat-center websites contain bibliographies and references including articles or videos in which scientists discuss their research or, in some cases, feature their own ad hoc researcher. Just as some anthropologists, psychologists, and other researchers have become facilitators or shamans in their own right, some local healers have also authored their own academic or quasi-academic texts. As scientific literature on ayahuasca has proliferated,[21] so has a certain mixed genre that combines travel writing, journalism, documentary film, and digital and artistic production. There seems to be an emerging international ayahuasca culture exhibiting certain common elements and blending concepts from vegetalismo and Western science. There has been an explosion of scientific and semi-scientific conferences to discuss ayahuasca and debate numerous issues, some of these interfacing with the international psychedelic movement.[22] Internet forums and list-serves allow researchers and enthusiasts to discuss, say, interactions between ayahuasca and mental health. Some jungle centers cultivate virtual online communities of "ayahuasca drinkers and readers" in what seems to be a new form of identity. Such spaces and networks generate hybrid activities at the interstices of experimentation, spirituality, therapy, research, service, and activism.

The internationalization of ayahuasca has also resulted in its "medicalization." Vegetalistas were historically classified as "traditional doctors" through a process of dialogue with hegemonic Western medical concepts. Now ayahuasca itself has assumed the status of transnational "sacred medicine." There seems to be a strong need on behalf of practitioners to establish the psychological and biomedical legitimacy of ayahuasca consumption.[23] In one particularly interesting adjacent case, the União do Vegetal ayahuasca religion in Brazil created an epidemiological surveillance system to monitor the incidence of mental health problems among its members.[24] Discourses proposing ayahuasca as a panacea against various evils of modernity—particularly against drug abuse, depression, and anxiety—must also be understood in the context of the proliferation of negative representations of ayahuasca as a dangerous hallucinogenic drug associated with fanatical religious sects.

A fertile area of contact and contagion exists between biomedical and native discourses. Psychiatric and vegetalista criteria become juxtaposed and shuffled together: witchcraft darts[25] and neurotransmitters live side-by-side as concrete realities experienced by ceremony participants. On occasion, both gringo and native shamans, influenced by Western biomedical concepts, have instructed contemporary ayahuasca drinkers to follow simultaneously two types of diets, the "vegetalista diet" (i.e., restriction of sex, alcohol, pork, etc.) and the "biomedical diet" (i.e., considering interactions with particular medicines and tyramine-containing foods). Some have attempted to find biomedical justifications for the vegetalista diets: the fact that it is necessary to diet, or that the diets are valid, is rarely questioned.

Ayahuasca samples have been sent to the laboratory for scientific analyses under the "shamanic" suspicion that the supplier is mixing other substances in the brew to harm the recipient. Doctors and psychologists have gained power in the contemporary scenario of vegetalismo, especially considering the large number of medications and unknown afflictions foreign patients and visitors bring with them. There are, to be sure, conflicts between the native and biomedical logic, especially in cases involving difficult health or behavioral problems. Pre-session interviews and medical forms have become frequent, even obligatory. Medical legitimacy and oversight can be evoked as an armament in shamanic disputes, or used as a differential factor to win over new clients. On the other hand, both native and gringo shamans will occasionally claim to heal certain mental or physical conditions, causing discomfort to those who follow medical etiquette and use politically correct language about potential harms and benefits of psychedelic drugs. Hence, communication and juxtaposition between both shamanic and biomedical logics is not always harmonious.

Ayahuasca and "Our Culture"

These contemporary developments within vegetalismo should be seen within the broader process of objectification of culture. Western representations about culture, including those in anthropology, are absorbed by traditional populations and manipulated politically in dialogue with the "Other." Native and mestizo curanderos appropriate foreign conceptions about "ayahuasca shamanism" and "the ancient knowledge of forest shamans" in order to emphasize their difference and benefit from it. Festivals celebrating indigenous cultures have proliferated in the Amazon, where myths, body painting, plant knowledge, and rituals are used as symbols of identity and ethnicity as well as terms of cultural and political negotiation. Regional populations have managed to create ties with a broader community of sympathizers, supporters, and NGOs. They have expanded their participation in national and international networks as part of a new strategy of survival and improvement of material and nonmaterial conditions. Such interest from foreigners can promote feelings of self-esteem and cultural pride that go beyond mere financial benefits.

The popularity of ayahuasca has led indigenous groups who did not traditionally use it to adopt this brew for their own rituals. In some cases, ayahuasca drinking has been associated with the emergence or reemergence of indigenous identity in groups that had historically ceased to consider themselves "Indians"; ayahuasca also plays a role in pan-indigenous alliances that may include additional participants such as shamanic facilitators, therapists, and Santo Daime adepts.[26] These new rituals appear to temporarily invert social hierarchies, with natives presiding at the top as professors over foreign guests. Yet, these processes also open the way for other kinds of reverse appropriation and the imposition of new kinds of inequality, as evidenced, for example, in the process of medicalization, or as will be discussed below.

Conflicts

The expansion of vegetalismo has resulted in several kinds of cultural and ideological conflicts. Various local beliefs and practices surrounding ayahuasca may be viewed as superstitious, backward, and primitive by Western visitors—for example, its use for love magic, for good luck in business endeavors, or to recover lost or stolen objects; the conflictive traditional universe of envy, witchcraft, and sorcery accusations; and the widespread traditional prohibition of menstruating women from taking ayahuasca. By the same token, local populations in Peruvian towns like Pucallpa are often shocked by the drug use, eating habits, and practice of nudism among foreign visitors. Perhaps the main area of misunderstanding and conflict has to do with gender roles and expectations and the ethics of sexual conduct. Such problems have been especially prevalent in the United States, where the relationship between the curandero and session participants has been interpreted through the lens of a puritanical ethos combined with feminist rights, a litigious culture, and the strict ethical standards enforced in the (non-shamanic) patient-therapist relationship, projected onto ayahuasca-related activities. There have been a growing number of denunciations of sexual harassment, assault, and abuse in regard to curanderos.[27]

By the same token, there is also a distinct tendency on behalf of foreigners to romanticize indigenous and mestizo peoples and traditional lifestyles. Many new visitors arrive with naïve notions about the Amazon and its "primitive" peoples, viewed as an inverted counterpart to the consumerism, ecological imbalance, and social inequality found in the capitalist West. Such idealistic representations are often not reflected in reality. Foreigners can be disappointed to learn that the supposedly "eco-friendly" natives do not, in fact, recycle, and even throw trash in the forest or in the river. They can become indignant when traditional curanderos, on tour in northern countries, express their desire to buy brand-name tennis shoes or video games. It can also be an unpleasant shock for a foreigner to have their feelings of cosmic consciousness interrupted by the theft of an expensive digital camera during a stay at an ayahuasca center. A critical and often bitter ayahuasca seeker—once enthusiast—emerges from the field as another typical category.

Increasingly, local populations are aware of foreigners' representations and expectations of them, sometimes adopting, for example, an environmental discourse, or recreating the image of the shaman as an incarnation of planetary ecological wisdom.[28] Most ayahuasca centers announce some kind of environmental conservation project or, at the very least, a botanical garden. The jungle is always central to presentations that introduce ceremonies. But, unlike the formal ecological discourse, the day-to-day reality of local people is much more preoccupied with practical concerns of development and "progress," shocking the expectations of some foreign visitors.

Traditional medical practices themselves, which include ayahuasca, herbal baths, diets, medicinal plants, and other treatments administered by curanderos, may conflict with some foreigners' concepts about health and illness, and thus encounter a degree of resistance. Patients who travel to Peru seeking treatment and cure for some kinds of illness may also displease their doctors at home, creating problems in their ongoing treatment. Correspondingly, local healers may find it difficult to relate to the medical concepts and treatment expectations of their patients. Brabec de Mori[29] notes that, in many cases, what Westerners would categorize as mental illness is classified by the Shipibo as antisocial behavior. Also, interactions between ayahuasca, mental health, prescription medications, and certain psychiatric conditions are an area of real concern and potential conflicts.

The main source of conflict in the expansion of vegetalismo has to do with asymmetric north-south relations. Exchanges between foreigners, natives, and mestizos take place in hierarchically differentiated sociolinguistic and economic contexts. Local people often feel exploited by foreign intermediaries, who charge in dollars and pay in *soles*, the Peruvian currency. According to some of those excluded by the expansion movement, the internationalization of ayahuasca drinking has only increased local income disparity, marginalizing the poor and making curanderos' services inaccessible for those who can't afford gringo prices. Inversely, ayahuasqueros involved in the business preach about the many local benefits, pointing out the lack of other viable economic alternatives while affirming that the attention of foreigners has awakened interest among local youths in traditional crafts and other practices. Ayahuasca centers and traveling shamans claim to support various projects in their home communities such as schools, hospitals, or forest conservation, though details about specific projects and locations can be rather vague. For those native and mestizo ayahuasqueros who manage to establish themselves in this market, their status as bearers of esoteric knowledge inverts economic hierarchies in the symbolic plane, allowing them to negotiate a materially better life. Moreover, many curanderos take advantage of colonial guilt on behalf of foreign visitors as a strategy of strengthening their demands.

Foreigners who dedicate themselves to building centers and promoting seminars can become frustrated with the lack of efficiency and professionalism of local actors, or become disappointed in relation to expected profits. Some resident foreigners integrate themselves into local communities while others remain isolated. Successful native curanderos tend to dedicate themselves increasingly to a foreign clientele, becoming estranged from local ties and criticized for being "shaman to the gringos." Some become romantically involved with or even married to foreign partners, maintain apprentices in other countries, and may end up spending much of their time traveling, or ultimately emigrating. There is still more research needed on this interrelated set of phenomena, beginning with an estimate of how many foreigners visit Peru each year seeking ayahuasca experiences, how many such centers exist, and the dimensions of the socioeconomic impact of ayahuasca internationalization.

There appears to be a contradiction between the commercial nature of some of these businesses and what might be called, broadly speaking, "the logic of shamanism." The commodification of the ayahuasca experience can be challenging, since ayahuasca's effects are hard to predict and stabilize. For example, some participants might not feel its effects, while others may suffer excessively unpleasant ones. A visitor who pays for a ceremony or diet may consider it is within his or her right, as a customer, to interrupt it or disobey ritual protocol that makes him or her uncomfortable; however, in most cases, the ayahuasquero will probably disagree. Tensions between economic pressures and traditional patterns of participation and apprenticeship may develop in this way.[30]

The traditional relationship between the *maestro* and apprentice implies a certain degree of tension. In the transnational context, this inherently ambiguous relationship gains additional complicating layers. Foreign apprentices can bring significant, direct financial support, aside from offering communication in several languages and access to networks that can open possibilities for overseas travel and to spaces to hold ceremonies internationally. Such advantages can provide a kind of "shortcut" in the process of shamanic initiation. Not all apprentices are able to offer such advantages to the ayahuasquero, which might lead to exclusion and favoritism. On the other hand, if the apprentices are native or mestizo looking, they might have more appeal to foreigners. Some criticize the proliferation of new ayahuasqueros who may not be fully prepared to conduct sessions on their own. Transparency and depth are said to be lacking in the training of the new generation.[31] This in turn feeds the traditional rivalry among local shamans. For example, it is common to hear one ayahuasquero, speaking about a new gringo apprentice who had previously apprenticed with another ayahuasquero, remark, "His body and energy were a real mess! It took a lot of work to reorganize him properly." One also hears frequent reference to "false shamans." It is worth remembering, however, that accusations of charlatanism predate the arrival of foreigners on the vegetalismo scene. Therefore, such accusations cannot be taken objectively as a sign that there is an increase in the number of "charlatans." Above and beyond conflicts surrounding commodification, some see the expansion of vegetalismo as leading to folklorization and vulgarization, concerns that are closely tied to notions about authenticity, indigeneity, and tradition, which will not be discussed here.

Legality and Identity

The worldview of new participants in vegetalismo is shaped by hegemonic Western concepts that divide licit from illicit drugs. A sense of secrecy permeates the ayahuasca scene in many countries, even where it is legal.[32] The concept of ayahuasca as a sacred medicine tied closely to the indigenous world comes into both dialogue with and opposition to the illicit recreational or experimental use of drugs. Ceremonies are developed and adjusted in order to adapt to the Western imagination about what the ayahuasca experience is all about. As noted above, there is a tendency to hyperformalize the ritual space, and to label the experience "sacred." This approach to the sessions may even be influenced, in part, by drinker communities' readings and appropriations of anthropological notions about ritual drug use and traditional social controls surrounding psychoactives. Yet, native practices and concepts sometimes defy Western expectations, as in the case of one curandero who prefers to hold his healing sessions slightly drunk, as well as the informal, matter-of-fact way local ayahuasqueros sometimes prepare or sell the brew.

Nonlocals can't always grasp the complexities of diverse plants used by the curanderos for medicinal, aphrodisiac, purgative, divinatory, dream inducing, and other purposes: everything ends up being subsumed under the category of "entheogen." Perhaps we can establish a parallel here with the Western category of "drunkenness," historically used to designate the effects of all psychoactive substances.[33] Aside from difficulties in understanding the local classification of plants beyond their psychoactive dimension, native concepts surrounding proscription of certain foods and sex abstinence are reinterpreted by foreign participants within their own cultural categories such as "the sacred," "holism," "purification," and "nature" without necessarily comprehending the animistic concepts that abound in Amazonia, which imply ontological and epistemological ruptures with their own worldview.[34]

Urban ayahuasca drinkers, especially in Europe, the United States, and Canada, have developed their own underground culture built around itinerancy and illegality or semilegality and characterized by a particular ethos, style of communication, and aesthetics. These groups experiment with and share specific techniques concerning the various stages of ayahuasca preparation and distribution: actual brewing techniques (more concentrated to occupy less space, with or without additional refining); bottling (plastic vs. glass, various types of containers, vacuum packing); storage (refrigerated or not, systems for avoiding fermentation); transportation and shipping (personally or by third parties; in luggage or not; by air, sea, mail, or couriers; how to disguise it or label it officially; postal and agriculture forms; etc.); discreet advertisement of the sessions (websites and email lists using euphemisms, phone trees, code words for use in public conversation, etiquette to introduce newcomers); means of payment (in cash, in advance); places to carry out the sessions (hotels, esoteric spaces, rented churches, private homes); ceremonial rules (discretion regarding neighbors, prohibition of going outdoors and vomiting publicly); and ritual paraphernalia (a portable ritual travel kit).[35]

Peruvian curanderos, as well as members of Brazilian ayahuasca religions such as Santo Daime who have gone to jail or been otherwise persecuted in Northern countries, have sent out mass mailings seeking support and donations for their legal representation. For example, Taita Juan Bautista Agreda Chindoy, an indigenous Kametsa *yagecero* from Colombia, was jailed for ayahuasca possession in Houston, Texas, and received donations totaling $30,000 to support his legal defense (personal communication, anonymous source involved in the legal team, 2012). Legal prohibitions, somewhat paradoxically, create a sense of identity and cultural resistance, strengthening ties within real and imagined communities. On the other hand, rivalries between shamans translate into the administrative and legal realm, in some cases even involving denunciations to law enforcement agents. References to the fact that a particular group is involved in problems are commonly turned into accusations that they are not fully legitimate: "That ayahuasquero is a charlatan, he was caught because he wasn't doing things properly"; "The organizers of his sessions are not trustworthy…they

Figure 8.3. Tobacco. Photograph by Alessandro Meiguins.

managed to jail him," "no wonder the post office refused to send his ayahuasca, as he has such a dark energy"; and so forth. Legal victories are transformed into stories of mystical significance and political power and recognition. Both the struggle for legal recognition and the choice to remain underground create forms of ritualization. The relationship between identity and legality remains to be studied.[36]

Cultural Heritage and Dilemmas of Regulation

Although international expansion has created legal problems in some countries, in Peru this has helped ayahuasca become recognized as national cultural heritage. Takiwasi Center, located in Tarapoto, was a key actor in this process. Takiwasi has promoted an ayahuasca-based regime of treatment for problematic use of drugs as well as other programs including diets, seminars, and ayahuasca sessions for foreigners. The center raises much of its operating costs by charging for these services for outsiders. Historically, Takiwasi was one of the main agents involved in promoting journeys to the Peruvian jungle for foreigners to get to know the "vine of the soul," and in raising awareness about vegetalismo. This center maintains strong ties with the provincial government of San Martín, and also has ties to national government agencies. Further, it has a wide range of international contacts, especially in France. Rosa Giove, who belongs to the board of directors, wrote a document[37] that resulted in the release of a formal report by the Direction of the Registry and Study of Culture,[38] and soon thereafter a resolution by the National Institute of Culture,[39] which recognized ayahuasca as Peruvian national cultural heritage.[40] Both governments' documents cite Giove's report.

The symbolic and discursive power of Takiwasi lies in its alleged promotion of a cure for problematic drug use employing traditional indigenous medicine. Such discourses center on the opposition between "master plants" or "plant teachers" (tradition, wisdom, cure) and "drugs" (modernity, the profane, addiction). Native, mestizo, and foreign ayahuasqueros and practitioners cite Resolution 836 as an emblem of the value of vegetalismo. The growing international interest in and popularity of ayahuasca are celebrated and incorporated by the state at the same time that the resolution and public debate warn about the danger of "decontextualized, consumerist, and commercially-motivated Western uses."[41] Paradoxically, since 1995, Takiwasi Center has frequently been mentioned in the reports by the French Ministerial Committee for Surveillance of Sects, which characterizes Takiwasi as incorporating a potentially dangerous combination of drug use and "brain-washing."[42]

The greatest challenge of the expansion of vegetalismo and the spread of ayahuasca into northern countries is the process of regulation. Groups make their own uses: medical, therapeutic, religious, recreational, aesthetic. It is difficult to draw clear distinctions between these modalities, and equally difficult to establish universally accepted ethical parameters for the consumption of ayahuasca within such a diverse context of communities. Legal disputes, ethical debates, and controversies have proliferated in a number of countries. In Peru, public debates about the expansion of ayahuasca occur especially when the news media focuses on a specific ayahuasca-related problem in some tourist lodge. Government oversight of tourism establishments and agencies that offer ayahuasca sessions is modest, and the organization of vegetalista associations is only just beginning.[43] Nevertheless, the process of expansion raises the question of what criteria should be considered necessary for individuals or groups to conduct ayahuasca sessions, and whether there should be some official recognition and certification of session leaders.[44] Meanwhile, unlike Brazil, the harvest of *B. caapi* and *P. viridis* remain unregulated in Peru. Some centers maintain their own plantations. It is probable that in the future sale, purchase, and shipping will be more tightly controlled.

It seems there should be certain modest regulations on behalf of the state, attenuated so as not to invade the privacy of individuals and the cultural autonomy of various ethnic groups. It is equally important to valorize the role of traditional and informal social controls and support indigenous knowledge systems. The process of regulation should be built through dialog with civil society, representative ayahuasca organizations, and researchers from various disciplines. Society does have the right to demand transparency in the process of training ceremonial leaders, to expect ethical conduct in their professional work, and to impose lawful taxation of their activities. The state should encourage and finance scientific research about the topic and support and subsidize the sustainable extraction and consumption of the plant species used in making ayahuasca.

Conclusion: Continuities and Ruptures

The internationalization of ayahuasca can be seen as a multidirectional process, "from the forest to the city," and likewise in reverse, "from the city to the forest." International networks have emerged in which subjects, substances, capital, images, and "sacred techniques" circulate. These exchanges are mediated by power relations and unequal economic conditions, and may be read as survival strategies on behalf of marginalized populations who have appropriated a potential source of power. However, these strategies do not always succeed.

In neo-vegetalismo, it is difficult to mark boundaries between shamanism, therapy, and tourism services; these spheres overlap and blend into one another. In one direction, there is a process of secularization and scientization as health sciences, psychology, and anthropology penetrate the vegetalismo universe. Simultaneously, the other way around, we find a "shamanization" of the world of the gringos, promoting a reverse colonization, and a new diaspora.

Scholars have argued that vegetalismo emerged in the contact between rubber tappers and indigenous and riverine populations—who were already strongly influenced by missionary activity—at the turn of the twentieth century. Thus vegetalismo was born out of population migrations and the engagement of multiple healing and spiritual systems.[45] Vegetalismo should not be thought of as a system of fixed contents, but rather as a way of establishing relationships between different levels and codes. The transformations that are taking place now represent both a rupture with tradition and a renewal of it; a new stage in the same process of dynamic reinvention through which vegetalismo was first born. Traveling shamans continue to navigate various worlds, and now arrive in distant foreign capitals. Ayahuasca rituals now, as always, mediate the relationships between whites and Indians, between colonizers and colonized,[46] presently on a global scale. Exogenous symbols and practices are appropriated and incorporated selectively and creatively, then return to their points of origin and are reelaborated once again. By means of such renovation and readaptation, continuity becomes possible. Just as shamans add new plants to the ayahuasca brew to "study" or test their spirits and properties, new cultural elements are also continuously added to and tested by vegetalismo, which comes to act as an especially fruitful agent for activating relationships and mediating communication between various spheres and actors. In this scenario, the powerful psychoactive effect of ayahuasca should not be underestimated; it seems to facilitate the accommodation of divergent cultural references and individual psychological projections into the vegetalismo's domain.

Notes

1. Luis Eduardo Luna, *Vegetalismo: Shamanism Among the Mestizo Population of the Peruvian Amazon* (Stockholm: Estocolmo, Almquist and Wiksell International, 1986).
2. See George E. Marcus, "Ethnography in/of the World System: The Emergence of Multi-Sited Ethnography," *Annual Review of Anthropology* 24 (1995): 95–117.
3. Beatriz C. Labate, "*Mamancuna merci beaucoup: internationalização e diversificação do vegetalismo ayahuasqueiro peruano*" (Ph.D. diss., Unicamp, 2011).
4. Throughout the chapter I use the term *mestizo* to refer to people of mixed heritage, which is to say Peruvians who don't identify themselves as indigenous. "Gringo" is used here as a synonym for foreigner, in contrast to *peruano* (Peruvian). Peruvian includes *nativos* or *indígenas* (natives, indigenous people), *mestizos* and *criollos* (white people of Spanish descent who were born in Peru, as opposed to "indios"). I adopt these terms in the same way that they are present in the local vocabulary, without intending to delve further into the semantics and politics of ethnic identity. These categories to describe people are used locally based on social and cultural aspects rather than on so-called racial classifications.

5. Jane Atkinson, "Shamanism Today," *Annual Review of Anthropology* 21 (1992): 307–30; Claude Lévi-Strauss, *Antropologia Estrutural vol. I* (Rio de Janeiro: Tempo Brasileiro, 1985).
6. Anthony Giddens, *Modernity and Self-Identity: Self and Society in the Late Modern Age* (London: Polity, 1991).
7. Beatriz C. Labate and J. C. Bouso, "Cura, cura, cuerpecito [Heal, Heal, Little Body]: Reflections on the Therapeutic Possibilities of Ayahuasca," *Erowid.org.*, accessed June 9 2011, http://www.erowid.org/chemicals/ayahuasca/ayahuasca_article3.shtml.
8. Benny Shanon, *The Antipodes of the Mind: Charting the Phenomenology of the Ayahuasca Experience* (New York: Oxford University Press, 2002).
9. Glenn Shepard, "Venenos divinos: Plantas psicoativas dos Machiguenga do Peru," in Beatriz C. Labate and Sandra L. Goulart, eds., *Ouso ritual das plantas de poder* (Campinas, Brazil: Meracado de Letras, 2005), 87–217.
10. Oscar Calavia Saéz, "A Vine Network," in Beatriz C. Labate and Henrik Jungaberle, eds., *The Internationalization of Ayahuasca* (Zürich: Lit Verlag, 2011).
11. Daniela M. Peluso, "For Export Only: Ayahuasca Tourism and Hyper-Traditionalism," in Nezar Alsayyad, ed., *IASTE 2006 Working Paper Series: Hyper-Traditions and "Real" Places,* 183 (2006): 482–500; Isabel Santana de Rose, "*Tata ndereko*—Fogo Sagrado: Encontros entre os Guarani, a ayahuasca e o Caminho Vermelho" (Ph.D. diss., Universidade Federal de Santa Catarina, 2010); Evgenia Fotiou, "From Medicine Men to Day Trippers: Shamanic Tourism in Iquitos, Peru," Ph.D. diss., University of Wisconsin-Madison, 2010); Anne-Marie Losonczy and Silvia Mesturini Cappo, "La Selva Viajera: Etnografia de las rutas del chamanismo ayahuasquero entre Europa y América," *Religião e Sociedade* 30, no. 2 (2010): 164–83.
12. See also Fotiou, "From Medicine Men to Day Trippers"; and Anne-Marie Losonczy and Silvia Mesturini Cappo's Chapter 5 in this volume.
13. Françoise Barbira Freedman's Chapter 6 in this volume.
14. Bernd Brabec De Mori, "Tracing Hallucinations: Contributing to a Critical Ethnohistory of Ayahuasca Usage in the Peruvian Amazon," in Beatriz C. Labate and Henrik Jungaberle, eds., *The Internationalization of Ayahuasca* (Zürich: Lit Verlag, 2011), 23–47; Glenn Shepard's Chapter 1 in this volume; Calavia Sáez, "A Vine Network"; and Peter Gow, "River People: Shamanism and History in Western Amazonia," in Nicholas Thomas and Caroline Humphrey, eds., *Shamanism, History and the State* (Ann Arbor: University of Michigan Press, 1994), 90–113.
15. Bernd Brabec De Mori and Laida M. S. Brabec, "Shipibo-Konibo Art and Healing Concepts: A Critical View on the 'Aesthetic Therapy,'" *Viennese Ethnomedicine Newsletter* 11, no. 2–3 (2009): 18–26. Ironically, the Shipibo may have adopted ayahuasca in historical times from neighboring groups; see Brabec de Mori's Chapter 9 in this volume.
16. Peluso, "For Export Only."
17. Carneiro Da Cunha, "Pontos de vista sobre a floresta Amazônica."
18. Frequently the sites quote the scientific names of these plants. They also transcribe observations made by various curanderos about each, but these other plants have no coherent, fixed public image at this point.
19. The language used in neo-vegetalista circles that probably best reveals this instrumentalization appears in the descriptions of the rituals, where practitioners may affirm that they follow the "Shipibo methodology," "design," "format," or "lineage."
20. Another place to observe the interface between science and ayahuasca is in the emergence of rituals designed for scientific research. Some research is carried out with subjects participating in rituals in natural settings, or settings adapted for the goals of the research. Other projects create "ritual experiments" in the laboratory, which might use freeze-dried ayahuasca. See Beatriz C. Labate, Isabel S. Rose and Rafael Santos, *Ayahuasca Religions: A Comprehensive Bibliography and Critical Essays* (Santa Cruz, CA: Multidisciplinary Association for Psychedelic Studies, 2009).

21. See Labate, Rose, and Santos, *Ayahuasca Religions*; Beatriz C. Labate and Clancy Cavnar, "The Expansion of the Field of Research on Ayahuasca: Some Reflections about the Ayahuasca Track at the 2010 MAPS 'Psychedelic Science in the 21st Century' Conference," in *International Journal of Drug Policy* 22, no. 2 (2011): 174–78.
22. See Labate and Cavnar, "The Expansion of the Field"; Beatriz C. Labate, "Conference Review: Notes on the 'International Congress of Traditional Medicine, Interculturality, and Mental Health,' Takiwasi Center, Tarapoto, Peru, June 7–10, 2009," *Anthropology of Consciousness* 2, no. 1 (2010): 30–46.
23. See Labate, Rose, and Santos, *Ayahuasca Religions*; Labate and Bouso, "Cura, cura cuerpecito."
24. Francisco Lima and Luis Tófoli, "An Epidemiological Surveillance System by the UDV: Mental Health Recommendations Concerning the Religious Use of Hoasca," in *The Internationalization of Ayahuasca*, ed. Beatriz C. Labate and Henrik Jungaberle (Zürich: Lit Verlag, 2011): 185–99.
25. Known as *virotes*, these short poisoned darts or arrows are reportedly made of various materials: rock, thorns, insects, feathers, or bone. They transmit witchcraft attacks, can be sent invisibly over great distances, and become lodged in the throat or spine of the victim. To cure witchcraft, the darts must be removed by a shaman and then returned to whoever sent them, supposedly with fatal consequences for the perpetrator.
26. Rose, "*Tata endy rekoe*—Fogo Sagrado"; Tiago Coutinho, "O *Nixi Pae* urbano: Uma possível interpretação junguiana do xamanismo amazônico" (Ph.D. diss., Universidade Federal do Rio De Janeiro, 2011); Pirjo Kristiina Virtanen's Chapter 3 in this volume; Mariana Pantoja's Chapter 2 in this volume.
27. See Peluso, "Ayahuasca's Attractions." Such denunciations have caused some curanderos to be censured by ayahuasca communities in various countries; but since curanderos come and go, and some of these figures are quite charismatic, and because ayahuasca is hard to obtain outside Amazonia, the period of censure tends to be short-lived and the offenders often return to the circuit.
28. The alliance between indigenous peoples and the ecological movement goes beyond shamanism and ayahuasca; see Manuela Carneiro Da Cunha and Mauro W. B. Almeida, "Populações tradicionais e conservação," in João Paulo R. Capobianco, et al, eds., *Biodiversidade na Amazônia brasileira: Avaliação e ações prioritárias para a conservação, uso sustentável e repartição de benefícios* (São Paulo: Estação Liberdade e Instituto Socioambiental, 2001), 184–93.
29. Bernd Brabec De Mori, "Words Can Doom, Songs May Heal: Ethnomusicological and Indigenous Explanations of Song-Induced Transformative Processes in Western Amazonia," *Curare Journal of Medical Anthropology* 32, no. 1–2 (2009): 123–44.
30. I gathered firsthand accounts of ayahuasca being used among stock market traders, Hollywood celebrities, and computer geniuses from the Silicon Valley. The concern about attending to this special kind of population and their need for privacy has created a special kind of category: "private ceremonies." These can cost up to $5,000. I heard stories about politicians and businessmen interested in ayahuasca as a way to gain power and money in various countries. Such ambitions are often associated with insinuations of sorcery, and are in line with local views on ayahuasca.
31. One Shipibo healer in Iquitos developed a training regime for apprentices from the United States and Canada that consisted of a "social diet": the full suite of traditional dietary and behavioral restrictions, but without the traditional period of isolation in the forest.
32. For a discussion of the legal status of ayahuasca and public debates around the world, see Brian Anderson et al., "Statement on Ayahuasca," *International Journal of Drug Policy* 23, no. 3 (2012): 173–75; Kenneth W. Tupper and Beatriz C. Labate, "Plants, Psychoactive Substances and the INCB: The Control of Nature and the Nature of Control," *Human Rights and Drugs* 2, no. 1 (2012): 17–28; Beatriz C. Labate and Kevin Feeney, "Ayahuasca and the Process of Regulation in Brazil and Internationally:

Implications and Challenges," *International Journal of Drug Policy* 23, no. 2 (2012): 154–61.

33. Henrique Carneiro, *Bebida, abstinência e temperança na história antiga e moderna* (São Paulo: Editora SENAC, 2010).
34. See Eduardo Viveiros De Castro, "Os pronomes cosmológicos e o perspectivismo Ameríndio," *Revista Mana* 2, no. 2 (1996): 115–44; Peluso, "Ayahuasca's Attractions"; Brabec de Mori, "From the Native's Point of View."
35. Due to the delicate nature of the subject, I provide no details about networks of purchase and sale of ayahuasca. In sum, there are many networks built around kinship, friendship, and personal loyalty and fewer that are exclusively commercial and impersonal.
36. See Beatriz C. Labate, "Paradoxes of Ayahuasca Expansion: The UDV-DEA Agreement and the Limits of Freedom of Religion," *Drugs: Education, Prevention & Policy* 19, no. 1 (2012): 19–26.
37. Rosa Giove, *Reconocimiento y declaratoria de las manifestaciones culturales vigentes como patrimonio cultural: Ritual de Ayahuasca* (Tarapoto, Peru: Centro Takiwasi, 2008).
38. Report no. 056-2008-DRECP/INC, May 29, 2008.
39. RDN (Resolución Directoral Nacional) Nº 836: Instituto Nacional De Cultura (INC), Declaración Patrimonio Cultural de la nación a los conocimientos y usos tradicionales del Ayahuasca practicados por comunidades nativas amazónicas (Lima, June 24, 2008).
40. Slightly before ayahuasca was so recognized, the geometric artistic patterns (*kené*) of Shipibo-Conibo art were also declared national culture heritage: see RDN (Resolución Directoral Nacional) No. 540: Instituto Nacional De Cultura Inc., Declaración Patrimonio Cultural de la nación al kene de la sociedade Shipibo-Koniba (Lima April 16, 2008). This event was followed by an exhibition on *kené* in Museo de la Nación in Lima in 2009 and the opening of the Museum of Sacred, Magical, and Medicinal Plants in Cuzco in 2011. However, *kené* are far less frequently mentioned than ayahuasca in discussions of national cultural heritage from Amazonia.
41. RDN, No. 836.
42. See, for example, MIVILUDES "Mission interministérielle de vigilance et de lutte contre les dérives sectaires," *Rapport annuel au Premier ministre: Année* 2009 (Paris: La Documentation Française, 2010).
43. Veronica M. Davidov, "Shamans and Shams: The Discursive Effects of Ethnotourism in Ecuador," *Journal of Latin American and Caribbean Anthropology* 15, no. 2 (2010): 387–410, notes that the creation of such associations has become an international trend, citing examples such as ASHIM (Asociación de Shamanes de Imbaburana) in Ecuador. Caicedo, in "Patrimonialización y consumo en debate," mentions ASMIK, Associación de Médicos Indígenas Yageceros Kofanes, and UMIYAC, Unión de Médicos Indigenas Yageceros da la Amazónia Colombiana, a group that was involved in blocking an attempt to patent ayahuasca.
44. Not directly related to the expansion process, the Peruvian Congress has debated a proposed law that would create a registry of recognized traditional, complementary, and alternative medical agents, allowing them to work in the public health system (Proyecto de Ley n. 2053/2007- CR; Rosario Jessica Quevedo Pereyra de Pribyl: "The Long Way Home: The Integration of Traditional Medicine into the Peruvian Healthcare System." Ph.D. thesis, University of Vienna, 2013).
45. Luis Eduardo Luna, "Xamanismo Amazônico: ayahuasca, antropomorfismo e mundo natural," in *O uso ritual da ayahuasca*, ed. Beatriz C. Labate and Wladimyr Sena Araújo (Campinas, Brazil: Mercado de Letras, 2004, 2nd edition), 181–200; Luis Eduardo Luna, "Narrativas da alteridade: a ayahuasca e o motivo da transformação em animal," in *O uso ritual das plantas de poder*, ed. Beatriz C. Labate and Sandra L. Goulart (Campinas, Brazil: Mercado de Letras, 2005), 333–52; Michael Taussig, *Xamanismo, colonialismo e o homem selvagem* (São Paulo: Editora Paz e Terra, 1993).
46. Taussig, "*Xamanismo, colonialismo e o homem selvagem.*"

References

Anderson, Brian T., Beatriz C. Labate, Matthew Meyer, Kenneth W. Tupper, Paulo C. R. Barbosa, Charles S. Grob, Andrew Dawson, and Dennis McKenna. "Statement on Ayahuasca." *International Journal of Drug Policy* 23, no. 3 (2012): 173–75.

Atkinson, Jane. "Shamanism Today." *Annual Review of Anthropology* 21 (1992): 307–30.

Brabec De Mori, Bernd. "Words Can Doom. Songs May Heal: Ethnomusicological and Indigenous Explanations of Song-Induced Transformative Processes in Western Amazonia." *Curare Journal of Medical Anthropology* 32, no. 1, 2 (2009): 123–44.

Brabec De Mori, Bernd. "Tracing Hallucinations: Contributing to a Critical Ethnohistory of Ayahuasca Usage in the Peruvian Amazon." In *The Internationalization of Ayahuasca*, edited by Beatriz C. Labate and Henrik Jungaberle, 23–47. Zurich: Lit Verlag, 2011.

Brabec De Mori, Bernd and Laida M. S. Brabec. "Shipibo-Konibo Art and Healing Concepts: A Critical View on the 'Aesthetic Therapy.'" *Viennese Ethnomedicine Newsletter* 11, no. 2–3 (2009): 18–26.

Caicedo Fernández, Alhena. "Patrimonialización y consumo en debate." *Revista Colombiana de Antropología* 46, no. 1 (2010): 63–86.

Calavia Saéz, Oscar. "A Vine Network." In *The Internationalization of Ayahuasca*, edited by Beatriz C. Labate and Henrik Jungaberle, 131–44. Zurich: Lit Verlag, 2011.

Carneiro, Henrique. *Bebida, abstinência e temperança na história antiga e moderna*. São Paulo: Editora SENAC, 2010.

Carneiro da Cunha, Manuela. "Pontos de vista sobre a floresta Amazônica: Xamanismo e tradução." *Mana* 4, no. 1 (1998): 7–22.

Carneiro da Cunha, Manuela, and Mauro W. B. Almeida. "Populações tradicionais e conservação." In *Biodiversidade na Amazônia brasileira: Avaliação e ações prioritárias para a conservação, uso sustentável e repartição de benefícios*, edited by João Paulo R Capobianco, Roberto B. Cavalcanti, José Maria Cardoso Da Silva, Luiz Paulo Pinto, and Silvio Jablonski, 184–93. São Paulo: Estação Liberdade and Instituto Socioambiental, 2001.

Coutinho, Tiago. "O *Nixi Pae* urbano: uma possível interpretação junguiana do xamanismo amazônico." PhD diss., Universidade Federal do Rio De Janeiro, 2011.

Davidov, Veronica M. "Shamans and Shams: The Discursive Effects of Ethnotourism in Ecuador." *Journal of Latin American and Caribbean Anthropology* 15, no. 2 (2010): 387–410.

Fotiou, Evgenia. "From Medicine Men to Day Trippers: Shamanic Tourism in Iquitos, Peru." Ph.D. diss., University of Wisconsin-Madison, 2010.

Giddens, Anthony. *Modernity and Self-Identity: Self and Society in the Late Modern Age*. London: Polity, 1991.

Giove, Rosa. *Reconocimiento y declaratoria de las manifestaciones culturales vigentes como patrimonio cultural: Ritual de ayahuasca*. Tarapoto, Peru: Centro Takiwasi, 2008.

Gow, Peter. "River People: Shamanism and History in Western Amazonia." In *Shamanism, History and the State*, edited by Nicholas Thomas and Caroline Humphrey, 90–113. Ann Arbor: University of Michigan Press, 1994.

Labate, Beatriz C. "Notes on the 'International Congress of Traditional Medicine, Interculturality, and Mental Health,' Takiwasi Center, Tarapoto, Peru, June 7–10, 2009." *Anthropology of Consciousness* 2, no. 1 (2010): 30–46.

Labate, Beatriz C. "*Ayahuasca Mamancuna merci beaucoup*: internacionalização e diversificação do vegetalismo ayahuasqueiro peruano." Ph.D. diss., Unicamp, 2011.

Labate, Beatriz C. "Paradoxes of Ayahuasca Expansion: The UDV-DEA Agreement and the Limits of Freedom of Religion." *Drugs: Education, Prevention & Policy* 19, no. 1 (2012): 19–26.

Labate, B. C., and J. C. Bouso, "Cura, cura, cuerpecito (Heal, Heal, Little Body): Reflections on the Therapeutic Possibilities of Ayahuasca." *Erowid.org*, accessed May 4, 2012, at http://www.erowid.org/chemicals/ayahuasca/ayahuasca_article3.shtml.

Labate, Beatriz C., and Clancy Cavnar. "The Expansion of the Field of Research on Ayahuasca: Some Reflections About the Ayahuasca Track at the 2010 MAPS 'Psychedelic

Science in the 21st Century' Conference." *International Journal of Drug Policy* 22, no. 2 (2011): 174–78.

Labate, Beatriz C., and Kevin Feeney. "Ayahuasca and the Process of Regulation in Brazil and Internationally: Implications and Challenges." *International Journal of Drug Policy* 23 (2012): 154–61.

Labate, Beatriz C., Isabel S. Rose, and Rafael Santos. *Ayahuasca Religions: A Comprehensive Bibliography and Critical Essays*. Santa Cruz, CA: Multidisciplinary Association for Psychedelic Studies, 2009.

Lévi-Strauss, Claude. *Antropologia Estrutural vol. I*. Rio de Janeiro: Tempo Brasileiro, 1985.

Lima, Francisco, and Luis Tófoli. "An Epidemiological Surveillance System by the UDV: Mental Health Recommendations Concerning the Religious Use of Hoasca." In *The Internationalization of Ayahuasca*, edited by Beatriz C. Labate and Henrik Jungaberle, 185–99. Zurich: Lit Verlag, 2011.

Losonczy, Anne-Marie, and Silvia Mesturini Cappo. "La Selva Viajera. Etnografia de las rutas del chamanismo ayahuasquero entre Europa y América." *Religião e Sociedade*, 30, no. 2 (2010): 164–83.

Luna, Luis Eduardo. *Vegetalismo: Shamanism Among the Mestizo Population of the Peruvian Amazon*. Stockholm: Estocolmo, Almquist and Wiksell International, 1986.

Luna, Luis Eduardo. "Xamanismo Amazônico: ayahuasca, antropomorfismo e mundo natural." In *O uso ritual da ayahuasca,* edited by Beatriz C. Labate and Wladimyr S. Araújo, 181–200. Campinas, Brazil: Mercado de Letras, 2004, 2nd edition.

Luna, Luis Eduardo. "Narrativas da alteridade: a ayahuasca e o motivo da transformação em animal." In *O uso ritual das plantas de poder*, edited by Beatriz C. Labate and Sandra L. Goulart, 333–52. Campinas, Brazil: Mercado de Letras, 2005.

Marcus, George E. "Ethnography in/of the World System: The Emergence of Multi-Sited Ethnography." *Annual Review of Anthropology* 24 (1995): 95–117.

MIVILUDES (Mission interministérielle de vigilance et de lutte contre les dérives sectaires). *Rapport annuel au Premier ministre: Année* 2009. Paris: La Documentation Française, 2010.

Peluso, Daniela M. "For Export Only: Ayahuasca Tourism and Hyper-Traditionalism." In *IASTE* 2006 *Working Paper Series,* edited by Nezar Alsayyad. *Hyper-Traditions and "Real" Places* 183 (2006): 482–500.

Pribyl, Rosario Jessica Quevedo Pereyra de. "The Long Way Home: The Integration of Traditional Medicine into the Peruvian Healthcare System." Ph.D. thesis, University of Vienna, 2013.

Proyecto de Ley n. 2053/2007- CR. Ley de la medicina tradicional, alternativa y complementaria y de los agentes que la ejercen. Congresso de La República del Perú, Lima, 2007.

RDN. Resolución Directoral Nacional N° 540: Instituto Nacional De Cultura (Inc). *Declaración Patrimonio Cultural de la nación al kene de la sociedade Shipibo-Koniba*. Lima, April 16, 2008.

RDN. Resolución Directoral Nacional N° 836: Instituto Nacional De Cultura (Inc). *Declaración Patrimonio Cultural de la nación a los conocimientos y usos tradicionales del Ayahuasca practicados por comunidades nativas amazónicas*. Lima, June 24, 2008.

Rose, Isabel S. "*Tata endy rekoe—Fogo Sagrado: Encontros entre os Guarani, a ayahuasca e o Caminho Vermelho*." Ph.D. diss., Universidade Federal de Santa Catarina, 2010.

Shanon, Benny. *The Antipodes of the Mind: Charting the Phenomenology of the Ayahuasca Experience*. New York: Oxford University Press, 2002.

Shepard, Glenn. "Venenos divinos: Plantas psicoativas dos Machiguenga do Peru." In *O uso ritual das plantas de poder*, edited by Beatriz C. Labate and Sandra L. Goulart, 87–217. Campinas, Brazil: Meracado de Letras, 2005.

Taussig, Michael. *Xamanismo, colonialismo e o homem selvagem*. São Paulo: Editora Paz e Terra, 1993.

Tupper, Kenneth W., and Beatriz C. Labate. "Plants, Psychoactive Substances and the INCB: The Control of Nature and the Nature of Control." *Human Rights and Drugs* 2, no. 1 (2012): 17–28.

Viveiros De Castro, Eduardo. "Os pronomes cosmológicos e o perspectivismo Ameríndio." *Revista Mana* 2, no. 2 (1996): 115–44.

9

From the Native's Point of View

How Shipibo-Konibo Experience and Interpret Ayahuasca Drinking with "Gringos"

BERND BRABEC DE MORI

In many cultural anthropological studies, "traditional" uses of the hallucinogenic brew ayahuasca among various groups in the Amazon rainforest have been subject to investigation.[1] Findings from such research are sometimes juxtaposed with so-called modern or internationalized uses of the same compound.[2] Although the positions of ayahuasca tourists, "apprentice shamans," or famous indigenous protagonists have been studied seldom, even if thoroughly,[3] there is still another important perspective hitherto almost untouched, which will be addressed in this chapter: the native's point of view regarding the transition from alleged "traditional" to "modern" uses of the substance. My survey will concentrate on the Shipibo-Konibo (also called Shipibo), an indigenous group comprising about fifty thousand individuals mainly dwelling on the Ucayali River in the eastern Peruvian rainforest. In both popular and academic literature, the Shipibo are often regarded as sophisticated specialists in using ayahuasca. This survey does not claim validity for other groups, indigenous or mestizo. It represents a pinpoint study of a certain discourse at a certain place (the central Ucayali Valley), during a certain span of time (the first decade of the twenty-first century).

Besides references to academic literature, the main source for this survey is my own ethnomusicological fieldwork in the Ucayali region, comprising five years of living with Shipibo people, as well as frequent telephone contact and short visits since then.[4] From 2001 to 2006, I lived in Puerto Callao de Yarinacocha near Pucallpa (the capital city of the Ucayali region) together with my Shipibo wife and children, among Shipibo people who had forsaken rural community life in order to pursue a new form of living in the semiurban slums of Puerto Callao. In the given context it might be important to note that between 2002 and 2004, I did not engage in fieldwork actively. I stopped making recordings, taking photographs, and asking annoying questions all day long. I had to take care of my children and worked as a teacher in Pucallpa, earning a standard Peruvian teacher's salary, about $250 a month, during these years. Some local Shipibo people were working as teachers, too, under similar terms, so I was soon viewed simply as one who lived there, part of the family, an incorporated *gringo*.[5] Thus I obtained a position of observation and experience most often closed to visiting observers as well as an emotional attachment I cannot shake off when writing about Shipibo people's opinions. In this chapter, I will adapt to a fairly colloquial style of writing, due to the fairly colloquial nature of Shipibo discourse that I aim to describe.

After a brief summary of ayahuasca use and its understanding during Shipibo history in the following section, a series of biographical sketches will be presented. These biographies relate the life and experiences of Shipibo healers who came into contact with Northerners[6] and therefore had to decide how to deal with them. On the basis of these narratives, the motivation for Shipibo people to work with visitors, as well as the visitors' motivations to drink ayahuasca, will be addressed. Some of the narratives indicate that an integration of Shipibo animist[7] ontology into a "modern," naturalistically understandable mode of using ayahuasca may be problematic. Ontologies and respective expectations regarding ayahuasca use will be juxtaposed and discussed. Finally, I will conclude this chapter with some thoughts about problems that arise from ayahuasca tourism among Shipibo people and the visitors' dreams about how the world could be made into a better place if they were to pursue a "shaman's" career.

A Brief History of Ayahuasca Use Among the Shipibo

The length of time Shipibo people and their forebears have been using ayahuasca is still open to dispute. A common popular assumption is that the brew has been used by Shipibo people, among many other Amazonian groups, for thousands of years, more or less in the way they use it today. This assumption is nowadays challenged by various scholars, namely by Peter Gow, Antonio Bianchi, Glenn Shepard, and myself,[8] who propose that the use of the hallucinogenic ayahuasca brew spread relatively recently through the Peruvian Amazon. Ayahuasca use among Shipibo seems not to be ancient, though still well established after two centuries of practice.

Among contemporary rural Shipibo, therapeutic use of ayahuasca still shows different structures compared to "modern" applications: in a common ayahuasca session, the healer (whom I refer to by the term *médico*, a word most often used by practitioners themselves) drinks the brew, but not the patient. Here, ayahuasca empowers the médicos' senses for diagnosis and action: in Shipibo ontology, the cause of an ailment mostly originates from sorcery by another médico, either human or nonhuman (like certain animals, plants, or demons *yoshin*). In this context, ayahuasca still serves mainly for warfare and hunting: for hunting down the person, human or nonhuman, who caused the illness. The patient will be able to recover only if the original cause is vanquished.

During the second half of the twentieth century, the structure of ayahuasca sessions was subject to the influence of Northern tourists and researchers.[9] William Burroughs, who arrived in Pucallpa in 1953, was the first ayahuasca tourist. This author published his experiences in a then-famous book.[10] Many young ethnographers were animated by Burroughs, or by Carlos Castaneda, Michael Harner, and other pioneers studying indigenous applications of psychoactives. This happened during the 1960s and 1970s, and "psychedelic" tourists followed in their footsteps. Shipibo people quickly recognized that sharing ayahuasca with a large group of participants, thus enabling the *gringos* to experience its effects, yielded notable advantages: attention, payment, and visitors who returned or recommended them, promising continuous economic growth.

Most Shipibo people in rural communities, and all the elders, remember very well when this transition happened. Most Shipibo agree that the "real" (*kikin*) médicos in former times (the *yobé* and the *meráya*) did not need ayahuasca for their healing and sorcery. However, today everybody seems to depend on it.

Figure 9.1. The living environment Shipibo people interact with. Photograph by Bernd Brabec de Mori.

Shipibo discourse about the transformation of ayahuasca use is a complex issue that cannot be easily generalized. In particular, engaging or not engaging in constant contact with visitors marks a bifurcation in discourse. "Official" and "unofficial" versions of narration have emerged when dealing with ethnomedical concepts, arts and singing, and daily life, which are in some way connected to ayahuasca use and tourism.[11] Notably, most Shipibo people do not distinguish between tourists, researchers, and "apprentice shamans." They all ask apparently similar questions, take photos all day long, and wish to explore the ayahuasca experience. Some stay longer, some may depart, and some may return, but the pattern is the same. We are all (mostly fairly pale) visitors from the North, we own great sums of money compared to local people, and our behavior is incredibly naïve.

In contemporary ayahuasca practice, Shipibo specialists trained in sorcery and healing most often call themselves médicos ("physicians"), reinterpreting this Spanish term. Additionally, there is another introduced word in use, *chamán* ("shaman"). This term is usually absent in vernacular language use; it is applied almost exclusively when facing Northerners. Therefore, it became common that specialists who prefer to work with visitors call themselves chamanes, while those who tend to work among local people view themselves as médicos. I will adopt this terminology for the remainder of this chapter.[12]

Sample Biographies

In the following text, six biographical sketches will be presented, in order to elucidate the enormous variety of individual decisions and attitudes toward the *rinko* people ("gringos": foreigners), and toward the blessings and curses they bring with them. The biographies belong to people who I know or knew well personally. Pseudonyms are used throughout because Amazonian magic is a delicate issue, especially when it comes to gossip. In order to present the protagonists' individual positions as truthfully as possible, I will use the phrase "it is said" in exact correspondence to the Shipibo narrative marker *-ronki*. "It is said" therefore indicates rumors and gossip, far from any evidence or firsthand information.

Case 1: Julián

Julián was born in 1957, in a provincial town that hosted a Shipibo minority among a mestizo majority. Julián's father was a yobé (Shipibo term for a médico specialized in dart warfare and healing) of high reputation, one of the "old school" who commonly worked without using ayahuasca. Julián never accomplished the formal training, which mainly consists of yearlong retreats and fasting (these retreats are called *dietas* in regional Spanish, *samá* in Shipibo). During his youth, he received some rather informal training and although he never worked professionally as a yobé like his father, he did some curing too, soon specializing in "ayahuasca shamanism." His subsequent success was mainly due to his jovial nature and well-tempered approach to visitors. He found his niche as an intermediate between renowned chamanes and visitors, friendly and funny with all of them. He also worked with NGOs in art and tourism projects. Guiding ayahuasca sessions was never his main interest, and he usually preferred to have one of his renowned relatives do this. In his own curing method he introduced foreign techniques, for example, acupuncture. His reputation among Shipibo peers was accordingly ambiguous. Although some people attributed a certain healing power to him, the majority perceived him as untrustworthy. His end was terrible and even his adversaries agree that nobody would deserve this: he was murdered by pirates in 2008. He was traveling in order to buy Shipibo art for tourists, carrying a (relatively) considerable sum of money. It is said that he boasted about that—though nobody really knows—and he never reached his destination.

Case 2: Pedro

Pedro was born in 1948 as the son of a renowned ayahuasca médico in a rural Shipibo community. During his youth, he pursued another career. He was already in his twenties when he started formal training to become a médico. At this time, his father served as the main informant for a Northern anthropologist who paid him fairly well. Pedro showed high talent in both ayahuasca healing and rhetoric toward visitors. He soon earned a reputation as a healer in his community as well as among visitors, who he always treated with great care. He was working in various NGO projects and as an informant for researchers. His expertise was well acknowledged. Pedro maintained a dual orientation for a long span of time: he cured locals in cases of illness for little or no money while at the same time hosting visitors. With the latter occupation he did well financially, and therefore many peers criticized him. It is said that he would not share and that he was an egoist. This culminated in a violent attack by anonymous rascals against him and his family. Thereafter, he moved to another place where he specialized in working with visitors, especially with "apprentice shamans." Shipibo people view him ambiguously, still. Though many admire him, some say he is miserable, betraying his people, selling their knowledge, and even abusing female visitors. The same ambiguity can be observed among apprentices: some trust him unreservedly while a few others claim he would have taken their money and stolen their diets.[13] Anyway, almost everybody attributes a fair amount of knowledge and power to him and he is still highly recommended, though nowadays almost exclusively among visitors.

Case 3: Antonio

Antonio was born in 1933 in a village close to a small mestizo town. His father was a médico, too. Unlike his brothers, he did not train from early on, but accomplished his dieting periods little by little, so it took longer for him to reach a high level. This level, however, is acknowledged by all Shipibo who know him as one of the highest among living Shipibo médicos. He was considered a meráya (Shipibo term for a médico who excels in transformation) of the "old school." He did not depend on ayahuasca for accomplishing transformations and healing successes, but he says that he drank ayahuasca in some instances. It is said that he was able to transform into a black jaguar "here," in the common world. He told me that around 1987 he retired from being a médico. From then on, he lived as a farmer and fisherman for about twenty years, until a Northern visitor who had read about him in an anthropological study asked him to teach him "ayahuasca shamanism." Antonio declined, recommending other médicos as good teachers, but the visitor insisted and eventually convinced him by promising that he would help pay for his family's education, help him build a better house, and so on. Therefore, Antonio again started to drink and administer ayahuasca in order to provide a better life for his children and grandchildren. It is said among Shipibo that the visitor is now building a hotel for ayahuasca tourists that he will manage himself, earning much money because of his teacher's high reputation. Recently, Antonio traveled to his apprentice's home country but decided to return to Peru after a few days and to stop drinking ayahuasca again because he felt very bad in the foreign country, and he did not enjoy drinking ayahuasca anymore. He also told me that the rinko's money has already caused much disagreement, jealousy, and even fighting among his adult children, his brothers, and fellow villagers—an observation that troubled him deeply.

Case 4: Wilder

Wilder was born in 1969 in a small upriver Shipibo community. There was no médico within his nuclear family, but when he was about twenty years old, he decided to take on training. He said that he saw much suffering, especially among children in his village, and so he decided to provide health service for them. Because he was already working as a primary school teacher, his training proceeded little by little. He was instructed by his father-in-law and by an uncle who lived in a community close to Pucallpa. This uncle had also recently started training in "ayahuasca shamanism." In reality, Wilder himself instructed the uncle; however, Shipibo rules of respect would not allow this to be uttered openly. When Wilder had reached a level at which he considered himself able to cure people, he was asked by his cousins, who also lived close to Pucallpa, to join them in a tourist project. The cousins built a botanical garden with accommodation services for "apprentice shamans." Wilder, though, was the only one in the family who could actually instruct and guide these visitors. As he declined, his cousins tried to insist, but Wilder left the community, together with his wife and children. He once again retired to a small rural community, where he could work as a teacher. He explained to me that his decision was a plainly moral one: he had studied to be a médico in order to cure ill people and not for selling his knowledge to visitors and actually cheating them, as he thought his cousins would do. He still lives in the small community, probably working as a teacher and applying his healing talents among the villagers.

Case 5: Clara

Clara was born in the early 1940s in a rural Shipibo community. According to her own account, her grandfather was a meráya, and she sometimes assisted in his sessions, listening to his curing songs. Thus she remembered some songs and learned the most important methods and techniques. She never practiced as a médica herself, but she is well known among her relatives for her vast knowledge of narratives and as an herbalist. Living a typical Shipibo family life in another rural community, she cured mostly children, usually with plant medicine, but also with magical songs, and sometimes by drinking ayahuasca. She came in touch with Northerners when she was recommended as a knowledgeable person to filmmakers who included her in a popular documentary about Shipibo people and traditions, with a focus on ayahuasca. When I was working with Clara in 2005, I especially acknowledged her excellent remembrance of "old songs" (*moatian ipaokani*); however, she did not define herself as an ayahuasca drinker. Via the contacts with filmmakers, she was subsequently invited to participate in a project created by visitors where exclusively female Shipibo ayahuasca drinkers guide ayahuasca sessions and instruct visitors from the North. This project is interesting in terms of gender mainstreaming in ayahuasca drinking: usually, among both Shipibo people and researchers, "ayahuasca shamanism" is considered a male profession. This project, involving only women chamanes, therefore occupies a niche in ethnomedical tourism, fostering professional chamanismo also among Shipibo women. Since then, together with fellow female ayahuasca drinkers, Clara has been working professionally in ayahuasca sessions devoted to providing experience and instructions for Northerners.

Case 6: Elmer

Elmer defines himself as mestizo. He was born in 1978 in a small mestizo town close to Pucallpa with a Shipibo minority. He never lived in a rural community.

His parents separated during his childhood and he was raised mainly by his aunt and her husband. Elmer finished secondary school and started to drink ayahuasca out of curiosity, with artists and visitors who he got in touch with via his uncle. This uncle also engaged in spiritualism studies, which may have influenced Elmer's knowledge in a small way, but he preferred to study with different Shipibo teachers and to lead his sessions in the Shipibo style of drinking ayahuasca and singing. By his own account, he is not very advanced in his studies, but is already able to guide ayahuasca sessions with visitors, and has done so for a few years now. He takes his work very seriously and tries to provide the best he can for the visitors. During the course of his work he met a Northern girl and they got married. With her help, he was able to visit her home country. Because of his school education and his constant contact with visitors and artists, he understands ayahuasca drinking entirely in the "modern" structure: all participants drink the brew, and the focus is not placed on curing illnesses via reciprocal sorcery, but on experiencing the effects of the ayahuasca and achieving spiritual and artistic advances on an individual scale. Starting a few months ago, he began to feel that he was involved in a struggle among competing médicos typical of indigenous ontology, which was probably due to his studies with Shipibo methods of fasting and instructions he received from various indigenous teachers. He thinks that he is being attacked and threatened during ayahuasca sessions by enemy médicos.

As can be observed in these paradigmatic stories that I chose out of thirty-five possible biographies of Shipibo médicos I have been working with (including three female médicas), it is not possible to generalize. Attitude toward tourists and the styles of the transformations made to the ayahuasca sessions are idiosyncratic to each médico. At the same time, Shipibo commoner's interpretations and attitudes toward those who work with visitors are also idiosyncratic and ambiguous. However, there are some tendencies that can be observed, and I am going to examine them here.

Money for the Shipibo

Motivations for Shipibo *médicos* to work with visitors shall be discussed first. Two main tendencies can be isolated. The first one is probably older, historically speaking, and occurs when a visitor investigates where and how he or she could drink ayahuasca. In case the visitor encounters a médico, the latter may accept or decline to work with the first, which is completely up to him. However, a visitor may "help" in the decision, as was shown in Antonio's story. If an ayahuasca-centered relationship between the médico and the visitor is established, the visitor is supposed to give something in exchange for the experience or instruction received, in most cases a certain sum of money or other economic provisions. Thereupon, the second motivation for starting to work with foreigners arises, mostly among younger Shipibo: as it is still very difficult to earn money in Ucayali regularly and legally, one possible option is to train to provide ayahuasca experiences for visitors. A paradigmatic case is represented in Elmer's story. It is worthwhile in this context to also recall Wilder's account, because he declined to work with foreigners. Unlike Elmer, Wilder can work as a teacher, which does not provide large sums of money but enables him to live fairly well compared to villagers in a rural community. Therefore, he does not have to charge patients. Usually, among rural médicos, small sums of money, food, or other services are provided by patients, but are no comparison to the high incomes of professional chamanes who work with foreigners. Elmer, on the other hand, lives in a town, and his contact with relatively rich visitors and urban populations suggests another scale of income comparability: in order to live well among his peers, he has to earn much more than Wilder, and curing local people (who are commonly very poor) could never yield such sums.

Antonio's story also sheds light on economic relations: during 2004–2006, he repeatedly told me that he was not interested in drinking ayahuasca anymore. On the contrary, he would be waiting for his brother (a médico, too) to take his magic knowledge from him, so he could again be free of what he perceived to be a burden. He was living in poor circumstances because his advanced age did not allow him to provide everything necessary for his extensive family. It was exactly at this point that the "apprentice shaman" could step in. It is a morally ambiguous situation; on the one hand, the visitor did not respect the old man's own decision and longed for an egoistic goal, insisting on being instructed by the one regarded most powerful instead of being content studying with any other médico. On the other hand, he could provide income for Antonio's family, at least for a certain time.

Fostering tourism does, of course, not only include income for chamanes. The women who produce most of the artwork can also earn considerably more selling their art to visitors than they can at the weak local market. In many cases, visitors also provide food, school materials, and other necessary things to the chamán's family or neighborhood, which creates a positive impression. However, the downside of growing economic power is shown in Julián's terrible story above, as well as in the violent episode in Pedro's biography. Also, Antonio's account is paradigmatic: the rinko's money causes disagreement and jealousy among his family. Antonio added that nobody wants to help him, an old man, for free anymore (as is common among Shipibo), because everybody thinks he owns a great deal of money. But his money is being spent on a hedonistic lifestyle by some of his very own children, who are in charge of administering his income. Antonio's decision to stop drinking ayahuasca again seems to be motivated to a great degree by this disillusion.

Figure 9.2. A Shipibo rural settlement, Comunidad Nativa. Photograph by Bernd Brabec de Mori.

Hard economic considerations are the most obvious reasons to start working with rinko people. However, one should not underrate the fact that dealing with visitors also results in external friendship. Many people in most South American countries (by no means limited to young Shipibo males) are eager to meet friends from Northern societies. Elmer found the friend many South Americans dream of: a partner to live with, originating from a Northern country. Although this implies favorable economic consequences in most cases, I would like to draw attention to the fact that rinko friends and partners can provide possibilities to emotionally partake in the globalizing world. Such opportunities are otherwise very limited in Ucayali, where education and economic baselines are very low, and reaching outward is almost impossible.

Money for the Whites

Northern visitors who first take up studying the ayahuasca experience may return and ask for more. Some of them wish to embark on training in order to become a chamán. This is the logical consequence of a general spiritual poverty in industrialized and postindustrial societies. It is easily imaginable and happens very often that visitors, who feel spiritually enhanced after drinking ayahuasca with Shipibo (or other) chamanes, wish to carry this experience further, for themselves and for other spiritual seekers in their home countries. The stories most often told—that somebody got cured from cancer or any other lethal threat by drinking ayahuasca—are actually those that almost never happen. Usually, Northerners feel "cured" in a more psychological way: "finding themselves," understanding spiritual issues, or exploring ecology via ayahuasca visions. This is nevertheless important: if one can provide such knowledge and experience to inhabitants of Northern countries, a more balanced understanding of the world and the universe may be fostered. This may sound naïve, but reports attesting to this kind of motivation for foreigner's interest in becoming shamans (chamanes) are very common. Of course, there are also egoistic motives, dreams of power, reputation, boasting, and exoticism, which go with the claim of being an "authentically" trained shaman who may rely on "year-long studies with real indigenous master shamans." Anyway, the issue is serious, and many rinko people are actually training in order to become shamans, each one motivated by her or his own individual imagination.[14]

When looking at these "apprentice shamans" from the native's point of view, one may observe that most people's attitude depends very much on whether they or their family do or do not have a relationship with "their own" rinko. However, there is a dominant consensus that does not lack relevance: many Shipibo people think that whites who buy artwork, make recordings, or take photographs "take away" their achievements in order to earn enormous amounts of money in their countries. This formulation seems naïve, too, but there is evidence of foreign people selling reproduced t-shirts with Shipibo designs, for example, or maybe earning modest sums with public slide shows. The mere difference of the amount of money circulating in Northern countries compared to rural Peru makes it a true observation, though enhanced with many imaginations. Therefore, it is also true for apprentice shamans who guide ayahuasca sessions outside the Amazon; although they may charge less than their teachers charged them, and they may be more concerned with helping people than with exploiting them, they will actually earn more money with one ayahuasca session than rural Shipibo earn in one month. It is important to stress that typical apprentice shamans neither exploit people nor earn millions. But there are some singular cases Shipibo people know about that are rather disturbing. Apprentice shamans will enter a community, build an ayahuasca hotel (*albergue*), and give ayahuasca to visitors by themselves. I remember a "white shaman" who, in 2007, charged €2,400 per person for all-inclusive three-week ayahuasca retreats in groups of almost a hundred people at a time. This is an extreme case, but it does happen, and these are the cases that are perceived and criticized by many Shipibo people. "Shamans" from Northern countries have a great advantage over chamanes from Shipibo communities: they can work on their own publicity, and organize all-inclusive trips from their country to the doorstep of their place in Peru. They have a better knowledge of what short-term experience-seekers wish to encounter, and they can travel on their own and do not depend on invitations, visa regulations, and funding. All of this is impossible for Shipibo natives.[15]

Shipibo people also observe that apprentice shamans invite their teachers to foreign countries. In general, it is imagined that these teachers guide groups of rich rinko people in ayahuasca sessions and earn incredible amounts of money. When they return and bring little back, it is said that they were betrayed by their own apprentices who became rich, regardless of what they claim. This is a sad tenor among many Shipibo people.

Because of the few cases in which this has proven true, a form of "cultural colonialism" is taking place. It is beyond the scope of this contribution to judge if these people have the right to do so. They may own this right in a Northern understanding (including law systems and moral judgments), but from the Shipibo's point of view, this is problematic. The Shipibo system of assessment is based on an animist world conception, with reciprocity being the most important principle for keeping the world in order. Exchange of food and sexuality, of knowledge and power, and of sorcery and healing among Shipibo "Real People" (*jonikon*) as well as with the "other"—including neighbor natives,

Figure 9.3. An urban slum, a shared space of Shipibo and mestizo Peruvians. Photograph by Pierre Urban.

mestizos, whites, animals, plants, and spiritual entities—is the key for understanding an animistic world.[16]

Missing Diets, and Sorcery

Elmer's story reveals a central point in the complex relations between an animist basis and "modern" applications of ayahuasca shamanism. His understanding of administering ayahuasca is centered in the "modern" style. Therein, all participants in a session drink the brew and the visionary experience is regarded as the central and cathartic process. Spiritual encounters with alien intelligence and "God" (in any interpretation) crown an ideal ayahuasca session. In Elmer's understanding, such alien instances are not projections of a person's mind (as in psychoanalysis, for example), but encounters with definitely existing others.

Elmer has studied ayahuasca shamanism on his own, with his spiritualist uncle, and has been instructed by a few moderately renowned Shipibo médicos. With the latter, he became involved with indigenous ontology, and by using and imitating indigenous techniques, he was drawn into the network of interrelating life-giving and life-taking forces as conceived by indigenous people, a network that relies on reciprocity among people in the same way as between people, animals, plants, and spirits. This network was coined a "cosmic food web" by Kaj Århem,[17] as a cosmic system of reciprocal giving and taking, and of healing by sorcery, depending on perspective: western Amazonian healing involves predation and warfare.

The "old-school" yobé and meráya commonly did not use ayahuasca for healing, but for fighting their enemies. A Shipibo médico is per definition at the same time both a healer and a sorcerer, because healing consists of neutralizing an enemy's action on the patient, and overthrowing this enemy by striking him with his own weapons. Only if the original cause is defeated can the patient's symptoms be cured, often with other techniques and plants, or by singing. Here it seems that the healer is doing something "good" because he is curing a suffering patient, but this also depends on his perspective: all healers are "good guys," while the enemies are always the "bad guys." By switching perspectives, it may appear that the enemy caused the problem (*daño*) while curing a patient himself, being the "good guy" for somebody else. Therefore, struggles go on among competing médicos, ever implying the subjective perspective of being the "good guy" oneself. Elmer now feels that the knowledge and abilities he obtained through fasting were "stolen," or he was "blinded" by an attacking enemy sorcerer. He reasoned that he would lack training, "diet power," and is now looking for a more powerful mentor who may "cure" him; with this, he will probably be drawn further into the médico's wars.

Sorcery is seldom mentioned in "modern" ayahuasca shamanism, but it appears now and again as the nemesis of well-wishing Northerners.[18] In Northern societies, the common Christian bias suggests that it is possible to "do only good things," and separate from anything "evil," which is what most apprentice shamans vow. It may be perfectly possible to conduct ayahuasca sessions without meddling with sorcery, in the way commonly performed by Northerners, but only when refraining from indigenous techniques. Elmer's account shows that at the point where indigenous concepts become involved, the principle of reciprocity kicks in and demands an (in Northern terms, "immoral") exchange of benevolence or violence. Healing and sorcery, or "good" and "evil," cannot be separated from each other in indigenous understanding.

In western Amazonian ontologies, "good" and "evil" are not absolute categories but depend on perspective: when delving into the animist conception of the world, a non-indigenous "shaman" may find that somebody else is challenging his or her individual or dogmatic definition of what is to be considered "good." Anyone delving into an indigenous animist ontology and into the "cosmic food web" will be confronted sooner or later with the "healing power" of others, who may perceive him or her as evil. Some may perish in the process, or survive by learning to kill. The médico's job is not an easy task. These are obvious reasons, in all instances I know, for "old-school" médicos to be at the same time admired and feared by their peers.

One of the main issues in Shipibo people's opinion about both young Shipibo chamanes training to work with foreigners and Northern apprentices, is their "missing diet," an alleged lack of training for surviving on the battlefield of an animist ontology. In the cases of Julián, Clara, and Elmer, it can be seen that they went to work with rinko people despite having a lack of training. One médico, who died in 2002, told me that without at least four to seven years of hard training and much experience, it is not possible to understand the many forces one encounters. Premature application of half-learned knowledge, he stated, could be more harmful than helpful. He used a metaphor to underline his position: in a hospital, doctors have to study many years before they are allowed to operate by themselves. When confronted with battling médicos, someone inexperienced may side with one party (with the "good guys," of course) and later be surprised by ambiguous situations and obviously cruel deeds that she or he never imagined the "good guys" would commit.

This moral ambiguity also appeared in Pedro's story. Some of his apprentices (the "good ones") admire him as a benevolent teacher and praise their own years of positive cooperation, while others (the "bad ones") left him in search of somebody else able to "cure" them from his sorcery attacks. It is impossible for me to judge what has happened, and I cannot say if Pedro is a "good" healer (*curandero*) or an "evil" sorcerer (*brujo*). All I know is that he studied within

Shipibo ontology and that his Northern apprentices also delve into it, in most cases without anticipating what this means. I collected such accounts not only from Pedro's Northern apprentices, but also from many other students: Northerners, mestizos, and Shipibo. This is the way it works: morality depends on perspective. From the teachers' point of view, "bad" students have to be rejected. Many médicos or chamanes accuse their "bad" students of not "dieting well," and therefore not advancing, but getting stuck in their own sorcery, because one who does not "diet well" is thought to become a sorcerer. From my own point of view, I observed such "bad" students' attitudes toward fasting compared to the "good" students' habits, and could not find any significant difference.

"My Gringos," or the Drug Addicts

Ayahuasca is praised in many studies for being effective in treating drug addiction. In these studies, grounded in Northern ontology, drug addiction is considered a serious illness or sociopsychological disorder. However, "drug addiction" (*drogadicción*), in a more colloquial and morally determined interpretation, is also a behavior observed by médicos or chamanes when confronted with apprentices, researchers, or experience-seeking tourists.

Common Shipibo people consider Northern apprentices to be promising candidates for becoming powerful chamanes, so long as they "diet well." The Shipibo are more concerned with the economic threat apprentices may pose by carrying away Shipibo-based knowledge and earning a lot of money on their own. This leads to a difficult paradox, because Shipibo people may try to find "their own rinko" in order to obtain economic favors in return for providing information or access to a chamán. At the same time, Shipibo people often try not to give too much, because they fear that it could be "taken away." Therefore, it is most secure to provide "official" information to the visitors, but to withhold "unofficial" knowledge (*mezquinar conocimiento*). "Official" knowledge includes, for example, that Shipibo artwork is intrinsically related to the ayahuasca experience; that the Shipibo cosmos is structured in four layers accessible in ayahuasca visions; and that ayahuasca constitutes the key element of Shipibo culture. The "unofficial" discourse, on the other hand, involves the consciousness that what is told "officially" is not exactly true but provides a bridge for the dilemma mentioned above: how to provide interesting things for "my rinko" without risking that she or he could take away what is considered valuable.

Chamanes also have to integrate the same paradoxical situation, but the level at which this is negotiated is different. Apprentices who "take away" knowledge are considered a threat, especially combined with the aforementioned sorcery. Every chamán manages the paradoxical situation according to individual preferences and emotional sympathies. In this arrangement, one's master teacher, like Pedro, may be a terrible sorcerer for somebody else.

Among médicos and chamanes (here, both terms apply), the "official" knowledge is also transmitted from the beginning: we are the "good" ones and there are also "bad" ones, drinking ayahuasca is the only way of learning how to be a chamán, one has to fast and sing *ikaros* (ayahuasca-related songs) while cooking ayahuasca, and so on. While doing so, all the médicos and chamanes I know declared that they observe "their rinko" closely in order to find out why he or she would be there. It is said that some rinko people are "*estudiosos de mágia*" (meaning they have had contact with esoteric or New Age spiritual techniques). The same visitors may be "*miserable*" (stingy, if they would not help the chamán's family accordingly), and finally there are also "*Buenos*," good ones. However, most of them are considered *drogadictos* ("drug addicts") because they like taking drugs and this is why they also like ayahuasca.

Laughing and Transforming

Visitors, then, are accepted, are instructed, and are the object of many laughs. I spent many delightful moments listening to Antonio's brother relating rinko stories (in their absence, of course) and laughing loudly about them and their strange behavior during his "modern style" ayahuasca sessions. Most fun is made of rinko people who drink high doses of ayahuasca and then suffer from uncontrollable effects. They may be seen "*revolcando*," rolling over when lying on the floor moaning, or begging for help. One, it is said, was seen taking off his clothes and starting to dance during an ayahuasca session, or others wanted to flee from the session because they got frightened. All this is commonly seen as a general weakness Northerners suffer from. In that spirit, médicos and chamanes seem to endlessly make fun of certain rinko people when their behavior was strange enough to be remembered.

Shipibo people can make great fun of us drug addicts during their "unofficial" discourse, when no visitors are present and experiences can be exchanged freely. Because of the high importance of joking in Shipibo discourse, making fun of somebody is actually a powerful tool for dealing with alterity, for incorporating the "other," or for one's own transformation into the "other" while maintaining a superior position. This is most obvious in the Shipibo song genre *osanti*.[19] Osanti are funny songs exclusively performed by médicos, sung from the perspective of animals the médico is supposed to be able to transform into. If the animals own a lower competence of perception and action than the Shipibo (tortoises, dogs, or howler monkeys, for example), the latter may laugh about them. Animals with higher competence than Shipibo (such as jaguars, birds of prey, and anacondas) are never subject to mocking. As long as médicos laugh about "their rinko," the power relationship is clear.

Transforming into the other (*naikiti*), mimesis of the other's appearance (*paranti*), and incorporating captured others into "Real People" (*ináti*) are probably ancient techniques used by Shipibo (and other) médicos to negotiate power relations between the many inhabitants of an animist ontology. These techniques are also used by powerful chamanes in order to obtain and maintain their subject positionality among "others," including rinko apprentices. I think they do so unconsciously, and it is possible to observe this only from outside their ontology. I think this because transformation was the task of meráya and yobé, who do not practice anymore, as was shown, for example, in Antonio's account. Possession by and possession of nonhuman others was once performed in rituals that are not executed anymore among western Amazonian people. Such techniques and rituals were probably entirely substituted by "ayahuasca shamanism" many decades ago, and are now long lost and seldom remembered by even the most knowledgeable elders. Gow similarly suggests that, "Prior to the rubber industry period, shamanism was rather different from its current form, involving possession by forest animal spirits."[20] Maybe the rituals and techniques performed for negotiating positionalities with the others have not disappeared but changed; and these changes were substantial.

Ritualization

Some Shipibo médicos also make fun of chamanes who construct fantastic ceremonies around ayahuasca sessions with rinko people. Many local mestizo curanderos, for example, always use a small *mesa*, a kind of altar in their ayahuasca sessions. Some say prayers or sing Christian hymns before drinking ayahuasca and after the session, thereby performing within a ritual framework. Quite contrarily, among Shipibo médicos, there is almost no ritual present. Shipibo médicos may sit at night among their relatives and patients, talking about family news, for example. At some point, they would take a bottle of ayahuasca, have a draft, put it away, and go on talking. Later on, electric light or the *lamparín* (a petroleum candle) will be turned off, and they'll start whistling and singing. During the whole session, relatives and patients may come and go. Some of them may fall asleep, or at times talk to each other about any topic and noisily kill mosquitoes without heeding the singing médico(s). All present would wear everyday garments, including médicos.

This usually changes drastically if ayahuasca sessions are staged for Northerners.[21] Participants often prefer to wear white clothes, and chamanes are supposed to dress up with painted or embroidered *tari* shirts and their feather crowns called *maiti*. Often, participants bring shirts or sheets that are painted or embroidered in Shipibo *kené* style as well. The session will be ceremonially opened and concluded by the chamán. During the session, in many cases there are certain rules to be followed, depending on the chamán's preference. For example, often a certain diet is to be maintained, both before and after the session. While cooking the ayahuasca brew, some chamanes chant certain songs in front of the observing Northerners, and will insist that one has to fast while collecting plant material and cooking it.

As should be clear by now, Shipibo people often share a fairly burlesque air among themselves. My brother-in-law (who is not an ayahuasca drinker), for example, would tell many médicos we met about some rules we once were subjected to while attending a chamán's ritualized ceremony; in particular, that participants should wear white clothes and, when suffering strong visions, should not talk to each other but bear (*aguantar*) the state by themselves.[22] Such reports commonly caused a good deal of amusement among Shipibo médicos who are not used to working with visitors. Antonio's brother told me another anecdote:

Figure 9.4. Shipibo art, used to "indigenize" a white shaman's ayahuasca lodge. Photograph by Pierre Urban.

he once helped a chamán prepare and guide a session with Northerners. When the chamán told the rinko people that, while cooking ayahuasca, they would have to fast, sing, and blow smoke on the cauldron in order to produce a good brew, he intervened and told the rinko people, "What bullshit! While my ayahuasca is boiling, I eat what I want and have sex with my wife multiple times, and I still see beautiful visions." With this, he torpedoed his fellow chamán's careful attempt to impress the visitors. And, in telling the anecdote, he scored by getting laughs among his Shipibo peers.

Following the theories of Stanley Tambiah,[23] rituals are essentially necessary for performing the cosmology of any society. This author mentions, for example, U.S. American celebrations of Independence Day as an example of a ritual that affirms a certain cosmology. Among Shipibo (or neighboring indigenous societies), it is fairly obvious that such rituals have, in most cases, been abandoned. Since a few decades ago, drinking feasts that include ritualized processes (as, for instance, the ritual killing of domestic animals), female initiations, or children's hair cutting rituals are not performed anymore. Most notably, the hitherto unknown *mochai* ritual,[24] which probably served to perform vital ontological connections between Shipibo people, sun and climate, and forest demons, is almost forgotten today. Therefore, no ritual has been available during the late twentieth and the early twenty-first centuries that would have served the purpose of (re-) defining and performing the Shipibo's positionality in cosmos. Highly ritualized ayahuasca ceremonies may well substitute for former rituals that are nowadays lost. Although "shamanistic" ayahuasca ceremonies conducted by Shipibo chamanes involving rinko people may originate from the visitor's expectations of ceremonial presentation, such ceremonies may nowadays also serve to aid the Shipibo's active positioning in the globalizing world. This is underlined by a historical observation: it seems that it has "always" been one of the main concerns of médicos among the Shipibo (and many other societies) to deal with the "other," to contact those different from the "Real People" (*jonikon*) because of apparent alterity or processes of alterization. This is well documented for indigenous societies across the Amazon rainforests, for example by Tânia Stolze Lima, Eduardo Viveiros de Castro, and Ernst Halbmayer.[25] For Shipibo people, any Northerners are *nawa*, "others," and it can be understood as a fairly natural process that médicos are among the most prominent ones to deal with them and to negotiate their mutual positionality in the colliding animist and naturalistic ontologies, respectively. When, in former times, médicos negotiated between "Real People" and demons (*yoshin*) of weather, hunting, and the forest by performing mochai rituals, for example, their social reputation was ambiguous, too. This is because, to a high degree, society's well-being depended on the outcome of the médico's negotiations, which could yield positive results but also devastating effects in case of failure. This is continued, as was shown in this chapter, in the ambiguous view Shipibo commoners have of the chamanes who now negotiate with rinko people via the ayahuasca ceremony-ritual. Nowadays Shipibo society—which is usually displayed as an "ethnic unity"—depends heavily on these negotiations of chamanes and rinko people that similarly can fail (as in Julián's case, for example) or succeed (as in Pedro's case).

Conclusions

In this chapter, aspects of Shipibo people's perceptions and experiences regarding the popularization and internationalization of ayahuasca were recounted. The first and foremost conclusion to draw from these descriptions is that the Shipibo have a highly ambiguous approach to the topic, in detail, mostly depending on each individual's positioning in the context. This ambiguity is similar in structure to the disparate positions that can be observed in Europe or North America when it comes to regulation, authorization, or the harms and benefits of ayahuasca use.

Finally, the emergence of "ayahuasca ceremonies" in ritual frameworks that were not performed in native contexts was discussed. These new ritual celebrations correlate at the same time with the Northerner's expectations of "indigeneity," and with the disappearance of other Shipibo rituals that were not connected to ayahuasca. Apparently, this new ritual serves for performing and (re-) creating the cosmos for both the visitors (including their audiences in their home countries) and the Shipibo. Shipibo people seem to be in need of a new performance of their positionality as an animist society that is now merging with the globalizing Northern (naturalistic) ontology.

A more secular consequence of ayahuasca tourism is the growing disparity of income and power among Shipibo people: Those who actively seek contact and catch (and at times incorporate) "their rinko people" can expect economic advantages. On the other hand, those who retain their life apart from ayahuasca tourism do not share in these possibilities. In 2011, those who live well on ayahuasca tourism are still a only a few dozen persons (author's estimate), while the difference is made up by around fifty thousand living Shipibo people who do not receive their share of the cake. This is, however, the "normal" impact of capitalism that, in the Shipibo's case, is closely related to ayahuasca. In other societies, it may be connected with a specific history, with ecological peculiarities, with production, extraction, or any other phenomena that can be exploited by capitalist structures.[26]

A majority of today's Shipibo people suffer from a lack of medical services. "Hospital medicine" in Ucayali is still poorly developed and, in most cases, far away and expensive—a huge barrier, especially for rural Shipibo. At the same time, many médicos transform to chamanes and, in some instances, refrain from working with poor natives because they get used to earning much more when working with foreigners. I am sure that such cases are very rare in an explicit sense, but the problem is the mere thought of many Shipibo commoners, "If I do not pay him well like the rinko people do, he will not cure me accordingly." Such thoughts reflect a loss of confidence in the médicos. In former times, healing failure could be explained in terms of the patient's missing diet, for example, or of repeated counterattacks by enemies that outnumber the healer, or similar renderings. Nowadays, patients may explain healing failure with the argument indicated above: the healer does not take the patient's problem seriously anymore because he is much more engaged in earning money with foreigners.

Whether these problems can be brought to a satisfactory end, with all sides winning, depends on the art of negotiation applied by chamanes and médicos and their rhetoric toward both their own people and the visitors. To a great extent it also depends on the sensibility of the Northerners who are engaging in ayahuasca tourism or working within "modern" ayahuasca formats. One indicator that many Shipibo still feel able to control the situation is the good-humored aspect of their discourse. In the course of this chapter, I have described various instances where fun is made of chamanes, apprentices, or inexperienced Northerners. In Shipibo ontology and understanding of magic relations, fun can be made of entities that have less competence in (magical) perception and action than those who laugh. As long as there is laughter, there is hope. In some instances, I was told by Shipibo médicos and chamanes that they tried to educate, or even "civilize" (*raeti* in Shipibo), rinko people to behave like "Real People." If successful, the "civilized ones" would regard reciprocity among humans and nonhumans (spiritually and ecologically, so to say) in their consumption and production habits. This actually coincides with the intention of the many apprentices who strive to bring this message to the North in order to save their societies and, consequently, the world from the looming threat of authoritarian domination by the finance sector. Although I do not think that this can be achieved by drinking and administering ayahuasca (which, on the contrary, facilitates the introduction of capitalism to native societies), maybe it does no harm if done consciously. Let us hope so, for the Shipibo's sake as well as our own.

Notes

1. Among many others, see Gerald Weiss, "Shamanism and Priesthood in Light of the Campa Ayahuasca Ceremony," in Michael Harner, ed., *Hallucinogens and Shamanism* (New York: Oxford University Press, 1973), 40–48; Norman E. Whitten, Jr., *Sacha Runa: Ethnicity and Adaptation of Ecuadorian Jungle Quichua* (Urbana: University of Illinois Press, 1976); or Bruno Illius, *Ani shinan: Schamanismus bei den Shipibo-Conibo (Ost-Peru)* (Tübingen: Verlag S & F, 1987).

2. For example, see various contributions in Beatriz Caiuby Labate and Wladimyr Sena Araújo, eds., *O uso ritual da ayahuasca* (Campinas, Brazil: Mercado de Letras, 2nd edition 2004); Kenneth W. Tupper, "Ayahuasca Healing Beyond the Amazon: The Globalization of a Traditional Indigenous Entheogenic Practice," *Global Networks* 9, no. 1 (2009): 117–36; or Marlene Dobkin de Rios and Roger Rumrill, *A Hallucinogenic Tea, Laced with Controversy: Ayahuasca in the Amazon and the United States* (Westport: Praeger, 2008) for differing perspectives on the transformation of the use of ayahuasca.
3. For example, see Evgenia Fotiou, "From Medicine Men to Day Trippers: Shamanic Tourism in Iquitos, Peru" (Ph.D. diss., University of Wisconsin-Madison, 2010) on ayahuasca tourists, or John L. Comaroff and Jean Comaroff, *Ethnicity, Inc.* (Chicago: University of Chicago Press, 2009), for a more global analysis of "ethnic tourism" and related issues of capitalism's impact on indigenous populations. These authors also mention "modern" Shipibo use of ayahuasca.
4. The most intense phase of fieldwork (2004–2006) was made possible by the Austrian Academy of Sciences granting economical funding (program "DOC"). All my field recordings are archived at the Vienna Phonogrammarchiv.
5. The term *incorporated* is used here as an indicator that indigenous people played an active role in this process. As was shown for example by Fernando Santos-Granero, "Amerindian Torture Revisited: Rituals of Enslavement and Markers of Servitude in Tropical America," *Tipiti* 3 (2005): 147–74, incorporation has a long history in vast parts of the Amazon and marks an inclusive process of dealing with the "other."
6. In this chapter I will substitute "Western" with "Northern" in order to underline the native perspective: "*gringos*" definitely originate from the north, not from the west.
7. Animist ontology as contrasted to the naturalistic ontology of northern societies follows the theoretical framework formulated by Philippe Descola, *Par-delà nature et culture* (Paris: Editions Gallimard, 2005).
8. Peter Gow, "River People: Shamanism and History in Western Amazonia," in Nicholas Thomas and Caroline Humphrey, eds., *Shamanism, History and the State* (Ann Arbor: University of Michigan Press, 1994), 90–113; Antonio Bianchi, "Ayahuasca e xamanismo indígena na selva Peruana: O lento caminho da conquista," in Beatriz Caiuby Labate and Sandra Lucia Goulart, eds., *O uso ritual das plantas de poder* (Campinas, Brazil: Mercado de Letras, 2005), 319–29; Glenn H. Shepard, Jr., "Psychoactive Plants and Ethnopsychiatric Medicines of the Matsigenka," *Journal of Psychoactive Drugs* 30, no. 4 (1998): 321–32, and his Chapter 1 in the present volume; Bernd Brabec de Mori, "Tracing Hallucinations: Contributing to a Critical Ethnohistory of Ayahuasca Usage in the Peruvian Amazon," in Beatriz Caiuby Labate and Henrik Jungaberle, eds. *The Internationalization of Ayahuasca* (Zürich: Lit Verlag, 2011), 23–47.
9. Bernd Brabec de Mori, "La transformación de la medicina Shipibo-Konibo: Conceptos etno-médicos en la representación de un pueblo indígena," in Eveline Sigl, Yvonne Schaffler and Ricardo Ávila, eds. *Etnografías de América Latina. Ocho ensayos* (Guadalajara: University of Guadalajara, 2013), 269–86.
10. William S. Burroughs and Allen Ginsberg, *The Yage Letters* (San Francisco: City Lights Books, 1963, 2nd ed., 1975).
11. Bernd Brabec de Mori and Laida Mori Silvano de Brabec, "Shipibo-Konibo Art and Healing Concepts: A Critical View on the 'Aesthetic Therapy'," *Viennese Ethnomedicine Newsletter* 11, nos. 2–3 (2009): 18–26; Bernd Brabec de Mori and Laida Mori Silvano de Brabec, "La corona de la inspiración. Los diseños geométricos de los Shipibo-Konibo y sus relaciones con cosmovisión y música," *Indiana* 26 (2009): 105–34.
12. I will use male forms throughout, because about 93 percent of practitioners I encountered in the field were male.
13. It is common in Shipibo ontology to understand knowledge and abilities as objects that can be obtained or taken away. Therefore, many tales are known about médicos who would instruct apprentices, only to steal their newly accumulated knowledge after the training diet had been accomplished.

14. Fotiou, *From Medicine Men to Day Trippers.*
15. There may be rare exceptions, such as Guillermo Arévalo, who has reached a certain independence and self-determination in that issue. However, he is the only Shipibo I know who achieved this.
16. The importance of interspecies exchange is formulated e.g., by Ernst Halbmayer, "Nahrung und Sexualität als Kommunikationsmedien des Identischen, des Sozialisierten und des Wilden bei den Yukpa Nordwest-Venezuelas," in Elke Mader and Maria Dabringer, eds., *Von der realen Magie zum magischen Realismus* (Frankfurt: Brandes & Apsel and Südwind, 1999), 67–90; and in more general terms by Kaj Århem, "The Cosmic Food Web: Human-Nature Relatedness in the Northwest Amazon," in Philippe Descola and Gísli Pálsson, eds., *Nature and Society: Anthropological Perspectives,* (London: Routledge, 1996), 185–204.
17. Århem, "The Cosmic Food Web."
18. Fotiou, *From Medicine Men to Day Trippers,* 216–37. This author recounts stories told by Northern shamans combined with her own ayahuasca experiences. Notably, these Northern shamans actually do engage in sorcery, but "only by fighting back" and thus never attacking themselves, representing the "good guys," too. This fits perfectly into Christian bias of Northern people, where one finally has to represent the "good."
19. See Bruno Illius, *Das Shipibo: Texte, Kontexte, Kommentare. Ein Beitrag Zur diskursorientierten Untersuchung einer Montaña-Kultur* (Berlin: Dietrich Reimer Verlag, 1999), 227–30; and Bernd Brabec de Mori, "Shipibo Laughing Songs and the Transformative Faculty: Performing and Becoming the Other," *Ethnomusicology Forum* 22, no. 3 (2013): 343–61 on *osanti* songs and the role of humor in constructing alterity; see also Joanna Overing, "The Efficacy of Laughter: the Ludic Side of Magic Within Amazonian Sociality," in Joanna Overing and Alan Passes, eds., *The Anthropology of Love and Anger: The Aesthetics of Conviviality in Native Amazonia* (London: Routledge, 2000), 64–81.
20. Gow, "River People," 109; see also Brabec de Mori, "Die Lieder der Richtigen Menschen: Musikalische Kulturanthropologie der indigenen Bevölkerung im Ucayali-Tal, Westamazonien" (Ph.D. diss., Vienna University, 2011).
21. For a detailed discussion of ritualization of ayahuasca "ceremonies" in more general terms, see Labate's Chapter 8 in this volume.
22. See also Fotiou, *From Medicine Men to Day Trippers,* 272–73.
23. Stanley Tambiah, *Culture, Thought and Social Action* (Cambridge: Harvard University Press, 1985).
24. The *mochai* ritual has been only briefly mentioned a few times in literature. In Bernd Brabec de Mori, "Die Lieder der Richtigen Menschen," 447–64, *mochai* rituals and their implications are described in detail.
25. See Tânia Stolze Lima, "The Two and Its Many: Reflections on Perspectivism in a Tupi Cosmology," *Ethnos* 64, no. 1 (1999): 107–31; Eduardo Viveiros de Castro, "The Forest of Mirrors: A Few Notes on the Ontology of Amazonian Spirits" (2004), http://amazone.wikia.com/wiki/The_Forest_of_Mirrors; and Ernst Halbmayer, *Kosmos und Kommunikation: Weltkonzeptionen in der südamerikanischen Sprachfamilie der Cariben* (Vienna: Facultas, 2010).
26. Comaroff and Comaroff, *Ethnicity, Inc.,* dedicate a broad analysis to the various possibilities of how "ethnic groups" can reproduce and exploit their "ethnicity."

Bibliography

Århem, Kaj. "The Cosmic Food Web: Human-Nature Relatedness in the Northwest Amazon." In *Nature and Society: Anthropological Perspectives,* edited by Philippe Descola and Gísli Pálsson, 185–204. London: Routledge, 1996.

Bianchi, Antonio. "Ayahuasca e xamanismo indígena na selva Peruana: O lento caminho da conquista." In *O uso ritual das plantas de poder,* edited by Beatriz Caiuby Labate and Sandra Lucia Goulart, 319–29. Campinas, Brazil: Mercado de Letras, 2005.

Brabec de Mori, Bernd. "Die Lieder Der Richtigen Menschen. Musikalische Kulturanthropologie der indigenen Bevölkerung im Ucayali-Tal, Westamazonien." Ph.D. diss., Vienna University, 2011.

Brabec de Mori, Bernd. "Tracing Hallucinations: Contributing to a Critical Ethnohistory of Ayahuasca Usage in the Peruvian Amazon." In *The Internationalization of Ayahuasca*, edited by Beatriz Caiuby Labate and Henrik Jungaberle, 23–47. Zürich: Lit Verlag, 2011.

Brabec de Mori, Bernd. "La transformación de la medicina Shipibo-Konibo: Conceptos étnomedicos en la representación de un pueblo indígena." In *Etnografías de América Latina. Ocho ensayos* (Colección Estudios del Hombre 30), edited by Eveline Sigl, Yvonne Schaffler and Ricardo Ávila, 269–86. Guadalajara: University of Guadalajara, 2013.

Brabec de Mori, Bernd. "Shipibo Laughing Songs and the Transformative Faculty: Performing and Becoming the Other." *Ethnomusicology Forum* 22, no. 3 (2013): 343–61 (Special Issue on *The Human and Non-human in Lowland South American Indigenous Music*, guest edited by Bernd Brabec de Mori).

Brabec de Mori, Bernd, and Laida Mori Silvano de Brabec. "La corona de la inspiración: Los diseños geométricos de los Shipibo-Konibo y sus relaciones con cosmovisión y música." *Indiana* 26 (2009): 105–34.

Brabec de Mori, Bernd, and Laida Mori Silvano de Brabec. "Shipibo-Konibo Art and Healing Concepts: A Critical View on the 'Aesthetic Therapy.'" *Viennese Ethnomedicine Newsletter* 11, no. 2–3 (2009): 18–26.

Burroughs, William S., and Allen Ginsberg. *The Yage Letters*. San Francisco: City Lights Books, 1963, 2nd edition, 1975.

Comaroff, John L., and Jean Comaroff. *Ethnicity, Inc*. Chicago: University of Chicago Press, 2009.

Descola, Philippe. *Par-delà nature et culture*. Paris: Editions Gallimard, 2005.

Dobkin de Rios, Marlene, and Roger Rumrill. *A Hallucinogenic Tea, Laced with Controversy: Ayahuasca in the Amazon and the United States*. Westport, CT: Praeger, 2008.

Fotiou, Evgenia. "From Medicine Men to Day Trippers: Shamanic Tourism in Iquitos, Peru." Ph.D. diss., University of Wisconsin-Madison, 2010.

Gow, Peter. "River People: Shamanism and History in Western Amazonia." In *Shamanism, History and the State*, edited by Nicholas Thomas and Caroline Humphrey, 90–113. Ann Arbor: University of Michigan Press, 1994.

Halbmayer, Ernst. "Nahrung und Sexualität als Kommunikationsmedien des Identischen, Sozialisierten und des Wilden bei den Yukpa Nordwest-Venezuelas." In *Von der realen Magie zum magischen Realismus*, edited by Elke Mader and Maria Dabringer, 67–90. Frankfurt: Brandes & Apsel and Südwind, 1999.

Halbmayer, Ernst. *Kosmos und Kommunikation. Weltkonzeptionen in der südamerikanischen Sprachfamilie der Cariben*. 2 volumes. Vienna: Facultas, 2010.

Illius, Bruno. *Ani shinan: Schamanismus bei den Shipibo-Conibo (Ost-Peru)*. Tübingen: Verlag S &F, 1987.

Illius, Bruno. *Das Shipibo: Texte, Kontexte, Kommentare: Ein Beitrag zur diskursorientierten Untersuchung einer Montaña-Kultur*. Berlin: Dietrich Reimer Verlag, 1999.

Labate, Beatriz C., and Wladimyr Sena Araújo, eds. *O uso ritual da ayahuasca*. Campinas, Brazil: Mercado de Letras, 2002, 2nd edition, 2004.

Lima, Tânia Stolze. "The Two and Its Many: Reflections on Perspectivism in a Tupi Cosmology." *Ethnos* 64, no. 1 (1999): 107–31.

Overing, Joanna. "The Efficacy of Laughter: The Ludic Side of Magic Within Amazonian Sociality." In *The Anthropology of Love and Anger: The Aesthetics of Conviviality in Native Amazonia*, edited by Joanna Overing and Alan Passes, 64–81. London: Routledge, 2000.

Santos-Granero, Fernando. "Amerindian Torture Revisited: Rituals of Enslavement and Markers of Servitude in Tropical America." *Tipiti* 3 (2005): 147–74.

Shepard, Glenn H., Jr., "Psychoactive Plants and Ethnopsychiatric Medicines of the Matsigenka." *Journal of Psychoactive Drugs* 30, no. 4 (1998): 321–32.

Tambiah, Stanley. *Culture, Thought and Social Action*. Cambridge, MA: Harvard University Press, 1985.

Tupper, Kenneth W. "Ayahuasca Healing Beyond the Amazon: The Globalization of a Traditional Indigenous Entheogenic Practice." *Global Networks* 9, no. 1 (2009): 117–36.

Viveiros de Castro, Eduardo. "The Forest of Mirrors: A Few Notes on the Ontology of Amazonian Spirits." http://amazone.wikia.com/wiki/The_Forest_of_Mirrors. Originally published in Portuguese as "A floresta de cristal: Notas sobre a ontologia dos espíritos Amazônicos." Cadernos do Campo (USP) 14 + 15 (2007): 319–38.

Weiss, Gerald. "Shamanism and Priesthood in Light of the Campa Ayahuasca Ceremony." In *Hallucinogens and Shamanism*, edited by Michael Harner, 40–48. New York: Oxford University Press, 1973.

Whitten, Norman E., Jr. *Sacha Runa: Ethnicity and Adaptation of Ecuadorian Jungle Quichua.* Urbana: University of Illinois Press, 1976.

10

Ayahuasca's Attractions and Distractions

Examining Sexual Seduction in Shaman-Participant Interactions

DANIELA PELUSO

Ayahuasca tourism is a rapidly growing set of enterprises in which participants and shamans become global tourists or visitors within their own towns or countries, or abroad, in an explosion of diverse encounters. This variable set of hosts and guests partakes in shamanic rituals in which the ayahuasca brew is consumed within ritual settings with the aim of producing hallucinogenic visions deemed to be personally beneficial to all participants.[1]

Whereas only a few decades ago, the ayahuasca experience required that a lone traveler make his or her way to the forests of South America, now notions of local, global, space, and place converge as shamans and tourists travel throughout the world to perform and participate in a diversity of ayahuasca ceremonies. For example, an eighty-year-old Shipibo shaman who once mostly healed within his community in Pucallpa, Peru, began to travel nationally and then around the world, while his apprenticing son began to appear in international films as a healer and opened a tourist's lodge. Some newcomers to the rituals, also interested in bringing ayahuasca to a larger public, have introduced it in dance raves.[2] Not only are more people eager to participate in ceremonies, but also more individuals want to become *ayahuasqueros* (shamans who heal with ayahuasca). Furthermore, the ingredients of the brew are now available for purchase on the Internet.[3] Moreover, many Euro-American ayahuasca tourists who have apprenticed shamans are now based in South America and travel throughout the world performing ayahuasca rituals. These are but a few examples of the novel expansion of ayahuasca ritual practices.

The inventive global expansion of ayahuasca rituals creates a set of encounters that bring together individuals with highly divergent epistemologies and experiences, creating a sundry montage of cognitive, emotional, and practical cultural systems rife with contradictions and potential misunderstandings. Although these are also settings for positive exchanges, as would be expected, the convergence of translocal and transnational flows of communication, knowledge, and practices also comes with its challenges.

This study focuses on a more obscure, yet growing, consideration of what happens when various belief systems are brought together within transnational ritual contexts by examining the relationship between sex, seduction, and gendered power relations in the context of ayahuasca rituals. By "sex" and "seduction," I refer to sexual imagery, meanings, attraction, arousal, and/or the physical sexual act in relation to the ayahuasca ceremony or ceremonial space. Initially, I will examine the historical, symbolic, and practical relationships between ayahuasca and sex. I will focus on how, in the historical and contemporary associations of sex with ayahuasca, the adoption and reinvention of ayahuasca rituals is part of the ongoing challenges that ayahuasca usage and practices undergo. Through an analysis of local and global narratives, the paper also engages with Amerindian epistemologies and theories of perspectivism, countertransference, and "the male gaze" to examine local concerns and interactions between shamans, their apprentices, and ayahuasca participants, and how they variably position themselves as authorities, intermediaries, and gendered individuals. In the broadest sense, I will explore gender relations between shamans and local as well as nonlocal participants and the resultant ensuing debates about sex and sexuality as discussed among locals and web-based audiences. Importantly, this discussion is not meant to detract from the legitimacy ayahuasca rituals deserve.

Ayahuasca Tourism

There is a growing literature on ayahuasca tourism from a social science perspective.[4] Several authors in this volume describe how ayahuasca rituals have spread in today's post-traditional environment, referring to the new non-indigenous contexts in which these rituals increasingly take place. By focusing on sex and gender, I hope to highlight how flexible, yet fragile, social interactions can be in the context of health and healing through ayahuasca ceremonies worldwide. I will examine the way in which many ayahuasqueros and participants creatively use or reinvent these rituals for accommodating or imposing local and global conditions and desires, including gender relations.

The central locus of this paper is Puerto Maldonado, Peru, a regional Amazonian capital and its environs, where I have conducted fieldwork over the last two decades, particularly among Ese Eja.[5] Most individuals interviewed either reside(d) in or visited this area, unless indicated otherwise. In this chapter I refer only to male ayahuasqueros. This does not imply that women do not drink or play key roles in ayahuasca ceremonies; merely that here, women do not identify themselves as ayahuasqueras.

Figure 10.1. Puerto Maldando, Madre de Dios, Peru. Photograph by Daniela Peluso.

I have previously provided an overview of the predicaments of ayahuasca tourism as a contribution toward understanding how ayahuasca tourism affects the localities in which such encounters take place.[6] I examined local concerns and interactions between shamans and participants regarding the recent proliferation of ayahuasqueros, the sanitization of rituals, and the discounting of potential roles of malevolence and conflict within ayahuasca tourist rituals. In forthcoming work, I describe ayahuasca ceremonies as *hypertraditions,* whereby the tradition flourishes and intensifies within a context of amplified contact and conflict, as occurs in global tourism.[7] In brief, my past research concluded that ayahuasca tourists tend to be uninformed about the local politics of ayahuasca and how their roles as tourists can negatively affect the local social and political economies of health, particularly as these traditions grow increasingly popular and widespread.

Ayahuasca and Sex

Although a discussion of sex and ayahuasca may appear provocative, it is not a novel subject, since sex has a historical context. Thus, before I discuss sex in terms of its relationship to the recent proliferation of ayahuasqueros and tourism, I will underscore the significant pan-Amazonian role sex has in ayahuasca symbolism, discourses, and practices. First, sexual abstinence is part of a broader pan-Amazonian epistemological outlook that acknowledges the existence of cross-realities replete with sexual imagery and an ethos of appropriate sexual behaviors, of which abstinence is only one. To comprehend this, one must understand how indigenous notions of personhood, agency, and transformation are intrinsic to Amerindian ontologies. This entails paying close attention to the invisible, intangible, and inalienable aspect of all "life." For instance, for Ese Eja, the world we live in is a Kantian inversion whereby humanity—who we really are—is but a symptom or intuition of reality. Ese Eja maintain that we do not perceive reality ("the world as it really is"); instead *it* perceives us through multiple invisible life forms. As such, animals and plants are seen as having personhood (with its ensuing sociality) and individual perspectives. Viveiros de Castro's theory of *multinatural perspectivism* clearly sets forth how, in Amazonia, intentionality and consciousness form the multiple subjects of humans, animals, plants, and spirits and their ability to see each other differently.[8] Concomitantly, multiplicity (the fluidity of human identity and the permeability between realities) and transformation (the ability to change between various singular and plural forms) are prominent themes among Lowland South Americans, as demonstrated through dreams and creation narratives.[9] The taking of ayahuasca, certain states of illness, dreams, solitary hunting, and extreme negative emotions are some of several states of consciousness that Amazonians consider to be crossing points between realities. This is why a person's behavior in ayahuasca visions is not considered to be exclusively hallucinatory, but rather a crossing over of one's self from one reality to another—realities that have implicit effects on one another. Hence, one way the otherwise invisible world of multiple personhoods that influence human reality is revealed, accessed, and consulted is through ayahuasca visions. Ayahuasca links the "seeing," "learning," and "knowing" that transpire through visions to ultimately see the world as it truly is.

Second, sexual abstinence is part of an overall *dieta* that indigenous and mestizo ayahuasca shamans undergo, restricting certain food and activities such eating sugar, strong spices, and having sex.[10] Sexual abstinence is expected of ayahuasqueros who are in training; it is a time in which they are focusing on acquiring and sharpening their skills and most likely enduring exigent trials and quests with other beings in nonvisible realities. For instance, it is common for novice Shuar shamans to refrain from sex for five to six months to ensure a successful apprenticeship whereby they will gain the power to harm or heal.[11] In turn, sexual restraint, for Machiguenga, demonstrates a commitment to socialize with the spirit worlds.[12] Usually, once shamans are initiated, they are no longer required to abstain from sex for such long periods of time, but may choose to do so when they undergo specific additional dietas they deem appropriate.

In light of perspectivism, which considers how nonhuman subjects see human activities differently from how humans see them, sexual abstinence can be understood as reflecting an awareness and sensitivity toward other selves, as an "expression for the bond of 'community' with the spirits."[13] Narratives about relationships between different types of beings indicate that sexual desire—its implications and consequences—defines much of human and nonhuman social relations. Abstinence can also deemphasize the incompatibilities between human and nonhuman others. For instance, abstinence avoids the alleged repugnant stench of human sex that other beings find offensive[14] and that might cause them to perceive human activity as something different from their own. This perspectivist outlook further concurs with why indigenous hunters often refrain from sex, claiming that the resulting stench interferes with their ability to seduce nonhuman beings; in contrast, they focus on smelling good and acts of cleanliness.[15]

Third, there is a complex relationship overall between sex and the ingestion of plants or animals, a relationship that many ethnographers have identified and explored.[16] One aspect of this relationship is expressed through sexual abstinence as a way to prevent food pollution, ensuring that food is appropriately collected and ingested. For instance, among Ese Eja, particular animal and plant foods harvested by adults must be entirely consumed before the harvester can have sex; otherwise the foods become pathogenic.[17] Once harvested, food must be stored away from places where people copulate so as to prevent contamination.

Figure 10.2. Human man with anaconda woman. Sketch by Sydney Solizonquehua, commissioned by Daniela Peluso.

People commonly express this threat by describing plants and animals as spirits prone to "jealousy" or "possessiveness." Amazonians take great precautions to abide by notions set forth by animal and plant personhood, what I have thus far attributed to perspectivism, in order to ensure their own safety and well-being.

The ayahuasca vine is widely recognized as being a female spirit and, in relation to shamans-in-training, is often referred to as being "jealous."[18] Sex can further taint the relationships that apprentices are attempting to form with nonhuman beings and the surroundings that the ayahuasca introduces them to in their visions. Among Amerindian peoples, jealousy is a key negative emotion that underpins most forms

Figure 10.3. Ayahuasca is widely recognized as being a female spirit. Photograph by Daniela Peluso.

of exchange, including gender relations. Yet jealousy, as Amazonians speak about it, can also be an admirable quality, especially when expressed in regard to children. For instance, in many contexts jealousy signifies a sense of caring for someone, guardianship, supervision, protection, or a feeling of responsibility. In this sense, the spirit of ayahuasca is seen as protecting its obliging apprentices.

The gendering of plants and animals is another significant, yet scantly addressed, topic[19] whereby shamans and ayahuasca participants can form allegiances with plant and animal spirits on the basis of their own notions of gender and kinship relations. Male shamans use notions of seduction to describe how they establish and negotiate affinity with invisible beings. These descriptions are not mere tropes but portray practical and strategic relations that mirror male attitudes toward women as they are narrated through stories about seducing women or hunting prey. These relations of exchange whereby sex and seduction are mediums to gain meat and women, or means to gain women through meat, have been referred to as an "economy of sex"[20] and are contentiously debated in the Amazonian literature.[21] Although there is no consensus, it is minimally agreed that sex is a figurative, metaphorical, and practical trope whose significance is conveyed in the everyday lives of Amazonian peoples.

Finally, notions of sensuality and seduction are also predominant within many ayahuasca visions and the discourses that surround them. Although seduction is a way of engaging in social relationships, sex with nonhumans simultaneously carries the potential threat of transgression and pollution. However, several shamans have described how, while under the influence of ayahuasca, their libidinal responses increase, which they experience through a state of arousal that they consciously control. One shaman described how, throughout his training, he was warned to avoid having sex with nonvisible others because they were probably traps set up by rivals or enemies who wished him to "fall" and "lose his power." Locally, shamans and participants alike are also cautioned to resist following beautiful beings appearing in their visions, since these beings will divert them from their intended path through inherently dangerous sensual temptations. There are many cautionary tales against having sex with nonhumans for fear of permanent transformation into another type of being no longer able to return to a human form.[22] One common narrative is that of mermaids attempting to seduce men, and of pink dolphins attempting to seduce women.[23] A Shipibo-trained shaman described how only very experienced shamans might one day, in their visions, meet and get to know a woman who, over time, will become his spiritual wife and sexual partner. However, there are strict rules that this relationship not interfere with the shaman's terrestrial life or produce any cosmic children. Although for shamans there is the possibility that sex or sensual experiences might lead to beneficial exchanges with other beings, it may also drain them of their vitality and cause their death.[24]

Tourist-centered ayahuasca ceremonies have transformed the legacies of local rituals through continuity and reinterpretation. For instance, when tourism websites refer to the "spirit of ayahuasca" as being jealous, they refer only to its possessive connotation; one website advises, "The conscious spirit of Ayahuasca desires our undivided attention when in her presence. Temporary sexual abstinence might also be seen as an offering of one's higher intention to the Divine."[25] This is a one-dimensional understanding of what jealousy and sexual abstinence mean in the local context. As already mentioned, rather than possession, jealousy can signify a caring form of protection.

Also, in local ayahuasca contexts, participants often abstain from sex as part of the diet they undergo for apprentice training or to treat difficult illnesses. Although most tourists are not training to be shamans, numerous ayahuasca tourism websites informing ayahuasca tourists of what to expect during ceremonies advise prolonged sexual abstinence. Perhaps the Western tourist's self-prescribed sexual abstinence suits the script of his or her own view of the ayahuasca quest as an adventurous exotic journey,[26] as indicated on numerous blog sites where ideas of celibacy complement New Age ideas about spirituality and self-healing, and individual self-empowerment is valued and emphasized.[27] Returning from an ayahuasca lodge in Puerto Maldonado, a female tourist exclaimed, "I am a shaman, I now need to diet like one. This will keep me pure." In an interview, she indicated that her assertive, self-imposed stance on celibacy was influenced by her Buddhist beliefs. Some websites also encourage sexual abstinence as a way to conserve energy and invest oneself fully in the ritual by focusing on spirituality rather than physicality.[28] In sum, Amazonian ideas of sexual abstinence are often combined with Western notions of purity, monkhood, and New Age enlightenment as tourists integrate themselves into local and global ayahuasca practices.

Similarly, references to seduction and arousal are common on blog sites.[29] One tourist interprets ayahuasca's attractions: "Seduced by the undulations of her serpentine body, I followed her willingly inside the rhythmic trance. She said coyly, 'Watch me dance.'"[30] Another reports the shaman chanting into the brew in the "high key of a tin whistle or courting bird, seducing the plant spirits to aid me."[31] Local and nonlocal participants alike link seduction to the desire to enlist nonvisible allies in a ritual that addresses health and well-being; yet seduction has its limits, since sex is resisted and proscribed.[32]

Shaman-Participant Seduction

As I have just discussed, sex is a highly charged subject in relation to ayahuasca and people's relationships to the nonvisible world. Sex, as a universal activity, seems to traverse human, cultural, and language barriers. Alongside the proliferation of ayahuasca shamanism and tourism, locally and abroad, ayahuasca settings bring together shamans and participants who have different imaginaries about each other and the reasons they wish to participate in a shared ritual. Among the increasing occurrence of such encounters, there is an alarming incidence of ayahuasqueros (and/or their assistants) making sexual advances toward their female participants during or following ayahuasca ceremonies.[33]

There are now many recorded cases of shamans who intentionally seek out sexual relations with participants, showing that, for these particular men, sex with participants is premeditated and part of a routine.[34] Individuals I have interviewed and on blogs have described how some shamans seem to "canvas the room" and target their attentions accordingly. One woman referred to a particular shaman saying he "has a predatory pattern of how he chooses women to attempt to seduce."[35] A male anthropologist described to me how, when he traveled with one of the young indigenous men from a community he worked in, the young man would pretend he was a shaman explicitly as a tactic for seducing women, mimicking the success his own village shaman had in seducing female ayahuasca tourists.

Some ayahuasqueros in the tourism circuit use particular substances to "aid in the seduction of female participants in rituals."[36] One shaman told me he had apprenticed under Shipibo shamans who knew particular herbs that could blur women's sexual boundaries. The Amazonian pharmacopeia includes charm spells used explicitly for seduction. They are meant to last only for a short time, unless renewed, creating a temporary lapse in rational thinking. Yet some described how ayahuasca itself, because of the sensual feelings it provokes, is deliberately used by some as a tool for seduction.[37] There are also rare, tragic cases in which shamans or their assistants stalk women and brutally force themselves on them.[38]

Typically, shaman-participant seductions take place as the ceremony is winding down, though sometimes they happen while the participant is experiencing the hallucinatory affects of ayahuasca. A young woman explained, "It's not so much about seduction: it is about sexual harassment. I got felt up by a shaman!" She explained that she went with a male friend and colleague, local to the Colombian Amazonian town she was staying in, to drink ayahuasca at the home of a well-established healer. On drinking, she found that the hallucinogen came on quickly and intensely: "I had full-bodied tingling and my vision blacked out and I was in space! My body was completely gone." She attributed her extraordinary visions to the recent death of a loved family member who she was mourning. Amidst her extraordinary visions she also felt violently ill.

> The shaman's assistant was helping several of the participants who were nauseous like me. He was helping a woman several people away from me. Then he came over to me and put his hands on my back. He had

> some great healing skills because he made my nausea go away. He spoke softly reassuring me that I would be well. He told me to lay down and he placed his hands on my tummy and it felt a lot better. Then, all of a sudden, his hands were down my pants! [She laughed incredulously] I had to physically fight him off and I was still under the influence of ayahuasca. He whispered 'tranquila, tranquila' (relax, relax) when I said 'no, no' and pushed away his hands. He tried to lie next to me but finally went off. I noticed that he went to help other young women, ignoring older women and men: The young women were all non-locals.

Some participants are seduced while they are experiencing visions and are thus in a hallucinatory state. A young woman who had participated in a ceremony in which she was the only nonlocal explained:

> I was so delighted that the shaman placed me next to him and that he began to pay special attention to me. When he began to rub my body I had no way of knowing what he intended but it soon became obvious when he... [she gestures where he placed his hands]... I pushed him away but felt extremely sad and confused and even wondered if it was part of my vision. I also felt somewhat frightened as the visions had only just started setting in and I felt abandoned by the person meant to guide my experience. I spent the whole time resisting the visions for fear that I might lose any sense of control. For ages I kept on thinking of what I might have done to make him think that this would be OK. He was a well-known and respected shaman. The only thing that makes sense is that either his opinion of Western women from cinema made him feel that we were all sluts or that somehow he interpreted my enthusiasm toward him to be sexual. That was it for me, I never drank ayahuasca again.

In another ceremony that took place in the United States with a Peruvian-based European shaman, one male participant expressed how strange he felt when he noticed that a woman was seemingly being seduced toward the end of an ayahuasca session. He described how it was dark and mostly a time for reflection and gentle speaking when he became aware of the shaman lying down next to a woman. They maintained a spooned position cooing to each other and simulating what appeared to be sexual foreplay or intercourse, leaving the participants who took notice confused and distracted.

Sexual harassment[39] also occurs within local or indigenous ayahuasca settings. Indigenous women are reticent to drink ayahuasca with an unknown shaman unless accompanied by family, friends, or their children. One indigenous friend in Puerto Maldonado described what happened when she drank with a local urban shaman:

> I arrived with my two boys. He looked at me. He said that I was very ill and in danger of dying, that people had done terrible things to me with *daño* (intentional harm). He put my boys in a separate room and then prepared a blanket for me to lie on. I immediately felt that his intentions were not good, that they were sexual. I gave it some time but every sign imaginable was there telling me that he was going to force himself on me: the tone of his voice, the way he looked at me, the way he touched me, and then separating me from my children. I never drank with him because I left before anything could happen. It has happened to me before, but I was stupid then, trusting in everyone.

Another indigenous friend described what happened with her when she drank with a famous indigenous healer in a native community who she knew had been desiring her for many years.

> He knew that I wanted nothing to do with him in that way; I had pushed him away many times, which was why I wouldn't drink [ayahuasca] with him. But this time there were many friends and family there and a gringo friend [male]. I drank and sat away from him even though he had asked me to be next to him. When my vision came it was amazing, so beautiful that I wanted to cry. I was on the verge of understanding [something] but then he came and stood in front of me and blocked my vision. It was like an eclipse! Afterwards, he told me: "If you want to 'see' then you need to drink with me alone." I knew what he meant by that and so now I am afraid of ever drinking.

Still, some urban Amazonian, Latin American nationals and even Western women who reported experiencing inappropriate sexual advances have simply brushed it off, claiming to give it very little importance. Many women have told me, generally, "This is how men are here; you just need to tell them that you're not interested. It's not a big deal." Others have said, "It's weak and insecure women who do not know how to handle these men." Perhaps sidestepping the question of ethics, these interviewees seem to presume that power relations are negotiable on the basis of strength of character and an understanding of local culture and gender relations.

However, in a few rare cases some women feel complimented by the shaman's sexual advances. One woman I interviewed expressed feeling empowered by the dedicated attention, and used the sexual encounter as a way to confirm her own sense of uniqueness and aspirations for divinity. Some shamans capitalize on this by offering obliging women a special status in ayahuasca ceremonies. On one blog thread that discussed a particular shaman's pattern of sexual advances on ayahuasca ceremony participants, a woman with a history of "falling in love" with shamans, and who proclaims herself to be shaman, expressed that sex was a potentially fulfilling aspect of the ayahuasca experience[40]:

> . . . I found his closeness very comforting and helpful to the sacred work I was sent to do with the Medicine . . . who is to say what is really appropriate or not when it comes to this kind of work? . . . if you can't take the heat stay out of the kitchen. . . . That's what I say anyway. . . . For me the experience was totality . . . and Completion with a Man on all levels. . . . [He] is a very talented conductor of sacred energies and has a strong Male Force that is God-Like in many ways, meaning beyond the ordinary realm of power . . . it was like a true Sacred Union and Divine merger. I had never in my life felt such completion. Being there was like being in the arms of God in Heaven. . . . I cannot describe this insatiable longing for Completion and Ecstasy. . . . There is no Shaman, no amount of money that one could pay to have this experience. So, for me, being with the Medicine in this way was completely priceless. . . ."

This narrative reiterates that some cases of seduction under the influence of ayahuasca are mutually consensual. Yet, as is argued on the blogs, many believe that the ultimate accountability lies with the shaman, who is responsible for resisting both arousal and star-struck women, to seek ways of healing that do not depend on his phallus. The blogs are in agreement, with a general consensus among shamans and serious students of shamanism.

Reactions to Sex and Seduction: Global and Local Considerations

For those immersed in ayahuasca circles, whether as shamans, participants, or scholars, the occurrence of sexual scandal has become common knowledge. Another well-known sex scandal concerns a key leader of the Santo Daime church, who was accused on multiple occasions of inappropriate sexual advances on women who had gone to him to be healed through *daime* (ayahuasca). The leadership's unwillingness to reprimand the "padrinho" leader in question resulted in many people leaving the church and describing it as an exploitative system of patriarchy.[41] In general, bloggers assert that these shamans are not fit for their profession.

Sexual harassment clashes with the variable reasons women want to drink ayahuasca. As Winkelman describes, most ayahuasca tourists are generally seeking "personal spiritual development; emotional healing; and the development of personal self-awareness, including contact with a sacred nature, God, spirits, and plant and natural energies produced by ayahuasca."[42] Furthermore, according to ayahuasca blogs, many participants interested in spiritual healing are themselves victims of childhood sexual abuse and thus find the sexual advances of shamans to be emotionally damaging and cruelly exploitative. This is compounded by a tendency to idealize shamans,[43] thus masking the usual boundaries ayahuasca tourists might normally encounter in hierarchical gender settings.

A common public response by bloggers who witness or experience shamans' inappropriate behavior is to claim that these men are not "real shamans" and are thus "inauthentic." Such responses are not limited to ayahuasqueros; they include any individuals who refer to themselves as shamans.[44] These positions do not take into account that shamans are humans who may have detrimental flaws; they also overlook the historical and ongoing possibility that indigenous women are sometimes sexually harassed within contexts of traditional ayahuasca shamanism, and they further ignore the necessary rewriting of a gendered landscape for many local practitioners who now frequently travel abroad, as well as the significant number of Western shamans and apprentices who are now fully aware of the Western allure and mystique surrounding ideas about shamans.

In sum, my study has found people generally respond negatively to a shaman's inappropriate sexual advances. Female participants feel vulnerable, ashamed, exploited, and betrayed. Male onlookers are also disturbed and confused. Both assume that the shaman or his assistants are taking advantage of their power and status, and the actuality that the participants are unsure of any of the roles, methods, and consequent boundaries. In these cases, people feel that the shaman has undermined the trust they have given him as a caretaker, guide, and healer. Furthermore, many feel that the experience of ayahuasca and their outlook toward it has been tainted.

If we are to regard shamans from a broad Western perspective, then clearly sexual advances toward participants are unethical. If we pay attention to local or indigenous perspectives, then we also find that such behavior is frowned on. In Puerto Maldonado, the indigenous and non-indigenous Amazonians whom I have interviewed and conducted fieldwork with over the last few decades do not feel that sexual relations of any degree are acceptable between shamans and their patients, unless these are preexisting or legitimate relationships that occur outside of the ayahuasca experience and ceremonial context. There is significant social criticism when such norms are violated. The women I have interviewed who have experienced such behavior clearly attribute it to an abuse of power both in terms of gender and community. They feel that particular men are imposing their physical and political dominance over women, and that as shamans they intentionally use their power to intimidate or try to seduce them. For these reasons, most women are reticent to drink ayahuasca with an unknown shaman unless accompanied by family, friends, or their children, and even then, as shown in an earlier narrative, sexual harassment may still occur.

Nonetheless, issues of trust are important to many ayahuasca healers and participants to the extent that, in the last several years, tourist websites for ayahuasca package tours have begun to address concerns about the potential seduction of female participants by ayahuasca specialists. One website resolves this problem by dealing exclusively with female shamans:

> Ayahuasca facilitation in Peru has typically been a male dominated world. It is not uncommon for male shamans in Peru to misuse their leadership role to seduce unsuspecting foreign women that come to them for shamanic healing. The fact that we almost exclusively work with elder, female Shipibo ayahuasca shamans provides a safe environment for women coming to the Amazon for ayahuasca experiences.... These Shipibo shamans represent the highest level of integrity that you can find anywhere in the Amazon region.[45]

In response to the sexual exploitation of women at ceremonies, one blogger questions tourists' general gullibility when searching for a shaman:

> Now, if you get met at the airport in Iquitos, don't speak Spanish, and decide that the taxi driver, who asked, "Ayahuasca? Ayahuasca? Mi Padre!" is your guiding light; well then, you're on your own. But if you've looked around, found out who's who and what's what by talking to people who have been there, then things will generally be pretty kosher.[46]

This narrative suggests that tourists themselves have a responsibility to be informed and not be trapped within their own idealizations and romanticizations of apparently non-Western worlds and practices. Yet, tourist encounters take place at the juncture of local and global gender relations that reflect a broad and diverse panorama of gender performances and practices. Locally, gender relations vary, but there is a predominant notion that, in most circumstances, women will surrender to male sexual advances if they find themselves in a vulnerable position or merely alone with a man, as such behavior is aligned with gender expectations. In most contexts, any time men and women are together, there is a constant barrage of sexual overtones that inform all verbal and nonverbal behavior. To circumvent vulnerability, indigenous women avoid smiling directly at men, laughing with them, paying too much attention to them, being in their presence without close kin nearby, and traveling alone. Not coincidentally, these precautions prescriptively describe most nonlocal female ayahuasca participants, particularly if they openly esteem the shaman, converse and laugh freely, are unhindered by local customs, and travel alone.

However, an explanation of mismatched gender codes cannot fully justify the increasing sexual exploitation of women by shamans. Further trends contradict this; first, nowadays, many of the most popular tourist-focused shamans are themselves Westerners who have apprenticed with local shamans and then gone abroad to allow others to experience ayahuasca; second, many shamans in traditional ayahuasca ritual settings have sexually harassed local and indigenous women; and last, many local shamans have now traveled extensively and are exposed to numerous forms of expression and understand that there are codes for gender relations in different places. Yet it is precisely this set of individuals from which the most active perpetrators of sexual harassment spring forth.

Before returning to the ambivalence implicit in gendered and unequal encounters and the disjuncture embedded in these translocal encounters in which the idea of the "other" is romanticized, I would like to turn to a discussion of ethics in the Western healer-practitioner relationship.

Countertransference

Trichter, in writing about his concerns that Western ayahuasca participants are not sufficiently informed about the traditional uses of ayahuasca, raises the point that in the ayahuasca healing rituals, shamans might experience countertransference toward their participants just as a therapist might with patients.[47] He also suggests that shamans might "project their erotic fantasies into their work with participants" and, consciously or not, may "wield their power over the participants in drug-induced states" or suggest sex as being part of the ayahuasca experience to a novice participant.[48] Although shamanism and psychoanalysis are two very different therapeutic traditions, the comparison between therapist-patient and healer-participant relationships raises questions about the ethics of sexual interactions between these actors.

In any vocation in which people rely on an individual for health and healing purposes, there is an ethical code of conduct, even if unwritten. The person being healed is in a position of vulnerability, and the healer is expected not to create further suffering or to entangle that individual within his own projected emotional issues, particularly his own erotic feelings.[49] According to psychoanalytic principles, transference is a misguided projection of emotions toward the therapist, commonly in the form of sexual attraction. For Freud, transference constitutes a healthy process within therapy by unearthing the patient's otherwise repressed emotions and allowing the therapist to address them and help the patient heal.[50] However, with countertransference, therapists unconsciously respond to the patient's transference onto them. According to psychoanalytic principles, cases of erotic countertransference that remain unchecked serve to heighten both the patient's and the analyst's neurosis,[51] causing the healer to become "locked into a position in which her own wounds cannot be used in service of the client, and the client's inner healing capacities are denied."[52] As Freud warned, "We ought not to give up the neutrality toward the patient, which we have acquired through keeping countertransference in place."[53] For these reasons, occurrences of countertransference need to be acknowledged and examined for successful treatment of the patient.

Ayahuasca visions have their own language and symbols whereby the explicit and obvious are determined by what is implicit and not obvious. Nonetheless, the implicit is intended to examine the participant's unresolved conflicts, not the healer's. There is no doubt that ayahuasqueros possess, wield, and aspire to hold increasingly more power. Their reasons and motivations are ideally for advancing personal spiritual growth and well-being, and the positive effects that ensue. Yet the sexual exploitation of female participants, alongside acts of sorcery, is certainly a reminder that shamanistic power is not always implemented for positive deeds and that shamans can be diverted from their path. Ayahuasca tourism can certainly serve as a setting for such a distraction, particularly when shamans are romanticized and treated with unrealistically high regard.

The Tourist Gaze, Perspectivism, and Critical Feminism

Gender relations need to be examined within the production and consumption of tourist experiences.[54] A useful concept is the "tourist gaze," the culturally constructed way tourists watch and transfix themselves on the places they visit.[55] Such a gaze repeatedly inscribes itself on local geographies of ayahuasca tourism,[56] and the advertising of these locales invites such a gaze—particularly the male gaze, with its emphasis on extreme adventures and quests amid general associations of the vacation as hedonistic outlet.[57] Furthermore, tourist destinations themselves are eroticized in such a way that tourism can depend on the "sensual mythologies of exotic places."[58]

I argue that ayahuasca tourism is a set of encounters whereby the tourist gaze does not go undeflected. In the ayahuasca tourism cases discussed earlier, the shaman can redirect the gaze away from himself and toward female participants through seductive desire. It is the familiar "male gaze," constituting an actively controlling patriarchal maleness voyeuristically invoked upon women as fetishized passive objects of desire.[59] Although Foucault[60] links the surveillance "gaze" to power rather than to gender, in feminist theory the male gaze reflects a nuanced gendered power asymmetry whereby men hegemonically impose their *unwanted* gaze on women.

The production of ayahuasca tourism privileges shamans as idealized, nearly supernatural beings. This is reflected in the propaganda, websites, and blogs that hail these men as celestial beings, obliterating their humanity and often their economic reality.[61] This corresponds with a general trend that privileges "masculinized themes" and glorifies "Great Men," scripting all other needs and desires as subservient to a male norm.[62] I argue that, in ayahuasca tourism, male and female tourists may render themselves into seemingly passive states, as is familiar in Western pedagogical learning when one is in the apprenticeship of an esteemed teacher[63] or a medical doctor.[64]

Figure 10.4. Maloca built for tourists, Madre de Dios, Peru. Photograph by Daniela Peluso.

Mulvey's ideas about the "male gaze" derive from critical cinema studies that characterize the male audience and camera as privileging an active male viewpoint and focus on passive women. Historically, and as elsewhere[65] in Amazonia, the exposure of local peoples to Western women is principally via the cinema and tourism. In the former, women are portrayed as sexually loose. In an earlier account, when an ayahuasca participant tried to make sense of her predicament, she articulated these conflicting notions of gender: "The only thing that makes sense is that either his opinion of Western women from cinema made him feel that we were all sluts or that somehow he interpreted my enthusiasm toward him to be sexual." Whereas Urry stresses how men are conditioned to see women of color as being sexually available, I suggest that non-Westerners of all shades are informed through the media that Western women are highly sexually driven and independent.[66] Compounded with this, as mentioned earlier, female tourists' gestures and fashion are often in conflict with local gender norms whereby Western customs can be misread and misunderstood. For instance, among many indigenous Amazonian people, making eye contact and smiling directly at a male is a sexual invitation, a code so implicitly understood that it is naturalized in terms of gender relations. Therefore, it would not even occur to a man that a woman, albeit a Western tourist, would not also subscribe to the same understandings.

Yet, as discussed earlier, in ayahuasca tourism settings, any misunderstandings concerning gender roles are further embedded within behaviors that are linked to the romanticization and idealization of the shaman. I argue that, in these contexts, including cases where women participants desire shamans, the male gaze deflects the female gaze and redirects it toward the participant through sexual desire.

Conclusions

In this chapter, I have reviewed historical, symbolic, and contemporary relationships between sex and ayahuasca through gender relations, shaman and local and nonlocal participants behaviors, and ideas of countertransference and the male gaze within the local-global contexts in which ayahuasca ceremonies currently take place. Yet, this analysis would be incomplete if it did not remark on the disproportional social, economic, and political inequality that generally tends to occur between shamans and their nonlocal and international participants, as well as their respective cities and countries, as part of the broader context in which ayahuasca tourism takes place.[67] Moreover, ayahuasca shamanism cannot be divorced from the economic incentives that further motivate its recent proliferation. As one European ayahuasquero pointed out to me, the new economic incentives can reshuffle the priorities that are usually in place when one practices shamanism. Furthermore, the emerging neo-shamans do not have adequate shamanic training or community vigilance to give them the tools necessary to maintain the integrity of their work. An experienced South American woman described how an itinerant Peruvian shaman she was well acquainted with had been tactically seducing women within the ceremonial context of ayahuasca for years: "He had sex with strategic women that could organize sessions for him, open doors, make contacts, etc. He would choose women with financial resources that were potentially ongoing participants and could bring new clients to his sessions or women who were just young and pretty, as it was revealed he had done for years."

Shamans using their special status to exploit women in a state of vulnerability within the ayahuasca ritual and its ceremonial spaces is part of a broader trend of South American–based men who prey on female tourists by using the currency of cultural legitimacy. In some instances, such men play off Western notions of authenticity to seduce vacationing women with displays of "Inca-nismo,"[68] as does the *birichero* who poses as a spiritually sensitive Inca descendant and typically plays Andean music and makes and wears jewelry and clothing from traditional natural materials and motifs. The birichero offers sex and mysticism in exchange for free meals, entertainment, and, hopefully, a ticket to visit the traveler abroad. Similarly, ayahuasqueros, even those who are Westerners, might flaunt local traditions and privileged knowledge to allure gringas. Such behavior reflects how global tourism tends to amplify economic and political inequities that some men directly challenge through their sexuality.[69]

With the advent of ayahuasca tourism, as ayahuasca rituals further transform, the unwritten codes of what are and aren't considered acceptable transgressions—codes normally dictated by culture, locale, and training—are pushed further and further into the background though local-global encounters between

Figure 10.5. Young man with a birichero-like appearance. Photograph by Miguel Alexiades.

particular shaman (be they weak, lost, greedy, perverted, or sexist) and particular participants (be they uninformed, delusional, romanticist, or idealist). Just as transference and countertransference can be valuable, so can the desire for transgression, but not when it is unchecked and unrestrained. In cases where seduction is attempted, the clash between variable shaman and participant imaginaries is blatant. As I have shown, such attractions and distractions align with historical continuities of shamanism and ayahuasca rituals. Yet, whereas Amazonian women tend to view shamans as humans who can potentially be abusive, uninformed Western women do not. Within the spectrum of shamans and participants, it is the coinciding of shamans who view women as easy prey with women who idealize shamans that exacerbates the trend of seduction within ritual contexts. For these reasons, this chapter is not meant to detract from the benefits and legitimacy of ayahuasca rituals, but rather to urge an awareness of the conditions that create these possibilities within ritual contexts. In conclusion, the increased incidence of inappropriate or unwelcomed seduction by shamans toward female tourists is a manifestation and repercussion of the conceptual and practical disjuncture between the global and the local dynamics of ayahuasca uses and practices, as well as underlying disparate notions of gender relations, healer-participant ethics, appropriate uses of power, and the broader economic and political contexts in which they transpire.

Acknowledgments

This chapter owes its existence to the encouragement I received from Bia Labate. I am thankful to all of the ayahuasqueros, assistants, and participants who granted me their time and thoughts, yet remain anonymous. I am further grateful to the countless bloggers who post their experiences on the Internet in hopes of sharing their ideas with a wider audience; indeed, they do achieve that. I am thankful to Miguel Alexiades and Bia Labate for their suggestions.

Notes

1. The brew combines a vine (*Banisteriopsis caapi*) and leaves (*Psychotria viridis*) that contain dimethyltryptamine (DMT), a tryptamine compound.
2. One such rave was organized on Facebook (http://www.facebook.com/group.php?gid=327741552347#) and mentioned in ayahuasca blogs: http://dawnontheamazon.com/blog/2011/02/24/proposal-an-ayahuasca-organization-for-iquitos/.
3. http://www.iamshaman.com/eshop/10Browse.asp?Category=Roots%20Barks:B%20Caapi.
4. See bibliography for Davidov (2010), Fotiou (2010), Holman (2011), Peluso (2006), and Tupper (2009).
5. Ese Eja are an indigenous Amazonian group who reside in Peru and Bolivia.

6. Daniela Peluso, "For 'Export Only': Ayahuasca Tourism and Hyper-Traditionalism," *IASTE Working Paper Series (Hyper-Traditions and "Real" Places),* edited by Nezar AlSayyad, 189 (2006): 482–500.
7. Daniela Peluso, "Altered States of Dislocation: Ayahuasca Tourism in the Peruvian Amazon," *Journal of Tourism and Culture Change* (forthcoming).
8. Eduardo Viveiros de Castro, "Exchanging Perspectives: The Transformation of Objects into Subjects in Amerindian Ontologies," *Common Knowledge* 10 (2004): 463–84.
9. Daniela Peluso, "'That Which I Dream Is True': Dream Narratives in an Amazonian Community," *Dreaming* 14 (2004): 107–19.
10. See bibliography for Chaumeil (1983) and Luna (2011).
11. Michael Harner, *The Jivaro: People of the Sacred Waterfalls* (Garden City, NY: Doubleday, 1972).
12. Dan Rosengren, "Transdimensional Relations: On Human-Spirit Interaction in the Amazon," *Journal of the Royal Anthropological Institute,* 12 (2006): 803–16.
13. Ibid., 892.
14. Luisa Elvira Belaunde, "Entrevista con Herlinda Agustín, mujer *Onaya* del Pueblo Shipibo-konibo," in *Ayahuasca y salud,* eds. Beatriz Labate and José Carlos Bouso (Barcelona: Los Libros de La Liebre de Marzo, 2013: 48–65).
15. Michael Brown, *Tsewa's Gift: Magic and Meaning in an Amazonian Society* (Washington, DC: Smithsonian Institution Press, 1985).
16. Miguel Alexiades, *Ethnobotany of the Ese Eja: Plants, Change and Health in an Amazonian Society* (Ph.D. diss., City University of New York, 1999).
17. Ibid.
18. Evgenia Fotiou, "From Medicine Men to Day Trippers: Shamanic Tourism in Iquitos, Peru" (Ph.D. diss., University of Wisconsin, Madison, 2010). Also, notwithstanding ayahuasca is occasionally attributed as being a male spirit.
19. See Alexiades, *Ethnobotany*; Barbira-Friedman (2010) in bibliography; and Fotiou's Chapter 7 in this volume.
20. Janet Siskind, "Tropical Forest Hunters and the Economy of Sex," in Daniel Gross, ed., *Peoples and Cultures of Native South America* (New York: Natural History, 1973), 226–40.
21. Brian Ferguson, "Game Wars? Ecology and Conflict in Amazonia," *Journal of Anthropological Research* 45 (1989): 179–206.
22. Peluso, "That Which I Dream Is True."
23. Eduardo Luna, "Indigenous and Mestizo Use of Ayahuasca: An Overview," in Rafael Guimarães dos Santos, ed., *The Ethnopharmacology of Ayahuasca,* (Kerala, India: Transworld Research Network, 2011), 1–22.
24. Fernando Santos-Granero, "Sensual Vitalities: Noncorporeal Modes of Sensing and Knowing in Native Amazonia," *Tipití: Journal of the Society for the Anthropology of Lowland South America* 4 (2006): 55–80.
25. http://www.biopark.org/peru/sqcleansing-01.html.
26. See bibliography for Davidov (2010), Holman (2011), and Peluso (2006).
27. For example, see Maria Guiterrez, "A Date with the Vine Spirit," posted Feb. 28, 2011, at http://www.suite101.com/content/my-summer-of-foggy--love-in-san-francisco-a357294 (accessed on July 1, 2011).
28. http://www.biopark.org/peru/sqcleansing-01.html.
29. http://www.ayahuasca.com/spirit/primordial-and-traditional-culture/mermaids-by-steve-beyer/ (accessed on July 1, 2011).
30. Georgina, New Mexico, June 2009, http://tierravidahealing.com/Testimonials.html (accessed on July 1, 2011).
31. Andy Isaacson, "Amazon Awakening," *New York Times,* Oct. 13, 2010.
32. Yalila Espinoza, "Erotic Healing Experiences with Ayahuasca" (presentation at the First International Psychedelic Science in the 21st Century conference, Multidisciplinary Association for Psychedelic Studies or MAPS, San Jose, CA, April 15–18, 2010), retrieved from

http://vimeo.com/15201056. Espinoza contradicts widespread indigenous knowledge that cautions mixing ayahuasca with sex. She proposes that ayahuasca is popularly pursued as a positive erotic healing experience, physically, through experiencing orgasm, and spiritually, by having sex with nonphysical beings. I suspect her data, which are unspecified, refer to New Age participants because of the explicit nudity and exhibitionist acts described, which are generally deemed inappropriate among indigenous peoples in relation to ayahuasca. Although many refer to the work of Reichel-Dolmatof (1971) to indicate the connection between sexual pleasure and ayahuasca, his descriptions explicitly refer to the symbolic.

33. Stephen Trichter, "Ayahuasca Beyond the Amazon: The Benefits and Risks of a Spreading Tradition," *Journal of Transpersonal Psychology* 42 (2010): 131–48.
34. "Peru AYAHUASCA—A Bad Trip!" http://forum.davidicke.com/showthread.php?t=37987; posted June 2007 by Space Lizard on the David Icke Official Forums. The comment generated fourteen pages of discussion.
35. This post is from an archived record of a conversation that took place on Saturday, June 7, 2007, on the Tribe.net website from a defunct stream entitled "CAUTION! Shaman acting inappropriately."
36. Marlene Dobkin de Rios and Roger Rumrill, *A Hallucinogenic Tea, Laced with Controversy: Ayahuasca in the Amazon and the United States* (Westport, CT: Praeger, 2008), 72.
37. Ibid.
38. "Joven Alemana fue violada y golpeada salvajemente durante una sesión de ayahuasca en Iquitos," *El Comercio*, Mar. 21, 2010, accessed June 15, 2011, http://elcomercio.pe/lima/450258/noticia-joven-alemana-fue-violada-golpeada-salvajemente-durante-sesion-ayahuasca-iquitos.
39. The term used is *"fastidiar"* (to annoy) implying normalized male behavior.
40. This post is from an archived record of a conversation that took place on August 19, 2007, on the Tribenet website from a defunct thread entitled "CAUTION! Shaman acting inappropriately."
41. Clancy Cavnar, "The Effects of Participation in Ayahuasca Rituals on Gays' and Lesbians' Self Perception" (Ph.D. diss., John F. Kennedy University, 2011).
42. Michael Winkelman, "Drug Tourism or Spiritual Healing? Ayahuasca Seekers in Amazonia," *Journal of Psychoactive Drugs* 37, no. 2 (2005): 209–18.
43. Peluso, "For 'Export Only'"; Trichter, "Ayahuasca Beyond the Amazon."
44. See, for instance, "New Age Frauds & Plastic Shamans" or NAFPS, an activist group of Native people and supporters whose website exposes fraudulent practitioners. NAFPS is "concerned about the fraud, deceit, money hunger, sexual abuse, racism, control, hunger for power and ego, and cult-like tendencies of the New Age movement and pseudo 'shamans.'" http://www.newagefraud.org/.
45. Winkelman, "Drug Tourism or Spiritual Healing?" 208. http://www.sacredperuadventures.com/programs/ayahuasca/2011_aya_intinerary.html (accessed on June 10, 2011).
46. Gorman, Peter, "A Couple of Thoughts on Ayahuasca in Peru," *The Gorman Blog*, Dec. 9, 2007. http://thegormanblog.blogspot.com/2007/12/couple-of-thoughts-on-ayahuasca-in-peru.html (accessed on June 5, 2011).
47. Trichter, "Ayahuasca Beyond the Amazon." Also, the notion of countertransference is close to the anthropologist's heart since it is considered as one of the potential pitfalls to avoid during ethnographic fieldwork (Robben and Sluka, 2007), whereby the ethnographer projects upon others his own worldview.
48. Trichter, "Ayahuasca Beyond the Amazon," 140.
49. Since the Hippocratic oath was first taken, it has been widely recognized that physicians, therapists, and counselors should not have sexual contact with their patients.
50. Sigmund Freud, *The Future Prospects of Psychoanalytic Therapy*, vol. 11 of *The Standard Edition of the Complete Psychological Works* (London: Hogarth Press, 1957 [1910]).
51. Ronald Britton, *Sex, Death, and the Super-Ego: Experiences in Psychoanalysis* (London: Karnac, 2003).

52. Jeffrey Hayes, "Playing with Fire: Countertransference and Clinical Epistemology," *Journal of Contemporary Psychotherapy* 32 (2002): 93–100.
53. Freud, "Future Prospects," 164.
54. Annette Pritchard and Nigel J. Morgan, "Privileging the Male Gaze: Gendered Tourism Landscapes," *Annals of Tourism Research* 27 (2000): 884–905.
55. John Urry, *The Tourist Gaze* (London: Sage, 1990).
56. Peluso, "Altered States of Dislocation."
57. Pritchard and Morgan "Privileging the Male Gaze."
58. Joanne Sharp, "Gendering Nationhood: A Feminist Engagement with National Identity," in Nancy Duncan, ed., *Bodyspace: Destabilizing Geographies of Gender and Sexuality* (London: Routledge, 1996), 212–33.
59. Laura Mulvey, "Visual Pleasure and Narrative Cinema," in Leo Braudy and Marshall Cohen, eds., *Film Theory and Criticism: Introductory Readings* (New York: Oxford University Press, 1999 [1975]), 833–44.
60. Michel Foucault, *Discipline and Punish: The Birth of the Prison* (New York: Pantheon, 1977).
61. Peluso, "Altered States of Dislocation."
62. Pritchard and Morgan, "Privileging the Male Gaze," 898.
63. Alex Moore, *Teaching and Learning Pedagogy, Curriculum and Culture* (Philadelphia: Falmer Press, 2001).
64. Christina Foss and Johanne Sundby, "The Construction of the Gendered Patient: Hospital Staff's Attitudes to Female and Male Patients," *Patient Education and Counseling* 49 (2003): 45–52.
65. Lynn Meisch, "Gringas and Otavalenos: Changing Tourist Relations," *Annals of Tourism Research* 22 (1995): 441–62.
66. Urry, "The Tourist Gaze."
67. Peluso, "For 'Export Only'."
68. Michael D. Hill, "Contesting Patrimony: Cusco's Mystical Tourist Industry and the Politics of *Incanismo*," Ethnos 72 (2007): 433–60.
69. Glenn Bowman, "Fucking Tourists: Sexual Relations and Tourism in Jerusalem's Old City," *Critique of Anthropology* 9, no. 2 (1989): 77–93.

Bibliography

Alexiades, Miguel. "Ethnobotany of the Ese Eja: Plants, Change and Health in an Amazonian Society." Ph.D. diss., City University of New York, 1999.

Barbira-Friedman, Françoise. "Shamanic Plants and Gender in the Healing Forest." In *Plants, Health and Healing: On the Interface of Ethnobotany and Medical Anthropology*, edited by Elisabeth Hsu and Stephen Harris, 135–78. Oxford: Berghahn, 2010.

Belaunde, Luisa. "Entrevista con Herlinda Agustín, mujer *Onaya* del Pueblo Shipibo-konibo." In *Ayahuasca y salud*, edited by Beatriz C. Labate and José Carlos Bouso. Barcelona: Los Libros de La Liebre de Marzo, 2013.

Blanco, Otorongo. *Ayahuasca SpiritQuest Spirituality, Healing and Cleansing Preparations for Traditional Shamanic Ayahuasca Ceremony in the Classical Style of the Peruvian Amazon*, 1996 http://www.biopark.org/peru/sqcleansing-01.html (accessed July 16, 2011).

Bowman, Glenn. "Fucking Tourists: Sexual Relations and Tourism in Jerusalem's Old City." *Critique of Anthropology* 9, no. 2 (1989): 77–93.

Britton, Ronald. *Sex, Death, and the Super-Ego: Experiences in Psychoanalysis*. London: Karnac, 2003.

Brown, Michael. *Tsewa's Gift: Magic and Meaning in an Amazonian Society*. Washington, DC: Smithsonian Institution Press, 1985.

Cavnar, Clancy. "The Effects of Participation in Ayahuasca Rituals on Gays' and Lesbians' Self Perception." Ph.D. diss., John F. Kennedy University, 2011.

Chaumeil, Jean-Pierre. *Voir, savoir, pouvoir: Le chamanisme chez les Yagua du Nord-Est Peruvian.* Paris: Editions de l'École des Hautes Etudes en Sciences Sociales, 1983.

Davidov, Veronica M. "Shamans and Shams: The Discursive Effects of Ethnotourism in Ecuador." *Journal of Latin American and Caribbean Anthropology* 15 (2010): 387–410.

Dobkin de Rios, Marlene, and Roger Rumrill. *A Hallucinogenic Tea, Laced with Controversy: Ayahuasca in the Amazon and the United States.* Westport, CT: Praeger, 2008.

Espinoza, Yalila. "Erotic Healing Experiences with Ayahuasca," Presentation at the First International Psychedelic Science in the 21st Century conference, Multidisciplinary Association for Psychedelic Studies (MAPS). San Jose, CA. April 15–18, 2010. Retrieved from http://vimeo.com/15201056.

Ferguson, R. Brian. "Game Wars? Ecology and Conflict in Amazonia." *Journal of Anthropological Research* 45 (1989): 179–206.

Foss, Christina, and Johanne Sundby. "The Construction of the Gendered Patient: Hospital Staff's Attitudes to Female and Male Patients." *Patient Education and Counseling* 49 (2003): 45–52.

Fotiou, Evgenia. "From Medicine Men to Day Trippers: Shamanic Tourism in Iquitos, Peru." Ph.D. diss., University of Wisconsin, Madison, 2010.

Foucault, Michel. *Discipline and Punish: The Birth of the Prison.* New York: Pantheon Books, 1977.

Freud, Sigmund. *The Future Prospects of Psychoanalytic Therapy.* Vol. 11 of *The Standard Edition of the Complete Psychological Works.* London: Hogarth Press, 1957 [1910].

Gorman, Peter. "A Couple of Thoughts on Ayahuasca in Peru." *The Gorman Blog.* Dec. 9, 2007. http://thegormanblog.blogspot.com/2007/12/couple-of-thoughts-on-ayahuasca-in-peru.html (accessed June 5, 2011).

Harner, Michael J. *The Jivaro: People of the Sacred Waterfalls.* Garden City, NY: Doubleday, 1972.

Hayes, Jeffrey A. "Playing with Fire: Countertransference and Clinical Epistemology." *Journal of Contemporary Psychotherapy* 32 (2002): 93–100.

Hill, Michael D. "Contesting Patrimony: Cusco's Mystical Tourist Industry and the Politics of *Incanismo.*" *Ethnos* 72 (2007): 433–60.

Holman, Christine. "'Surfing for a Shaman': Analyzing an Ayahuasca Website." *Annals of Tourism Research* 38 (2011): 90–109.

Hutchins, Frank T. *Ecotourism in the Amazon: Commodification of Culture and Nature.* Paper presented at the 28th Midwest Conference on Andean and Amazonian Archaeology and Ethnohistory, Indiana University-Purdue University, Fort Wayne, 2000.

Kosovych, Danylo. "Non-Native Ayahuasca Use." Master's thesis, George Mason University, 2010.

Luna, Luis Eduardo. "Indigenous and Mestizo Use of Ayahuasca: An Overview." In *The Ethnopharmacology of Ayahuasca,* edited by Rafael Guimarães dos Santos, 1–22. Kerala, India: Transworld Research Network, 2011.

Meisch, Lynn A. "Gringas and Otavalenos: Changing Tourist Relations." *Annals of Tourism Research* 22 (1995): 441–62.

Moore, Alex, 2001. *Teaching and Learning Pedagogy, Curriculum and Culture.* Philadelphia: Falmer Press, 2001.

Mulvey, Laura. "Visual Pleasure and Narrative Cinema." In *Film Theory and Criticism: Introductory Readings,* edited by Leo Braudy and Marshall Cohen, 833–44. New York: Oxford University Press, 1999 [1975].

Peluso, Daniela M. "'That Which I Dream is True': Dream Narratives in an Amazonian Community." *Dreaming* 14 (2004): 107–19.

Peluso, Daniela M. "For 'Export Only': Ayahuasca Tourism and Hyper-Traditionalism." *IASTE Working Paper Series (Hyper-Traditions and "Real" Places),* edited by Nezar AlSayyad, 189 (2006): 482–500.

Peluso, Daniela M. "Altered States of Dislocation: Ayahuasca Tourism in the Peruvian Amazon." *Journal of Tourism and Culture Change* (forthcoming).

Pritchard, Annette, and Nigel J. Morgan. "Privileging the Male Gaze: Gendered Tourism Landscapes." *Annals of Tourism Research* 27 (2000): 884–905.

Reichel Dolmatoff, Gerardo. *Amazonian Cosmos: The Sexual and Religious Symbolism of the Tukano Indians*. Chicago: University of Chicago Press, 1971.

Robben, Antonius, C. G. M., and Jeffrey A. Sluka. *Ethnographic Fieldwork: An Anthropological Reader*. Malden, MA: Blackwell, 2007.

Rosengren, Dan. "Transdimensional Relations: On Human-Spirit Interaction in the Amazon." *Journal of the Royal Anthropological Institute* 12 (2006): 803–16.

Santos-Granero, Fernando. "Sensual Vitalities: Noncorporeal Modes of Sensing and Knowing in Native Amazonia." *Tipití: Journal of the Society for the Anthropology of Lowland South America* 4 (2006): 55–80.

Sharp, Joanne P. "Gendering Nationhood: A Feminist Engagement with National Identity." In *Bodyspace: Destabilizing Geographies of Gender and Sexuality*, edited by Nancy Duncan, 212–33. London: Routledge, 1996.

Siskind, Janet. "Tropical Forest Hunters and the Economy of Sex." In *Peoples and Cultures of Native South America*, edited by Daniel Gross, 226–40. New York: Natural History, 1973.

Trichter, Stephen. "Ayahuasca Beyond the Amazon: The Benefits and Risks of a Spreading Tradition." *Journal of Transpersonal Psychology* 42 (2010): 131–48.

Tupper, Kenneth W. "Ayahuasca Healing Beyond the Amazon: The Globalization of a Traditional Indigenous Entheogenic Practice." *Global Networks* 9 (2009): 117–36.

Urry, John. *The Tourist Gaze*. London: Sage, 1990.

Viveiros de Castro, Eduardo. "Exchanging Perspectives: The Transformation of Objects into Subjects in Amerindian Ontologies." *Common Knowledge* 10 (2004): 463–84.

Winkelman, Michael. "Drug Tourism or Spiritual Healing? Ayahuasca Seekers in Amazonia." *Journal of Psychoactive Drugs* 37 (2005): 209–18.

11

Yage-Related Neo-Shamanism in Colombian Urban Contexts[1]

ALHENA CAICEDO FERNÁNDEZ

Yage, also known as ayahuasca, is a psychotropic, or as it is now called "entheogenic," beverage, traditionally used by various ethnic groups from the Colombian Southwestern Amazonian Piedmont (Ingas, Kamentsá, Kofán, Siona, and Coreguaje). It is made from a vine also called yage (*Banisteriopsis caapi*) and the *chagropanga* (*Dyplopteris cabrerana*) plant. It is mainly used for healing and shamanic learning.[2] During the last fifteen years, ritual consumption of yage has spread widely not only through various Colombian cities, but also through social groups that previously did not have any contact with these kinds of practices. Although yage and the therapeutic traditions associated with it have been present in large Colombian cities for at least forty years—as research by Pinzón, Suárez, and Garay has shown[3]—it was mainly used by lower classes of migrating peasants. This constituted the traditional scenario of hybridization and crossbreeding of health systems and exchange networks of knowledge and medicinal plants among *mestizo* healers and indigenous yage specialists (*curacas* or *taitas.*[4]) However, even though yage arrived in the cities a long time ago, it has only recently been noticed by urban elites and the middle classes.

The practice of urban yage consumption commonly occurs in what are known as "yage sessions." These are private gatherings where the psychotropic substance is consumed ritually under the guidance of a taita, who is often from the Putumayo region, the area traditionally inhabited by yage-drinking ethnic groups. Understood as a practice commonly associated with traditional indigenous medicine, the sessions are presented nowadays as a therapeutic or healing alternative with a significant spiritual component.[5] In this sense, yage sessions have become new settings where therapeutic and religious spheres interface.

The elites' growing interest in these practices started in the 1990s. At that time, curacas and yage taitas began to appear in such cities as Pasto, Bogota, Cali,

Medellin, and Pereira. They would guide the sessions for small groups of intellectuals, scholars, and artists. The taitas, who came from Putumayo, were invited by friends belonging to such circles, and moved to the city for short periods of time in order to offer ceremonies.[6] In this manner, traditions that, for a long time, belonged to popular classes and were considered "cheap superstitions," "witchcraft," or "sorcery," were reevaluated as they were taken up by these groups. Soon, yage sessions started to gain supporters among university students and the middle classes as the taitas' invitations and visits became more frequent. Gradually, this type of yage consumption became an important source of income and status for yage taitas. As the new millennium arrived, yage consumption flourished. Many members of the middle class also became interested in traditional indigenous medicine rituals that were offered as therapeutic alternatives. Not only did the more well-known and influential taitas start to travel periodically from the rainforest to the cities to distribute yage, but other indigenous people also began to organize their own sessions, especially young indigenous men with less experience or education than the curacas.

In just a few years, a growing number of yage sessions were offered and new ways of inviting people appeared: small groups of ten or twenty friends became big groups of hundreds of people. In many cases, indigenous authorities from various ethnic groups decided to offer yage sessions themselves as a political and identity-vindication strategy.[7] Thus, in less than a decade, yage consumption acquired an unprecedented level of visibility and legitimacy among indigenous practices.

The visibility and success of these sessions has been transformed rapidly in recent years. On the one hand, the economic success of the taitas who lead urban yage sessions has revitalized apprenticeship and promoted new generations of young *yajeceros*. This has also contributed to the migration of many indigenous people to the cities to try their luck as improvised shamans.[8] Alongside the evolution of this phenomenon, intermediaries started to gradually appear, acting as "bridges," mediating the relationship between the urban population interested in these practices and the indigenous curacas and their communities.[9] In fact, this interface of intellectuals, scholars, artists, and pro-indigenous activists who invited taitas to the city allowed the creation of new forms of mediation when a number of these intermediaries were initiated into careers as yage taitas under the guidance of curacas. The phenomenon of expanding ritual consumption therefore includes a new modality created by the appearance of new yage taitas initiated in indigenous traditions and living in cities. These shamans—as most of them refer to themselves—have capitalized on urban demand as they offer the ritual practice of a yage session that, without breaking from traditional indigenous heritage, incorporates new language and ritual elements directed mostly toward an urban public.

This chapter offers a general overview of the current yage phenomenon based on some representative cases in cities like Pasto,[10] and seeks to identify new dynamics or processes related to yage sessions. It follows four new yage taitas who started practicing in the city in the mid-1990s and who are now widely recognized in urban circles. Although I do not pretend to make a thorough analysis of each one of these scenarios, I seek to contribute to a better understanding of the cultural reach of this growing phenomenon, which has expanded yage use in Colombia. To this end, I explore the most significant features of new forms of ritual yage consumption that, in comparison to more traditional ways of consumption, reveal the continuities and discontinuities in the process of diversification behind new urban uses of yage.

Javier Lasso[11]

Less than an hour away from Pasto and in front of the great Lake La Cocha, almost three thousand meters above sea level, is the Maloca de la Cruz del Sur. Inspired by the traditional design of indigenous communal houses of the Amazonian rainforest, this magnificent structure is built on land that belongs to Javier Lasso, a professor, fine artist, and well-known shaman. The maloca was built in 2003 and since then has functioned as a ritual space for an important group of yage traditionalists led by the Lasso family. Born in Pasto to urban middle-class parents, Javier Lasso is a thin, bearded, forty-five-year-old white man who is married and has two children. According to many of his followers, his physical appearance unavoidably reminds one of the actor who played Jesus Christ in the Italian director Franco Zeffirelli's film *Jesus of Nazareth*. His initiation as a yage taita started in the 1980s under the guidance of two indigenous shamans from the Putumayo region. His main teacher and mentor was the taita Pacho Piaguaje, a Siona elder from Buenavista in the Putumayo lowlands.[12] In fact, the maloca was built in honor of this well-known taita from the region who, invited by Lasso, would frequently travel to Pasto to carry out healing sessions alongside his initiated sons. After the taita passed away in April 2007, his sons continued traveling to the highlands to conduct ceremonies in the maloca. Today, Lasso shares the ritual calendar of the yage sessions in the Cruz del Sur with his mentor's sons. This place has become the main non-indigenous ritual space for the indigenous taitas belonging to the Siona lineage of the Piaguaje, who also make and supply the yage consumed there.

During the mid-eighties, Javier Lasso met taita Pacho Piaguaje in Pasto, where the former had arrived to participate in a forum about traditional indigenous medicine at the Universidad de Nariño. Lasso experienced yage for the first time in a session guided by taita Pacho, where the grandfather predicted: "I have seen

Figure 11.1. Map of Colombia.

here that medicine needs to be taken. I will tutor someone. Tomorrow he will be the one sitting here and everyone will see the power of yage. He will be in my maloca for a month. He will die and be resurrected." After this, taita Pacho would regularly send half a bottle of yage from the lowlands to Javier. Thus Javier started to discover the plant and its lessons by himself and to practice using a bunch of eucalyptus leaves as a ritual broom or *waira*.[13] At the same time, following some friends' recommendations, Javier began taking yage with taita Kamentsá Martín Agreda in Sibundoy in the Putumayo highlands. Sometime later, he felt the need to leave Pasto and went to Buenavista in the Putumayo lowlands, where taita Pacho lived. He spent a month there, and according to Javier, they took yage on at least twenty-five nights. At the end of the month, he was not scared of yage anymore; he was able to endure the "trips." At that point the taita told him: "Behind you, rivers of people are coming and you are a bridge between us; the Indians and the whites, who are the sick ones. You have become a disciple and your task is to communicate, to be a bridge."

Javier built the Cruz del Sur in honor of his mentor and his family, but also to have a space where he could perform his duties as a yage taita. Later on, some of his brothers and friends—all middle-aged men—started on the path toward shamanism just as he did, under the guidance of taita Pacho and the Piaguaje lineage.[14] Some became apprentices, while others acted as helpers in the ceremonies carried out in the maloca. They are also part of the maloca's guard. This group is always present in yage sessions and is in charge of logistics, monitoring and accompanying the ritual. Some of them are even part of the musical group popularly known as "Combo Chuculero," which plays instruments during the yage sessions and sings songs already known to the maloca regulars.

One of the particular characteristics of the yage sessions carried out in this maloca is that they are part of the "Siona Indigenous School." Given the Cruz del Sur's close relation to the Piaguaje family, all the ritual prescriptions of the Siona culture are adhered to as faithfully as possible. This is a fundamental part of its ceremonial style, which attempts to preserve indigenous heritage and tradition in the use of yage. Likewise, the followers undergo a strict education in the yage tradition taught to Javier by taita Pacho during his years as an apprentice. This reflects how thoroughly the "traditional" precepts are followed, since these are supposed to be applied throughout all the yage ceremonies carried out by the Putumayo lowlands ethnic groups. Among other things, the yage session ritual space is considered predominantly male. Pregnant and menstruating women are not allowed to enter the maloca. During the rituals, men and women must be separated, and the yage is served in separate containers for each gender. Both men and women must remain silent during the ceremony.

Regardless of the "traditional Siona" mandate, the most noticeable characteristic of these sessions is the strong link they have with Catholicism. In fact, the sessions in Cruz del Sur are ceremonies in which Catholic representations and practices are omnipresent. Images of Jesus Christ and the Virgin Mary are always present in the ritual space. Also, the taita sings Catholic hymns to summon the forces of yage. Usually, the ceremony starts with prayers such as the Lord's Prayer and Hail Mary, and hymns sung by the collaborators in order to praise the Catholic God, the Virgin Mary, and the Saints, as well as the older taitas represented by taita Pacho. The sessions are well known in the city, and sixty to seventy people attend each ceremony. Without a doubt, the role of Catholicism in these ceremonies is one of the main reasons the rituals are successful.

The Cruz del Sur, or as it is also known, "La Cocha's maloca," is nowadays a major point of reference in Pasto's "yage scene." Although there is no official calendar, the yage ceremonies are carried out more or less every two weeks, or when Siona taitas from the Putumayo lowlands are visiting. The assistants, for the most part adults of both sexes from the middle class, come looking for yage as an alternative healing method because they have embarked on a spiritual journey or because they are attracted by the fame of the Siona mestizo maloca. It is also common to find foreigners and people from other urban social backgrounds there. Nevertheless, in recent years the attendance of peasants from neighboring towns has increased. Also, many of the regular participants are patients referred by physicians in Pasto who promote these therapeutic alternatives as complements to their regular treatments.

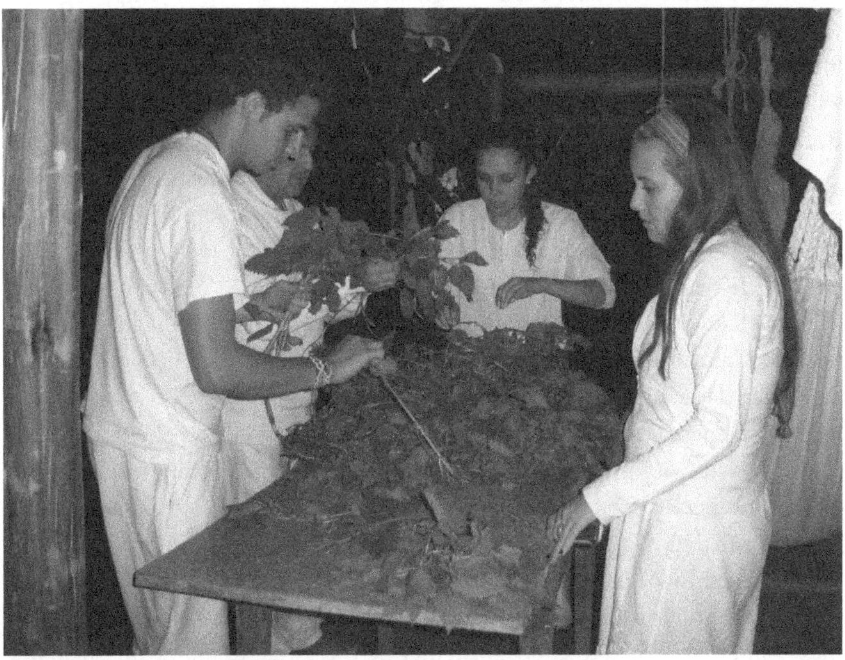

Figure 11.2. Urban ayahuasca users making nettles wairas for the yage rituals. Photograph by Alhena Caicedo.

Kajuyali Tsamani

Kajuyali Tsamani-Wichapishinteton Luta-Mama Nabi is the sacred Sikuani-Lakota-Kogui name of Colombian anthropologist and shaman William Torres.[15] He started on the shamanic path following in the footsteps of his maternal grandfather, who was always interested in indigenous knowledge. He studied anthropology at the Universidad Nacional and, while a student, started visiting indigenous territories throughout Colombia, researching Amerindian peoples' ancestral knowledge. His first mentor on this journey was Grandfather Muinane Juan Garcia, by whom Kajuyali was initiated into the coca and tobacco traditions. Garcia insisted that he learn other shamanic traditions, and sent him to the Sebundoy Indians from the Sibundoy Valley in the Putumayo highlands, to learn from ayahuasca. Under the guidance of taita Martín Agreda, a Kamentsá elder from Sibundoy, he started his apprenticeship with yage. During a yage session, he had a vision in which the taita took him to the jungle and showed him a vine around a tree. The plant told him that he was going to begin his journey there. Sometimes William went to Sibundoy; sometimes he invited the taita to the city. After almost ten years, taita Martín gave him a *waira* and a crown and told him "I have taught you all I can. You can cure now. You can do your job."

Sometime later, William went to Buenavista in the Putumayo lowlands, where he asked Siona taita Pacho Piaguaje to teach him about jungle yage. He worked for five years alongside this mentor, visiting him in the Putumayo or inviting the taita to officiate at yage sessions in Bogota with university students who were reading Carlos Castaneda's books and were interested in shamanism. Both taitas visited Bogota for the first time because Torres invited them.

For Kajuyali, the shamanic path is closely linked to knowledge of the indigenous power plants. Therefore, he also learned the *yopo* tradition. *Yopo* (*Anadenanthera peregrina*), like yage, is a sacred plant that grows in the eastern plains of Colombia. He began his yopo initiation more than fifteen years ago with two elders from the Sikuani indigenous group. Recently, his son was initiated into this tradition too. Kajuyali is also interested in shamanic traditions from the Sierra Nevada de Santa Marta, and for three years he followed the teachings of some Kogui *mamos* (shamans) with whom he is still in the process of initiation. For a long time, Kajuyali lived two lives: one as a university professor of philosophy, anthropology, and ethno-literature, and another as a mestizo shaman, pioneer, and reference source for all the young university students interested in shamanism and its powers.

According to William, after he had worked for some time in Pasto, the yage's spirit told him it was important to build a maloca—a sacred place for ceremonies—and that he had to choose whether he was going to follow the shamanic path or not. So he left his job as a university professor and started the Fundación de Investigaciones Chamanistas (Shamanic Research Foundation). In the late nineties, he met the coordinators of a Dutch foundation, and this enabled him to get funding to build the maloca on the outskirts of Pasto. Since then, he has worked with this foundation in order to cover the expenses of the maloca and its activities. He also travels regularly to the Netherlands, where he also organizes yage sessions and other shamanic rituals.

Nabi-nunhue, "the jaguar's house," in the Kogui language, is the Fundación de Investigaciones Chamanistas' maloca in Chachagüí (20 kilometers from Pasto). In the maloca, a sacred space dedicated to yage that opened in 2002, sessions are conducted once a month during the full moon. The sessions held here are unusual because some of the rituals are conducted during the day, which is exceptional with regard to the deeply rooted tradition of nighttime ceremonies. Also, Kajuyali is one the few yage taitas who allow menstruating women to participate in the sessions. The yage consumed is either provided by Kamentsá taitas who bring it from the jungle or produced by Kajuyali from vines bought in the lowlands. Kajuyali leads the sessions, while Kajuyali's ten-year-old son, Tsamani, who has been initiated by his father in the use of yage, blesses the yage.

Yage sessions are not the only activity that is conducted at the site. This maloca was conceived as a space to explore multiethnic shamanism, diverse shamanic techniques and ritual practices linked to the consumption of various psychotropic substances. One follower describes it as "a great campus of shamanic experimentation." Rituals and ceremonies from the founding traditions of the maloca are conducted periodically. These include rituals that were introduced to Kajuyali during his initiation experiences among a number of ethnic groups: yage sessions, yopo rituals from the Sikuani tradition, Kogui ceremonies, and, recently, various ceremonies from the Lakota tradition in North America, such as the *inipi* (sweat lodge), vision quests, and the *lowampi* (spirit ritual), and *chanupas* (or peace pipes) rituals. The latter are ritual practices that the maloca adopted after a 2005 visit from a Lakota shaman called Tunka Hota Winyan, who "gave" Kajuyali and his family permission to conduct them. These rituals are organized by the maloca at least once a year, when shamans and assistants are summoned from around the world.

Recently, a group of followers of the foundation and its maloca has emerged. These followers take part in ceremonies and consider themselves apprentices of the four main traditions practiced there (Lakota, yopo, yage, and Kogui traditions). The group is composed mostly of middle-class people from Pasto, including foreigners. Within this group, many are young women who attend the ceremonies with their small children at least once a month. These followers are not only initiated in these practices under the guidance of Kajuyali but are also in charge of the maloca's logistics and preparing its activities.

The Fundación de Investigaciones Chamanistas is known for its maloca, Nabi-nunhue, which is open to the public. The maloca and its rituals are well known in the city, with yage sessions and Lakota inipis being the activities that attract the most people. People of all ages, from children to elderly people, come from Pasto, nearby towns, and other areas of the country to attend these spaces. They come looking for cleansing and healing, or on a spiritual quest. Nevertheless, regular followers are, for the most part, North Americans and Europeans who come seasonally to take part in the activities offered. Aside from having a group of faithful followers from both sides of the Atlantic, Nabi-nunhue also offers tourist packages that promote the foundation's activities in Pasto and in Europe.

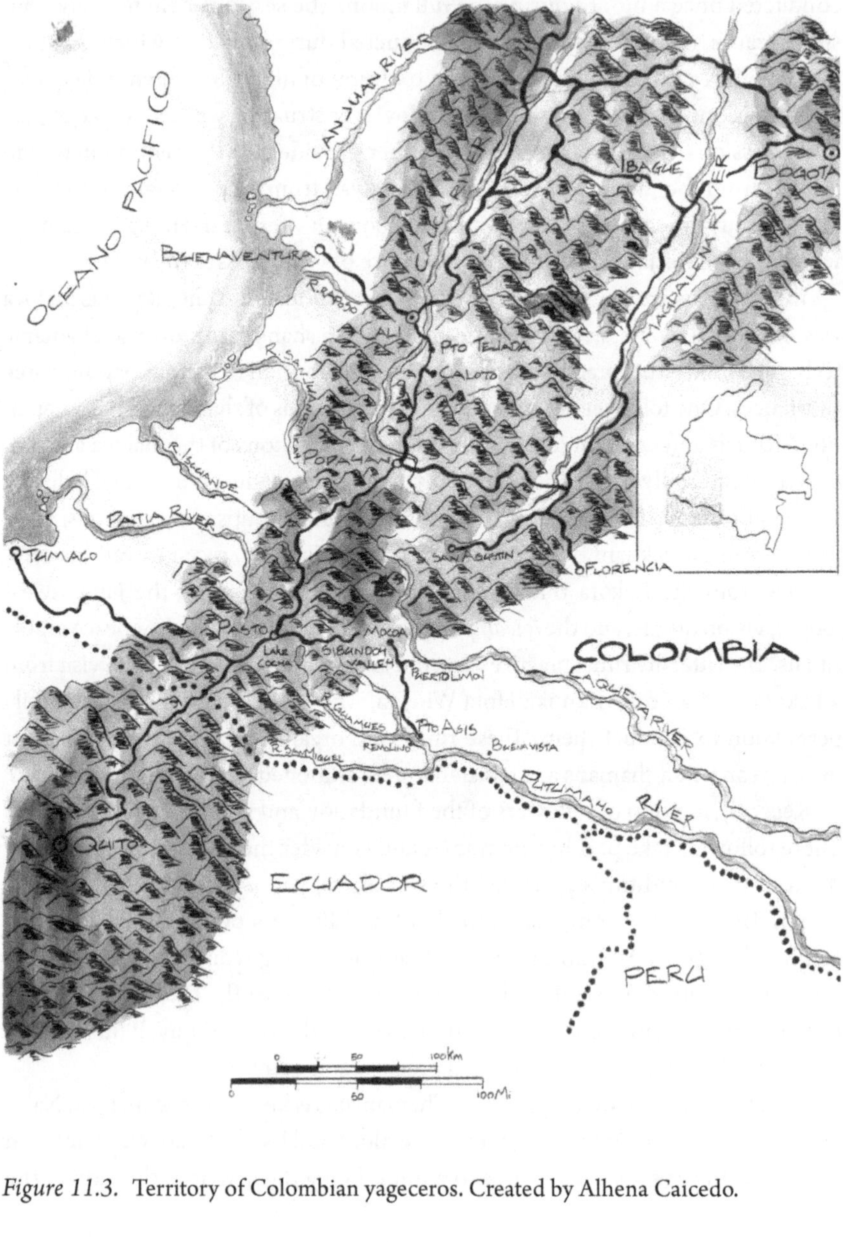

Figure 11.3. Territory of Colombian yageceros. Created by Alhena Caicedo.

Some Reflections on the New Scenarios of Urban Yajeceros

The cases described above reflect just a few of the urban tendencies found in Colombian yage circles. However, without oversimplifying the diversity of the phenomenon, these cases reveal diverse trends, specializations, and features leading me to the conclusion that this is a heterogeneous phenomenon, although both cases also share certain features and characteristics.

A common denominator of their identity is that yajeceros call themselves "yage taitas." Each claims a source of authority and power from the indigenous traditions in which he was initiated, particularly with regard to their apprenticeship and friendship connections with elder curacas from the Putumayo highlands and lowlands, who continue to live in their territories and who are recognized by their communities. Without exception, their legitimacy is linked to indigenous authenticity founded on the idea of continuing the "yage tradition."[16] Therefore, their taita status must be recognized by an indigenous authority that not only endorses the initiation process itself, but also legitimizes it by giving them healing abilities through the bestowal of certain traditional objects imbued with shamanic yage power, such as the feather crown, the waira, etc. One can also highlight the fact that both of the aforementioned urban practitioners were initiated as taitas after the generation of famous yage curacas who made yage visible in urban settings during the 1990s. The elder grandfathers from various groups in the Putumayo, who were the first yage taitas to go to the city and to be endorsed by non-indigenous specialists, appeared in national and international media, and were the informants for the majority of work on the topic. Both Lasso and Torres started their training as followers of these curacas during their trips to the city, and their initiations were relatively short compared with their mentors'. Nevertheless, being a new yage taita has no relation to ethnic filiation; nor is it a condition that excludes mestizo or non-indigenous people. On the contrary, far from associations of this kind, the new taitas are defined more by their profile as practitioners and by the place each one has in the Colombian yage circle. What makes them different from their mentors, and at the same time characterizes them as a growing phenomenon, is this intermediary role. Despite their differing autobiographical narratives, they consider that, unlike the first taitas who came to the cities and made traditional yage medicine visible, their position in the "historical juncture of traditional medicine's expansion" is as a *bridge* between the urban and indigenous worlds. In that sense, articulating themselves between tradition and a growing urban demand is what differentiates them from other yage practitioners and allows them a polyvalent flexibility to introduce reinventions and adaptations of rituals, language, meaning, etc.

Although urban yage sessions contribute to an expansion of these indigenous rituals, the urban character of the phenomenon is not defined only by their being carried out in the city, since the urban aspect has to do with cultural and class factors that characterize the audience they attract. In this sense, certain sessions are also urban even if they are conducted in rural areas.[17] Likewise, it is the semantic and ritual reinventions that have been introduced by some taitas that determine this new modality.

Most urban yage followers are middle-class and elite adults between twenty-five and fifty years old. They have a high education level; most are college graduates or students. As will be discussed later, this has not stopped lower classes from getting involved. Unlike other new religious movements where women are the majority,[18] and yage ceremonies conducted inside indigenous communities where mostly men participate, in the new yage spaces, the percentages of men and women are nearly equal.

City people are attracted to these spaces for various reasons. The majority arrive because of curiosity regarding a psychedelic experience, because a friend or relative recommended it to them, as part of an existential search, or simply with the intention of trying new things. The label "traditional indigenous medicine," under which these practices appeared in the city—a label introduced by scholars who started the urbanization-elitization process of yage sessions—became the main term used to promote legitimate and legal ritual consumption of yage. In this sense, social representations that consider indigenous people to be bearers of an alternative way of relating to the world and to nature, and custodians of forgotten ancestral knowledge that must be saved, are the main motivations for people who come to these new alternative spaces.[19]

Although the promise of "traditional medicine" is the lure, there are at least three dimensions by which the yage session followers give meaning to this practice: the sacred, the traditional indigenous, and the therapeutic dimensions. Yage is considered sacred and is understood to be a means to access God and divinity ("yage's path is God's path," "yage enables a direct connection with God and divinity"). Yage comes from a centuries-old indigenous tradition; it is an ancestral patrimony shared by the taitas from Putumayo, the greatest bearers of knowledge that needs to be recovered ("elder grandparents are those who keep yage knowledge"). Finally, through the consumption of yage, one gets *healed*. In these networks, yage is considered a sacred medicine. In fact, inside the yage circle, it is commonly known as the "remedy." Session followers consider this practice an alternative source of health. Consequently, ritual consumption of yage is a therapeutic practice that provides a regular bodily, mental, and spiritual decontamination. Thus, in a broad, multidimensional sense, it is a cleansing exercise where sickness is swept away by consuming the psychotropic ("yage cleans," "yage shows you what is wrong"), suffering is soothed ("yage teaches," "yage tests you") and health, well-being, and happiness are achieved ("yage allows you to live more peacefully and with greater awareness").

Within this framework, health is understood not as the lack of physical sickness, but as a state of equilibrium that involves the physical, emotional, and spiritual dimensions, and that must be constantly renewed. "Yage is medicine for the body and soul," "yage allows you to know yourself," "yage helps you make decisions," and "yage shows you things as they really are" are some of the recurring claims we hear from followers. This is exactly why it is hard to establish a formal differentiation between urban followers' conceptualizations of yage sessions with regard to its purely therapeutic and purely spiritual aspects. Most urban yage takers do not make a distinction between these dimensions. For them, there is an important interrelation between the emotional, the spiritual, and the physical dimensions: "therapeutic summoning of the sacred, or sacred summoning of the therapeutic."[20] The fact is that urban yage takers' motives reveal a syncretism that includes a number of aspects: on the one hand, social representations of the indigenous self and the indigenous world, combined with the health-sickness conceptualization as an indivisible unit of the physical and the emotional; and, on the other, of course, the Catholic element.

As mentioned before, this phenomenon's recent transformations are also influenced by the increasing participation of middle- and some lower-class public in yage sessions. These groups' participation is, without a doubt, related to the new place Catholic representations and practices have gained within the sessions. References to the Catholic pantheon, iconography, and hymns, among other things, are common in yage sessions. Although the indigenous curacas' reference to Catholicism is a legacy from the conquest era, in many of the new urban spaces the Catholic realm plays an even greater part. For example, Mass may be celebrated before yage sessions. Although the Catholic Church has never been in favor of this set of practices because they are seen as sacrilegious, it is interesting to see how "indigenous traditional medicine" has gained legitimacy and prestige from the acknowledgment of the elites, and how this has also influenced the recent acceptance of these practices among some lower-class Catholic groups.[21] Even so, we cannot overestimate the fact that there are equally strong tendencies that exclude religious references from these spaces. Such is the case of yage scenarios influenced by transnational trends such as agnosticism and other tendencies related to the New Age that mostly attract middle- and upper-class groups.[22]

One must keep in mind that "maloca" does not refer only to the physical space built as a ceremonial site. The fact that a site is called maloca is a linguistic mark of indigenous authenticity. On the other hand, the malocas have created groups around them, central communities of followers of a certain type of yage sessions that, in general, revolve around the preferences of the particular taita who is the owner of the maloca. For this reason, it is important to highlight how the evolution of new urban yage settings points to institutionalization concerned with constituting ceremonial spaces, configuring more or less permanent groups around these sites, and consolidating an emphasis or a particular trend linked to a ritual style that identifies taitas and their followers.

The consolidation of all these groups has been spontaneous and gradual. Although each claims to follow an alternative approach, the type of articulations between the practice of ritual yage consumption and the particular concept of well-being differ in every case. The public profile of each maloca is partially defined by how it contrasts with tradition. Thus the Maloca de la Cruz del Sur proclaims itself an heir to Siona ancestral traditionalism, making indigenous authenticity an element that connects yage consumption and popular Catholicism.[23] In the case of the Nabi-nunhue maloca, the multiethnic shamanism it advocates relies more on New Age paradigms and is explicitly foundational, independent from any culture, universal, and detached from any particular context. Thus ritual yage consumption becomes one of many possibilities for accessing alternative forms of well-being. Other well-known malocas, such as El Sol Naciente (under the guidance of new taita Orlando Gaitán in Bogota), emphasize therapeutic aspects and healing practices. Although constantly reinforcing Catholic representations as well as images of indigenous people as a radical healing alterity, this maloca offers a wide variety of health services through the Carare Foundation. At its diagnosis and medical treatment center, directed by the taita, the main treatment consists of yage sessions. In this way, the emphasis on the therapeutic efficacy of this maloca is reinforced by focusing on the image of the indigenous taita as a healing agent.

Figure 11.4. Cleansing ritual at the Shamanic Research Foundation (Fundación de Investigaciones Chamanistas).

In spite of the adjustments and reinventions introduced by the new taitas, the yage rituals maintain a similar form, which the new taitas have inherited from their indigenous mentors. This form is related to both the ritual and its purpose. Yage sessions are carried out either for therapeutic purposes or as initiation into esoteric knowledge. With some exceptions, as mentioned above, they are always conducted at night, involve a group and a ritual procedure, and, above all, are always carried out by a specialist celebrant (taita, curaca, etc.). Although there are many variations regarding style, the ritual sequence is maintained. Every yage session has three stages: preparation, intake, and ending. These three phases are put together in sequential scenes that impart order to the ritual event as a whole.

The consolidation of each maloca's style and its gradual institutionalization also reveals various types of membership within groups of followers. At yage sessions, one can find two kinds of public. On the one hand, there is a sporadic public that fluctuates and has a tangential relation to these spaces. These people go every now and then, and they consider their participation incidental. In general, they take part as a way of earning prestige in circles in which a "yage session" gives them status. On the other hand, there are the regular followers who initially attended as the former, but continued to attend regularly. This audience can be considered *yajecera*, or "yage-centered," and is made up of consistent participants who frequently attend ceremonies and, in general, belong to a group that follows a particular style and a particular taita. This kind of urban yage taker usually identifies with the esoteric knowledge associated with yage; therefore they are commonly called "followers of the yage path" or "followers of the path of traditional medicine." Within this group, the most committed yage takers are generally those who have already been initiated as taita apprentices.

Although every maloca offers yage sessions open to the public, groups of followers who are apprentices of a yage taita are also associated with each of these ceremonial sites. Initiation processes are restricted, and only experienced male and female yage takers have access to them, subject to the taita's approval. It is relevant to emphasize gender because in these spaces—contrary to the indigenous yage tradition—women of reproductive age are allowed. This fact reveals a trend found in some malocas of displacing the taita-patient dichotomy in favor of the taita-apprentice relationship. For many of these urban yage takers, "following the yage path" means becoming your own healing agent; in other words, becoming your own taita. This ideal of becoming one's own healer is central to New Age philosophy. Some of the opposing ideologies connected with yage use in Colombia include the contradictions that arise from a practice that, on the one hand, regards the taita as a necessary external agent, in the sense that very few people would accept taking yage without an expert, and on the other hand manifests an increasing tendency to manage without the taita and focus on a purely individual process.

The mechanisms that regulate access are another important characteristic of these new spaces. Participation in the sessions is usually dependent on physical and psychological preparation, since these are considered the key to having a successful experience. Aside from these kinds of general recommendations, urban sessions attest to the relevance of some traditional ritual prescriptions and interdictions, though new meanings may also be attributed to them. In the majority of these new spaces, the regulation of the presence and participation of menstruating women is enforced both in the physical sites associated with yage and in the maloca, the taita's house, the places where he attends to people, or where yage is prepared. These prohibitions are usually justified as precepts from the "yage culture"[24] according to which two female conditions, the menstrual period and pregnancy, are considered contaminating. Both are associated with a particular energy that "damages" the session, harms the participants, and affects the taita's power. Although there are exceptions, many spaces nevertheless do not observe this prohibition. For Kajuyali, for example, these interdictions have a cultural character that can be isolated from the ritual's purpose. This claim is associated with the concept of yage's ritual use as a practice that must be understood as one of many practices of "shamanism." According to Kajuyali, "Shamanism is universal and goes beyond any cultural order. In this sense, any restriction to access is mediated by cultural considerations that are just matters of form."

Another common condition in these spaces is related to the yage itself. In fact, yage consumed in urban sessions comes from the jungle in the Putumayo-Caquetá region, since the production of the psychotropic still depends on indigenous and mestizo people who know the traditional procedures for producing the beverage.[25] Like other plants, yage has historically circulated between the Putumayo-Caquetá lowlands and the Andean cities and central region of the country through exchange networks of knowledge and products between indigenous people and mestizos. The Inganos have historically been recognized as an important part of these networks because of their tradition as traveling medicinal plant merchants and carriers of specialized botanical and medicinal knowledge.[26] Starting approximately ten years ago, the increase in yage sessions in urban centers, and the greater demand it produced, not only caused periods of product scarcity within the networks but also changed yage circulation and distribution strategies.[27] These are active networks; those who work in the cities depend on their families and initiation relationships for their supplies, and they maintain friendships and alliances with taitas in the lowlands who produce yage. Nowadays, yage is transported by courier services from the Putumayo, mainly to Bogota. There are also middlemen who distribute the yage they get from the jungle in a number of cities.[28] On average, a liter of high-quality yage is worth 100,000 Colombian pesos (40 Euros, more or less). Currently, the legal status of yage is undefined. Although Colombia is a signatory to the international treaties

Figure 11.5. Nabi-nunhue (jaguar's house): Kajuyali's maloca in Chachagüí, near Pasto. Photograph by Alhena Caicedo.

prohibiting psychoactive substances such as DMT, there is no express prohibition of the internal distribution or consumption of this psychotropic; this is due to a lack of legal clarity regarding the traditional use of yage by indigenous groups. At the moment, yage is being exported to places such as Spain, Belgium, and Holland under legally dubious conditions, since in some of these countries the components of yage (especially DMT) are prohibited. Private interests have also tried to establish patents on the vine on various occasions.[29]

Although urban adaptation has widened the circle of yage consumption, these new trends still depend on traditional networks for supplying the tea, and these are still controlled by indigenous and mestizo yage producers from Putumayo-Caquetá.

By Way of Conclusion

In recent years, the emergence of new urban yage use shows that the yage field in Colombia is flexible to some extent. In countries like Brazil,[30] the field of yage, or ayahuasca, is not only wider but also shows a variety of urban uses, including several churches and dissident groups.[31] In Colombia, the new yage consumption trends are still linked to the traditional indigenous matrix centered on the Putumayo-Caquetá region. Within the networks connected to the Putumayo, yage is still a form of power, not only in material terms, depending on yage supply networks, but even more so in symbolic terms, linked as it is to the image of the *indio* from Putumayo as the source of shamanic legitimacy and power.[32]

Figure 11.6. Curacas from Putumayo region: Highland curaca (Inga) with lowland curaca (Kofán). Photograph by Alhena Caicedo.

As was pointed out at the beginning of this chapter, the rise of new urban trends has evolved quickly: the current urban yage landscape is very different from the one seen five years ago. It may be that the growing trend of institutionalizing urban yage consumption around malocas is just a sign of a more complex phenomenon that will emerge in the long run. By considering how styles are consolidated, in terms of the patterns of articulation between traditional yage uses and the urban audience's expectations, we can see the seeds of diversification that germinate through a continuous reinvention of the uses of this psychotropic substance.

Although one could claim that this phenomenon is a positive sign of the traditional yage networks growing, one must take into account that the emergence of new trends within this matrix almost always involves tension and conflict. The institutionalization of malocas and consolidation of varying ritual styles have introduced new tensions into the traditional hierarchies. These stresses affect exchange, production, and circulation within the yage networks, as well as the symbolic and material monopoly of the psychotropic, which have traditionally been the preserve of indigenous peoples. At the same time, these new trends also open the discussion regarding the problem of controlling other uses of yage in the present context of economic globalization.

Notes

1. This chapter is the result of the research completed for my doctoral thesis at the École des Hautes Études en Sciences Sociales in Paris (EHESS) titled "New Spaces for Shamanism in Colombia." My research aims to account for the reconfiguration of the field of yage use by analyzing the expansion in consumption of yage in the main urban centers. From this perspective, I consider in depth the process of urbanization and the elitism connected with consumption of this psychotropic drink from the Amazon, the current mechanism for legitimization of this practice, and the changes generated by the widening of the network of consumers. The research has a particular emphasis on the emerging new generations of young yajeceros (people who work with yage) who act as intermediaries between traditional shamanic practices of yage use and the new scenarios of urban consumers. The fieldwork for this research was completed between 2006 and 2010 in the Amazon region of Putumayo-Caquetá, mainly in the Sibundoy Valley and in the towns of Mocoa and Puerto Asis, and in the cities of Pasto and Bogota with the urban followers of the practice.
2. Germán Zuluaga, *El aprendizaje de las plantas: En la senda de un conocimiento olvidado; Etnobotánica medicinal* (Bogota: Seguros Bolívar, 1994).
3. Carlos Pinzón and Rosa Suárez, "Los cuerpos y los poderes de las historias: Apuntes para una historia de las redes de chamanes y curanderos en Colombia," in *Otra América en construcción. 46 Congreso Internacional de Americanistas. Memorias del simposio identidad, cultura, medicina tradicional y religiones populares. Universidad de Ámsterdam 1988* (Bogota: ICAN, 1991), 136–84; Carlos Pinzón and Gloria Garay, *Violencia, cuerpo y persona: Capitalismo, multisubjetividad y cultura popular* (Bogota: Equipo de Cultura y Salud-ECSA, 1997).
4. *Curaca* is a word introduced soon after the arrival of the Spaniards. It is widely used in the Colombian Southwest to refer to a person who knows or specializes in managing yage, a shaman in classical anthropological terminology. In the case of *taita* ("father" in the Quechua language), this term is traditionally used among various indigenous communities to refer to older men who must be respected (fathers, grandfathers, authorities). Also, an older *curaca* is called a *taita*. In the urban contexts described here, the word *taita* is preferred to refer to yage experts. The term *curaca* is not used in these contexts, since it is associated with popular representations of witchcraft among Amazonian indigenous people.
5. Jorge Ronderos, "Neochamanismo urbano en los Andes Colombianos: Aproximaciones a un caso; Manizales y el eje cafetero Colombiano," (paper presented at the Jornadas sobre chamanismos in Barcelona, Spain, Nov. 17–18, 2001); Carlos Alberto Uribe, *El yajé como sistema emergente: Discusiones y controversias* (Bogota: Departamento de Antropología, Universidad de los Andes, 2002); Jimmy Weiskopf, *Yajé: El nuevo purgatorio* (Bogota: Villegas Editores, 2002).
6. Weiskopf, *Yajé*, 409–53.
7. This is the case of the Kofán Zio-a'i Foundation (interview with Sebastian Jansasoy, director of the Kofán Zio-a'i Foundation, September 2006).
8. This is a particularly sensitive issue if one takes into account that the places of origin of most of these indigenous people are border regions, isolated by armed conflict and completely ignored by the state.
9. Alhena Caicedo Fernández, "Les séances de yajé à Bogotá, Colombie: Dynamiques d'une tradition indigène dans la Modernité. Mémoire du DEA" (master's thesis, L'École des Hautes Études en Sciences Sociales or EHESS, 2004), 26.
10. Pasto is the Southernmost Colombian city, and has historically been the only crossroad between the Andean world, the Amazonian Piedmont, and the jungle. From early on in the colonization process, its strategic position became a scenario for strong miscegenation, or *mestizaje*, between Andean and Amazonian indigenous traditions and the popular culture of the rising city. This tradition of miscegenation explains the fact that the flourishing of

urban yage communities not only started in Pasto before anywhere else but also gained special importance. The majority of its population has not perceived this as a break from the set of practices and beliefs that have historically circulated there. Because Bogota is the capital city, it is traditionally one of the most important destinations for rural migrants.

11. All the stories presented here are based on field notes and interviews with leaders and followers carried out during the research process.
12. Esther Jean Langdon, "Shamans and Shamanism: Reflection on Anthropological Dilemmas of Modernity," *Revista Vibrant 4*, no. 2, (2007): 27–48. http://www.vibrant.org.br/downloads/v4n2_langdon.pdf
13. The *waira* or *wairasacha* is one of the most important ritual elements of a yage taita. Generally, it is made of a bunch of *Olirya latifolia* leaves used as a broom to sweep away bad energies.
14. Regarding the case of taita Pacho Piaguaje, see Langdon, "Shamans and Shamanism."
15. The introduction of the term *Shaman* to the field of yage consumption is relatively recent and related to the elitism of this practice in urban settings. In this context "shaman" and "neoshaman" are used interchangeably.
16. The concept of tradition is central to the analysis of representations of the expansion of yage's ritual use. Under this framework, tradition is evoked by making reference to an origin generated by a self-affirmation of the new yage taitas' authenticity.
17. Weiskopf, *Yajé*, 418–19.
18. Christian Ghasarian, "Santé Alternative et New Age à San Francisco," in Raymond Massé and Jean Benoist, eds., *Convocations thérapeutiques du sacré* (Paris: Éditions Karthala, 2002), 143–63.
19. Alhena Caicedo Fernández, "Neochamanismos y modernidad: Lecturas sobre la emancipación," *Revista Nómadas* 26 (2007): 114–47. These new representations of the indigenous self and the indigenous world are supported by various records circulating nationally and internationally that revalue the ethnic indigenous condition: the rise of the environmental discourse and neo-indigenous movements, the laws created by the Colombian Constitution of 1991 in which ethnic and cultural rights where recognized, among others. See Astrid Ulloa, *La construcción del nativo ecológico: Complejidades, paradojas y dilemas de la relación entre movimientos indígenas y el ambientalismo en Colombia* (Bogota: ICANH-Colciencias, 2004).
20. Raymond Massé, "Rituels thérapeutiques, syncrétisme et surinterprétation du religieux," *Convocations thérapeutiques du sacré*, eds. Raymond Massé and Jean Benoist (Paris: Éditions Karthala, 2002), 5–12.
21. It is also interesting to see how, in certain urban spaces for yage sessions in which the Catholic elements are very strong, the ritual openly involves Catholic proselytism against new Christian churches. Nevertheless, this phenomenon has to be studied in relation to the rise of new forms of Catholicism that veer away from the official line and that are mainly organized around prayer groups (from field notes taken in 2006).
22. Alhena Caicedo Fernández, "Nuevos chamanismos, nueva era," *Revista Universitas Humanistica* 68 (2009): 15–32.
23. Popular references to Catholicism are present in most yage rituals, from the traditional setting in an indigenous community to the new urban ritual consumption.
24. Zuluaga, *El aprendizaje de las plantas*, 66.
25. Both the yage vine (*Banisteriopsis caapi*) and the *chagropanga* (*Diplopterys cabrerana*), another plant used in yage production that is responsible for the visionary effect (the "pinta"), grow mainly in the jungle. Although there are varieties adapted to higher altitudes, they grow slowly and, in general, are not used to make the beverage.
26. Esther Jean Langdon, "Interethnic Processes Affecting the Survival of Shamans: A Comparative Analysis," in *Otra América en construcción. 46 Congreso Internacional de Americanistas. Memorias del simposio identidad cultural, medicina tradicional y religiones populares. Universidad de Ámsterdam 1988* (Bogota: ICAN, 1991), 44–65; Carlos Pinzón, Rosa Suárez, and Gloria Garay, *Mundos en red: La cultura popular frente a los retos del siglo 21* (Bogota: Universidad Nacional de Colombia, 2005).

27. Recently, Kofan yage production has increased. Several taitas working in cities depend on personal relationships with Kofan taitas who sell them yage. Nevertheless, the majority of yage consumed in cities such as Bogota, Medellin, and Cali comes from production and distribution networks in Mocoa, the capital city of the Putumayo department, and is mainly controlled by Inganos from the lowlands.
28. Not surprisingly, this kind of commercial distribution is considered detrimental to yage. Within the yage universe, the beverage is considered "jealous," which means one must meticulously follow the prescriptions for preparing the psychotropic, including observing the ritual rules of concoction, the prohibition of it coming into contact with menstruating women, keeping it in isolated and secure places, etc. Moreover, one must avoid overmanipulation and commercialization, since all these conditions affect the quality of yage's visionary power.
29. Regarding patent registration cases, see Weiskopf, *Yajé*, 653–68.
30. Beatriz Caiuby Labate, *A reinvenção do uso da ayahuasca nos centros urbanos* (Campinas, Brazil: Editorial Mercado de Letras, 2004).
31. Joseph María Fericgla, "El peyote y la ayahuasca en las nuevas religiones mistéricas Americanas," in *Antropología en Castilla y León e Iberoamérica: Aspectos generales y religiosidades populares*, ed. Ángel Espina (Salamanca, España: Instituto de Investigaciones Antropológicas de Castilla y León, 1998), 325–47.
32. Pinzón, Suárez, and Garay, *Mundos en red.*

Bibliography

Caicedo Fernández, Alhena. "Les séances de yajé à Bogotá, Colombie: Dynamiques d'une tradition indigène dans la modernité". Mémoire du DEA. Master's thesis, L'École des Hautes Études en Sciences Sociales (EHESS), 2004.

Caicedo Fernández, Alhena. "Neochamanismos y modernidad: Lecturas sobre la emancipación." *Revista Nómadas* 26 (2007): 114–47.

Caicedo Fernández, Alhena. "Nuevos chamanismos, nueva era." *Revista Universitas Humanistica* 68 (2009): 15–32.

Fericgla, Joseph María. "El peyote y la ayahuasca en las nuevas religiones mistéricas Americanas." In *Antropología en Castilla y León e Iberoamérica: Aspectos generales y religiosidades populares*, edited by Ángel Espina, 325–47. Salamanca, Spain: Instituto de Investigaciones Antropológicas de Castilla y León, 1998.

Ghasarian, Christian. "Santé alternative et New Age à San Francisco." In *Convocations Thérapeutiques du Sacré*, edited by Raymond Massé and Jean Benoist, 143–63. Paris: Éditions Karthala, 2002.

Labate, Beatriz Caiuby. *A reinvenção do uso da ayahuasca nos centros urbanos*. São Paulo: Editorial Mercado de Letras, 2004.

Langdon, Esther Jean. "Interethnic Processes Affecting the Survival of Shamans: A Comparative Analysis." In *Otra América en construcción. 46 Congreso Internacional de Americanistas. Memorias del simposio identidad cultural, medicina tradicional y religiones populares. Universidad de Amsterdam* 1988, 44–65. Bogota: ICAN, 1991.

Langdon, Esther Jean. "Shamans and Shamanism: Reflection on Anthropological Dilemmas of Modernity." *Revista Vibrant* 4, no. 2 (2007): 27–48. http://www.vibrant.org.br/downloads/v4n2_langdon.pdf.

Massé, Raymond. "Rituels thérapeutiques, syncrétisme et surinterprétation du religieux." In *Convocations thérapeutiques du sacré*, edited by Raymond Massé and Jean Benoist, 5–12. Paris: Éditions Karthala, 2002.

Pinzón, Carlos, Rosa Suárez, and Gloria Garay. *Mundos en red: La cultura popular frente a los retos del siglo* 21. Bogota: Universidad Nacional de Colombia, 2005.

Pinzón, Carlos, and Gloria Garay. *Violencia, cuerpo y persona: Capitalismo, multisubjetividad y cultura popular*. Bogotá: Equipo de Cultura y Salud-ECSA, 1997.

Pinzón, Carlos, and Rosa Suárez. "Los cuerpos y los poderes de las historias: Apuntes para una historia de las redes de chamanes y curanderos en Colombia." In *Otra América en construcción. 46 Congreso Internacional de Americanistas. Memorias del simposio identidad cultural, medicina tradicional y religiones populares. Universidad de Ámsterdam 1988*, 136–84. Bogota: ICAN, 1991.

Ronderos, Jorge. "Neochamanismo urbano en los Andes Colombianos: Aproximaciones a un caso: Manizales y el eje cafetero Colombiano." Paper presented at the Jornadas Sobre Chamanismos in Barcelona, Spain, Nov. 17–18, 2001. http://www.etnopsico.org/index.php?option=content&task=view&id=78.

Ulloa, Astrid. *La Construcción del nativo ecológico: Complejidades, paradojas y dilemas de la relación entre movimientos indígenas y el ambientalismo en Colombia*. Bogota: Icanh- Colciencias, 2004.

Uribe, Carlos Alberto. *El Yajé como sistema emergente: Discusiones y controversias*. Bogota: Universidad de los Andes, 2002.

Weiskopf, Jimmy. *Yajé: El nuevo purgatorio*. Bogotá: Villegas Editores, 2002.

Zuluaga, Germán. *El aprendizaje de las plantas: En la senda de un conocimiento olvidado; Etnobotánica medicinal*. Bogota: Seguros Bolívar, 1994.

INDEX

Photographs, illustrations, and maps are indicated by italic page numbers.